ALSO BY BETTY BOLES ELLISON

*The Early Laps of Stock Car Racing: A History of the
Sport and Business through 1974* (McFarland, 2014)

The True
Mary Todd Lincoln

A Biography

BETTY BOLES ELLISON

McFarland & Company, Inc., Publishers

Jefferson, North Carolina

LIBRARY OF CONGRESS CATALOGUING-IN-PUBLICATION DATA

Ellison, Betty Boles.
The true Mary Todd Lincoln : a biography / Betty Boles Ellison.
p.   cm.
Includes bibliographical references and index.

ISBN 978-0-7864-7836-1 (softcover : acid free paper) ∞
ISBN 978-1-4766-1517-2 (ebook)

1. Lincoln, Mary Todd, 1818–1882.   2. Presidents' spouses—United States—
Biography.   3. Lincoln, Abraham, 1809–1865—Family.   I. Title.
E457.25.L55E45 2014   973.7092—dc23   [B]   2014003651

BRITISH LIBRARY CATALOGUING DATA ARE AVAILABLE

On the cover: Oil portrait of a twenty-year-old Mary Todd
painted in 1928 by Katherine Helm, a niece of Mary Todd Lincoln
and daughter of Confederate General Ben H. Helm.
It is based on a daguerreotype taken in Springfield by
N.H. Shepherd in 1846; a companion daguerreotype is the earliest
known photograph of Lincoln (courtesy of the Abraham Lincoln Library
and Museum of Lincoln Memorial University, Harrogate, Tennessee)

Manufactured in the United States of America

*McFarland & Company, Inc., Publishers
Box 611, Jefferson, North Carolina 28640
www.mcfarlandpub.com*

For Sofia E. Franklin

Table of Contents

Acknowledgments

Interest in researching a biography of Mary Lincoln began years ago with my involvement in the restoration and operation of her girlhood home as a board member of the Kentucky Mansions Preservation Foundation (KMPF). The house was rescued from demolition by former Kentucky first lady Beula C. Nunn.

It is my good fortune to be surrounded by a most supportive and loving family and a close circle of friends who share my interest in the wife of the sixteenth United States president. They were always willing to read manuscript drafts, provide assistance, make suggestions, offer criticism and advance encouragement. They have been the bedrock of this endeavor. In particular, Kathleen Wills-Ellison's astute and perceptive copyediting on our Friday nights together for many months made the book so much better. My appreciation to Margaret for always being there and willing to go the extra mile.

The name Mary Lincoln seems to have the same magical ring for archivists and librarians as it does for my family and friends. From Lincoln librarians to archivists at the National Archives, all were very helpful, but none more so than Jane Gastineau, librarian at the Lincoln Financial Foundation Collection, Allen County Public Library, Fort Wayne, Indiana. Jane always had an answer to my questions through endless emails. Her assistance is most appreciated.

Lou Holden, a long-time curator of the Mary Todd Lincoln House and KMPF board member, has been a wonderful sounding board for my ideas. Lou shared the extensive work she did on the relationships of various members of the Todd family.

Michelle Ganz, archivist at the Abraham Lincoln Library at Lincoln Memorial University, Harrogate, Tennessee, was kind enough to provide a copy of a 1928 painting done by Katherine Helm, Mrs. Lincoln's niece. Mary Ann Pohl, at the Abraham Lincoln Presidential Library and Museum, Springfield, Illinois, made available information on the first lady's jewelry and the sale of her Springfield home.

Frank Stanger and William Marshal, from Special Collections at the University of Kentucky in Lexington, were always helpful in locating material for a number of years. Lisa Thompson, archivist in the Kentucky Department of Libraries and Archives, in Frankfort, always offered assistance. B.J. Gooch, archivist and director of Special Collections, Transylvania University, Lexington, provided material on the early Todd family and their close connections in establishing the university. The reference and Kentucky Room librarians at the Lexington Public Library answered questions and provided material in a most helpful manner.

Anthony B. Willson, archivist at the Twickenham Museum in Middlesex, England, guided me through the complex ownership of York House by the d'Orleans family. Mary Lincoln met Louis-Philippe d'Orleans, the Comte de Paris, at the Executive Mansion in 1861, and later visited him and his family in Europe.

Terry Langford, curator, and Chuck DeCroix, park ranger, at Mammoth Cave National Park were helpful in unearthing material about the park at the time of Mrs. Lincoln's visit in 1876. Gwen Thompson, the current curator of the Mary Todd Lincoln House, provided insight into the relationship between the Todd family and their slaves. The encouragement of Dr. Thomas F. Schwartz, director of the Herbert Hoover Presidential Library and former Illinois State Historian, is appreciated. My gratitude is extended to Dr. Humbert Nelli, retired history professor at the University of Kentucky, for his always helpful advice and for believing in my abilities.

Preface

If she was not a favorite as first lady of the land—lacking that indefinable quality in which her husband excelled—surely that was no reason why her less fortunate traits should be magnified to the neglect of others not only more numerous, but lovely and winning. There is nothing in our history more unmanly, more cruel than the treatment of that noble woman by a prying, gossiping press, which pursued into her lonely years. Here at last is the testimony of one who knew her, bearing witness to her worth as a woman, her loyalty as a wife and her service to her country, and bespeaking for her— what will not always be denied—a place beside her husband in the grateful and venerate memory of the Republic.
—*Personal Recollections of Abraham Lincoln*, by Henry B. Rankin, 1916

For decades, Mary Lincoln has been denied what Henry B. Rankin, who knew the Lincolns in Springfield, Illinois, sought for her: a fair appraisal. Herein is the fair appraisal that Rankin wanted. This biography examines the totality of her personality—the admirable traits as well as those not so commendable.

Mary's principal denigrator, William H. Herndon, Abraham Lincoln's last law partner, was a viperous and vindictive man who has been allowed to define the sixteenth president's wife as having few if any redeeming characteristics. For portions of three centuries, Mary's life story has been distorted by Herndon's jaundiced accounts. This work uses archival documents, overlooked for decades, to establish clear evidence to substantiate that while her husband was deified by the nation she has been unjustly vilified.

A widely held concept is that Mary Lincoln was crazy; she must have been since she was placed in an insane asylum. She was there because her physician generously dosed her with chloral hydrate, which can cause patients to become disoriented and incoherent and exhibit paranoid behavior. That same physician was the principal witness at her 1876 insanity hearing. Afterwards, she outsmarted some of the country's best legal minds, including a sitting associate Supreme Court justice, in not only obtaining her release but having her sanity, property and legal rights restored. The stigma of having been declared insane at the instigation of her only surviving son, unfortunately, remained with her the rest of her life.

It is undeniable that David Davis, whom Lincoln appointed to the Supreme Court, was the power behind the scenes of Mary's committal to the asylum. His accomplices were her son Robert Lincoln along with Leonard Swett, his lead counsel, and Isaac Arnold, two men her husband called "friends." They decided she was insane, set up a sham of a trial, and foisted an attorney—Arnold—off on her who cross-examined none of the witnesses Robert Lincoln had carefully assembled and presented no defense in her behalf. In addition, Swett

watched as Arnold searched her petticoats for her bonds and money before sending her off
to an asylum, smugly satisfied they had done their job so well that she would never surface
again.

The saga of how Mary endured her incarceration and obtained her release bears witness
to Mary's inner strength and intelligence. Despite living in isolation, her letters being censored, having no available funds to hire an attorney and being under supervision twenty-
four hours a day, Mary outsmarted Davis, Robert, Swett, Arnold and the asylum staff. She
lulled them into thinking she was acquiescing to the court's decree by displaying a meek and
obliging demeanor expected of a nineteenth century woman. With unbelievable guile, she
created a network of friends who worked for and gained her release. This book presents the
entire sordid story of her incarnation prompted by her son and abetted by her late husband's
so-called friends. It challenges and repudiates the accusation that Mary Lincoln spent public
money recklessly. Other biographers of Mary Lincoln neglected to follow the money trail
found in archived government documents for the $20,000 Congressional furnishings
allowance.

Since 1862, when her refurbishing of the Executive Mansion was complete, Mary has
been accused of being a spendthrift because she not only allegedly exceeded the $20,000
Congressional allowance for furnishing the residence by $6,858, but did so during the Civil
War. This biography refutes that accusation by documenting that William S. Wood, interim
commissioner of public buildings, was writing checks to himself out of the furnishings
account. In July and August 1861, Wood's checks to himself totaled $7,700, which would
have more than covered Mary's expenditures. As for the hue and cry over her furnishing
purchases, the Lincoln bed remains the Executive Mansion's most famous piece of furniture.
Succeeding presidents use the china service and crystal she selected. Mary Lincoln regarded
the restored Executive Mansion not only as the peoples' house but as an indication to European nations, leaning toward supporting the Confederacy, that the Union was strong and
would withstand the challenge.

Mary Lincoln knew the social world as well, perhaps better, than the Washington elites
who scorned her. Despite their slings and arrows, Mary enacted her revenge, not only succeeding as first lady but doing so in an exceptional manner under circumstances no other
president's wife has ever experienced.

Another popular concept is that Mary spent extravagantly on clothing. Certainly, she
spent money on clothes but it was hardly excessive given her position as the president's wife.
However much money she did or did not spend on her clothes was the Lincolns' concern.
Authors since 1932 have made erroneous assumptions about her expenditures. New York
department and specialty store accounts included clothing and accessories for the entire
family. When they moved to Washington, Willie and Tad were growing boys and Lincoln's
physical build precluded his wearing suits off the rack. Consequently, all those expenditures—her critics like to rave about—were not just for Mary.

From March 1861 through March 1865, Mary attended at least 106 official functions
that required formal dress. She usually purchased fourteen or fifteen new gowns a year, which
indicates she made alterations on some of her gowns and wore them more than once. Her
second inaugural gown was a gift. Mary required additional clothes for less formal activities,
traveling, visiting wounded soldiers in hospitals in and around Washington, troops in the
field and riding in Army ambulances.

Euphoria reigned supreme when her critics discovered that she bought white kid gloves,

300 pairs at a time. Such actions, they screeched, were a sure sign of her extravagance; perhaps even insanity. Buying the gloves in bulk, this book indicates, was actually a frugal move on Mary's part. Both she and Lincoln wore those gloves to greet guests at two inaugurations and their twice weekly levees and receptions in the Executive Mansion during the Washington social seasons 1861–1865. On those occasions, they shook hands with 4,000 to 10,000 guests in an evening. Considering that not everyone then practiced the cleanliness that is prevalent today, those numbers required constant glove changes. Her critics failed to distinguish between the number of gloves purchased in her small size and the larger ones her husband wore.

Everything else aside, what really rankled Illinois and Washington politicians was that Mary Lincoln refused to fit their stereotype of a nineteenth century woman who was supposed to be only seldom seen and never heard. Mary grew up in the tempestuous and acrimonious world of slavery-emancipationist politics in Kentucky. She learned the art of politics firsthand at her father's dinner table from guests like Henry Clay, Garrett Davis, Richard M. Johnson and other national figures. Encouraged by her father, Mary seldom hesitated in speaking out concerning political matters. Her husband recognized her astute political mind and she became his worthy partner, in politics as well as in their marriage, as Rankin pointed out. Mary received an extraordinary education because her father recognized her unusual intellect. Her nineteenth century education was the equivalent of a twenty-first century graduate degree. During her last years in France, she ordered a five-volume French history from a Paris bookstore and read it in the original language. This volume describes in detail her Kentucky childhood, her abhorrence of slavery, generous heart, unselfish nature and the strength of character she exhibited in not publicly answering her critics but succeeding beyond their expectations.

Some of Lincoln's supporters accepted her participation in political matters but others, such as Davis, resented her for not knowing her place. Davis, as Lincoln's administrator, prolonged the settlement of his estate until Mary was forced, for lack of funds, to give up her Chicago home, where she wanted to raise her young son Tad. Consequently, they lived in hotels and boarding houses the rest of their lives. Davis, this biography documents, was quite liberal in providing extra estate funds to Robert Lincoln. Hard as he tried, neither Davis, his confederates, her son nor the tragedies she suffered were able to break the proud, indomitable spirit of Mary Lincoln.

In the end, her tiny body wore out; her superlative mind did not.

CHAPTER 1

Mary Spreads Her Wings

Mary Todd was sassy, politically savvy, sophisticated, sarcastic, intelligent, temperamental, sensitive, attractive and, with all those attributes, it was not surprising that Abraham Lincoln fell in love with her when they met in Springfield, Illinois, in 1839. Just as Robert Todd saw traits in his daughter that led him to provide an advanced education for her, Mary saw something special in the rough-hewn frontier lawyer that others, including her family, failed, or chose not, to notice.

Two previous visits to Springfield had introduced Mary to the town's social circle. In 1835, she traveled to Springfield with her father and sister, Frances, to visit their elder sister Elizabeth Todd Edwards, wife of Ninian W. Edwards. The Edwardses had moved to Springfield two years earlier after he graduated from Transylvania Law School. The 1834 appointment of Edwards as Illinois attorney general by Governor John Reynolds was seen as a springboard for the young man's political career.[1]

Edwards' father, also Ninian Edwards, had been the chief justice of Kentucky court system for four years before being appointed territorial governor of Illinois from 1809 to 1818. The senior Edwards served one term in the United States Senate and was governor of Illinois from 1826 to 1830.[2]

The son Ninian W. Edwards seemingly benefited from his father's career and influence. According to a fellow attorney, Usher Linder, originally from Elizabethtown, Kentucky, Edwards deemed himself to be "naturally and constitutionally an aristocrat and he hated democracy when I first knew him as the devil is said to hate holy water."[3]

Elizabeth Todd Edwards, who also considered herself an aristocrat, introduced her sisters to Springfield society in hopes of finding them husbands. But, those men had to meet the family's approval. The Illinois visits took her sisters out of the highly-charged, dictatorial atmosphere that their stepmother, Betsy Todd, had established in their new home in Lexington, where she was raising her own children.[4]

The Edwards family lived in the Italianate-styled house of his father, who died in 1833, and they entertained a great deal for social and political reasons. Their home at Second and Jefferson streets was near the state capitol.[5]

After the 1835 summer visit to Springfield, Mary returned to Lexington with her father and Frances. She continued her studies at Mme. Mentelle's school. Two years later, she went back to spend three months with the Edwardses. Mary was comfortable meeting new acquaintances, many of whom had Kentucky roots and connections in common. Not considered beautiful but certainly attractive with light brown hair, blue-green eyes and an engaging personality, Mary was a popular addition to Springfield's social life.

Springfield, an energetic, bustling frontier town in 1837, with a population of around 1,500, had just been made the state capital through the efforts of a young legislator, Abraham Lincoln, and the "Long Nine," a group of seven house members and two senators who were all over six feet tall and from Sangamon County.[6]

An incident during that legislative session indicated that Abraham Lincoln was no dull-witted backwoodsman. The "Long Nine" held the balance of legislative power and a dominant issue was the location, or relocation, of the state capital that, by statute, had to be decided in that session.[7]

When the state capital was moved from Kaskahia to Vandalia in 1820, another legislative vote had to be taken on its location in twenty years. After postponing the required vote several times, many of the legislators left the capital during the final 1837 session. When supporters of the Vandalia location discovered they had the majority with a bare quorum of members present, the presiding officer brought the matter up for a vote. A burly sergeant-at-arms guarded the only door to prevent any departures.[8]

"Lincoln took the floor, only to find out how powerless the minority was," a *New York Times* reporter wrote. "The situation looked hopeless. The tall, gaunt figure nodded to his followers and hurried to a corner window. A wooden sill, twenty-inches wide, made a projection beyond the wall. Before his purpose could be divined and officers of the house could reach him, Lincoln had stepped through the window, let himself down until he hung by his hands from the sill. The distance to the ground was less than five feet. Lincoln dropped."[9]

"'No quorum,' the Springfield minority shouted. Proceedings were blocked for the time being. Subsequently, when the absentees (legislators) had returned and when the session was about to close, it was impossible to further postpone the vote. Springfield won."[10]

The Springfield legislators celebrated. In July 1837, a dinner

Portrait of Mary Lincoln painted in 1928 by her niece, Katherine Helm, from a daguerreotype taken in Springfield, Illinois, by N.H. Shepherd in 1846. The portrait was commissioned by Henry E. Bullock from Lexington (photograph courtesy of Abraham Lincoln Library and Museum of Lincoln Memorial University, Harrogate, Tennessee).

was held at Spottswood's Rural Hotel to commemorate their legislative victory. The *Sangamo Journal* quoted Lincoln's toast at the dinner. "All our friends. They are too numerous to be now named individually, while there is no one of them who is not too dear to be forgotten or neglected."[11]

Lincoln was one of a coterie of young Kentucky lawyers, teachers and businessmen who had moved to Springfield. In 1830, Robert W. Scott, from Frankfort, Kentucky, received a letter from John J. Hardin, a Frankfort native and Todd relative who had moved to Illinois, describing migration to the state. The letter was passed around the Todd family and Mary remembered hearing her father read it aloud. "Our country at present is swarming with travelers. It appears as if the flood gates of Kentucky had broken loose and her population set free had naturally turned their course to Illinois and Missouri." Hardin added that many decided to settle in Illinois and not continue on to Missouri.[12]

"Our society is composed of every nation, tribe and kindred. We have a considerable English Colony settled in one of the finest parts of the country, ten or twelve families arrived this summer direct from England and who started for this place. These, with those we had before, will make 40 or 50 families. The population of the county is about two-thirds Kentuckians, many of them men of standing and wealth in Kentucky."[13] Hardin noted that the elected offices were mostly held by eastern people. "Edwards, when sent here as territorial governor, supposing it was a free state it would be settled by western people, to keep them in favor appointed eastern men for judges, etc., these appointed their clerks of the same stamp."[14]

Hardin spent the remainder of the letter complaining about the lack of marriage-age women in Illinois. "We have some sprightly ladies in town though they are few and indeed when this state is compared to yours in that respect it falls short indeed.... It has occurred to me that a considerable speculation might be made by a qualified person who would bring out a cargo of ladies. You recollect in the first settlement of Virginia a cargo of that description was brought in and sold for 150 pounds of tobacco per head. If they should be landed here shortly they might command in the market at least several head of cattle apiece. Besides, it would be a very great accommodation to many young ladies of my acquaintance who have been a long time trying to make an equal swap but as yet have not succeeded."[15]

Mary reminded Hardin of his words about the scarcity of women after she arrived in Springfield. "Well, little cousin," Hardin said, "while you are one of a belated cargo, you are not too late to help some poor fellow fight the battle of life."[16]

Ninian Edwards, Mary's brother-in-law, was a native of Frankfort, Kentucky. Lincoln was born near Hodgenville, Kentucky. John Todd Stuart, Lincoln's first law partner and another Todd cousin, was born in Lexington. Stephen Trigg Logan, Lincoln's second partner and another Todd cousin, was a Franklin County native. Ward Hill Lamon was from Louisville. O. H. Browning came from Cynthiana. William H. Herndon, Lincoln's last law partner, was from Greensburg, Kentucky.[17]

Springfield was a place where young lawyers could further their political careers and many of them, not just from Kentucky, paid court to Mary. Stephen A. Douglas, a native of Brandon, Vermont, first settled in Winchester, Illinois, as a teacher until he finished his law studies and was admitted to the bar. The loquacious James Shields, forever tied to the Lincolns through a duel that never occurred, was a native of Altmore, County Tyrone, Ireland. Another suitor was Edwin B. Webb, a Springfield lawyer who was a widower with two small children.[18]

Not all members of the group were lawyers. Mentor Graham was a teacher from Greene County, Kentucky. Col. Robert Allen, another Greensburg, Kentucky, native, initially opened Allen and Blankenship mercantile establishment before becoming one of the state's largest mail contractors. Allen, whose wife, Jane, was the first woman teacher in Illinois, ordered his stage coaches from a Nashville firm and owned as many as 500 horses at a time. Allen was a director of the old State Bank.[19]

Along with the Edwardses, the Allens also entertained on a large scale. During her 1837 visit, Mary attended a ball at the Allen home. She had no idea that one of her dance partners at the Allens' ball would, decades later, eviscerate her reputation and brand her with a hideous image that lingers today. William H. Herndon, just out of college, asked Mary to dance. During the dance, he allegedly remarked that she glided through the waltz with the ease of a serpent. "Mr. Herndon, comparison to a serpent is rather severe irony, especially to a new-comer," Mary supposedly replied.[20]

Katherine Helm, in her biography of her aunt, did not repeat the serpent story told by Herndon. However, in a draft of the book she wrote, "As he (Herndon) did not have 'social relations' with any of Miss Todd's circle of friends, it is unlikely that she ever danced with him and the serpent story is probably like the wedding account, a fabrication."[21]

Whether the Allens invited another popular young lawyer, Abraham Lincoln, to their ball in 1837 is unknown. In June 1836, while Lincoln was campaigning for a seat in the legislature, Col. Allen made known that he was in possession of facts which could scuttle the legislative elections hopes of Lincoln and Ninian Edwards. Lincoln's reply to Allen about his statement demonstrated his elegant but concise thought process. "I find myself wholly unable to form any conjecture of what fact or facts, real or supposed, you spoke but my opinion of your veracity will not permit me for a moment to doubt that you at least believed what you said. I am flattered by the personal regard you manifest for me; but I do hope that, on more mature reflection, you will view the public interest as a paramount consideration, and therefore determining to let the worst come. I here assure you that the candid statement of facts on your part, however low it may sink me, shall never break the tie of personal friendship between us."[22]

It was difficult to believe that Lincoln, a budding master wordsmith, would turn into a bumbling, stumbling man searching for words in the presence of or corresponding with women. His letters to Mary Owens, with whom he earlier contemplated marriage, and women friends such as Mrs. O. H. Browning, not only exhibited a deft hand with words but had a very persuasive, convincing tone.[23]

Historian Paul M. Angle marveled at Lincoln's grasp and command of the spoken and written word. "With less than a year of formal schooling, and that of a character which today would be laughed out of our schools, he became one of the great masters of the English language," Angle wrote. He used Lincoln's Gettysburg and Cooper Institute addresses to prove his point. Few, he contended, knew much about the actual Battle of Gettysburg or the significance of the Cooper Institute speech. "The numbers pale in comparison to those who carry the words, four score and seven years ago, in their minds." The same, he wrote, applied to the Cooper Institute speech in New York, where Lincoln said, "Let us have faith in that right makes might and in that faith let us to the end dare to do our duty as we understand it."[24]

Mary's correspondence style, much different from Lincoln's, echoed her enthusiasm and exuberance for life but her pen could turn into a rapier of wit and sarcasm, skewing her target with few words. Oft times, her trenchant wit and demand for excellence extended into her conversations which, on occasions, were not well received by some of her admirers. Lincoln, from all indications, appreciated that part of her personality. The expectation for excellence among their associates was a trait they shared. In an 1863 letter to James C. Conkling, who had married Mary's best friend, Mercy Levering, Lincoln wrote, "I am mortified to find the letter to you, botched up, in the Eastern papers, telegraphed from Chicago. How did this happen?"[25]

Lincoln was part of a group of young Springfield men competing for Mary Todd's attention. David H. Donald, a Lincoln biographer, wrote, "The Edwards entourage included the most attractive young women in Springfield. From time to time, Ninian Edwards welcomed a relative, such as his niece, the beautiful and pious Matilda Edwards. Julia Jayne, daughter of a Springfield doctor, nearly always attended the Edwards' parties as did Mercy Ann Levering, when she was visiting from Baltimore. But nobody in the Edwards' circle attracted more interest than Mrs. Edwards' younger sister, Mary Todd. She was variously described as attractive, dashing, witty, graceful, cultured, sarcastic, witty, haughty, aristocratic and an excellent conversationalist. It was no surprise that she became the belle of the town."[26]

Why did the nineteen-year-old social sensation return to Kentucky to further her education for two more years? She was certainly old enough for marriage. Elizabeth Todd was engaged to Ninian Edwards when she was just sixteen. If life with her stepmother in the Todd household was so unpleasant, there were other close Todd relatives whom she could have visited or lived with in Ohio, Virginia and Missouri.

It is possible that Mary Todd felt she needed more education and her father was agreeable. If that was the case, perhaps life in the family home, on Lexington's West Main Street, was not that difficult anymore. John Ward, whose academy Mary attended as a youngster, was conducting a seminary for young ladies and she spent the next two years there.[27] The scope and depth of Mary Todd's education would be equivalent today to a graduate degree in the arts.

While Mary was at Dr. Ward's seminary, her sister, Frances, who was a year older, moved to Springfield. Robert Todd paid Elizabeth Edwards $150 a year for her room and board. Frances married Dr. William Wallace in May 1839, and her departure left a vacancy in the Edwards household for another Todd sister looking for a husband.[28]

Springfield was such a small town that Mary and Lincoln could have seen each other in the three months she was there in 1837. In April of that year, Lincoln and John Todd Stuart, Mary's cousin, became partners in a Springfield law firm. Their announcement read, "J.T. Stuart and A. Lincoln Attorneys and Counselors at Law will practice conjointly in the Courts of this Judicial District—Office No. 4 Hoffman's Row, upstairs Springfield, April 12, 1837."[29]

Mary Todd and Abraham Lincoln became attracted to each other after she returned to make her home in Springfield. She was twenty-one and he was thirty-one years old. They both had pasts that included flirtations, romances and, possibly, thoughts of marriage with other people.

After dancing with Mary at the Edwards home one evening, Lincoln made an appointment to call the following night. Mary's niece, Katherine Helm, would later write of the event, "It pleased him that she understood and discussed politics with subtle discernment. From that time they were on all occasions drawn irresistibly together. They discovered new bonds in common."[30]

Regardless of the difference in the economic and educational backgrounds, Mary and

Lincoln each brought traits to the relationship that were lacking in the other. With her formal education and social background, Mary recognized a steely resolve and determination in Lincoln that certainly made him attractive as a future husband. After all, she had told her young friends in Lexington that the man she married would be president of the United States.

"He was in the appearance a dreamer, yet from his records, practical, and ready to take advantage of every opportunity to improve himself," Helm wrote.

> He was certainly not the ill-dressed man some people said he was (Mary attached importance to dress), but was as conventionally clad as all the other young men she met. She might have known, of course, that her cousin John Stuart would hardly have taken into his office for a partner a man whose appearance or manner would cast a reflection on the dignified firm. Also, of course, when Lincoln was traveling through the country electioneering he was shrewd enough to know, having been a back woodsman himself that broadcloth even if frayed and dusty would not win as many votes among the farmers as jeans.[31]

The relationship between Mary and Lincoln progressed to the point where he was comfortable to call on her at will in the Edwards' house in the winter and early spring of 1840. Helm recalled one evening after dinner he appeared as they were having coffee and cake. The conversation he joined was about Fridays being unlucky days. "You see," she quoted her aunt as saying, "my sister and I are part Scotch and we believe in fairies. I have hunted for the magic circle where they dance, and I am sure I have heard that faint elusive music of fairy bells."[32]

Lincoln told them he believed in fairies, too. Looking at Mary he said, "I am sure that one of them must have been your godmother. She fell in love with you in your cradle and showered you with all her choicest gifts."[33]

Elizabeth Edwards, later in the conversation, mentioned that Mary was planning to visit her uncle, Judge David Todd, in Columbia, Missouri, and attend the Whig gathering at Rocheport in honor of candidates William H. Harrison and John Tyler for the office of president and vice-president. "Mary and Mr. Lincoln exchanged a quiet glance, he had heard of this contemplated visit," Helm wrote, "and together they had conceived a romantic plan to meet each other during this political rally."[34]

Their plan was not without its faults.

Lincoln had planned speeches on Harrison and Tyler's behalf in southern Illinois before going to Rocheport and on to Columbia. According to Earl S. Miers' *Lincoln Day by Day: A Chronology 1809–1865*, on August 17, 1840, "Ed. Baker, Lincoln, Governor Duncan and myself [A. P. Fields] are going to spend all our time in the southern counties discussing the principles of our party ... and challenge these men to a fair discussion of this administration, organize our friends, circulate documents amongst them and in this way, my word for it, we must succeed."[35]

The next day, the group started for Belleville, in southwestern Illinois. However, Miers was unable to locate Lincoln's whereabouts for four days, August 18 to August 22. He wrote that he believed Lincoln and Field were meeting with Whig leaders in county seats in southern Illinois.[36]

Judge David Todd, his daughter, Ann, and Mary Todd traveled by steamboat from Columbia to the Whig meeting at Rocheport, attended by about 8,000 people. Lincoln had also booked passage on a steamboat but his craft became stuck on a sandbar, according to Helm. Along with judge Todd, the speakers included Daniel Webster's son Fletcher Webster, artist and politician George C. Bingham, and Major James Rollins, the best man in the wedding of Mary's friend Cassius Marcellus Clay to Mary Jane Warfield. Clay was later Lincoln's minister to Russia.[37]

It was a Kentucky reunion of sorts, but apparently Lincoln was not there to enjoy it or participate in the speaking. Along with cannons, music and banners, the Whigs from Boone and Howard counties built a log cabin to represent Harrison's early years. Guests were invited to walk through the cabin and partake from the barrel of hard cider inside. Everybody drank the cider from a communal gourd dipper and talked about the snarling raccoon chained inside the cabin.[38]

Lincoln, according to Helm, did not allow a steamboat stranded on a sand bar to keep him from the assignation with Mary. Somehow or other, he managed to get to Columbia. "The next Sunday," she wrote, "he and Mary were occupying the Todd pew in the Presbyterian Church."[39]

Mary's visit to Columbia extended over several weeks. A month before the Rocheport Whig rally, she wrote Mercy Levering about all the social activities, how beautiful it was in Columbia and meeting several young men she knew in Kentucky. She told Levering, "When I mention *some letters*, I have received since leaving S—you will be somewhat surprised as I must *confess* they were entirely *unlooked for*. This is *between ourselves*."[40]

An adept story teller, Mary entertained her family in Springfield with anecdotes about her trip to Missouri. Her uncle, Dr. John Todd, was delighted to hear about his brother, David, who was her host. "Every day after dinner," she said, "and before returning to the courthouse, it was uncle's custom to take a short nap. On account of company for dinner one day, he was deprived of his forty winks. One of the lawyers was making a long argument to the jury and Uncle David went to sleep on the bench. He awoke in a moment and interrupted the lawyer in his argument said, 'Mr. Clerk, enter a fine of ten dollars against David Todd for contempt of court. I'll break this habit of going to sleep in daylight or I'll break the court.'"

In December 1840, Mary replied to a letter from Mercy Levering apologizing for not writing due to being busy with a formidable amount of sewing for the coming winter. She wrote about Ninian Edwards' cousin, Matilda Edwards from Alton, coming to spend the winter with them. "We expect a very gay winter," she wrote, "evening before last my sister gave a most agreeable party, upwards of a hundred graced the festive scene." She talked about a planned excursion to Jacksonville for a couple of days in the following week. "Mr. (John J.) Hardin & (O. H.) Browning are our leaders the van brought up by Miss Edwards, my humble self, Webb, Lincoln and two or three others whom you know not, we are watching the clouds most anxiously trusting it may snow, so we may have a sleigh ride—Will it not be pleasant?"[41]

One evening at the Edwards' house, Stephen T. Logan teased Mary about her beaux, saying, "I hear the Yankee, the Irishman and our rough diamond from Kentucky were here last night. How many more do you have on the string, Mary?"[42]

"Are they not enough?" she replied.[43]

"I fear I am in grave danger of having to welcome a Yankee cousin," Logan quipped.[44]

"Never," said Mary. "The Yankee, as you call Mr. Douglas, differs from me too widely in politics. We would quarrel about Henry Clay. And Jimmie Shields, the Irishman, has too lately kissed the Blarney Stone for me to believe he really means half of his compliments and the rough diamond."[45]

"The rough diamond is much too rugged for your little white hands to attempt to polish," Logan said, interrupting.[46]

"To polish a stone like that," Mary said, "would be the task of a lifetime but what a joy to see the beauty and brilliance shine out more clearly each day! The important thing is the diamond itself, clear and flawless under its film."[47]

"Whew," Logan replied, "You don't mean you would seriously consider it?"[48]

"Why not?" she countered. "He is one of your best friends. You have told me time and again you never met a man with more ability, more native intellect."[49]

"Mary is not thinking of Mr. Lincoln in the light of a lover, Cousin Steve," Elizabeth Edwards announced firmly. "He is merely one of her most agreeable friends and not one whit more agreeable than Mr. Douglas or several others." Francis Wallace joined in the chorus of disapproval of Lincoln as husband material for their sister.[50]

Both sisters knew their younger sibling had a mercurial personality and that she chafed at restrictions being placed on her. Mary was in Springfield, Illinois, not in Lexington, Kentucky, where she could always depend on Grandmother Parker's support regardless of the situation. She was undoubtedly, for the moment, overwhelmed by their opposition. But, given her nature, would do exactly as she pleased.

Lincoln knew about her family's opinion. He probably had doubts about being able, in the short term, to give Mary the life to which she was accustomed due to his income. His law partner, John Todd Stuart, contributed to the situation. Stuart was serving in Congress and the success of their law practice was entirely dependent on Lincoln while he was away.

Elizabeth Edwards may have considered her opposition to Mary's relationship with Lincoln in her sister's best interests, however, it was a recipe for disaster.

Lincoln was late in arriving at the Edwards' house to take Mary to a party one evening in December. She had left without him. When he arrived at the event, she was dancing with Douglas. Seeing Lincoln come in the room, she paid him back for his tardiness and flirted even more outrageously with her partner. Lincoln was stunned and left.[51]

The Edwardses had their usual family dinner on New Year's Day. After the guests left, Lincoln called on Mary. She was flabbergasted that her flirting with Douglas had cut Lincoln so deeply. That, coupled with the Edwardses and other family members' opposition to any future marriage caused him to ask for a release from their understanding. Mary was heartbroken. Lincoln was nearly incapacitated from the situation, according to a portion of his January 23, 1841, letter to his law partner, John Todd Stuart, regarding Stuart running for re-election to Congress.[52] Lincoln wrote,

> For not giving you a general summary of news, you *must* pardon me, it is not in my power to do so. I am now the most miserable man living. If what I feel were equally distributed to the whole human family, there would not be one cheerful face on earth. Whether I shall ever be better I can not tell; I awfully forebode I shall not. To remain as I am is impossible; I must die or be better, it appears to me. The matter you speak of on my account, you may attend to as you say, unless you hear of my condition forbidding it. I say this, because I fear I shall be unable to attend to any business here, and a change of scene might help me. If I could be myself, I would rather remain at home with Judge Logan. I can write no more. Your friend, as ever, A. Lincoln.[53]

Lincoln's words were so deeply poignant and heart-rending one cannot imagine how he managed to function for the previous twenty-three days, not to speak of all the days that lay ahead. Lincoln suffered another loss. Joshua Speed, his best friend, had sold his store in Springfield in January 1841 and returned to Louisville to run Farmington, the family plantation. Speed's absence made things doubly difficult for Lincoln in this critical time.[54]

Mary Todd was also suffering. In a June 1841 letter to Mercy Levering, she wrote, "The last two or three months have been of interminable length, after my gay companions of the past winter departed, I was left much to the solitude of my own thoughts and some *lingering regrets* over the past, which time can alone overshadow with its healing balm, thus has my *spring time* passed, summer has again come, and the prairie land looks as beautiful as it did in the olden time, when we strolled together & derived so much of happiness from each other's society."[55]

She wrote of Joshua Speed, Lincoln's best friend, returning to Kentucky at his mother's request to help with her affairs. Judge John Speed, his father, died in March 1840. Mary indicated that she occasionally received letters from Speed. "In his last he spoke of his great desire of once more inhabiting this region & of his possibility of soon returning—*His* worthy friend [Lincoln] deems me unworthy of notice as I have not met *him* in the gay world for months, with the usual comfort of misery, imagine that others were as seldom gladdened by his presence as my humble self, yet I would that the case were different, that he would once more resume his Station in Society, that 'Richard [Lincoln] should be himself again, much, much happiness would it afford me."[56]

Lincoln, in a June 19, 1841, letter to Speed, was still using the affectionate name, Molly, in referring to Mary Todd, as he told Speed about the news from Springfield. The chief personages in the current local drama, he wrote, were Archibald Fisher, who was supposed to be murdered and Archibald, Henry and William Trailor, who were supposed to have murdered him. "[Ellis] Hart, the little drayman that hauled Molly home once," Lincoln wrote, "said it was too damned bad to have so much trouble and no hanging after all."[57]

Lincoln was referring to Mary having walked to call on some friends near the Edwards home. A heavy rain fell while she was visiting, turning the street into a sea of mud. Preferring to keep her clothes and shoes clean and dry, she flagged a passing dray, driven by Hart, to take her home. She smiled and waved to friends as she sat on the cart and was criticized for her unseemly actions.[58]

Two months later, Lincoln did escape his problems in Springfield. He went to Louisville to spend six weeks, from early August to the middle of September, with Speed at his family's Farmington plantation. While Lincoln was there, Speed began dating the daughter of a local landowner, Fanny Henning. When he returned to Springfield, Speed accompanied him.[59]

According to Helm, Mary's family received the news of the breakup with unalloyed joy. "For a year and a half after the broken engagement the two remained apart, thinking often of each other, but neither able to take the first step toward a reconciliation," Justin Turner wrote in *Mary Todd Lincoln: Her Life and Letters*.[60]

After he returned from Louisville, Lincoln poured out his soul in an extensive correspondence with Speed, who was having second thoughts about his relationship with Fanny Henning. The two broken-hearted swains were giving each other advice that failed to satisfy either of them.

In his January 3, 1842, letter to Speed, Lincoln began by saying, "Feeling as you know I do, the deepest solicitude for the success of the enterprise you are engaged in, I adopt this as the last method I can invent to aid you, in case, (which God forbid) you shall need any aid." Lincoln acknowledged that Speed was not feeling well physically but promised he would improve.[61] The advice Lincoln gave his friend could have well mirrored his own circumstances: "I know what the painful point with you is," he wrote, "at all times when you are unhappy. It is an apprehension that you do not love her as you should. What nonsense!— How came you to court her? Was it because you thought she desired it; and that you had given her reason to expect it.... Did you court her for her wealth? Why, you knew she had none. But you say you *reasoned* yourself *into* it. What do you mean by that? Was it not, that you found yourself unable to *reason* yourself out of it? Did you not think, and partly form the purpose, of courting her the first time you ever saw or heard of her? What had reason to do with it, at that early stage?"[62]

A month later Fanny Henning became ill and Speed wrote Lincoln of his concerns. Lincoln replied, "You know well that I do not feel my own sorrows much more keenly than I do yours, when I know of them; yet I assure you I was not much hurt by what you wrote me of your excessively bad feeling at the time you wrote. Not that I am less capable of sympathizing with you now than ever; not that I am less your friend than ever, but because I hope and believe, that your present anxiety and distress about *her* health and *her* life, just and will forever banish those horrid doubts, which I know you sometimes felt, as to the truth of your affection for her."[63]

Lincoln pointed out that if Speed did not love Fanny Henning he would face the situation more calmly. "You know the Hell I have suffered on that point, and how tender I am upon it." Lincoln adds that he was recovered from his hypochondria and was "even better than I was along in the fall."[64]

Lincoln had not recovered from his broken romance with Mary Todd, as he used the present tense in his statement about his suffering and the tenderness of his emotions. Speed, however, took his friend's advice and married Fanny Henning on February 14, 1842. In congratulating Speed on his marriage, Lincoln wrote, "I hope with tolerable confidence, that this letter is a plaster for a place that is no longer sore. God grant it may be so." In a post script, Lincoln added, "I have been quite a man since you left."[65]

Lincoln wrote Speed again on February 25, 1842, congratulating him on his marriage and saying he was somewhat jealous that the couple would be so wrapped up in each other that he would be forgotten entirely. Lincoln wrote that he would be very lonesome without Speed who decided not to return to Springfield, but his sense of humor was returning. In a post script, he told Speed about the death of the Sangamon circuit clerk Marvelous Eastman: "They say he was very loth to die."[66]

While celebrating his friend's good fortune in his marriage, Lincoln very much had Mary Todd on his mind.

"I am not going beyond the truth," Lincoln wrote Speed in a March 27, 1842, letter, "when I tell you, that in the short space it took me to read your last letter, [it] gave me more pleasure, than the sum total of all I have enjoyed since that fatal first of Jany. '41. Since then, it seems to me, I should have been entirely happy, but for the never-absent idea, that there is *one* still unhappy whom I have contributed to make so. That still kills my soul. I can not but reproach myself, for even wishing to be happy while she is otherwise. She accompanied a large party on the Rail Road cars to Jack-sonville last Monday; and on her return, spoke, so that I heard of it, of having enjoyed the trip exceedingly. God be praised for that."[67]

Mary Todd was on Lincoln's mind during the summer of 1842, and even more so after he continued to learn of the success of Speed's marriage, for which he claimed a small portion of credit. "I believe God made me one of the instruments of bringing you and Fanny together, which union, I have no doubt He had fore-ordained. Whatever he designs, he will do for *me* yet. Stand *still* and see the salvation of the Lord is my text just now."[68]

Speed, in a role reversal, became the advisor and not the advisee and had given Lincoln his opinion on his relationship with Mary. Lincoln replied:

> As for my having been displeased with your advice, surely you know better than that. I know you do; and therefore I will not labour to convince you. True, that subject is painful to me; but it is not your silence, or the silence of all the world that can make me forget it, I acknowledge the correctness of your advice too; but before I resolve to do one thing or the other, I must regain my confidence in my own ability to keep my resolves when they are made. In that ability, you know, I once prided myself as the only, or at least the chief, gem of my character; that gem I lost—how, and when, you too well know. I have not yet regained it; and until I do, I can not trust myself in any matter of much importance. I believe now that, had you understood my case at the time, as well as I understood yours afterwards, by the aid you would have given me, I should have sailed through clear; but that does not afford me sufficient confidence, to begin that, or the like of that, again.[69]

His best friend and chief confidant was in another state, but there were those in Springfield who were also interested in bringing about reconciliation between Lincoln and Mary. One of those was Dr. Anson G. Henry, Lincoln's physician and personal and political friend. Henry apparently acted as a go-between for the two, delivering Mary's assurances of her continuing devotion to Lincoln.[70]

Simon Francis, editor of the Whig newspaper the *Sangamo Journal*, and his wife, Eliza, were convinced that Mary and Lincoln belonged together, the Edwardses notwithstanding. The Francises arranged a surprise dinner party and invited Mary and Lincoln. Neither knew the other would be a guest until they arrived. Mrs. Francis advised them to be friends and a new chapter in their life began. They met secretly in their friends' home and revived their marriage plans, away from the Edwardses prying eyes.[71]

While they were rebuilding their relationship, Lincoln became involved in events leading up to his being challenged to a duel by State Auditor James Shields, the Irishman Steven Logan referred to in his list of Mary's suitors.

Shields, a Democrat, refused to honor the currency of the state bank after it failed in February 1842. Shields' action was in the best interests of the state but a clerk in his office, Milton H. Wash, had embezzled $1,161 in state funds. Lincoln picked up on the ideas from previous "Rebecca" letter writers and wrote an August 27, 1842, letter to the newspaper, which was printed on September 2, about the fiscal problems of a fictional couple, Peggy and Jeff, from the Lost Townships, and asked whether Shields was a Whig or Democrat: "It may help to send the present hypocritical set to where they belong and to fill the places they now disgrace and take a fewer airs while they are doing it. It ain't sensible to think the same men who got us into trouble will change their course; and yet its pretty plain, if some change for the better is not made, it's not long that neither Peggy or I, or any of us, will have a cow left to milk or a calf's tail to wring. Yours truly, Rebecca."[72]

The auditor went ballistic. Both he and Lincoln were traveling but they exchanged letters on the matter. Shields, on September 17, 1842, wrote Lincoln that, due to his public business, they would have to postpone their matter of private considerations a little longer. "I had hoped to avoid any difficulty with anyone in Springfield while residing there, by endeavoring to conduct myself in such a way amongst my political friends and opponents, as to escape the possibility, if any."[73]

Shields added that, while he abstained from provocation, he had been the object of slander and vituperation and abuse. His close friend, Gen. John Whitesides, erred when he told Shields that Lincoln had written the last two or three "Rebecca" letters that appeared in the *Sangamo Journal*.[74]

Lincoln answered Shields' letter on the same day, saying the auditor was presumptive in his charges. "Now, sir," he wrote, "there is in this so much assumption of facts and so much of menace as to the consequences, that I cannot submit to answer that note any farther than I have, and to add that the consequence to which I suppose you allude, would be a matter of as great regret to me as it possibly could be to you."[75]

In his second letter of the day, Shields backed off accusing Lincoln of writing the earlier "Rebecca" letters and asked again if he wrote the "Lost Township" letter that appeared in the September 2, 1842, *Sangamo Journal*. According to Dr. Elias H. Merryman, a friend of Lincoln's, he read Shields' note carefully and verbally told Gen. Whitesides that he did not think it consistent with his honor to negotiate for peace with the auditor unless Shields withdrew his former letter, which Lincoln considered offensive.[76]

Lincoln told Shields he did write the August 27 "Lost Townships" letter but none of the others. "I had no intentions of injuring your personal or private character or standing as a man or a gentleman; and I did not think, and do not now think that that article, could produce or has produced that effect against you and had I anticipated such an effect I would have forborne to write it. And I will add, that your conduct toward me, so far and I knew, had always been gentlemanly; and that I had no personal pique against you and no cause for any."[77]

The possibility of a duel might have ended there if Mary and her friend Julia Jayne had not needled Shields with still more rhetoric in the newspaper. They made fun of Shields by saying he was going to demand satisfaction for the insults he had received from an unusual source. They had "Aunt Rebecca" saying, "Let him come here and he may squeeze my hand.... If that aint personal satisfaction, I can only say that he is the furst man that was not satisfied by squeezin' my hand." Then the two women posted another missive, signed Cathleen, announcing that Shields had proposed marriage to 'Rebecca, the widow.'"[78]

In announcing the supposed nuptials of "Rebecca" and Shields, they wrote, "Ye jews-harps awake! The A's [auditor] won-Rebecca, the widow has gained Erin's son, The pride of the north from the emerald isle Has been woo'd and won by a woman's sweet smile."[79]

That did it. There was going to be a duel on September 22, 1842.

As the one challenged, Lincoln had the choice of date, weapons and place. After careful consideration, Lincoln selected cavalry broadswords, which he had used in the Black Hawk War. He knew Shields was a dandy shot with pistols and, of course, chose the weapon that would provide him with the most advantage. Lincoln was six feet, four inches tall, giving him a seven-inch reach over Shields. Lincoln selected the place, "Within three miles of Alton, on the opposite side of the river."[80]

In addition, Lincoln laid out a careful grid for the duel that was also to his advantage. "A plank ten-feet long and from nine to twelve inches broad to be firmly fixed on the edge, on the ground, as the line between us which neither is to pass his feet over upon forfeit of his life. Next, a line drawn on the ground on either side of said plank and parallel with it, each at the distance of the whole length of the sword and three feet additional from the plank; and the passing of his own such line by either party during the fight shall be deemed a surrender of conflict."[81]

In the days before the duel, Mary had to be concerned about Lincoln whether or not her part in events leading up the challenge was a factor. She had seen, as a young girl in Lexington, how dueling resulted in broken family ties and devastated friendships. The brothers of Mary's close friends Catherine Trotter and Mary and Margaret Wickliffe, George Trotter and Charles Wickliffe, were drawn into a duel over slavery and their fathers' opposition to and support of the institution. The two young men were best friends until a disagreement over slavery led to Wickliffe challenging Trotter.[82] Trotter shot Wickliffe, and he died from his wounds.[83]

Mary's feelings were about events leading up the duel have been lost in time. Twenty-three years later, after the death of two sons and seeing her husband murdered as he sat beside her, she gave a rather murky account of the incident in a letter to Mrs. Gideon Wells, whose husband was secretary of the Navy in Lincoln's cabinet.

> Gen Shields, a kind hearted, impulsive Irishman, was always creating a sensation & mirth by his drolleries. On one occasion, he amused me exceedingly, so much so, that I committed his *follies* to rhyme and very silly verses they were, only, they were said to abound in sarcasm causing them to be very offensive to the gen. A gentleman friend carried them off and persevered in not returning them when one day, I saw them, strangely enough in the daily paper. Genl Shields called upon the Editor and demanded the author. The Editor, requested *a day* to reflect upon it—The latter called upon Mr. Lincoln, to whom he knew I was engaged & explained to him that he was certain I was the Author—but M L. then replied, say to Shields that, "I am responsible."[84]

That was not exactly the way it happened, as Lincoln told Shields he only wrote the "Rebecca" letter that appeared in the September 2, 1842, newspaper, none of the others.

Lincoln prepared himself for the duel by training in the use of broadswords with Albert Taylor Bledsoe, a Frankfort, Kentucky, native who was a West Point graduate and had spent two years on the frontier as a brevet second lieutenant in the Seventh Infantry. A brilliant attorney, Bledsoe brought a varied background to his Illinois law practice from being the chairman of the mathematics department at Miami University, Oxford, Ohio, to an assistant to the Episcopal Bishop of Kentucky. But, it was his West Point expertise that Lincoln sought prior to his duel with Shields.[85]

All the principals—Lincoln, Shields, Whiteside, Merryman, Bledsoe, and Butler—arrived at the dueling site, known as Bloody Island, on September 22, 1842. A considerable crowd gathered on the Illinois side of the river. During what could be called a warm-up session, Lincoln, broadsword in hand, reached over Shields' head and clipped a branch off a tree in one quick stroke.[86]

One can only imagine what was going through Shields' head as he realized how absolutely outclassed he was with an unaccustomed clumsy weapon.

Most historians appear to agree with David Herbert Donald that the duel was stopped by John J. Hardin and Dr. R. W. English. "As friends of both parties," Donald wrote, "they persuaded Shields to withdraw his insulting note so that Lincoln could disavow any intentions of injuring the auditor's 'personal or private character or standing ... as a man or gentleman' and claim that he wrote the 'Lost Township' correspondence 'solely for political effect. With that, the parties shook hands and returned to Illinois."[87]

Bledsoe's daughter, Sophia Bledsoe Herrick, a journalist and editor, gave another version in *The Century Illustrated Monthly Magazine* in 1892. She wrote that her father, grandfather, Moses O. Bledsoe, and Merryman, Lincoln's second, made the overnight trip to the dueling site together. Like the historians, Herrick does not give particulars about the meeting other than to say the duel would fall flat if the combatants just apologized. "So, they put a log of wood prostrate in a canoe and covered it with General Shields' cloak or something equally effective and clustered around the supposed victim, one fanning another, supporting, etc., till the crowd on the opposite bank was worked up to a great pitch of excitement and sympathy. When the log was lifted out, the dueling party had effectively turned the laugh on themselves."[88]

Lincoln said, "To tell you the truth, [Usher] Linder, I did not want to kill Shields and felt sure I could disarm him, having had a month to learn the broadsword exercise; and furthermore, I didn't want the damned fellow to kill me, which I rather think he would have done if we had selected pistols."[89]

The broadsword referred to in the dueling documents was probably an 1840 heavy dragoon saber, according to retired Marine Corps Lt. Col. Michael Wills, from Florence, Kentucky. The saber blade was slightly less than thirty-six inches long and 1.25 inches wide. "The 1840 saber had the nickname of the 'Old Wristbreaker,'" according to the Fort Scott National Historic Site, in Fort Scott, Kansas, "because it was fairly easy for the soldier to break his wrist in combat if he held the saber wrong. The proper way to hold the saber was inverted and away from the body."[90]

After the duel that never was, questions about the length of the weapons lingered for some time. On May 13, 1843, Lincoln wrote John J. Hardin asking him "to measure one of the largest swords we took to Alton and write me the length of it, from the tip of the point to the tip of the hilt in feet and inches. I have a dispute about the length."[91]

Lincoln wrote Speed on October 5, 1842, about Shields challenging his friend William Butler to another duel. "The town is in a ferment and a street fight somewhat anticipated," Lincoln wrote. He added that the duel was not the real reason for the letter but he had something to ask Speed.[92] His question concerned Mary Todd.

"The immense suffering you endured from the first days of September till middle of February you never tried to conceal from me, and I well understood. You have now been the husband of a lovely woman nearly eight months. That you are happier now than you were the day you married her I well know; for without, you would not be living. But I have your word for it too; and the returning elasticity of spirits which is manifested in your letters. But I want to ask a closer question—'Are you now, in *feeling* as well as *judgment*, glad you are married as you are?' From any body but me, this would be an impudent question not to be tolerated; but I know you will pardon it in me. Please answer it quickly as I feel impatient to know."[93]

Whatever Speed's answer was, Mary Todd and Abraham Lincoln were married a month later on November 4, 1842. Initially they intended to be married in the home of Dr. Charles Dresser, an Episcopal minister. Helm wrote they chose that location because they both feared further opposition from Mary's family.[94]

Ninian Edwards, when Lincoln told him of their wedding plans, insisted that the ritual be held at their house. After discussing the matter, Mary and Lincoln agreed and Dr. Dresser married them in the Edwardses parlor. Mary wore a white gown. The tucked bodice had a round neckline, leg-of-mutton sleeves and came to a point in front. The embossed white skirt was given Mary by her sister, Frances.[95]

It was a small gathering of relatives and friends who witnessed Abraham Lincoln slipping a wedding ring, engraved with "Love Is Eternal, A.L. to M.T. Nov. 4 1842," on Mary Todd's finger.[96]

Mary Todd's niece and biographer, Katherine Helm, omits the wedding ring inscription from the book about her aunt. However, in a draft of her manuscript, Helm clearly expressed the deep well of anger the Todd family felt about those they believed criticized Mary unfairly. Helm, in the draft, excoriated Gamaliel Bradford for an article, "The Wife of Abraham Lincoln," he wrote in a September 1925 issue of *Harper's Magazine*. Bradford suggested the inscription inside the ring might have been Mary's idea. "Mr. Bradford, speaking of the ring given Mary by Mr. Lincoln in which was engraved, 'Love is eternal,' sneeringly suggests that the sentiment might have emanated from Mary. If it did, she was never for one instant false to it."[97]

"Nothing new here," Lincoln wrote Samuel D. Marshall a week after their wedding, "except my marrying, which to me is a matter of profound wonder."[98]

CHAPTER 2

Deeds Not Words

It was not surprising that Mary Todd defied her family in marrying the man she loved. In brushing aside their objections and persistently following her heart, she exhibited the ruthless determination demonstrated by her Scottish and Irish ancestors who fought against oppressions of their freedoms. It was a multi-faceted characteristic in her personality, encouraged by her father Robert Smith Todd, which served her well at times and in other situations was not necessarily an asset.

Acumen for political discourse drew Abraham Lincoln to Mary, whose Scottish ancestors believed in adhering to one's principals regardless of the cost. Among those principals was the free expression of opinion, the right to engage in political dialogue and the freedom to practice one's chosen religion. Mary Todd's seventeenth century Covenanter forbearers, in defiance of royal edicts, stood a chance of becoming slaves themselves in the American and Caribbean colonies if their cause was lost. Consequently, the Todds' healthy dose of family pride was passed down through the generations, along with a spirited defense of society's underdogs.

The Robert Smith Todd family's Scottish coat of arms depicted a fox proudly sitting atop a line of bars surrounded by an oval border inscribed "Deeds Not Words." There were several English variations of the Todd coat of arms. One had three foxes' heads arranged around a shield. Another also used the fox with the motto, "By Cunning. Not by Craft." In both Scotland and England, the word tod or todd was associated with the fox.[1]

The Scottish family of Tods, a contentious and scrappy lot, lived up to that motto when they sacrificed their lands and their lives in the fight against English monarchs and the Church of England for the right to practice their chosen religion, Presbyterianism. Although they were forced to leave Scotland, the Tods brought that same deeply ingrained belief in religious and individual freedoms with them when they escaped to Ireland, came to America, helped to settle Kentucky and opened the western frontier.

On February 28, 1638, a massive crowd of Presbyterians met in Greyfriars Kirkyard in Edinburgh, Scotland, to sign a revival of the Covenant of 1581, which established Presbyterianism as the state religion. After Charles I came to the English throne in 1625, he convened a general assembly of Scotland to determine what the national religion would be and agreed to accept the body's decision. When the assembly decided to abolish the Anglican episcopacy, Charles refused to honor his commitment and a war broke out that lasted four decades.[2]

After warring back and forth across the Scottish-English border, a Covenanter army in 1639 captured Newcastle, and Charles I, unable to raise enough support to resist the Scots, agreed to the Covenanters' demands to stop meddling in Scotland's church. Between 1661 and 1688, an estimated 18,000 Covenanters died for their cause.[3]

Robert Tod, of Fenwich Parish, and James Tod, of Dunbar Parish, were among the Covenanters engaged in the June 1679, Battle of Drumclog, where they defeated the English forces. Confident they would prevail, more than 1,000 Covenanters assembled in Edinburgh to plan their next move. A few days later at the battle of Bothwell Bridge, eight miles from Glasgow, they were defeated by massive English forces.[4]

About four hundred of the Covenanters, including the Tods, were kept under guard at Greyfriars Kirkyard for five months with little shelter and less daily subsistence, four ounces of bread and water. Other Covenanters were held in Cannongate and Edinburgh prisons.[5]

Many starved to death at Greyfriars, others died from their battle or torture wounds and some signed an oath of allegiance to the English monarch. The Tods were among the prisoners left to shiver through the cold Scottish autumn and await their fate.

By November 1679, the number of prisoners had decreased to 257. The Covenanters were gathered up by William Paterson, an Edinburgh merchant involved with the slave trade, and loaded on *The Crown of London*, commanded by Captain Thomas Teddico. The captain set sail for the American colonies on November 27 with the intent of selling the prisoners as slaves. There were 257 Covenanters in the hold of Teddico's ship built to hold only a 100 men.[6]

"Originally two vessels were to have been provided but for unexplained reasons only the *Crown* arrived in Leith and it was into her that all the unfortunate Covenanters were crammed," David Ferguson wrote in *Shipwrecks of Orkney, Shetland and the Pentland Firth*. "The wretched prisoners had been banished as rebels to 'some one or another of our plantations in America,' as King James II put it in a letter to the Scottish Privy Council."[7]

The October 6, 1988, Scottish newspaper, *The Orcadian*, recalled the Covenanters "had survived the months of confinement without Greyfriars Churchyard in Edinburgh finding they would escape death only to be transported to the new colonies in America where they would be sold as slaves."[8]

Two weeks after leaving port, Capt. Teddico's ship sailed through the North Sea headed for the Orkney Islands, en route to the North Atlantic, when a December blizzard struck. The captain put into port on Deerness, on one of the Orkney Islands. He ordered the hold's hatches battened down and locked to prevent any prisoners from escaping.[9]

The captain refused the pleas of the prisoners to release them from the hold. "At 10 p.m.," the article continued, "the inevitable happened. The straining anchor snapped conclusively allowing the ship to be carried unprotesting on to the treacherous saw-tooth rocks sending the majority of the prisoners to watery graves. Whatever, the entire crew escaped alive by cutting down the mast and using it as a bridge to shore, although when the prisoners attempted a similar crossing they were beaten back and forced into the water. About fifty prisoners escaped only to be recaptured and sold as slaves in Jamaica and New Jersey but James and Robert Tod were not among them."[10]

A third brother, John Tod, either eluded capture at Bothwell Bridge or was not in that battle. According to family lore, John Tod fled persecution in Claverhouse, Scotland, and sought refuge in Northern Ireland. Two of his grandsons, Andrew and Robert Tod(d), brought their families to America in 1737, and settled in Montgomery County, Pennsylvania, before moving to Virginia and later to Kentucky.[11]

John Todd's son, Robert, was born in Ireland in 1697, and first married Jean Smith.

That union produced two sons, David and John. The third son of David and Hannah Owen Todd, Levi, married Jane Briggs. Their son, Robert Smith Todd, married Eliza Ann Parker and they were the parents of Mary Todd. The Irish Robert Todd's second wife was Isabelle Bodley and their branch of the family produced a daughter, Elizabeth, who married General Andrew Porter. Their daughter, Elizabeth Rittenhouse Porter, married her cousin, Robert Parker, and they were the parents of Eliza Ann Parker, Mary Todd's mother.[12] Mary Todd's parents shared the same great-grandfather, Robert Todd, from Ireland.

Todds, from the early days in America, recognized just how important an education was and would be to future generations of their families. First, they needed to build a solid financial foundation through the acquisition of vast amounts of land. John, Robert and Levi, sons of David and Hannah Todd, were educated in Virginia, in the classical school of their uncle, the Rev. John Todd, known as Parson Todd. Levi and John Todd studied law and were surveyors. Robert married a daughter of Parson Todd, who never came to Kentucky County. He used his political influence to obtain the charter for Translyvania College from the Virginia legislature and gave the institution its first library.[13]

All three brothers fought in the Revolutionary War. In 1780, Thomas Jefferson, governor of Virginia, divided Kentucky County into three divisions, Lincoln, Jefferson and Fayette counties. John Todd was given the highest appointment, that of colonel of the Fayette County militia, by Jefferson. When the Virginia legislature created the Court of Quarterly sessions for Kentucky County in 1777, at Harrodsburg, Levi Todd was appointed clerk.[14]

A fervent advocate for more protection for Kentucky County settlements, Levi Todd's letters to three Virginia governors, Patrick Henry, Benjamin V. Harrison and Edmund Randolph, were a constant plea for additional troops, arms and ammunition. In a September 9, 1782, letter to Harrison, he complained that the frontier was left open and unguarded and emphasized the need for 200 soldiers and artillery.[15]

In December 7, 1786, and February 14, 1787, letters to Randolph, Todd complained about the gloomy conditions in Kentucky and how badly the militia needed equipment. Settlements in Jefferson and Mercer counties, he said, were being abandoned and Indians had killed one man at Limestone (now Maysville) and another in Jefferson County.[16]

As head of the Fayette County militia, Major Todd, who succeeded his brother, John, had the authority to take matters into his own hands. He advertised in the April 25, 1788, *Kentucky Gazette* that he would contract with any person who would furnish provisions for men ordered on duty to protect the county.[17] In the same year, as a member of the Danville Constitutional Convention, Levi Todd objected to certain powers being invested in Congress for fear the frontier would lose navigation rights to the Mississippi River.[18]

Mary Todd's other grandfather, Major Robert Parker, was also a surveyor and city clerk. He later owned a grocery store and operated a mill in Lexington on Versailles Road. The Parkers, while not as wealthy as the Todds, equaled or eclipsed them in prominent forebears. Her maternal great-grandfather, Gen. Andrew Porter, was on George Washington's staff during the Revolutionary War. One of his sons, David Rittenhouse Porter, was the first constitutional governor of Pennsylvania and the state's first surveyor general, he turned down an appointment by President James Madison to be his secretary of war.[19]

An aide to Gen. Andrew Lewis at the Battle of Point Pleasant in 1774, often called a prelude to the Revolutionary War, John Todd joined Benjamin Logan and John Floyd at Logan's Station, in Lincoln County. He explored and surveyed land from there south into what is now Tennessee. In 1777, Todd was one of the first two burgesses sent to the Virginia legislature from Kentucky County, and he introduced bills to emancipate slaves and set aside land grants for educational institutions. That same year, John Todd moved to Lexington, where he was joined by his younger brother, Levi, who first settled in Harrodsburg. Their brother, Robert, joined them in Lexington.[20]

Mary never knew her paternal grandfather and uncle, Levi and John Todd, who were among the larger landowners and influential citizens of Fayette County. Their fortunes came from slaves, lands awarded them in Revolutionary War grants, land warrants purchased from other veterans and the choice lands they surveyed for themselves. An examination of land records indicated the Todds often sold or traded lands with each other but always selected family members to handle their estates. The Rev. John Todd, in 1794, gave his nephews Robert and Levi power of attorney to represent him in all actions pertaining to his estate.[21]

Levi Todd, an astute businessman, also administered the estates of John Preston, James Dorchester, William Moyers and Patrick Ryan in 1780–1781.[22]

Virginia governors issued grants with such largess their excessiveness exceeded the existing land area of Kentucky County, which covered approximately 42,750 square miles.[23] Many land grants were vague and overlapped each other. Revolutionary War veterans, depending on their rank, were eligible for up to 5,000 acres in land warrants. Surveys often had undependable boundaries. Consequently, disputes over land ownership in Kentucky began and remained in mass confusion for more than a century. John and Levi Todd also accumulated vast acreages in Illinois and Tennessee.[24]

John Todd's widow and his infant daughter Mary Owen inherited his vast holdings when he was killed at the Battle of Blue Licks, the last engagement of the Revolutionary War. According to those who claimed they saw John Todd's will, his estate and holdings were to revert back to his brothers, Robert and Levi, if his daughter died without issue. It was said Mary Owen Todd was the richest female in Kentucky before she could walk. On December 20, 1780, Virginia governor Patrick Henry signed a treasury warrant giving Mary Owen Todd 400 acres of prime land along the waters of Elkhorn Creek in Fayette County. After her father's death on August 18, 1782, Henry signed treasury warrant number 666 on July 22, 1783, giving the child 1,000 more acres along the Elkhorn.[25]

The Todds, essentially Levi and his son, Robert Smith, who was a merchant, politician, banker and businessman, advised Jane H. Todd and her daughter in handling their fortune. Both women refused to heed their advice in their choice of husbands. Col. Todd's holdings, after his daughter's second marriage, became enmeshed in a bitter legal battle that consumed more than a decade and eventually ensnared Mary, her husband and her siblings.

Levi Todd had a vision for Kentucky settlement as well as a new government. In February 1784, he wrote his brother-in-law, John McCuloch, "I wish for a few more of your Pennsylvania Patriots to be mingled with our Virginians that we may find out the most free as well as the most safe way to govern and be governed." He outlined a vision he did not live to see. "People who have been confined to Forts are now entering the Woods, beginning the World; stately houses in a few years will be reared where the small Log Cabins have stood; Wheat Fields and meadows where cane brakes now grow."[26]

In 1787, Col. John Todd's fort was demolished as the threat of Indian attacks had lessened. Lexington/Fayette County tax rolls in 1789 indicated 9,670 horses (fifty stallions), 2,522 slaves, and a population of 834 in the city and 18,670 in the county. According to a 1791 plat of Lexington, the Todds and Parkers were owners of choice lots, measuring 17.5 by 40 poles (289' by 660'), reaching from what is now Short Street to Second Street. By

1808, there were 104 brick houses, ten stone residences and 187 framed houses in Lexington.[27]

Levi Todd began building Ellerslie, reputed to be the first brick house in Fayette County, in 1787. It was possible that Todd named his home for what is said to be the birthplace of William Wallace, who struggled for years to free Scotland from England in the thirteenth and fourteenth centuries. According to architectural historian Clay Lancaster, Ellerslie originally contained six rooms, plus a basement. Around 1792, Lancaster said Todd doubled the size of the house, when he purchased 100 acres to add to his estate from that of his late brother, John Todd.[28]

The residence, with a five-bayed façade and a wide transomed doorway, contained seven chambers (bedrooms), ten fireplaces and eighteen windows. There was a library for Levi Todd's considerable collection of books, a drawing room and a parlor. The furnishings were not lavish but were comfortable and well used.[29]

The Todd families lived in an affluent manner similar to their peers. Levi Todd, a prominent figure in Kentucky County's political world, was not only well educated for his time but prosperous and well-liked.

Robert Smith Todd, one of Levi Todd's eleven children, was born at Ellerslie on February 25, 1791. With the depth of education he absorbed at Parson Todd's school, Levi Todd saw that his children had the best education available. Robert entered Transylvania when he was fourteen. When he finished at Transylvania, he studied law under George M. Bibb, chief judge of the Kentucky Court of Appeals, who later served in the U.S. Senate and was secretary of the treasury in President John Tyler's administration. Todd was admitted to the bar in 1811, and had a lucrative law practice. He spent more than twenty years as the clerk of the Kentucky House of Representatives, served three terms in the House of Representatives and one in the Senate, ran various businesses and was a bank president.[30]

Another son, John, became a doctor. Levi Todd's daughters married well. Hannah married the Rev. Robert Stuart, the pastor of Walnut Hill Presbyterian Church. They were the parents of John Stuart Todd, Abraham Lincoln's first law partner in Illinois. Elizabeth Todd was the wife of Charles Carr, Fayette County's first sheriff and later a member of the state House of Representatives. Nancy Todd wed one of her cousins, Dr. John Todd, from Danville. Jane Briggs Todd married Judge Daniel Breck and Margaret married Col. William Rodes.[31]

James Clark Todd, the only child of Levi Todd's second marriage to Jane Holmes, wed Maria Blair, whose father, Samuel Blair, was one of Fayette County's early pioneers. They were the parents of Dr. Lymon Beecher Todd, one of the attending physicians at President Abraham Lincoln's bedside in April 1865, after he was shot.[32]

Levi Todd's children managed, probably with his assistance, to elude one of the biggest problems on the frontier, obtaining and keeping legal titles to their lands. A phrase he used in a 1784 letter indicated he was quite aware of the problems in securing sound property deeds to land. "Cousin Bob," Todd wrote, "has been dabbling in the Landmonger Business. I suppose he will be silent on the Head until he knows the event but he seems well suited with his prospect scarcely begun." The cousin he was referring to was probably Robert Parker, Fayette County's first surveyor and Mary Todd's maternal grandfather.[33]

Land ownership perplexities created problems for hundreds, including Daniel Boone and Thomas Lincoln, who were unable to retain ownership of their lands. They experienced drastic changes in their fortunes as they lost their lands from overlapping land warrants, faulty surveys or to greedy land speculators. It was this problem that allegedly spurred angry landowners, in 1803, to burn Levi Todd's clerk's office, destroying wills, deeds and lawsuits over landownership.[34]

In nineteenth century agrarian Kentucky, the practice of burning public buildings in general, courthouses in particular, to destroy both civil and criminal records was relatively commonplace. The practice, which lasted more than a century, further compounded land ownership problems. When Levi Todd built Ellerslie in 1787, he constructed a small stone building in his back yard to use as the clerk's office. Why the clerk's office was not located in the first courthouse, a two story log structure built in 1782, is a mystery.[35] Perhaps Levi Todd used his prominence to keep the clerk's office in his back yard because he did not want to make the short trip into Lexington every day.

Unanswered questions proliferated about the burning of a stone building, whose walls were probably ten or twelve inches thick. The sturdy building burned during the night of January 31, 1803.[36] Granted, a candle might have been left burning or a spark might have fallen out of the fireplace. On the other hand, it was just as likely to have been arson considering consequent events.

Documents lost in the 1803 clerk's office fire victimized the Todd family, as well as others, for decades. The wills, deeds, and other documents which could be reconstructed were resurrected and were referred to as the "Burnt Records." There was no index listing in the Burnt Records of Col. John Todd's will but there were four property transfers of land by his estate's trustees.[37]

The good name of his family was important to Levi Todd. In 1806, Todd bristled at a printed accusation in a Frankfort newspaper, *Western World*, that his brother John had been involved in a 1781 meeting connected to the "Spanish Conspiracy." In the sixteen years between Kentucky legally becoming part of Virginia and the commonwealth joining the union in 1792, settlers, Levi Todd included, were frustrated over the lack of protection and long awaited judicial appeals being conducted between Kentucky County and Virginia's capital in Richmond. Spain, having refused to recognize America's independence, was eager to form an alliance with that part of the western frontier. Gen. James Wilkinson, who was eventually booted out of the Continental Army by Gen. George Washington, came to Kentucky looking for wealth. He convinced Harry Innes, Kentucky's first federal district judge, John Brown, Kentucky's first U.S. Senator and Benjamin Sebastian, an appellate judge, to join him in working out a deal with Spain for Kentucky to secede not only from Virginia but from the Confederation of States.[38]

A representative of the newspaper, Thomas Allin, acknowledged the publication's error concerning John Todd and the Harrodsburg meeting in question. The "Spanish Conspiracy" was remarkably unsuccessful but Wilkinson, Brown, Innes and Sebastain were more than adequately rewarded with pensions from the government of Spain.[39]

A historian specializing in early Kentucky families, Thomas M. Green, wrote that Levi Todd "was a solid, substantial, enterprising citizen; a sensible, intelligent, well-educated man; a consistent Presbyterian; a valuable and faithful public servant; a good soldier." He died at age fifty-one in 1807, having lived through the American Revolution, Indian battles, opening of the frontier and the establishment of the commonwealth.[40]

Undoubtedly, Levi Todd had occasions where he cut corners in his personal and professional transactions, as did many living on a frontier which, for decades, was without specie, had little or no political framework and less law. He was no better and no worse than numerous other prominent citizens in Fayette County. It has become Levi Todd's misfortune that his granddaughter's marriage to the sixteenth president cast him into a historical spotlight.

One author, in his book about Mary, claimed that her grandfather Levi Todd, along with several other relatives of Mary, died in insane asylums. His sources were a couple of other biographers of Mary, two family letters, and he cited historian Michael Burlingame's research as evidence that Levi Todd died in an insane asylum. Levi Todd died in September 1807, at his home, Ellerslie. There was no facility for the mentally ill in Lexington at that time. The Fayette Hospital, begun in 1817, was never completed due to the financial panic of 1819. Gov. John Adair purchased the building and property for the commonwealth and Eastern State Hospital, said to be the first asylum west of the Alleghenies, which opened in 1824 with thirty-three patients.[41] Obviously, Levi Todd was not one of them.

A Kentucky statute, enacted in 1793, provided for the mentally ill to be supported out of their estates. If a mentally ill person was unable to provide for their own care, a conservatory fund was established under supervision.[42] There was no evidence in Levi Todd's probate documents in the Fayette County clerk's office to indicate any personal funds were provided for such care or that he was ever a ward of the commonwealth.

Levi Todd's estate inventory revealed that he lived very well. He owned what was then considered an extensive library with ninety-three volumes on the law, books on Greek grammar and English and Roman history, French and Latin dictionaries, and Mary Wollstonecraft's *A Vindication on the Rights of Women*, written in 1792. Levi Todd owned twenty-one slaves, a large assortment of tools, eight horses, four cows, fifty-six hogs and forty sheep along with a more than ample supply of corn and grains. Ellerslie was filled with fine furnishings, silver plate, bed-hangings, carpets, linens, china and crystal.[43]

Todd's personal estate, less the real property he owned, was estimated at approximately, $13,000, the equivalent of $240,000 in 2012 dollars.[44]

Without a doubt, some of Levi Todd's possessions found their way into his son's first home on Short Street, where Mary Todd was born. After his admission to the bar, Robert S. Todd's courtship of Elizabeth Parker, daughter of Major Robert and Elizabeth Rittenhouse Porter Parker, turned serious. Her family referred to her as Eliza. When Eliza Parker's father died in 1800, his entire estate was left to his wife with one stipulation, "That all my children shall be carefully brought up and well educated." There is no reason to believe that the Widow Parker, as she was known, failed to follow her late husband's wishes.[45]

Two of the Parkers' sons, James and John, were Transylvania College trained physicians. Alexander Parker was an attorney. The two Parker daughters, Eliza and Mary Ann, probably attended Mary Beck's academy, which opened in Lexington in the early 1800s, or one of the other academies. Said to be something of a beauty, eighteen-year-old Eliza Parker had completed her education and was enjoying social activities afforded by her family's status. Among her suitors were Transylvania students Robert S. Todd and Stephen F. Austin, later known as the founding father of Texas. Mary Ann Parker, unlike her sister, waited until she was in her twenties to marry J. C. Richardson, a long-time Fayette County sheriff.[46]

John Parker, Eliza's brother, wrote Henry Clay in Washington on December 7, 1811, asking the Congressman to promote a commission in the army for his nephew, Robert S. Todd.[47] In August 1812, Robert S. Todd and his company of militiamen joined the Lexington Light Infantry, under the command of Captain Nathan Hart, Henry Clay's brother-in-law, and marched off to fight the British in the War of 1812. The army was led by General Henry Proctor and the Shawnee Chief Tecumseh's Indian Confederation. The war began three months earlier after American seamen were impressed by the British and other international events forced the confrontation. Also at issue was which nation would control the Great Lakes and land expansion beyond the Mississippi River.[48]

Marching through rain, Todd came down with pneumonia and was eventually brought back home by his brother, Samuel. He recovered and, before leaving, he and Eliza Parker were married on November 26, 1812, at her mother's brick home on Short Street.[49]

Robert and Samuel Todd rejoined their unit and marched north for the disastrous Battle of the River Raisin in what is now Michigan. Hart and half of his company were killed in the battle. The Todd brothers were more fortunate. John and Samuel were wounded and captured. John ran the gauntlet and escaped. Sam was adopted by the Indians and remained with them for a year before he was ransomed for a barrel of whiskey. Robert escaped unscathed.[50]

Todd built a two-story home, similar in style to Ellerslie, on his lot next door to the Widow Parker's home. Nearby on Cheapside was the grocery and mercantile establishment, Smith and Todd, he owned with another War of 1812 veteran, Bird Smith. Henry Clay lent Smith and Todd the money to start their business.[51]

In a December 13, 1817, newspaper advertisement, Smith and Todd stated they would travel to foreign markets to procure dry goods, staples, fruits and vegetables and a wide range of wine, brandy, gin and whiskey.[52]

Legal documents indicated Todd had a thriving law practice and among his clients were two banks. David Todd executed a deed of trust (an instrument of mortgage) in 1815 to Robert S. Todd to satisfy repayment of notes over three thousand dollars to the Bank of Kentucky, which was chartered by the legislature in 1806, and partly owned by the commonwealth. David Todd's note for $3,000.00 also included two other prominent Lexington men, John H. Morton and Thomas Bodley, as co-signers. Robert S. Todd co-signed another note for $820.00. The deed of trust included David Todd's slaves, library, household furnishings, silver, linens, horses and wagon.[53]

Todd, in 1815, handled a transfer of mortgaged property from John Hart to Henry Clay for the Bank of Kentucky.[54] In 1816 and 1817, he acted as the attorney for the Kentucky Insurance Company, one of Kentucky's first banking institutions, in collecting on a defaulted note of John Bobb in the amount of $400.00. Todd was to oversee the sale of Bobb's slave, animals and household goods. Monies left, after satisfying the loan, Todd was to return to Bobb.[55]

Robert S. Todd was elected clerk of the state House of Representatives in 1813 and held the position for twenty-two years. The office of clerk, second only in power to the speaker of the House, was a prestigious position, as he kept track of legislation, certified passage of all bills and resolutions, attested to legislative documents, made reports to the Senate and had custody of all records. Todd's competency and popularity was evidenced by the fact House members elected him to that post sixteen times by a unanimous vote.[56] The position of clerk of the House enabled Todd to gain clients for his law practice and solidify a base for future political and business ambitions.

On December 13, 1818, Mary Ann Todd was born in the brick house on Short Street. She was the fourth child born to Robert and Eliza and was named for her mother's only sister. In her early years, she played with her siblings, Elizabeth, Frances, and Levi, in the commodious yard connecting the two houses. Her second brother, Robert Parker Todd, died in 1822, when she was four. Another daughter was born in 1824 and was named Ann

Maria, for Robert Todd's sister. Mary's second name was dropped. She used her full name only when signing legal documents.[57]

In July 1825, while Lexington was celebrating the nation's birthday with such luminaries as Gen. Winfield Scott and the new secretary of state, Henry Clay, Eliza Parker Todd was giving birth to another son. George Rogers Clark Todd never knew his mother. She died the next day from what was commonly called child birth fever. The most prominent physicians in Lexington, Dr. Benjamin Dudley and Dr. Elisha Warfield, attended the woman whose body was ravaged from birthing seven children in thirteen years. The six Todd children were kept in the Widow Parker's house and probably did not know their mother was dead until the next morning when the Todds' butler, Nelson, delivered funeral notices to family and friends: "Yourself and family are respectfully invited to attend the funeral of Mrs. Eliza Parker, Consort of Robert S. Todd, Esq., from his residence on Short Street, this evening at 4 o'clock. July 6, 1825."[58]

Mary's features are often compared to those of her father. There are no surviving likenesses of Eliza Parker Todd for comparison.

CHAPTER 3

A New Mother

With all his responsibilities as an attorney, businessman, family financial caretaker and father to a brood of six motherless children, Robert S. Todd, thirty-four, had his hands full and desperately needed a second wife. Eliza Parker Todd's death had an impact far beyond her family's initial grief. New family allegiances would be formed, her children had to become accustomed to a new mother they never cared for and some of their wounds never healed.

In her grief, young Mary Todd was surrounded by those she held most dear: her father, siblings, her maternal grandmother and the Parker and Todd families, aunts, uncles and cousins, friends and household slaves she had known her entire life.

Of course, the death of her mother deeply wounded the six-year-old. If she saw her in death repose, the image would be difficult to erase from her consciousness. Kentucky funeral customs in 1825 called for the deceased to be washed, dressed and laid out in their home for viewing of family and friends. Since Eliza Todd died in July, the warm weather required that she be buried as soon as possible. Ishbel Ross, in the 1973 book, *The President's Wife: Mary Todd Lincoln*, wrote, "After seeing her mother's still face, she was never again able to face death without showing convulsive grief."[1]

However, young children have marvelous recuperative powers. Mary Todd was in the middle of seven children. Mary Ann Parker stepped in to care for her sister's children with the support of her mother, brothers and their families. The huge Todd extended family also did their share.[2]

In later years, Mary Todd remembered those who were kind to a young girl who had just lost her mother. She wrote her cousin, Eliza Stuart Steele, a sister of John Todd Stuart and who married the Rev. Samuel Steele, "The memory of earlier years and the memory of those who were so kind to me in my desolate childhood is ever remembered by me."[3]

Being the middle child, Mary Todd was in a difficult position. Her older sisters, Elizabeth and Frances, with only two years' difference in their ages, had already bonded. Ann Marie Todd was the favorite of the paternal aunt for whom she was named. Levi and George were expected to carry the mantle of the next generation of the family. Mary, if she turned to her father for solace, found he had even less time for her than before her mother's death. Consequently, the vulnerable middle child sought and received comfort from her grandmother Parker.

Elizabeth Porter Parker understood very well her young granddaughter's loss and emotions. Her mother and namesake, Elizabeth McDowell Porter, who married Gen. Andrew Porter in 1767, died when she was about the age Mary was when Eliza Todd passed away.

There were three older brothers and a younger daughter. Soon after his wife's death, Gen. Porter married Elizabeth Todd in 1777, and they had eight children.[4]

How Elizabeth Porter, as a child, coped with her mother's death and, within a year, adjusted to a stepmother was not known. That life experience must have given her a particular insight in handling a similar situation with her own granddaughter. Mrs. Parker, as a result of her childhood, should have understood the circumstances and made some allowances for her son-in-law. Grief, however, differs with the personality.

The Todd clan in Lexington was considerable and, after Eliza Todd's death, they arranged social events for the children. There were outings with the Stuarts at Walnut Hall, the Russells on the Mansfield Track on Richmond Road, the Carrs and other collateral relatives. Between family and friends, such as the Bodleys, Breckinridges, Warfields, Trotters and Wickliffes, there were social activities of all kinds: dancing parties, barbeques, picnics, sleigh rides, watermelon and peach eating contests, hunting for nuts and blackberry picking. For the rainy days, there was reading, quilting and needlework.[5]

Aside from her siblings, Mary Todd had playmates such as John Cabell Breckinridge, who was U.S. vice-president 1857–1861 and one of her future husband's opponents in the 1860 presidential election. Breckinridge, whose grandfather, John Breckinridge, was credited with drafting Kentucky's first constitution and whose uncle, Robert Jefferson Breckinridge, was Kentucky's first superintendent of public education, was born at Thorn Hill, an early nineteenth century house at Limestone and Fifth Street, about five blocks from the Todd home.[6]

One of Mary Todd's close friends was her cousin Margaret Stuart, who lived in Stuart House, near Ellerslie. During gatherings there, young Mary Todd often entertained the family with skits and parts in plays. Margaret and Mary Wickliffe, daughters of Robert Wickliffe, were also her friends. The Wickliffe girls grew up on Howard's Grove Plantation and later moved into her cousin's home on Second Street after their father married Mary Owen Todd Russell. Mary Jane and Julia Warfield, daughters of Dr. Elisha Warfield, prominent physician and thoroughbred breeder, were other friends who then lived in the Ridgely House at the corner of Market and Second streets.[7]

Another friend of Mary Todd's was Catherine Cordelia Trotter, who lived with her family at the Woodlands. Much more palatial than the Todd home, Woodlands boasted four octagonal flankers capped by bonnets and baroque finials on each corner of the building. The residence was an ideal place for children's parties, especially in the winter. Isabel Bodley, another friend of Mary Todd's, lived in Bodley House on the corner of Market and Second streets. Bodley House featured an open, soaring three-story staircase and cost an amazing $10,000 to build in 1814. Where the Todds had tutors for their children, the Bodleys employed a French governess and an English head nurse.[8]

A very conventional man, Todd, despite rigid nineteenth century mores, lost no time in looking for a new wife and mother for his children. His ignoring the conventional mourning tradition, the initial period of one year and a gradual resumption of social activities in the second year, indicated his desperation. As a male surviving spouse, according to traditions, he could resume his business activities immediately. Todd, however, resumed everything.[9]

From all indications, he began seeing Elizabeth "Betsy" Humphreys, from a politically and socially prominent Frankfort, Kentucky, family, shortly after his wife died. Born in Staunton, Virginia, in 1800, to Dr. Alexander and Mary Brown Humphreys, she was nine years younger than Todd. A Scottish Covenanter, Dr. Humphreys, was educated at Edinburgh

University, served as a surgeon during the Revolutionary War, trained young surgeons such as his brother-in-law, Samuel Brown, and Ephraim McDowell, and was chairman of the board of the Staunton Academy. After his death in 1802, Mary Humphreys moved her family to Frankfort, where her brother, John Brown, lived. Mrs. Humphreys build the first house on Second Street in Frankfort. The marble doorstep was dated 1803, when the spacious brick residence was completed.[10]

Betsy Humphreys was twenty-six and never married. Whether that was by choice, the lack of suitors or being rejected by prospective mates is not known. According to customs of the time, she was, so to speak, on the shelf, far beyond the usual marriage age. Elizabeth Todd, Mary's oldest sister, was engaged to Ninian Edwards when she was sixteen.[11]

Todd was not looking for a young bride. He needed an older woman like Betsy Humphreys to run his household, take care of his children, entertain his friends and provide him with additional offspring. Betsy Humphreys came from wealth and was well educated, attractive and had political connections that could further Todd's career. He worked hard to convince her to marry him.

Betsy Humphreys' uncles, Preston and Samuel Brown, were prominent physicians. Samuel Brown in 1819 chaired the Department of Theory and Practice in the Transylvania College of Medicine. Preston Brown practiced medicine in Woodford, Franklin and Jefferson counties before he was accidentally killed in 1826.[12]

Another uncle, John Brown, studied law with Thomas Jefferson and George Wythe, represented Kentucky County in the Virginia senate in 1783, was the Kentucky County delegate to the Continental Congress in 1787 and 1789, and served two terms as a United States senator. He was president pro tempore of the Senate during the Eighth Congress.[13]

His younger brother, James Brown, served two terms in the Senate, 1813–1817 and 1819–1823, from Louisiana. During his latter term, James Brown chaired the Committee on Foreign Relations. While Robert S. Todd was courting and marrying Brown's niece, Brown served as Minister to France, 1823–1829.[14]

Betsy Humphreys having uncles as prominent as John and James Brown would do nothing to hinder the political career of Robert S. Todd. Where most young lawyers chose to stand for elective office, Robert S. Todd took another route to political power, clerk of the Kentucky House of Representatives.[15] When the January 1826 legislative session opened in Frankfort, Todd was again elected to the powerful position of clerk of the House of Representatives. By that time, he had been courting Betsy Humphreys for several months.

Todd's courtship of Betsy Humphreys came to the attention of the Widow Parker, who was not happy about the situation. The Parkers' disapproval of Todd's conduct of the romance so soon after their daughter and sister's death could have had a bearing on Betsy Humphreys' decision to visit relatives in Louisiana in February 1826. While she was in Louisiana, Robert Todd sent her a miniature of the portrait he commissioned from Lexington artist Matthew Jouett, one of the most significant antebellum portrait painters.[16]

The Widow Parker was not without resources, both financially and socially, and she was a formidable adversary.

In his letter accompanying miniature, Todd warned Betsy Humphreys of the gossip and rumors circulating about them in Frankfort and Lexington and said people were attempting to create mischief. "May I be permitted to put you on your guard against persons of this description," he wrote. "Not that I wish to stifle fair enquiry, for I feel in review of my past life a consciousness that such would not materially affect me in your estimation, although there are many things which I have done and said, I wish had never been done—and such I presume is the case of every one disposed to be honest with himself."[17]

Whether Mrs. Parker publicly articulated her opposition to her former son-in-law's pursuit of the Frankfort spinster is not known but it would be no surprise if she had. Elizabeth Rittenhouse Porter Parker was no shrinking violet. She spent two months after her marriage in 1789 riding across the mountains from Pennsylvania to Kentucky. Widow Parker enjoyed a high level of respect in Lexington and could have used that position to emphasize her opposition to the marriage.

By October 1826, Todd was encouraging Betsy Humphreys to set a date for their wedding. "I am sure if you knew my situation, you would not hesitate to comply with my wishes in fixing a day for our marriage in this or the early part of the ensuing week," he wrote on October 23.[18] Two days later, Todd wrote her that John J. Crittenden, if unmarried, would be his best man and that he would be in Frankfort on November 1, 1826 for their wedding.[19]

Mary Brown Humphries had reigned over Frankfort society for decades and gave her daughter an elegant wedding. Betsy Humphreys' only attendant was Maria Innis Todd, whose late husband, John Harris Todd, son of Associate Supreme Court Justice Thomas Todd, had died on February 7, 1826, and left her with three small children. She was the daughter of Harry Innis, who was involved in the Spanish Conspiracy. Crittenden and Marie Innes Todd had their own wedding in Frankfort on November 13, 1826.[20]

Neither Maria Innis Todd nor John J. Crittenden, a former U.S. senator and state representative who was then practicing law in Frankfort, observed the proper period of mourning, marrying only nine months after the death of her husband. She was the second of Crittenden's three wives.[21]

The older Todd children's and the Parkers' reception of Betsy Todd were unknown but later events indicated they were rather chilly. The Todd daughters, supported by the Widow Parker, presented a formidable front for the new bride and Betsy Todd waded into the fray with less than stellar results. At the sophisticated age of twenty-six, she had learned from her mother how to rule a household with an iron hand. Betsy Todd had been taught that it took a family seven generations to produce a lady. Her attitude indicated that she found the Todd daughters sadly lacking in that respect.[22]

A miniature of Betsy Todd, displayed in the Mary Todd Lincoln House in Lexington, portrayed a woman with cool blue eyes, rather stringy light brown hair and a haughty air of self-importance. The impression the miniature gives is of a woman accustomed to getting her way and who expected that to continue in the new stepmother role.

In her assessment of her stepchildren, Betsy Todd perhaps decided that, given their ages, Elizabeth and Frances would soon marry and leave home. Ann Marie was still young enough to be malleable. Levi could be left to his father, and George, at eighteen months, was too young to create any immediate problems. Obviously her biggest problem would be Mary, the middle child, who wanted what she wanted when she wanted it.

An incident Katherine Helm related in the book about her aunt illustrated how absolute Mary Todd was in having her way. At thirteen, she rode her pony out to Henry Clay's mansion, Ashland, so the Whig politician could admire her new pony. When she was informed by a slave that Mr. Clay was entertaining some gentlemen, she insisted on seeing him. On being told that Clay asked to be excused, she said, "I've come all the way out to Ashland to show Mr. Clay my new pony. You go right back in there and tell him that Mary Todd would like him to step out here for a moment."[23]

Clay and his guests came outside to see what the impetuous young lady wanted.

"Look, Mr. Clay," she said, "my new pony. Father bought him from those strolling players that were stranded here last week. He can dance—look." She touched him with her quirt and the animal reared up gracefully on his hind legs.[24]

"Mr. Clay," Mary gushed, "my father says you are the best judge of horseflesh in Fayette County. What do you think about this pony?"[25]

"He seems as spirited as his present diminutive jockey," Clay said as he lifted her down from the saddle. "I am sure nothing in the state can outdistance him. You are just in time for dinner." The Gallant Harry, as he was often called, handed the pony's reins to a stable boy and escorted Mary into the elegant dining room at Ashland. Mary listened attentively to animated political discussion around the table.[26]

During the meal, she told her host, "Mr. Clay my father says you will be the next president of the United States. I wish I could go to Washington and live in the White House. I begged my father to be president but he only laughed and said he would rather see you there than to be president himself. He must like you more than he does himself. My father is a very, very peculiar man, Mr. Clay. I don't think he really wants to be president."[27]

Clay laughingly replied, "If I am ever president, I shall expect Mary Todd to be one of my first guests." The young girl is said to have replied, "If you were not already married, I would wait for you."[28]

"So, I must go now," Mary said. "Poor mother is sick in bed, Father is in Frankfort. Mammy told me I might ride the pony for a little while in front of our house. I've been gone a long time. Mammy will be wild! When I put salt in her coffee this morning she called me a limb of Satan and said I was loping down the broad road leading to destruction. But, Mammy is a good old soul and promised to let me hold Baby Sam for ten or fifteen minutes if I didn't squirm too much. You have seen our new baby, Mrs. Clay? Don't you think he is too soft to be very healthy? I can't help but think he needs more starch. Teeny-weeny Margaret is all right, but Sam is flimsy."[29]

"Thank you so much for your charming hospitality," she said, executing a demure curtsy, "I've had a most delightful time."[30]

Such behavior was certainly a headache to Betsy and the slaves responsible for Mary. Todd failed to help the situation any by giving her the pony. Whether he gave his other children such gifts is not known. Early on in the father-daughter relationship there was an exceptional connection between the two of them that lasted until Todd's death in 1849.

One solution for handling the precocious Mary was to send her to day school and, before 1826 was over, she was enrolled in classes at Dr. John Ward's academy at the corner of Market and Second streets three blocks from the Todd Home. Dr. Ward came to Lexington eight years earlier from North Carolina as rector for Christ Church. A strict disciplinarian, Dr. Ward's classes began promptly at five in the mornings during the summer. An educational innovator, he instituted co-educational classes. About 120 boys and girls from Lexington's best families attended.[31]

On one particular morning before dawn, a new Irish night watchman noticed a young girl scampering up Second Street with a bundle in her arms. Deciding she was keeping an assignation with some unseen lover, he took off after her, club in hand, determining to spoil such plans. Mary Todd, fleet of foot, barely escaped the watchman as they burst into the classroom, much to the delight of the other students. Dr. Ward saw little amusement in the disturbance.[32]

Mary either took her lunch with her or returned home for the noon meal. There was homework to do and interactions with her siblings when she was not in class. She probably attended dancing classes with some of her friends in Mathurin Giron's ballroom or one of the other academies that taught dance.[33]

She likely visited the Widow Parker, just a few steps away, on a daily basis. Consequently, she was perhaps not underfoot during her starchy stepmother's daily routine but there were evenings and weekends when they probably clashed. Elizabeth, being the oldest of Eliza's children, was a substitute mother and looked after her siblings. Elizabeth, as she would prove in later years, was the peacemaker in her family, which was often a thankless task. Whether she was a successful buffer between Mary and Betsy is not known. In later years, Mary found Betsy Todd at times to be obliging and accommodating. "But, if she thought any of us were on her hands again, I believe she would be *worse* than ever," she said.[34]

Katherine Helm, in the biography of her aunt, handled the conflict between Mary Todd and her siblings and Betsy Todd is a very delicate manner. "Very calmly and competently she undertook the care and training of the six stepchildren, ranging in age from eighteen months to fourteen years," Helm wrote. "Mrs. Todd took very pardonable pride, for since Mary was a romping 'tomboy' of eight years she had trained her in all the social graces."[35]

Just how much training in the social graces Betsy Todd gave her young stepdaughter was unknown. From the time of her marriage in 1826 and until Mary left home the last time in 1839, Betsy Todd was rather busy birthing seven children, supervising a move into a new house and entertaining her husband's political friends and associates. It is more likely, prior to going to boarding school where she attained much of her old world manners, the rest came from her older sisters, her grandmother, and observing and participating in the events themselves.

Where Mary and her siblings referred to Betsy Todd as "Ma" in their correspondence, Helm had them calling Betsy "Mother" in her book.[36]

There were two explanations for Helm's careful handling in her manuscript of the conflicts between Mary Todd and her stepmother. Betsy Todd was Helm's grandmother and, even if she had to commit the sin of omission, she was not going to criticize her. Helm's mother and the Lincolns' oldest son Robert were exceptionally close after Mary's death and, if he did not provide funds for publishing her book, he certainly made the arrangements for the publication. Through their legal counsel, Frederick N. Towers, Robert Lincoln and his wife vetted Helm's manuscript very carefully, taking out sections that did not meet with their approval. Consequently, except for rare references, such as Mary's 1848 letter dealing with her extended visit in Lexington and visceral descriptions of Betsy Todd in later legal documents, a one dimensional impression of the stepmother emerged.[37]

While ruling her stepchildren with an iron hand, Betsy Todd was busy overseeing the work of the household slaves. Chaney was the cook, Sally was the children's nurse and there were other slaves overseen by Nelson, the butler, who also did the marketing. Eventually, Betsy Todd brought in one of her own slaves, Jane, trained by her mother.[38] While she did not sew, Betsy Todd did knit and required the girls in the family to apply their knitting needles and do ten rounds on socks every evening before they went to bed.[39]

Mary developed her sense of fashion at a young age. Elizabeth Humphreys, who spent several months with her aunt and shared Mary's room, recalled Robert Todd bringing back some beautiful embroidered pink muslin from a buying trip to New Orleans. "Much to Mary's delight," Elizabeth wrote, "Aunt allowed her to direct the sewing woman how to make the frocks." It was the beginning, Elizabeth recalled, of the development of Mary's dress-making talents. "Mary was the only one of the family of girls who ever learned to use her needle with skill."[40]

Aside from her household duties, Betsy Todd repeated the life that Eliza Parker Todd had led, bearing a child about every two years from 1827 to 1841, for a total of nine children. Her first child, Robert, died in infancy in 1827. In 1828, Margaret was born, followed by Samuel in 1830; David in 1832; Martha in 1833; Emilie in 1836; Alexander in 1839; Elodie in 1840, and Katherine in 1841.

Once his domestic situation was in the hands of his new wife, Todd was free to devote his attention to business and political affairs and his expanded family's finances. Todd was challenged in the race for House clerk in 1828. He beat out a challenger for the office, John M. McCalla, also from Lexington, by only one vote, 49–48. McCalla, a particularly vicious Democrat operative, collaborated with Robert Wickliffe and James Gutherie in scandal mongering about Henry Clay's gambling.[41]

How much attention Robert S. Todd gave to his first family of children aside from Mary is not known. However, an assumption can be made that he left, for the most part, those responsibilities to his new wife.

CHAPTER 4

The Unsavory Business of Slavery

From the time she was small, Mary Todd's father allowed her to join the adults at the dinner table for dessert.[1]

The dinner guests were a who's who of political luminaries. They included John J. Crittenden, the best man at Todd's second wedding and who was later governor of Kentucky and U.S. senator; Henry Clay, the nation's leading Whig, secretary of state, speaker of the house and senator; Garrett Davis, another U.S. senator; Richard M. Johnson, vice-president under Martin Van Buren; Robert J. Breckinridge, Presbyterian cleric and educator; judge George Robertson, an eminent jurist; and emancipationist Cassius Marcellus Clay, who lived with the Todd family during his last year at Transylvania. She heard amazing arguments and conversations. National businessmen who came to Lexington were often entertained in the Todd home.[2]

Robert Todd saw something very special in his young daughter that led him to include her in these adult discussions. There were no indications that her older sisters, Elizabeth or Frances, were accorded this privilege, nor her older brother Levi. Was it the bright intelligence brimming from her blue-green eyes? It could have been her proclivity to ask piercing questions far beyond her years. Since there was a vivid facial resemblance between Mary and her father, it is possible Robert Todd felt a special bond with this child. Whatever the reason, that very special father-daughter bond continued through his life.

Many of those after-dinner conversations concerned slavery and all the problems the peculiar institution created, including dueling to settle political arguments about the subject. Todd and his guests would also have discussed colonization, which closely touched his family. Mary Todd was exposed to all sides of slavery from the benevolent relationship with her nurse, Mammy Sally, to those liberated by the colonization societies, to the cruelty and death inflicted on their slaves by their owners, families she knew in Lexington. There were similar incidents she read about in southern newspapers. To put it bluntly, Mary Todd grew up in a slavery cauldron bubbling with emancipationist-pro-slavery arguments and duels in Lexington. Those experiences formed her opposition to the practice and accounted for the friendship and kindness she later extended to slaves and freedmen.

Whether or not she fully understood those after dinner conversations depended on her age but she was far more advanced intellectually than most girls of her time and possessed a remarkably retentive memory.[3]

Katherine Helm, drawing from the recollections of her pro-slavery mother, Emilie Todd Helm, described the family's house slaves. Running the household was Nelson, the butler who was also the coachman, did the marketing and was said to make the best mint juleps in

Lexington. Nelson, by negotiating with grocers, saved enough money out of the household accounts to buy himself a horse. Jane Sanders, a young slave trained by Mary Humphreys and given to her daughter, was described as a jewel. Chaney was a delightful cook but grumpy.[4]

One of the central figures in Mary Todd's early life was her nurse, Mammy Sally, who ruled the nursery with an iron hand. There were times when the mischievous child would hide her slippers and place salt where the sugar should be so that Sally would use it in her coffee. Consequently, Mammy Sally made up stories that such pranks were the works of the devil and shamed the miscreant into confessing.

"Mary and I wondered if Mammy ever wanted to be free," Elizabeth Humphreys later wrote. "We concluded she did not. How could we do without Mammy and how could she exist without us? It would just about kill her to give up bossing her white 'chillun.' She was part, and a very important, loved and venerated part of our family."[5]

She recalled that Mary, who was reading one night, heard a knocking noise and asked Mammy Sally what it was. The nurse replied that it might be a runaway slave who was hungry. She had placed a mark on the fence indicating the Todd house would provide them with food. "Oh," cried Mary, springing up, "you know Mammy that it is against the law to help runaway slaves but I will go down and give him food myself." Elizabeth Humphreys said Mammy Sally restrained Mary by explaining runaway slaves would only take food from other slaves.[6]

The Todd household slaves perhaps had better living conditions and treatment than many, but that did not alleviate their bondage. Certainly, they would have preferred freedom and the opportunity to decide who they wanted to work for and to negotiate their wages. The Todd family, like their peers, had no hesitation in using slaves to make their households run more smoothly and free them from mundane chores.

Todd, William Barr, William Rodes and John Todd in 1839 purchased a slave boy, Henry, about eight years old from the sale of Samuel B. Todd in Jessamine County. The four men, through a deed of gift, sold Henry for one dollar to Edmund Barr, the trustee for Caroline Todd, Samuel B. Todd's wife. The sale document made it quite clear that Henry was the property only of Caroline Todd, her heirs and/or representatives, not her husband.[7]

Charles W. Todd, John Todd (not Col. John Todd) and Thomas J. Todd manumitted slaves in 1825, 1827 and 1824, respectively.[8]

Todd women and those in their extended family also freed slaves. Mary Owen Todd Russell purchased a male slave from Stewart Walter in September 1802. She manumitted one male and two female slaves in September 1808. The same month she purchased another male slave.[9]

On the maternal side of Mary Todd's family, Alexander Parker manumitted a female slave in 1810. Elizabeth L. Parker manumitted a female slave in 1830. The Widow Parker, who died in 1850, not only manumitted her three slaves, Prudence, Ann and Cyrus, upon her death but directed that Prudence be paid twelve dollars a year as long as she lived.[10]

Mary Humphreys, Betsy Todd's mother, freed nine of her slaves in her will when she died in 1836, in Frankfort. However, their manumissions dates (when they were legally free) were not immediate and ranged from four to twenty years in the future.[11]

Mary Owen Todd Russell came to depend on Robert S. Todd for financial assistance with her slaves. The daughter of Col. John Todd, a brother to Levi and Robert Todd, she was faced with many difficult situations concerning not only her lands and slaves but other issues. One of those situations involved a young slave boy who was thought to be her mixed-race grandson.

During those early years, Richard M. Johnson, a U.S. senator from 1819 to 1829, congressman from 1829 to 1837, and vice-president 1837 to 1841, was a frequent guest in the Todd home. Johnson, like Robert S. Todd, attended Transylvania, was admitted to the bar and served in the War of 1812. Johnson is noteworthy in Mary Todd's window to slavery because of his personal life. Johnson never married, but sired two daughters, Imogene and Adaline, with Julia Chinn, a mixed-race slave he inherited from his father's estate. Johnson saw that his daughters were well educated and, when he was in Washington, Julia Chinn was left in control of his Blue Springs plantation.[12]

Todd and Johnson, according to William Townsend, had a political disagreement over Henry Clay's part in the "Corrupt Bargain" in the 1824 presidential election but remained personal friends.[13]

It is not known if Mary Todd ever met Johnson's two daughters but she certainly knew about them because every time Johnson ran for political office opposing candidates had a field day, albeit unsuccessfully, recycling his personal life in party newspapers.[14]

Mary saw, heard or read about local owners treating their slaves with extreme cruelty and about similar incidents in the south. Judge Fielding L. Turner and his wife Caroline lived in a mansion out in the county, between Frankfort and Versailles pikes, filled with house slaves. In 1825, Todd purchased a lot at the corner of Short and Mechanic streets from the judge. Caroline Turner, said to be from a prominent Boston family, was a large overbearing woman. She beat their slaves with such violence that her husband said six of them died. In early 1837, Mrs. Turner threw a small male slave out a second story window, crippling him for life. Community outrage was such that the judge had her committed to the lunatic asylum for her own protection. Before a Circuit Court jury, composed of Robert Todd and eleven others, could inquire into the state of Caroline Turner's mind at the trial, she convinced the asylum commissioners to release her from custody. She was killed several years later after whipping a chained slave who broke loose and choked her. He was hanged.[15]

Elizabeth Humphreys wrote that she and Mary were appalled after reading an article from the April 11, 1834, *New Orleans Bee* about the New Orleans riots that broke out after a fire at Dr. and Mrs. Louis LaLauries' French Quarter mansion. Dr. LaLaurie was accused of conducting medical experiments on slaves chained in their attic. His wife, said to be a homicidal maniac, assisted. When flames broke out in the mansion, fire fighters found the attic awash with blood, human limbs strewn around and seven slaves who were barely alive chained to the walls. When the word spread about the LaLauries' treatment of their slaves, riots broke out, and rioters tossed the LaLauries' expensive furniture out the mansion's windows. Damages were estimated at $40,000. The LaLauries barely escaped with their lives and sought refuge in France.[16]

Elizabeth Humphreys recalled the newspaper article and said, "We were horrified and talked of nothing else for days. If one such case could happen, it damned the whole institution, though in our own family, I think the slaves rather managed us and we heard of no cruelty to the slaves of our friends who seemed to love and trust their servants as we did ours."[17]

There was no way Elizabeth Humphreys or Mary Todd could have been unaware of the activities of Caroline Turner and the pain, suffering and death she inflicted on her slaves in Lexington. In chronicling that recollection, it should be remembered the author, Katherine Helm, was the daughter of Confederate General Benjamin Hardin Helm, who was killed at the Battle of Chickamauga. Wherever she discussed slavery in the biography of her aunt,

Five generations of a slave family on the Smith Plantation in Beaufort, S.C. (Library of Congress Prints and Photographs Division).

Mary Todd Lincoln, Helm presented the benevolent or paternal side of the peculiar institution, especially where the Todds were concerned.

One of Kentucky's efforts to deal with the problems of slavery was the Non-Importation of Slaves Act. The intent of it was to rid Kentucky of slavery in the next three or four decades. The law was debated for four years in the legislature before finally passing in 1833. From 1830 to 1840 the percentage of the Kentucky slave population decreased thirty percent.[18] Had the act not been repealed in 1849, the law might have actually accomplished its intent.

Consequently, the price for slaves after the act's passage increased to as much as $1,400.00 each. None fought the law more fiercely than Robert Wickliffe, who was one of the four or five largest slave owners in the commonwealth, with more than 200 slaves. Wickliffe called the act a tinderbox in abolitionists' efforts to make Kentucky a battleground state and did everything he could to have the law repealed and was eventually successful in 1849.[19] Wickliffe had a deep-seated fear someone would take away his slaves. He once accused Henry Clay of helping to steal all the slaves who had run away from their Kentucky owners.[20]

Unable to import young slaves, some slave owners turned to breeding slaves for sale after the act became law. Lewis Clarke, an escaped Madison County, Kentucky, slave, wrote in his narrative, "The common price for females is about $500 to $700 when sold for plantation hands, for house hands or for breeders." Clarke said the major crops produced in Kentucky in the 1830s were, "Corn and hemp, tobacco, oats, some wheat and rye, slaves, mules, hogs and horses for the southern market."[21]

Mary Todd probably saw groups of shackled slaves driven through the street, in front of her home, to auction, separated from their families and later shipped downriver. She was aware of the slave jails in the vicinity of her home on Short Street, including one in the next block. The *Lexington Western Luminary* in 1833 chronicled a slave drive. "Last week, a number of slaves were driven through the main street of our city, among them were a number manacled together, two abreast, all connected by and supporting a heavy iron chain, which extended the whole length of the line."[22]

Millie Crawford and Alfred Russell, the two slaves belonging to her cousin Mary Owen "Polly" Todd Russell, were never marched through the street chained but were eventually removed from their home in a manner almost equally as cruel. They were fixtures in the Todd extended family for years, as Mary's father played a pivotal role in their lives.

Both Mary Owen Todd Russell and her mother Jane Hawkins Todd Irvine, through the mismanagements of their husbands, had been forced to sell parts of the vast lands left them by their father and husband, John Todd. However, there was an enormous amount of property remaining. Although Mary Owen Russell was her father's only heir, her mother received dower rights, meaning she was entitled to one-third of the estate.[23]

Around 1797, a slick, good looking but not well-heeled Englishman, James Russell, appeared in Lexington looking for a wife, preferably a wealthy one. At seventeen, rather unattractive and certainly inexperienced in worldly ways, Mary Owen Todd allowed the Englishman to sweep her off her feet. Russell was described as being not poor but not wealthy, neatly and fashionably dressed but suffering from epilepsy.[24] Among Russell's possessions were a number of books stamped with the coat of arms of the House of Bedford, whose seat, Woburn Abby and its original 16,000 acre estate, had been in the Russell family since 1619.[25]

Even though the Todd family advised against the marriage, one of the Todds drew up a marriage contract, which Russell apparently signed.[26] The agreement was short lived. After the wedding, in the throes of marital love and faith in her mate, Polly Russell supposedly tore up the contract. The couple built a large log house and improved the grounds on the Mansfield Tract she inherited from her father.[27]

The marriage rapidly turned sour. Polly Russell was allegedly verbally and physically abused by her husband, who ran up numerous debts she only discovered after his death in 1802. She was left with a two-year-old son, John Todd Russell. After several years, she finally paid off the debts incurred by her husband.[28]

Around 1806, she built a home on Second Street, where her son was tutored in preparation for entering Princeton. Before leaving for college, John Russell visited his maternal grandmother in Louisville. There he met Millie, a beautiful octoroon who was one of Jane Todd Irvin's house slaves, fell in love with her and supposedly left her pregnant. A son, Alfred

Francis Russell, was born to Millie in August 1817. After two years at Princeton, young Russell returned home.[29]

There was no definitive evidence, only gossip, that Alfred was John Russell's son. Mary Owen Russell's subsequent actions regarding Alfred and his mother were another matter. She established patterns of interest, actions and expenses far beyond that of a mere slave owner. Gossip about the mixed race child did not fade and reoccurred fifteen years later in a lawsuit that involved Mary and her siblings.

In October 1822, John Russell, struck with a sudden illness while visiting relatives in Gallatin County, began his final journey home. In Shelbyville, he became too ill to continue. His mother rushed to his bedside and arrived just before he died, according to Mme. Mentelle. William H. Townsend presented a different picture. When he realized the end was near, Townsend wrote that John Russell "acknowledged Millie's boy Alfred to be his son, thought of him in the last throes of life and did what he considered necessary to insure the freedom and respectability of the child."[30]

In 1825, when Jane Todd Irvin died in Louisville, her brother, B. N. McIwaine, became the sole owner of Millie Crawford and Alfred Russell. Mary Owen Russell desperately wanted to purchase Millie and Alfred but she was short of money. McIwaine was in a rush to convert the slaves to cash and intended to sell them. Mrs. Russell turned to Robert Todd for assistance. He accompanied her to Louisville on April 8, 1825, and they purchased the two slaves for $625. Todd paid McIwaine $125 in cash and gave him his note for the remaining $500. McIwaine made the bill of sale out, not to Robert S. Todd, but to Mary O. Russell.[31]

By appealing to her cousin for assistance, it was obvious that Mary Owen Russell made her own business decisions. From 1802 until her second marriage in 1826, she bought and sold property as a femme sole, an unmarried woman of legal age, who required no guardian. During that period, she engaged in sixty transactions of land and slaves that included 1,197 acres and portions of twenty-five lots in Lexington.[32]

Todd and John M. McCalla, an owner of the *Kentucky Gazette*, co-signed a note for her to borrow $300 for four months. She had been forced to defend herself over a contested land grant she inherited from her father and had to pay Henry Clay for legal representation in the *May Heirs v. Russell* lawsuit.[33]

On November 3, 1821, Mrs. Russell signed an agreement to pay Clay $1,000 if he successfully defended in the Court of Appeals her claim to the 400 acres at the heart of the lawsuit.[34]

From all indications, the lawsuit against Mary Owen Russell was perpetuated by one of the most litigious lawyers around, Robert Wickliffe, whose office was several blocks down Second Street from Mrs. Russell's home. He was the father of two of Mary's friends, Margaret and Mary Wickliffe. Wickliffe claimed that John Todd was merely holding the land grant in trust for John May, to whom he maintained the land actually belonged. Mary Owen Russell testified the land belonged to her, as her father's only heir, and was left to her in his will. She swore that the will was duly proved, recorded and remained in the clerk's office until the building was destroyed by fire in 1803.[35]

Wickliffe, then in the Kentucky House of Representatives, attempted to persuade the court that Jane Todd Irvin had destroyed her husband's will. Regardless of his desperate arguments, Wickliffe lost the case in Fayette Circuit Court in October 1823 and again in the Court of Appeals in December 1824.[36]

Wickliffe accumulated much of his fortune through such litigation as the Mays case, which was finally settled forty years after John Todd was killed at the Battle of Blue Licks.[37] From all indications, Wickliffe decided Mary Owen Russell's lands could be acquired easier through matrimony than litigation. Wickliffe was a widower with seven children, some of them small, and he needed a wife and housekeeper. Her lands and slaves would further enhance his fortune. The match, however, was not without difficulties.

Wickliffe convinced her to marry him October 27, 1827, and insisted on her executing a most amazing pre-nuptial agreement. On September 12, 1827, she deeded all her property and Wickliffe deeded some of his property to a third party, Richard H. Chinn, an attorney friend. To complete the tripartite deed, Chinn deeded all the property in question back to Wickliffe. According to law, Mary Owen Wickliffe had to be questioned in private by the court clerk or his representatives to ascertain if she understood the document she was signing and if any duress had forced her decision.[38]

Unable to go to the courthouse to be examined, clerk J.G. Rodes appointed justices of the peace John Bradford, who published Lexington's first newspaper, and Oliver Keene, a prominent businessman, to examine Mrs. Wickliffe at her home. She assured them that she understood what she was doing.[39]

The most puzzling aspect of the tripartite deed was that, once she married Robert Wickliffe, all her property, unless otherwise encumbered, became his under Kentucky law. That property included Millie and Alfred. Robert Wickliffe, however, was not satisfied that one tripartite deed would protect the lands and slaves his wife conveyed to him. In 1835, he used William Owsley, from Franklin County, as the straw man instead of Richard H. Chinn, to execute a second such deed. If there was additional money owed the late Col. John Todd from his military service, Wickliffe wanted that too. In March 1832, Robert and Mary Owen Wickliffe signed an agreement with Thomas Bodley to collect from the Commonwealth of Virginia and the United States any money owed for the military service of Col. Todd. Bodley was to get half of whatever he collected.[40]

If Robert Todd was asked and advised Mary Owen Russell against the second marriage, she ignored his advice, as she did Levi Todd's before her first marriage. Mme. Mentelle indicated arguments were made against the marriage but did not say by whom. "She spoke of some arrangements that she had made as to her property; told me that her servants should never pass into any other family and many other things in justification for her entering to the married state and ending by repeating, 'I love him.'"[41]

Alfred Russell was twelve years old when Mary O. Russell purchased him and his mother from her uncle. She gave the child the basis of a good education. Whether his education continued after the Russell and Wickliffe households were combined was not known. Alfred Russell, however, did not remain in Lexington long after his grandmother's remarriage.

Colonization in Kentucky, although legal, was seldom considered by owners who looked on their slaves as chattel, part of their wealth. In the case of the Wickliffes, sending Millie and Alfred and their assorted relatives to Africa was the answer to what had become an increasing social embarrassment to their family. Earlier, in 1828, Robert Wickliffe was one of the organizers of the Kentucky Colonization Society, an affiliate of the American Colonization, whih Henry Clay helped found in 1821.

In 1833, Mrs. Wickliffe sent Millie Crawford and Alfred Russell and five of their relatives to Liberia. Mary Owen Wickliffe stated that she asked her husband to manumit and send Millie and Alfred and Millie's sister Lucy and her four children to Liberia, "at my request (& also theirs)."[42]

The travel arrangements, presumably conducted by Wickliffe, were made through Louisiana cotton factor (cotton broker) Nathaniel Cox and the Sierra Leone Colonization Society.[43] The slaves' passage was booked on the *Brig Ajax* out of New Orleans. Millie's name was listed as Amelia Crawford, thirty; Alfred Russell, fifteen; Lucretia (Lucy) Russell, twenty-nine, and Lucy's four children, ages five to thirteen. The slaves' owner listed in the ship's manifest was not Wickliffe but his wife.[44]

The Wickliffes' largess did not include transportation to Louisville to catch the boat to New Orleans. The slaves walked the eighty miles from Lexington to Louisville in March 1833 to board the *Mediterranean* riverboat for the trip down the Ohio and Mississippi rivers. At Frankfort, Mary Owen Wickliffe made arrangements for their lodging and food with a Mr. Gray. Millie Crawford, on March 10, 1833, wrote Mrs. Wickliffe of the kindness they were shown in Frankfort but expressed concern there was no man to protect them. "But we try to put our trust in the Almighty and go in his strength whatever betides us." She promised to write her again from Louisville.[45]

They arrived in Liberia in July 1833 and were among the 146 new settlers. Apparently the Wickliffes did send them money through missionary G.W. McElroy but Alfred Russell, in an 1855 letter to Wickliffe, reported the group did not receive the stipends.[46]

Alfred Russell was probably one of the better examples of the colonization efforts. Beginning as a missionary and teacher, he later became a coffee and sugarcane grower on his large farm along the St. Paul River in Montserrado County. He served in the Liberian senate and was elected vice-president with Anthony Gardner heading the ticket in 1881. When Gardner resigned in January 1883, Russell served out his term and died a few months after leaving office in 1884.[47]

Mary Todd, in addition to the newspaper accounts she read of horrible treatment of slaves and heard about her neighbors' actions in that realm, was an inside observer of the peculiar institution. The slaves mentioned in the June 5, 1833, *Lexington Western Luminary* probably passed her new home on West Main Street. Slavery was a multi-faceted situation that not only tore black families apart but ripped apart white relationships as well: something Mary Todd had earlier experienced with her family and friends.

The peculiar institution created a traumatic jolt to Mary's circle of friends in 1829, a blow that changed their lives forever. Mary often joined her friends, Mary and Margaret Wickliffe and Catherine Trotter, for parties and dance lessons for the cotillions they would later attend. Mary and Margaret's brother Charles and Catherine's brother George took the girls for drives in their family's conveyances. Charles Wickliffe and George Trotter were best friends, although their fathers were on opposite ends of the slavery debate.[48] That relationship would soon end in a tragic duel.

Men had been attempting to settle their differences with duels long before Kentucky became a state. The duels began with knives and then advanced to the more sophisticated practice of killing each other with matched sets of pistols, some with hair triggers.

Nearly a decade before Mary was born, Henry Clay fought a ridiculous duel with fellow Kentucky legislator Humphrey Marshall about members wearing only clothing made in America. The argument reached the point where Clay, usually a dandy dresser, wore a homespun suit to the assembly. Not to be outdone, Marshall appeared the next day in a suit of the finest English broadcloth. After bickering about details of the duel, the pair met, with their seconds and surgeons, across the Ohio River at Shippingport on January 19, 1809. Marshall, a former U.S. senator, had the misfortune of his pistol misfiring on the first encounter and Clay shot him in the stomach area. Both men's pistols misfired on the first shot at ten paces. When the third command was given, Clay missed his opponent and Marshal shot Clay in the thigh.[49]

Robert Todd saw no sense in men randomly placing their lives at risk. In 1818, the year of Mary's birth, he attempted to find a solution. Todd, newspaper publisher John Bradford, attorney Robert Wickliffe, holster John Postlethwait and numerous physicians, theologians and businessmen met to discuss how they could stop the practice of dueling. All the eighty-four men could do was issue a statement that differences of opinion should be settled by deliberation rather than deadly combat.[50]

Other duels, more serious than the Clay-Marshall encounter, were involved with the issue of slavery. Public discussions of slavery, once held at on oratorical level, descended into mortal combat.

Robert Wickliffe, father of two of Mary's friends, was pro-slavery's leading advocate. He made a long and contemptuous speech in the Kentucky legislature against the passage of the Non-Importation of Slaves Act. His vitriolic remarks were so stinging they required an answer from the other side. Robert J. Breckinridge, Cassius Marcellus Clay and other friends, who were personal friends and political allies of Todd, launched equally divisive replies against Wickliffe's position in the anti-slavery publication *Kentucky Gazette*.[51]

Wickliffe's son Charles felt a compelling need to answer his father's critics. He wrote, under the pen name of Coriolanus, a vicious rebuke to the emancipationists calling them a "Set of malevolent, black-hearted men." His article appeared in the March 4, 1829, issue of the pro-slavery publication *Kentucky Reporter*. Young Wickliffe maintained his father was an independent, upstanding, honest man who was being attacked unjustly. John M. McCalla, one of the *Kentucky Gazette* owners also writing under an assumed name, suggested that young Wickliffe name the men to which he referred and shamed him for not using his real name. Angered at McCalla's insinuations, young Wickliffe stormed into the newspaper office armed with two pistols, but McCalla was not there.[52]

Thomas Benning, the newspaper's editor, was there. Wickliffe demanded the name of the man who criticized his article. Benning refused and the argument turned heated. Benning told Wickliffe his defense of his father did not cover him with glory. Incensed, Wickliffe charged the editor, who only had a walking cane as a defense. Wickliffe took away the walking cane and pulled out a gun. Benning headed for the back door of the office. Wickliffe shot him in the back. Hearing the shot, several other men ran into the office to see what the ruckus was about. Wickliffe pulled out his other gun, threatened them and stumbled out the front door. Benning died the next day.[53]

The shooting of Benning was no duel—that came later—it was out and out murder.

Wickliffe was indicted for murder and his trial began June 30, 1819. His father spared no expense in the legal defense of his son. He retained Henry Clay as lead counsel. Assisting Clay were John J. Crittenden and Richard H. Chinn.[54]

It was no accident that the jury was predominantly pro-slavery. They held onto every word Clay uttered. Clay had not lost a criminal case in Lexington for thirty years. The jury took less than ten minutes to decide Charles Wickliffe was not guilty.[55]

Lexington's anti-slavery faction was furious and the affair might have ended there but for the actions of Charles Wickliffe. Posturing, strutting and bragging about his acquittal, he left the courthouse as if he had not a care in the world and was supremely proud of his behavior.[56] The rhetoric over Wickliffe's actions simmered and stewed through the summer. Everybody, including Mary, suspected the incident was not over.

George Trotter, once young Wickliffe's good friend, assumed editorship of the *Gazette*. In September, Trotter wrote an editorial attacking the court for allowing the jury to be packed with pro-slavery members and for exhibiting their prejudice in finding Wickliffe not guilty. Trotter called Wickliffe a coward for shooting Benning in the back. By the end of the month, Trotter's raw words forced Wickliffe to challenge him to a duel. Since Wickliffe issued the challenge, Trotter had the choice of weapons, firing distance, location and date.[57]

Duels, for the most part, were fought under a strict rules codified in books such as John L. Wilson's *The Code of Honor or Rules for the Government of Principals and Seconds in Dueling*.[58]

Turner chose pistols at a distance of eight feet between combatants, which was about the same distance between Wickliffe and Benning. From a distance of eight feet, it would take a person unfamiliar with pistols, suffering from vision problems or experiencing a high degree of nervous tension to miss their target. Trotter chose the old dueling grounds on the Fayette-Scott county line, about seven miles north of Lexington, on October 8, 1829.[59]

On command, the pair fired. Wickliffe's hip was grazed but Trotter was untouched. How could a man miss a target only eight feet away? Wickliffe, according to the code, had the right to demand a second shot. Again, Wickliffe missed. Trotter's bullet lodged in Wickliffe's abdomen. He died the next day a victim of his own recklessness, a ridiculous code and his father's inflammatory political rhetoric.[60]

Wickliffe was buried on his father's plantation, Howard's Grove, outside of Lexington. It is unknown if Mary or any of her family attended the funeral, although her cousin, Mary Owen Russell Wickliffe, was his stepmother. The duel was the talk of Lexington.

Trotter's conduct on the field of fire was questioned by Wickliffe' friends, who claimed it was not in accordance with the Code Duello. "These questions continued to be debatable subjects for weeks to follow in Lexington tavern, livery stables, drug stores and other gathering places while both sides took depositions and statements relative to the case," Coleman wrote.[61]

Finally, Trotter, fed up with all the quasi-legal maneuvering, answered his critics in November 1829, by suggesting they might want to finish what Charles Wickliffe started. No one answered his challenge.[62]

CHAPTER 5

The Todds Move

Robert S. Todd needed no urging from his wife to realize his house on Short Street was too small for a rapidly growing family, now numbering three new children; his five children from his first marriage; Betsy Todd's relatives whose increasing visits sometimes extended into years, and their household slaves. By 1832, Betsy Todd, to her credit, had spent six years trying unsuccessfully to live in peace with the Widow Parker just next door.

That year was pivotal for the family as well as for Mary. In February 1832, Todd entered into a partnership with Edward Oldham and Thomas Hemingway in the Oldham Todd and Company Woolen Mills, which manufactured fabrics for garments. Their business eventually covered several states and was quite successful. Todd did much of the traveling selling their products and collecting debts. A clause in the partnership agreement stated if one of the partners died, his surviving spouse could draw $1,000 annually from his shares until his estate was settled. For Robert S. Todd, that clause provided some security for his wife and growing family.[1]

Oldham Todd's offices were later located at the corner of West Main and Locust streets. Nearby was the Sign of the Eagle (originally the Sign of the Green Tree) Tavern, built by William Palmateer around 1803–1805. Palmateer, whose business was declining, advertised the property for sale in 1827. "Principal building—16 rooms, 10 of which have fireplaces, dry cellar underneath whole house, excellent kitchen with lodging for servants, a spring house, wash house and smoke house, all under one roof. A stable, carriage and cow house, all built of stone and the whole enclosed by a stone wall. A good well of never failing water with a pump."[2]

The tavern keeper found no buyer. He experienced continuing financial difficulties, defaulted on his mortgage and a commissioner's sale was held. Robert S. and Elizabeth Todd purchased the 5,076 square-foot house and 66 by 91 foot lot for $1,760 in March 1832. He financed the purchase through the local branch of the Bank of the United States and agreed to make annual payments of $440.57 for the next three years.[3]

The Todds sold their house on Short Street and a lot on Cheapside to John Kirkpatrick after they moved into the larger house.[4] The four story, including basement, building was erected of brick laid in both Flemish Bond and common bond patterns in the Georgian style. The exterior walls were thirteen inches thick and the interior ceilings' heights, in the house's main block, were over ten feet. An ell extended into the back yard.[5] Octagonal-shaped bricks lined the walks around the house, which set back only a few feet from the street.[6]

Architectural historian Clay Lancaster indicated Todd did some remodeling of the

46

house after his purchase. Lancaster found one of the presses, beside the fireplace, had been removed in the northeast room, a parlor, and a door cut in the wall leading to a garden. Town Branch, a tributary of Elkhorn Creek, ran through the property, which also had a garden and greenhouse-conservatory. The home's eight bedrooms on the second and third floors were ideal for the large family and their visitors.[7]

Robert and Betsy Todd now had room to do more elegant entertaining. The first floor, not including the ell, which contained the kitchen and a breakfast room, was a block of four large rooms with fireplaces and a wide entrance hall. Upon entering the front door, to the left was a parlor and behind it a second parlor or library. To the right of the hall was the family sitting room and the dining room. Either large pocket or hinged doors separated the front rooms from the back ones on each side of the hall.

Carpets covered the floors in the parlors and hallways. Heavy red damask draperies hung in the parlors over Venetian blinds and lace curtains. The parlors were furnished with sofas, chairs, card tables, lamps, étagères, paintings, secretaries, and bookcases for the more than 400 volumes the Todds owned. There were eighteen mahogany chairs for the mahogany dining table. A sideboard held the crystal, china, decanters and Betsy Todd's fine silver, a wedding gift from her uncle, Samuel Brown. Smaller serving tables completed the dining room.[8]

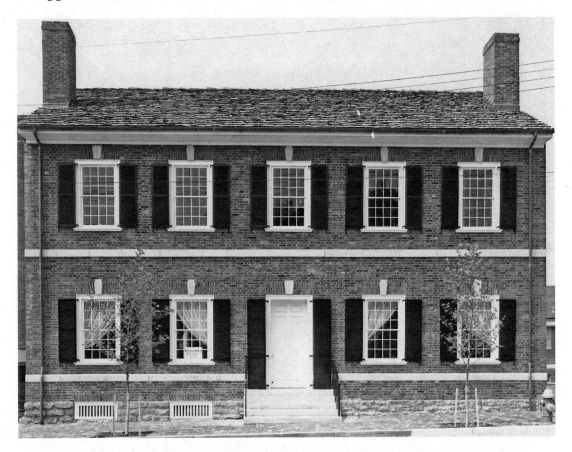

Mary Lincoln's restored girlhood home, the first shrine in America to honor a president's wife, opened June 9, 1977, in Lexington, Kentucky. The three story brick home was originally built as a tavern (Kentucky Department of Public Information, Frankfort).

Top, left: **One of the Twin Parlors.** *Top, right:* **Dining Room.** *Bottom, left:* **Sitting Room.** *Bottom, right:* **Mary Todd Lincoln's Bedroom** (all photographs, Kentucky Department of Public Information, Frankfort).

The bedrooms were furnished with beds containing mattresses or featherbeds, bureaus, bookcases, chairs and tables, carpets, wardrobes in those which did not have presses, washstands and window treatments. Each of the four major bedrooms on the second floor had fireplaces. The nursery in the second floor ell was heated with a small stove and had a bathtub. The two bedrooms on the third floor, probably used by the boys in the family, had no heat source.[9]

The kitchen was dominated by a five and a half foot fireplace and a half-dome oven in the throat of the brick flu. The huge fireplace hearth at the time of the house's restoration in 1976–1977 had long since disappeared into the basement. It was possible the Todds, soon after moving into the new house, converted from cooking over an open fireplace to wood or coal cooking stoves which were then available.[10]

As successful as Todd had been in business, politics and providing for his family, his station was not on the level with many of Lexington's elites, who came from other states and who exhibited their fortunes by building or buying imposing and luxurious homes. The Hunt family lived for several generations on the wealth accrued by John Wesley Hunt, a New Jersey native who began with a general store on Richmond Road in 1795. Hunt, said to be the commonwealth's first millionaire, made his fortune from hemp manufacturing, marketing and shrewd investments. His elegant home still stands at the corner of Mill and Second streets.[11]

Nearby on Mill Street, John M. McCalla, a lawyer, Democrat operative and veteran of the War of 1812, built Mount Hope in 1819, a grand brick Greek Revival home, later known as the Benjamin Gratz house. It was McCalla who almost defeated Todd in the race for clerk of the House of Representatives in 1828.[12]

Another Lexington millionaire, William Morton, built what was called the most elegant home in the city in 1810, at Limestone and Fifth streets. Morton came to Lexington from Baltimore, Maryland, and his commercial enterprises were so successful they enabled him to live in such a grand manner that townspeople referred to him as "Lord" Morton.[13]

Around 1817, Roger Quarels, a wealthy Virginian, purchased 190 acres on Georgetown Pike and built Hurricane Hall, described by architectural historian Clay Lancaster as the most engaging residence in Fayette County. The hand-blocked parlor wallpaper depicted scenes along the Tiber River. The elaborate presses, above built-in drawers beside the chimneys, were patterns for other houses. Sen. John Pope built an Italianate villa on what is now Grosvenor Avenue from plans reputedly drawn by Benjamin Latrobe, one of the U.S. Capitol architects. Thomas Lewis, another wealthy Virginian, built the rambling Lewis Manor on Viley Road. Judge Thomas Hickey purchased the sprawling Coolavin, on Sixth Street, in 1822.[14]

While the owners of these ostentatious homes had much more money than the Todds, they lacked, for the most part, that family's credentials of having helped establish the commonwealth in general and Lexington in particular and their deep involvement in politics. That distinction leveled the social playing field and placed the family's third generation, including Mary, among Lexington's elite.

Mary, who shared a bedroom in the new house with Elizabeth Humphreys, lost one of her champions, her older sister Elizabeth. In February 1832, Elizabeth married her long time suitor Ninian W. Edwards. The Edwardses may have lived with the Widow Parker after their marriage while he finished college. As soon as Edwards completed his law studies at Transylvania, the couple moved to Illinois. Mary had little time to enjoy the spacious new home with her family. In what was perhaps a mutual arrangement between the fourteen-year-old girl, her father and stepmother, she was sent to the Mentelle boarding school. In later years, she recalled the experience, "My early home was truly at a *boarding* school."[15]

Augustus Waldmare and Victorie Charlotte LeClere Mentelle first settled in Gallipolis, Ohio, then, like many of their countrymen, migrated to Lexington in the early 1800s. By the time they arrived in Lexington, they were almost penniless and took any work they could get. She was the daughter of a physician and he was the son of a Royal Academy professor who was historiographer to King Louis XV. To raise money, Mme. Mentelle wrote and published a book about their journey from France. Todd and Henry Clay each purchased four of her books and Levi Todd bought two. She began her career in 1802 at Mary M. Beck's Academy teaching French, dancing and drawing. M. Mentelle operated a stoneware kiln, was a surveyor, taught French at Transylvania and did private tutoring.[16]

The Mentelles opened their academy in 1820, when Mary Owen Todd Russell gave them some land and a large cottage on her Richmond Road property across from Henry Clay's plantation, Ashland. The house was large enough to accommodate the Mentelles, their five children and boarding students. Fees for the Mentelles' School for Young Ladies were six dollars per quarter for day students and $120 per year for those who boarded from Monday morning through Friday afternoon. Fees were paid quarterly in advance. Students, in addition to French, were given what Mme. Mentelle called "a solid English education in all its branches.[17]

Nelson, the Todds' butler and coachman, drove Mary to the Mentelles each Monday morning and returned for her on Friday afternoons. Elizabeth Humphreys recalled attending a French play given by the academy students. Mary "was the star actress of the school and I was thrilled with her talent." Nelson drove Elizabeth and Jane, Betsy Todd's slave, to the school. Jane was holding a cake which was Mary's contribution to the event. Elizabeth took some tea roses she had cut.[18]

"Mary was waiting impatiently at the door as we drove up and flew at me like a whirl-wind," Elizabeth wrote. "I had not seen her for a week and I thought she had grown during that period, she looked so dainty in her fresh muslin frock and silk sash! Her cheeks were as pink as the tea roses I had gathered for her. Her blue eyes were sparkling with excitement, her pretty chestnut curls were bright and glossy."[19]

Mary asked if M. Giron had made the delicious cake and Jane indignantly replied that Aunt Chaney, not the Frenchman, made the cake. Mathurin Giron was one of Mary's favorite people in Lexington. Barely five feet tall and heavy set, Giron came to Lexington in 1811 and brought with him a talent for making and keeping friends. He married Philberte Vimont, whose father, Louis Vimont, was a prominent merchant and landowner in Bourbon County. Giron was a culinary genius and catered parties, weddings and official events such as the visits of Gilbert du Motier, the Marquis de LaFayette and President James Monroe. "When Aunt was arranging a dinner or party," Elizabeth wrote, "we always begged to be allowed to take the written order to Monsieur [Giron] that we might feast our eyes on the iced cakes decorated with garlands of pink sugar roses or the bride's cakes with their fountains of clean, spun sugar pyramiding in the center veiling tiny fat cupids of little sugar babies. Mary chatted to Monsieur in French much to his delight." She added they spent their small allowances at the confectionery.[20]

Mary, always up to mischief, decided to tease Aunt Chaney about the cake when she arrived at the Todd house. "I am going to insist that Monsieur Giron made the cake; then when Aunt Chaney flies into one of her fierce rages and bangs the pans and kettles and orders me out of the kitchen, I am going to give her the red and yellow bandana I bought for her and tell her that Monsieur with all his icing and spicing could not make a cake so confectionary as hers. She will fairly eat me up for praising her cake so highly."[21]

Called one of the most intelligent girls at Mme. Mentelle's school, Mary always had the highest marks and took the biggest prizes. One of her former classmates recalled her as being "a merry companionable girl with a smile for everybody. She was really the life of the school, always ready for a good time and willing to contribute even more than her own share in promoting it."[22]

Mme. Mentelle was something of a chameleon in her political opinions of America in general and Kentucky in particular, but she was smart enough to know that her livelihood depended on the people she held in contempt and so confined her comments in letters to French relatives. "She was a gentlewoman, the cultured lady who opened her home to those interested in playing and hearing good music or in meeting French visitors to the city, the gifted headmistress of the most fashionable boarding school for young ladies in the area," Dr. Lindsey Apple wrote in the 1983 *Journal of the Kentucky-Tennessee American Studies Association*.[23]

"She spoke of flatterers and parasites, an interesting statement, given her dependence on the very group she was criticizing," he continued. "Kentuckians possessed many and great vices and no discernible virtues. Her strongest words condemned the lack of true society." She also had an opinion on the nation's constitutional concept of liberty. "But, that seems so ridiculous, so absurd, when compared to the enslavement of the negro." In discussions about slavery with her neighbors, Mme. Mentelle said it was like listening to fools who thought they were speaking rationally.[24]

Nor did she have a good impression of the state the Todds helped found. "We float always between good and bad in this Kentucky, this Paradise. The land is beautiful but what is beautiful? Trees, trees and more trees," she wrote. From all indications the longer the Mentelles remained in Kentucky, the more they longed for France.[25]

Whether Mme. Mentelle conveyed her true opinions of Kentucky and democracy to her students was not known. In a letter to a prospective parent, Charles C. Moore, Mme. Mentelle listed the price of boarding and tuition at $120 (paid quarterly in advance) and vacation days. She taught every subject needed for a good education, French would be taught if preferred and books were to be selected and paid for by parents. She told Moore she paid particular attention to the subjects of morals, temper and health.[26]

How much influence the four years studying with Mme. Mentelle had on Mary Todd is unknown. The Frenchwoman is portrayed in a miniature at the Mary Todd Lincoln House as being an imposing, determined woman. Without a doubt those years cultivated Mary's love of French, literature, the theater, and poetry. Historian Jean H. Baker wrote that the Mentelle years provided Mary Todd with distaste for Lexington, female independence, aristocratic snobbishness and individual eccentricity, and a fascination with royalty.[27]

Mary Todd was born independent. An early example of her independence is found in the ride out to Ashland to show Henry Clay her pony and demanding that he come out to examine the animal. Mary was later the quintessential independent woman as she inserted herself into the national scope of nineteenth century politics when it was a closely guarded male bastion. If there was distaste for Lexington's inhabitants, it certainly evaporated when she moved to Springfield, Illinois, which was full of people from Lexington and Kentucky. She spent several months in Lexington in 1848, after a lengthy visit in November 1847 with her husband. Mary returned again after the death of her father in 1849 and twice in the 1850s. In 1876, before her final trip to Europe, she came to Lexington for one last visit. As for her fascination with royalty, some of her friends in Europe, when Americans, for the most part, turned their back on the president's widow, were from the French royal Orleans family, who opened their home and hearts to her in England.[28]

An aristocratic snob would hardly have gone out of her way to stop a carriage and get out not only to speak to the dirty, vagrant William Solomon but also to give him money to supplement what she knew was a paltry income. In the summer of 1833, Lexington was struck with a cholera epidemic. Out of a population of 6,383, the death toll reached 502, and was beyond the town's infrastructure to handle. A mild winter led to a warm spring with heavy rains which caused shallow privies to overflow and contaminate the ground water supplying the town.[29]

It was not clear why the Todd family was in Lexington during the epidemic, as they usually spent the hot summers at Buena Vista, near Frankfort, or at Carb Orchard Springs Spa in Lincoln County.[30] Businesses were closed and there was a mass exodus from Lexington.

Not even Elizabeth Humphreys spent the summer of 1833 in Lexington. Helm quoted Mary's recollections of the tragic summer. "I will never forget that terrible time. The choking fumes of tar that mother made Nelson burn all through the house, the lime and white-wash over everything. The deadly quiet was everywhere. When the baby cried it seemed as if it must be heard all over town. Nothing on the streets but the drivers and horses of the dead carts piled high with bodies of those who had just died, the relatives of the dead were too frightened to make decent burial clothes, the poor bodies wrapped in sheets and blankets, many of them just as they were dressed when the plague caught them."[31] There were not enough coffins for the dead, Mary said, and her father had boxes and trunks taken from their attic to be used as coffins. "Other people did the same," she recalled, "and still so very, very many had to be buried in trenches, just dumped in like old dead dogs."[32]

The family was not allowed to eat any fruits and vegetables, just beaten biscuits, boiled milk and boiled water. Mary slipped outside and ate some mulberries. Aunt Chaney caught her and told Betsy Todd, who sent for a doctor. Mammy Sally held Mary's nose and poured ipecac, which induced vomiting, down her throat.[33] "But what was worse than all," Mary continued, "everybody was frightened to death, talking in whispers, almost afraid to breathe and poor, brave old sol going along as if nothing terrible was happening and just doing everything he could." She told Elizabeth that she was so ashamed of herself for once making fun of the man, laughing at his ragged clothes and his being sold as a vagrant.[34]

Mary was talking about the hero of the 1833 cholera epidemic, William "King" Solomon, who had fallen on hard times. Solomon once had a thriving excavation business and owned a brick residence on Upper Street for which he paid $737.50 in cash in 1814. After his wife died, Solomon turned to drink, lost his business and his home and he was auctioned off as a vagrant. A freed slave, Aunt Charlotte, who had grown up with Solomon in Virginia and made her living selling fruit and baked goods at the open market, purchased him and set him free. Her arrangement with Solomon was he could live at her house but would have to turn over his wages—about seventy-five-cents a day made from digging sewers, cellars and basements—for her to manage. Aunt Charlotte gave him back a little spending money but never enough to buy whiskey.[35]

As Mary was returning with Elizabeth from Mme. Mentelle's, she saw Solomon on the street. Mary ordered Nelson to stop the carriage so they could speak to him. "Get out with me, Elizabeth," Mary urged, "we must not pass him by without shaking hands and I know he needs a little piece of money for tobacco. I wish I could give him a cake of soap instead if it would not insult him." Nelson muttered, loud enough for Solomon to hear that he was going to tell Miss Betsy as soon as they got home about them shaking hands with white trash. "Howdy Miss Mary," Solomon said, "you ain't never too proud to speak to me." Mary replied, "Too proud to speak to you. I am proud when you speak to me! I will never forget last summer when you were the bravest man in town when you worked all night and day digging, digging, digging graves for those poor people who died like flies from the cholera. You dug the graves of some of my best friends. You were not afraid! You are a hero!"[36]

Mary was not the only person in Lexington who considered Solomon a hero. Portraitist Samuel W. Price painted his likeness. When he died in 1854, he was given ceremonies worthy of a hero. Governor Lazarus W. Powell, local officials and prominent members of the community attended his funeral and heard the novelist James Lane Allen give the oration. "On the day when King Solomon was laid here," Allen said, "the grass began to weave its seamless mantle across his frailties; but out of his dust sprang what has since been growing—what no hostile hand can pluck away, nor any wind blow down—the red flower of a man's passionate service to his fellow-men when they were in direst need of him."[37]

Mary, even as young girl, was as comfortable shaking hands and talking with Solomon as she was speaking French fluently with the Mentelles. From all indications, the Mentelles made their boarding students a part of their family. In the evenings, M. Mentelle would play the violin and Mme. Mentelle and their daughters would teach the students to dance.[38]

Elizabeth Humphreys recalled that dancing was one of Mary's favorite pastimes which she learned well from the many practice sessions with the Mentelles. But, she did not allow her love for dancing to interfere with her other studies, especially French. "For as long as I knew her [she] continued to read the finest French authors," Humphreys wrote. "At different times, French gentlemen came to Lexington to study English and when one was fortunate enough to meet her, he was not only surprised but delighted to find her perfect acquaintance with his language."[39]

Mary enjoyed the orchestra and dancing held on the summer evenings at Crab Orchard Springs Spa in Lincoln County during the Todd family's annual summer pilgrimage there. The spa was located at the end of Logan's Trace on the Wilderness Road, over which settlers in the 1770s followed Daniel Boone's path through the Cumberland Gap.[40]

Known as the "Saratoga of the South," the spa, a rambling wood complex with a main building, dining room, ballroom and stables, accommodated about 500 guests, social elites of the South who came each season to take the cure in the mineral water springs. The spa's seventy-seven rustic landscaped acres offered, at one time or another, shady walks, woodland nooks, overhanging rocks and rippling springs, double-decked gazebos, horseback riding, boating, cockfights, cards and even roulette. The charges were five dollars per week per person, children were half-price, and two dollars per week was charged for servants and horses.[41]

A week at the spa for his family, slaves and horses cost Todd between $60 and $75. Converted into 2012 dollars, that expenditure would be approximately $1,700 per week. If they remained at the spa longer than a week, the amount, of course, would be much more. Business at Oldham Todd and Company was indeed going well.

Crab Orchard Springs Spa had eight springs that contained a cornucopia of minerals. Two springs were chalybeate or iron impregnated, two were saline and the other three were filled with white, red and black sulfur. Water from the springs was advertised to cure diseases of the liver, kidneys, bowels, indigestion and general debility, such as Betsy Todd reportedly suffered.[42] Nearby Spring Hill Race Course offered spring and summer racing.[43]

Katherine Helm provided a graphic description of the Todds' trips to the spa. "The bustle of preparation; the piles of fresh little muslin dresses; the carriages filled with children and babies and nurses, for only the older boys who objected to going were left at home; the long drive; the meeting with old friends and acquaintances; the new arrivals each day driving up in state with jingling harness and prancing horses; the finely dressed ladies stepping mincingly down the carriage steps in mortal dread of showing their ankles; the beaux flocking around to greet those they knew and perchance to gain a fleeting glimpse of those same carefully guarded ankles. The negro fiddlers, the candlelight flickering from innumerable sconces over the bright, filmy ball dresses of the belles and the courtly bowing and scraping of the beaux."[44]

Often Betsy Todd's brother, Alexander Humphreys, and his family came from St. James Parish, Louisiana, to meet them at Crab Orchard Springs. Sometimes, the Humphreys children remained with the Todds in Lexington until cooler weather permitted them to return to Louisiana.[45]

Other summers Mary spent some time with her family at Buena Vista, the Humphreys' summer home on Leestown Pike, eighteen miles west of Lexington. Buena Vista was near Duckers' Station, where the Lexington and Ohio Railroad provided service after 1834. The Todds lived only a short distance from the depot in Lexington and the L&O enabled Robert S. Todd to travel back and forth to Buena Vista while attending to his business at Oldham and Todd.[46]

Mary Todd's years at the Mentelles were interrupted with a trip to Springfield, Illinois, to visit her sister, Elizabeth Todd Edwards. As the business of Oldham Todd and Company expanded, Todd traveled extensively. In May 1835, Mary and her sister, Frances, accompanied their father to Springfield.

Historian Thomas F. Schwartz, in an article in the Winter 2005 *Journal of the Abraham Lincoln Association*, discovered the 1835 visit. He found in Deed Book H in the Sangamon County, Illinois, clerk's office a document noting that Mary Ann Todd and Frances Todd were witnesses to a land transaction where Samuel Wiggins, from Cincinnati, Ohio, purchased property from their brother-in-law, Ninian W. Edwards.[47]

When Mary returned from Illinois, she continued her studies at the Mentelles' academy. Her father, however, made a change in his business life. In January 1835, Todd sent a letter to the Kentucky House of Representatives expressing his appreciation for having been allowed to serve that body as clerk for more than twenty years. Todd said he declined to again run for reelection due to indispensable engagements.[48] The Lexington man had something else in mind beside politics, although he had been a member of the Lexington City Council and had a long record of service on the Fayette County Court.[49]

At this time his second family numbered three. Combined with five children from his first marriage and all the Humphreys relatives who came to visit and seemed to never leave, Todd was constantly looking for business opportunities. In addition to the manufacturing business of Oldham Todd at Sandersville, of which he was president, the company had a wholesale store in Lexington that supplied outlets in Illinois, Indiana, Ohio and Missouri.[50]

He had represented the Kentucky Insurance Company, the commonwealth's first banking institution organized in 1817. Succeeding this company in 1822 was the Bank of Kentucky, which was partly owned by the state. The bank was ordered closed in 1822, but all its business was not phased out until 1835.[51]

Through his duties as clerk of the House of Representatives, Todd had a front row seat in which to network and observe various pieces of banking legislation as it moved through the General Assembly. Todd was an astute enough attorney and businessman to wait until the banking business was on a more stable fiscal footing before becoming actively involved.

In 1835, the Northern Bank of Kentucky in Lexington was chartered by the legislature with four branches. It was no surprise that Todd was the first president of the Lexington institution. That was one of the "indispensable engagements" he mentioned in his letter declining to run again for clerk of the House.[52]

In 1837, Mary finished her course of studies at the Mentelles' academy and planned another visit with Elizabeth and Ninian Edwards in Springfield, Illinois. It was there she met and married Abraham Lincoln.

CHAPTER 6

Married Life Begins

There was no honeymoon or grand tour for the newly wed Lincolns. They settled down, like many of their Springfield contemporaries, into quarters at the Globe Hotel, often referred to as the Globe Tavern. Living at the Globe certainly did not afford Mary with the comforts she enjoyed in the Edwards home or in her father's house in Lexington, but she had the man she wanted as her life partner. She was an intelligent woman and knew that, given Lincoln's traveling the circuit half of the year, most of the sacrifices needed to make the marriage work would come from her side of the union.

"We are not keeping house," Lincoln wrote Joshua Speed, "but boarding at the Globe Tavern which is very well kept by a widow lady of the name Beck." He added that the board was only four dollars a week. "Mary is very well and continues her old sentiments of friendship for you. How married life goes with us I will tell you when I see you here, which I hope will be very soon."[1]

The Globe, as described by Dr. James T. Hickey in a 1963 *Journal of the Illinois State Historical Society* article, was a residence hotel. Hickey used the word *rooms*, not *room*, to describe their domicile. "The Wallaces [Mary's sister Frances and her husband Dr. William Wallace] stayed [at the Globe] more than three years and it was into their recently vacated rooms that the Lincolns moved."[2]

Hickey's description indicated the couple had a suite consisting of a sitting room and a bedroom. The Globe was a two-story frame edifice. A back wing, with two floors, had porches on each side. Public parlors, with carpet, settees, chairs, tables and lamps were on the first floor. The dining room and kitchen, also on the first floor, could serve fifty to a hundred diners. The word *tavern* used in connection with the Globe may be a misnomer. A *Sangamo Journal* advertisement on February 18, 1840, referred to the establishment as the Globe Hotel and boasted it was a temperance house. The Lincolns' rooms, heated by a fireplace or stove, faced Adams Street.[3]

An 1840 inventory indicated the Globe's rooms were sparsely furnished. There would have been a bed, with either a mattress, featherbed or a tick filled with straw, bed linens, a washstand, chairs, tables and lamps, although many used candles. In the entire inventory, only two bureaus, or chests, were listed.[4] Many of the long-term residents probably supplemented the rooms with their own furnishings. The Lincolns may have done the same, picking up inexpensive pieces here and there. They had both been tenants, so to speak, before their marriage. She lived in the Edwards home and he roomed at William Butler's. They had little or no furniture.

Had Mary been married out of her home in Lexington, her father, the Widow Parker and their extended families—the Bodleys, Bullocks, Stuarts, Carrs and others—would have contributed ample furnishings for them to begin housekeeping. In addition, there would have been wedding gifts from her family, the Breckinridges, the Trotters and the Clays and other personal and political friends.

But, she was married in Springfield, to the man she loved, over the objections of her sisters, her only immediate family there, aside from a long list of cousins. Returning to Lexington for a wedding was out of the question due to the time frame of travel, not to mention the expense.

It was not unusual for newlyweds to begin their married life at the Globe. In addition to the Wallaces, a number of their friends, all prominent residents of Springfield, lived at the Globe. Lincoln's first law partner and Mary's cousin, John Todd Stuart, and his wife, the former Mary Virginia Nash, began their married life there in May 1839. Alfred Taylor Bledsoe, who schooled Lincoln in the use of the broadsword when he was challenged to a duel by James Shields, and his wife Harriet Coxe Bledsoe were also Globe residents. Dr. Richard F. Barrett, at one time an owner of the Globe, lived there with his family.[5]

From all appearances, the Lincolns were happy. He was busy with his law practice. Lincoln left John Todd Stuart's firm two years earlier to become Steven Trigg Logan's junior partner. Logan was another Todd cousin. Three months in the spring and three months in the fall Lincoln traveled the Eighth Judicial Circuit which comprised fourteen counties in Central Illinois.

Mary occupied her days with sewing, reading and making social calls while he was away. She and Lincoln went to concerts, plays and a traveling circus. "She looked forward with

Left: Abraham Lincoln, circa 1860–1861 (Library of Congress, Prints and Photographs Division). *Right:* Mary Lincoln, circa 1861–1862 (Brady-Handy Collection, Library of Congress).

eagerness to the little home they would have together," Helm wrote. "Dreaming of this, she contentedly lived at the tavern, received her callers without complaint and made no apologies for her un-lovey surroundings." Helm mentioned the parties and family dinner with the expanding Todd family. "Best of all [were] the quiet evenings together when they talked and made plans for the future."[6]

Without a doubt those long evenings included discussion and plans for Lincoln's political future, which he began envisioning years before they met. Both were astute students of politics and knew exactly what they wanted. Reaching that goal, however, was another matter and included sacrifices that Mary, who had lived a pampered existence up to that time, was obviously willing to make. While she brought additional political connections and monied interests to the marriage, Mary was the one who experienced a drastic change of lifestyle. She knew how to entertain, sew, knit and embroider but milking a cow, cooking, keeping a house clean, washing and ironing were not included in her training manual. She made a valiant and successful effort to learn. Raising a family was something she previously observed from afar.

William Butler beat the expectant parents in announcing the arrival of their first child by telling Joshua Speed that Mary and Lincoln were expecting. "In relation to the 'coming event' about which Butler wrote you, I had not *heard* one word before I got your letter," Lincoln wrote Speed in May 1843. "But I have so much confidence in the judgment of a Butler on such a subject that I [am] inclined to think there may be some reality in it. What day does Butler appoint? By the way, how do 'events' of the same sort come on in your family?"[7]

Speed inquired about the possibility, if the Lincolns' child was a son, if he would have a namesake. Lincoln replied, "About the prospect of your having a namesake at our house can't say, exactly yet."[8]

Lincoln told Speed that he and Mary would be unable to visit them in Louisville. "Besides poverty and the necessity of attending to business, those 'coming events' I suspect would be some what in the way. I most heartily wish you and your Fanny would not fail to come. Just let us know the time a week in advance and we will have a room provided for you at our house and all be merry together for a while."[9]

The "coming event" arrived on August 1, 1843, when Mary, with an anxious Lincoln waiting, gave birth to their first son, Robert Todd Lincoln. "Mary Lincoln, who presumably could have spent her confinement in her sister's commodious home, elected instead to have her child amid the stark surroundings of the Globe," Justin G. Turner and Linda L. Turner wrote. "Assuming that the choice had been hers, that decision to go it alone gives evidence of the streak of stubborn independence that was then such an important facet of her nature."[10]

Lincoln was the typical nervous expectant father. "When my wife had her first baby, the doctor, from time to time, reported to me that everything was going as well as could be expected under the circumstances. That satisfied me he was doing his best but still I felt anxious to hear the first squall. It came at last and I felt mighty relieved."[11]

"My darling husband was bending over me with such love and tenderness," Mary said later, recalling the birth of their first child.[12] More than love and tenderness were needed to take care of a newborn infant and his mother. There were feedings every three to four hours, a mountain of dirty diapers and baby clothes, the possibility of colic and the noise of arriving and departing stage coaches was not conducive to an infant's sleep.

Mary's three sisters in Springfield, one of them a doctor's wife, surely offered her some assistance during her pregnancy and after the child's birth, though there is no way of documenting their involvement. There was ample documentation that Harriet Bledsoe, the wife of Albert T. Bledsoe, cared for the infant and his mother very well. Mrs. Bledsoe went to their rooms every day for several weeks to bathe and dress the baby, clean up, and care for Mary until she recovered from birthing their first child.[13]

Abraham Lincoln never forgot Harriet Bledsoe's kindness toward his wife in her time of need. When she asked for his assistance in obtaining clothing for her children during the Civil War, Lincoln granted her a pass although her husband was the assistant secretary of war in President Jefferson Davis' Confederate cabinet. The pass read, "Allow the bearer, Mrs. Harriet C. Bledsoe, to pass our lines with ordinary baggage and go south. A. Lincoln. Jan. 16, 1865."[14]

The Globe was no place for a young, squalling infant and the Lincolns moved in the fall of 1843 to a rented three-room cottage on South Fourth Street.[15]

"Joshua Speed did not get the namesake he and Lincoln had joked about," Ruth Painter Randall wrote. "There was Mary's affection for a father who was good to her and her pride in the family name of Todd. And most people would agree that Robert was a more pleasing name than Joshua. Also Mr. Todd apparently did not look down on Lincoln as some other members of the family had done. According to family tradition he said, 'I only hope that Mary will make as good a wife as she has a husband.'"[16]

Robert Smith Todd came to Springfield in March 1844 for a visit and to see his namesake. During his visit, he deeded eighty acres of land in Sangamon County to Mary. The purchase price was one dollar. Elizabeth (Betsy) Todd co-signed the deed that Lincoln had drawn up.[17]

Robert Todd, after that visit, began providing the Lincolns with $120 per year until his law practice was firmly established. However, from 1844 until his death in 1849, Todd, according to his estate records, had advanced the Lincolns $1,157, which was an average of $231.40 per year.[18] That money certainly helped pay for the missing necessities such as hired help for Mary, buying furniture and subscribing to newspapers and periodicals that were so essential to both a rising young politician and his wife.

Todd also gave his daughter, Frances Wallace, a deed to eighty acres of land at the same time. Interestingly enough, he did not give Elizabeth Edwards the same as Mary and Frances. Instead, he deeded eighty acres to his granddaughter, Julia Edwards, Elizabeth's daughter. Another eighty acres was probably deeded to another daughter, Ann Todd Smith. Henry Pratt, in his book on Lincoln's finances, wrote there were 240 acres in the tract of land Todd purchased.[19]

Aside from assisting the Lincolns financially, Todd saw potential in his favorite daughter's husband and recognized his congressional ambitions. Undoubtedly, Mary had written her father about her husband's political plans before his visit to Illinois. In a March 1844 letter to Ninian Edwards from Lexington, Todd was appreciative of Lincoln's efforts in Illinois on behalf of the Whigs. "I can use my influence here if Mr. Clay is elected (of which there can be no doubt) to procure some appointment for him out of Congress until his monied point of view will enable him to take a stand in Congress. *Such as district attorney or judge.* I will write him in a few days.[20]

Despite Todd's declaration, Henry Clay was not elected in 1844. James K. Polk, a Jacksonian Democrat from Tennessee, became president. Betsy Todd wrote to Mary describing how Clay took the news of his defeat at a wedding party they attended when the New York mail arrived in Lexington around ten o'clock in the evening.

As the hour approached for the arrival of the mail, I saw several gentlemen quietly leave the room, and knowing their errand I eagerly watched for their return. As soon as they came in the room I knew by their expression of each countenance that New York had gone Democratic. The bearers of the news consulted together for a moment, then one of them advanced to Mr. Clay who was standing in the center of the group, of which your father was one, and handed him a paper. Although I was sure of the news it contained, I watched Mr. Clay's face for confirmation of the evil tidings. He opened the paper and as he read the death knell of his political hopes and life-long ambition, I saw a distinct blue shade begin at the roots of his hair, pass slowly over his face like a cloud and then disappear. He stood for a moment as if frozen. He laid down the paper, and, turning to a table, filled a glass with wine, and raising it to his lips with a pleasant smile, said: "I drink to the health and happiness of all assembled here." Setting down his glass, he resumed his conversation as if nothing had occurred and was, as usual, the life and light of the company. The contents of the paper were soon known to every one in the room and a wet blanket fell over our gaiety. We left the wedding with heavy hearts. Alas, our gallant "Harry of the West" had fought his last presidential battle.[21]

In surmising Clay had fought his last battle for the presidency, Betsy Todd was wrong. Clay contested another Kentuckian, Zachary Taylor, for the Whig nomination for president in 1848, and lost. Even then, he was not finished. Clay was again elected to the Senate in 1849, and died in office in 1852.[22]

Mary and Abraham Lincoln both realized Clay's presidential aspirations were finished after the 1844 defeat and they supported Taylor. That decision came back to bite them after Taylor's election and they discovered that, while out of office, Clay still wielded enormous influence. Lincoln had an interest in the position of commissioner of the General Land Office. So did another Whig, Chicago attorney Justin Butterfield, who had supported Clay. Butterfield got the job.[23] Neither of them, however, relinquished the dream of Lincoln holding national office. In fact, their ambitions were only whetted.

The law firm of Logan and Lincoln was doing very well. In 1842, their partnership averaged over 400 cases. The surge in business undoubtedly came from the Bankruptcy Act in 1841. The firm represented debtors in seventy-two bankruptcy cases the next year in federal court. In 1844, when Lincoln left Logan, who wanted to take his son into the practice, to start his own firm, their annual case load was over 300.[24] Lincoln established his own law firm and took William H. Herndon as his junior partner.

Another change came when they bought a house in Springfield. The Lincolns' furnishings from the small cottage did not fill the story-and-a-half home at the corner of Eighth and Jackson streets that they purchased from the Rev. Charles Dresser, who married them. Some of their new furniture was made by Daniel E. Ruckel, a Springfield cabinetmaker.[25]

According to the sale contract for the house and lot, the purchase price was $1,500.

The said Dresser is to convey to, or procure to be conveyed to, said Lincoln, by a clear title in fee simple the entire premises (grounds and improvements) in Springfield, on which said Dresser now resides, and give him possession of said premises on or before the first day of April next— for which said Lincoln at or before the same day is to pay to said Dresser twelve hundred dollars, or what said Dresser shall be at his own option accept as equivalent thereto; and also to procure to be conveyed to said Dresser, by clear title in fee simple, the entire premises (ground and building) in Springfield, on the block immediately West of the Public square the building on which is now occupied by H. A. as a shop, being the same premises some time since conveyed by N.W. Edwards and wife to said Lincoln & Stephen T. Logan.[26]

At the sales contract signing, Lincoln paid Dresser $750 and deeded him the lot, which was worth $300.[27] Three months later, on May 2, 1844, Lincoln paid Dresser the remaining $450, and he and Mary received the deed to their very own home.[28]

The house contained five rooms and a sleeping loft. The back portion was a simple flat-roofed wing with a side porch with an entrance to a partial basement, which the Lincolns used as a root cellar. There was both a cistern, providing water for laundry and bathing, and a well for drinking water and cooking. If not installed at the time the Lincolns purchased the house, pumps were later added for the cistern and well. Outbuildings eventually included a privy, washhouse, stable, barn and woodshed, where firewood was stored that Lincoln chopped for stoves and fireplaces.[29]

The house was certainly large enough for a couple and a toddler. With the new home came enormous responsibilities for Mary, who had to cook three meals a day, see that groceries and provisions were stocked, care for her young son, keep a larger house clean, do the laundry, make draperies, bed linens and clothes for the family, as well as keep Lincoln apprised of national political events from the newspapers she read. Emilie Todd Helm recalled her half-sister reading and reviewing books for her husband when she visited them as a young girl. "I heard him say he had no need to read a book after Mary gave him a synopsis," she said. "He had great respect for her judgment and never took an important step without consulting her."[30] For six months each year while Lincoln was on the court circuit, Mary functioned as a single parent and homeowner.

The Lincolns, like most couples, divided some of the chores at home. For a while they had a cow, which Lincoln milked. Lincoln's duties, when he was at home, were to provide a ready supply of firewood and to bank the fires in the stove and fireplaces in the evening so Mary could shake out the ashes and have hot coals to rekindle the fires the next morning with fresh split wood in the house. Often Lincoln forgot both chores.[31] Apparently, she tried several methods of impressing on him the necessity of heat in the cold Illinois winters mornings for both warmth and cooking.

A number of times, the fires had died out completely because he forgot to bank them. Lincoln, armed with a shovel, would go to a neighbor house and asked to borrow some hot coals. On one of those occasions, a neighbor woman told him she had no hot coals but offered him some matches.[32]

Mary found a solution to that problem.

A. L. Bowen, in a 1925 speech, outlined her strategy. "A morning chore was to split wood for the breakfast fire. Mrs. Lincoln, impatient to get the day's program started, found it necessary to prod her liege lord to greater activity. From the kitchen door would issue the loud proclamation of 'Fire! Fire! Fire!' The neighborhood understood its application and was not alarmed. Lincoln understood the need for wood in the kitchen and his acknowledgment was contained in the simple, mild reply, 'Yes Mary, yes Mary.'"[33]

Mary, according to Katherine Helm, enjoyed her new responsibility as a homeowner, in addition to being a wife and mother. "Mary passionately loved beautiful and desirable things, because of the cost, she had to collect her furniture and rugs very slowly and although she loved to make herself pretty and dainty for her husband, she did not burden him by incurring heavy debts."[34]

For years, her father had given her lovely, and expensive, pieces of Meissen porcelain. Without a doubt, she took them to Illinois with her in 1839.[35] Consequently, she had something to build her home's décor about. Mary was an excellent seamstress but all her sewing—

which included curtains and draperies, bed linens, towels, table linens, clothes for Robert and herself and Lincoln's shirts—was done by hand. Mary bought ticking and twenty-one pounds of feathers from John Irwin and Company to make their pillows. While she made Lincoln's shirts, his suits were tailored in Springfield by Benjamin R. Biddle.[36]

Their first large expenditure at Irwin's mercantile establishment on March 16, 1843, was material for a suit for Lincoln. Two yards of black wool, three yards of cashmere and thread, trim and interfacing came to $36.37. Biddle's tailoring fee was nine dollars for a total of $45.37. Six months later, they purchased more material—2.75 yards of heavy felted wool and three yards of cashmere—for Lincoln's winter suit. More expensive trimmings were used and Biddle increased his tailoring charge to $9.50.[37]

Irwin's store was much more than just a dry goods establishment. John Irwin had one of the few iron safes in Springfield and his business also functioned as a bank. Lincoln deposited funds with Irwin that drew twelve percent interest, which was credited to his account.[38]

In 1845, the first full year they lived in their own home, Mary purchased ninety-six yards of various fabrics from Irwin's store alone. Thread, needles, trim, interfacing and other items necessary to home sewing were included in those purchases. She was producing an enormous amount sewing for their home and her family while cooking, cleaning, child rearing and reading various newspapers and periodicals for her husband.[39]

There was, however, another way to augment her wardrobe. The sister, Ellen Marie Smith, of her next door neighbor, Mrs. Thomas Alsop, was the same size as Mary and they often wore each other's dresses. "The exchange was welcomed by both," A. L. Bowen said. "Neither seemed to feel any fear of social ostracism for being recognized in the gown of the other."[40]

Home sewing machines did not go into mass production until the 1850s.[41] One can only imagine the vast amounts of time and energy Mary put into sewing for her family and home when Lincoln was on the circuit. She often sewed in the evenings, her illumination coming from candles or an oil lamp, because she had other duties to fulfill during her days. Sewing by such a dim light could have led to one of her painful headaches but she did not let that stop her. Years later her hands were still hardened from the toil—sewing, washing, scrubbing and cleaning—from the early days of her marriage. A gentlemen who shook hands with her at a presidential reception in 1861 remarked, "We are pleased with her. She had gloves on and put out her hand. It is not soft."[42]

If there was something Mary Lincoln felt she needed to know, she found a source for the information and became competent in the application. She was not the kind of person to wring her hands in despair for the want of knowledge.

Not being as adept at cooking and housekeeping as sewing, Mary, on December 31, 1846, purchased *Direction for Cookery in Its Various Branches* and *The House Book: A Manual of Domestic Economy for Town and Country*. Both were written by Eliza Leslie, a Philadelphia native who grew up in England. She had also written one of the earliest American cookbooks, *Pastry, Cakes and Sweetmeats*, in 1828. For that book, authorship was attributed to "A Lady From Philadelphia."[43]

The Leslie cookbook contained a recipe that became a favorite of Lincoln's, fricasseed chicken, which Mary cooked often. The book gave precise instructions for preparing and cooking venison, pork, beef, lamb, rabbit, quail, grouse, vegetables, salads, breads, desserts, fruits and even ice cream. There was a recipe for ginger beer which was served at the Lincolns' wedding reception.[44]

Mary Lincoln loved her southern foods, especially breads. While in France in 1879, she lamented that a nation without "waffles, batter cakes, egg cornbread, biscuits, light rolls, buckwheat cakes was a gastronomic desert."[45]

From all indications, Mary Lincoln began preparing meals in their new home using an early cooking stove in her kitchen. Two cooking stoves were listed in Dr. Hickey's inventory of the furnishings of the Globe Hotel, indicating kitchen cooking stoves were available in Springfield at that time.[46] Regardless, Mary Lincoln not only learned to cook but mastered the art.

Attorney Isaac Arnold, who with O. H. Browning and others were frequent guests in the Lincoln home, described their dinners there in a speech to the 1881 Illinois State Bar Association.

> I recall, with sad pleasure the dinners and evening parties given by Mrs. Lincoln. In her modest and simple home everything was orderly and refined, there was always, on the part of both the host and hostess, a cordial and hearty Western welcome, which put every guest perfectly at ease. Mrs. Lincoln's table was famed for the excellence of many rare Kentucky dishes and, in season, it was loaded with venison, wild turkey, prairie chickens, quail and other game which was abundant. But it was her genial manners and ever-kind welcome and Mr. Lincoln's wit and humor, anecdotes and unrivaled conversation which formed the chief attraction.[47]

The *Home Book* provided a look at how Mary Lincoln, or some of the women who helped her, conducted such household chores as doing laundry or ironing and how her kitchen was likely furnished. Leslie suggested that kettles and tubs be placed at a proper height so the woman doing the washing would not have to bend over. It was a physical enough task without wearing out the back. "Each of the women engaging in washing," she wrote, "should be provided with one of the well-known grooved or fluted boards, which, by standing them up in tubs of suds, and rubbing the clothes on them will greatly save the hands and expedite the work." Even the best advice was unable to prevent knocking the skin off the knuckles and roughing the hands, which served as agitators in the process of rubbing clothes up and down the board. She also advised using a long hickory stock, flattened on one end, to stir clothes while they were boiling in a kettle over the fire, and a forked stick was used to lift them out of the hot water to avoid burns.[48]

When it came time to iron the laundered clothes, Eliza Leslie advised having four irons available during the process. One iron was in use while the other three heavy implements were heating on the stove. Her book had a long list of instructions for ironing various articles of clothing in different fabrics. She advised summer was the best time for washing blankets so they could dry in the fresh air. She had some rather dramatic suggestions for the process. She advised having three tubs of soapy water to wash the blankets in and called for using a beetle, a wooden board, to beat them. If a beetle was not available, the next best thing was to get into the tubs and trample them with one's feet. Once the blankets were dried, she wrote, they should be stored with bits of tobacco or camphor in the folds.[49]

Many of the cooking accoutrements Eliza Leslie mentioned in her 1844 book may have been in Mary Lincoln's kitchen. The furnishings included a large work table and a smaller one for meals; chairs, stools and a rocking chair; a sink; a marble slab for pastries and a safe for protecting foods. A kitchen safe was a wooden cabinet with perforated tin inlays in the doors and sometimes on the sides to allow air to pass through while protecting the prepared food from flies and other insects. Most important, Leslie advised, was an ice box, which the Lincolns had on their side porch.[50] Basic kitchen implements included pepper, coffee and spice mills, sugar snippers, colanders, egg beaters, graters, kettles, skillets, wooden tubs and buckets and griddles.[51]

The year 1846 was an exciting one for the Lincolns. Their second son, Edward Baker Lincoln, was born on March 10, 1846. Busy with his law practice, growing family and congressional campaign, Lincoln's correspondence with Joshua Speed was less frequent but not necessarily for that reason. As with many good friends, as well as families, the issue of slavery was beginning to erupt in a serious manner splitting them apart. Speed, at the time, was operating the family plantation in Louisville with slave labor. After discussing some legal business with Speed, Lincoln, in October 1846, wrote, "You, no doubt, assign the suspension of our correspondence to the true philosophical cause, though it must be confessed, by both of us, that this is rather a cold reason for allowing a friendship, such as ours, to die by degrees. I propose now, that, upon receipt of this, you shall be considered in my debt and under obligation to pay soon, and that neither shall remain in arrears hereafter. Agreed?"[52]

Lincoln told Speed about the birth of their second son seven months earlier on March 10, 1846. For such close friends, that was a long time not to correspond with each other. In describing the new baby and his older brother, Lincoln wrote,

Edward D. Baker, Lincoln's close friend from his circuit riding days, and for whom the Lincolns' second son was named. Baker also became a dear friend of Mary's (Library of Congress Prints and Photographs Division).

He is very much such a child as Bob was at his age—rather of the longer order. Bob is "short and low," and, I expect, always will be. He talks very plainly—almost as plainly as anybody. He is quite smart enough. I some times fear he is one of the little rare-ripe sorts, that are smarter at about five than ever after. He has a great deal of that sort of mischief, this is the offspring of much animal spirits. Since I began this letter a messenger came to tell me Bob was lost; but by the time I reached the house, his mother had found him and had him whipped—and by now, very likely he is run away again. Mary has read your letter, and wishes to be remembered to Mrs. S. and you, in which I most sincerely join her. As ever yours—A. Lincoln[53]

Although Joshua Speed had been a close friend of Lincoln's for years, he and Mary chose to name their second son after Edward D. Baker, a Springfield lawyer. The short and stout Baker, Lincoln's physical opposite, had served with him in the Black Hawk War. Their friendship deepened over the years and Mary was included in that bond. During a political debate between Baker and Josiah Lamborne, Lincoln became concerned for his friend's safety. He picked up a stone water jug and threatened to break it over the head of the first man who made a move toward Baker.[54]

An agreement had been reached by

Hardin, Baker and Lincoln in the early 1840s that each would take a turn at running for Congress as the Whig candidate from their district. Hardin ran and was elected in 1843. Baker was the district's congressman in 1845. When it became Lincoln's turn, Hardin, who wanted the position back, proposed in the *Morgan Journal* a new system—replacing the convention process with a polling process within the district—for selecting the candidate. It was intended to cut Lincoln out of their agreed upon rotation. In February 1846, Lincoln wrote a long letter to Hardin stating, "Now, if my proposition had been that we (yourself, Baker and I) should be candidates by turns, and that we should unite our strength throughout to keep down all other candidates, I should not deny the justice of the censurable language you employ; but if you so understood it, you wholly misunderstood it. I never expressed, nor meant to express, that by an arrangement, any one of us should be, in the least restricted in his right to support any person he might choose, in the district; but only that he should not himself be a candidate out of his turn."[55]

Without a doubt, Lincoln discussed his opposition to Hardin's plan with Mary. He urged his newspaper friends, Benjamin F. James, who published the *Tazewell Whig*, and Simeon Francis at the *Sangamo Journal*, to publicly oppose Hardin's idea of changing the nomination process and they did.[56]

Lincoln not only won the Whig nomination but beat the Rev. Peter Cartwright, a popular Methodist circuit riding minister, by 1,511 votes in the August 1846 general election. Despite being a minister, Cartwright and his supporters, hoping to paint his opponent in a bad light, circulated charges that Lincoln did not belong to a church and questioned his belief in God. Lincoln put out a handbill saying, "That I am not a member of any Christian church is true but I have never denied the truth of the Scriptures; and I have never spoken with intentional disrespect of religion in general or of any denomination of Christians in particular."[57]

Cartwright continued to hammer Lincoln about his religion, or the lack thereof, and played into the lawyer's hands. Lincoln made a speech in Springfield one Sunday and went to the church where Cartwright was preaching that evening. At the end of his hell-fire and brimstone sermon, Cartwright asked all who expected to go to heaven to stand. Those attending stood. Lincoln remained seated. Then, he asked all who expected to go to hell to stand. Nobody stood. "I have asked all who expect to go to heaven to rise and all who expect to go to hell to rise," Cartwright thundered, "and now I should like to inquire, where does Mr. Lincoln expect to go?"[58]

Lincoln stood up, smiled and, with a twinkle in his eyes, said, "I expect to go to Congress."[59]

Harry Pratt, in his book *The Personal Finances of Abraham Lincoln*, quoted Joshua Speed as saying Whig supporters raised $200 for Lincoln's election and Speed handed him the money. After the election, Lincoln returned $199.25 and requested it be given back to the subscribers. "I did not need the money," Lincoln was quoted as saying. "I made the canvas on my own horse, my entertainment being at the houses of friends, cost me nothing; and my only outlay was $.75 for a barrel of cider, which some farmhands insisted I should treat them to."[60]

Pratt noted, however, that Speed sold his store in Springfield in 1841 and removed to Kentucky and it was improbable that he was present in 1846 to hand the money for Lincoln."[61] It was not necessary that Speed be in Springfield to personally hand the money to Lincoln. In conducting his legal business, Lincoln sent money back to Speed in Louisville,

Kentucky, by trusted friends such as John Irwin. Speed could also have just as easily sent the money to Lincoln by a friend who was traveling to Springfield.

Mary Lincoln saw her husband's election to Congress as only the beginning of his national political career. They were going to Washington by way of Lexington, where she could show off her successful husband. She packed their bags, Lincoln rented their house to Cornelius Ludlum for $90 a year while reserving a room upstairs to store their furniture and they began their trip to Washington in the fall of 1847. An especially joyous part of the trip occurred at Scott's Hotel in St. Louis, where they were met by Joshua Speed and had a wonderful reunion. It must have been a bittersweet occasion for Speed, since he and Fannie never had any children, to see the Lincolns interacting with their sons.[62]

The trip from St. Louis to Lexington was by steamboat down the Mississippi to Cairo, Illinois, and up the Ohio River. Randall wrote that the Lincolns' boat left the Ohio at Carrolton and followed the Kentucky River to Frankfort. "From there they traveled to her hometown on the Lexington and Ohio Railroad's steam locomotive pulling a single coach," she wrote. Lexington lawyer and Lincoln collector William H. Townsend maintained the party arrived by steamboat in Louisville, where they took a train to Lexington. Regardless, they got to Lexington. According to Betsy Todd's nephew, Joseph Humphreys, who was coming to visit, the Lincoln boys created havoc on the train. "Aunt Betsy," he said, arriving at the Todd house, "I was never so glad to get off a train in my life. There were two lively youngsters on board who kept the whole train in an uproar and their long-legged father, instead of spanking the brats, looked pleased as punch and aided the older one in mischief." Before she could reply, the Todd carriage stopped in front of the house and the Lincolns got out. "Good Lord," Humphreys said, "there they are now." He decided to visit other relatives in Lexington as the Todds saw nothing of him during the Lincolns' visit.[63]

Emilie Todd Helm recalled seeing her twenty-nine-year-old half-sister for the first time carrying Eddy as the family lined the hallway to greet them with the slaves in the rear.

> To my mind she was lovely. Clear, sparkling, blue eyes, lovely smooth white skin with a fresh, faint wild-rose color in her cheeks; and glossy light brown hair, which fell in soft, short curls behind each ear. Mr. Lincoln followed her into the hall with his little son Robert Todd in his arms. He put the little fellow on the floor, and as he rose I remember thinking of Jack and the Beanstalk, and feared he might be the hungry giant of the story, he was so tall and looked so big with a long full black cloak over his shoulders and he wore a fur cap with ear straps which allowed little of his face to be seen. Expecting to hear the "Fee, fi, fo, fum!" I shrank closer to my mother and tried to hide behind her voluminous skirts. After shaking hands with all the grown-ups, Mr. Lincoln turned and, lifting me in his arms, said, "So this is little sister." I was always after that called by him "little sister." His voice and smile banished my fear of the giant.[64]

Three weeks allowed Mary ample time to visit, introduce her husband to family and friends and to be entertained by the extended Todd-Parker relatives and numerous political associates. Some of their time was spent with the Widow Parker, who was not in the best of health. In the vicinity of the Parker home on Short Street were a number of slave jails. Over the wrought iron fence that separated the Parker property from Pullum's Slave Jail, on Mechanics Alley, Lincoln could see into the yard, where the shipping post stood in one corner. The new congressman probably heard cries of agony from Pullum's slaves during the nights. Further down Short Street was Megowan's Slave Jail, where slaves were held before being shipped south.[65]

Lincoln may have been unaware, before his visit, that the Lexington firm of Bolton,

Dickens and Company was one of the largest slave traders in the south. The firm had branch offices in Memphis, Charleston, Natchez, St. Louis and New Orleans.[66] Mary, due to Lexington being a small, gossipy town, knew about the business of Bolton, Dickens and Company and probably enlightened her husband.

While Mary visited friends, Lincoln availed himself of the Todds' large library, reading the *Niles Registers* and poetry. "I do not recall how long the visit lasted," Emilie Todd Helm said, "but I remembering playing with Bob and that Mr. Lincoln was so absorbed in books that our noisy play never seemed to disturb him." The library also held Shakespeare in eight volumes, *The Decline and Fall of the Roman Empire, The Messages of Presidents, The Life of Oliver Cromwell, Elegant Extracts, or Useful and Entertaining Passages from the Best English Authors and Translations* and the numerous books of poetry he and Mary loved. He also explored the town, going to the courthouse and visiting attorneys in their offices on Jordan's Row and frequently accompanying Mary's brother Levi to Oldham, Todd and Company's factory at Sandersville, where he was assistant manager and bookkeeper.[67]

Mary, while they were in Lexington, had the opportunity of introducing her husband to Henry Clay at his Ashland estate. Lincoln heard Clay argue the Singleton will case in court, which lasted three hours. Lincoln, and probably Mary, heard Clay speak at the Lower Market House where he was flanked on the dais by Judge George Robertson and Robert S. Todd. Clay blamed President James K. Polk and Gen. Zachary Taylor for starting the Mexican War, where his son, Henry Clay, Jr., was killed. Accompanying the Todds to the First Presbyterian Church, Lincoln met the Rev. Robert J. Breckinridge, a close Todd friend for decades.[68] Neither suspected how their paths would cross again thirteen years later.

As Mary packed their luggage to continue the trip to Washington, she would miss, just by days, the heroic welcome her father arranged for their friend Cassius M. Clay when he returned home a hero from the Mexican War. The Lincolns took the stage from Lexington to Maysville, where they boarded a steamboat arriving in Washington on December 2, 1847. They initially stayed at Brown's Hotel before moving into Ann G. Sprigg's boardinghouse on Capitol Hill. They had wondrous adventures visiting, for the first time, the historic landmarks of the national capital. Across from the boardinghouse was a park where Mary could walk with the boys, weather permitting. Theaters offered more sophisticated drama than was available in Springfield.[69] The Lincolns went to the theater whenever possible. At the old Washington Theatre, sometimes referred to as Carusi's Salon, they saw a group called the Ethiopian Serenades.[70]

Dolley Madison, living across Lafayette Square from the Executive Mansion, often assisted Sarah Polk in her official entertaining. Mary Lincoln probably met Dolley Madison, whose first husband, the Quaker attorney John Todd, Jr., was a distant relative.[71]

Living in a boardinghouse with two small children, Mary could hardly reciprocate social calls.

It was unlikely that the Lincolns were invited to the Executive Mansion after December 22, 1847, when Lincoln, from the floor of the House, called on President Polk to answer eight questions about where the unpopular Mexican War's first casualties occurred, on Mexican or American soil. Lincoln claimed Polk attempted to escape the results of his own conduct of the war. The president, Lincoln said, "Talked like an insane man. His mind, taxed beyond its power, is running hither and thither, like an ant on a hot stove."[72]

Lincoln's opposition to the Mexican War was not received well by his constituents in Illinois. In addition, the family had a more pressing personal matter which required a decision.

CHAPTER 7

Letters Tell Their Story

Whether it was tension created from two adults and two rambunctious boys, Bobby just turned four and Eddy not quite two, crowded into one room in a boardinghouse during a dark Washington winter, boredom that led to Mary's temper tantrums or the demands she was making on her husband that distracted him from his Congressional business, it was time for the Lincolns to try something else.

Their house in Springfield was rented for the duration of Lincoln's term. Returning to the Edwards home was evidently not an option or even something Mary would consider. The Widow Parker would have welcomed them into her home, even with two rowdy boys.

They found a solution through the largess of Robert Todd. Mary, Bobby and Eddy returned to Lexington in the late winter or early spring of 1848 for an extended visit with her father and stepmother, the Widow Parker and the large extended Todd-Parker families.

No details of the arduous journey from Washington back to Lexington were found. With two young children and a mountain of luggage, the trip must have exhausted Mary long before she arrived at her father's home.

The Lincolns were not happy with the separation but there were advantages once she arrived in Lexington. Mary had help, either someone she hired or the Todd slaves, with their two boys. Bobby and Eddy had space to romp and play both indoors and out. With ease, she slipped back into her old social life of making calls and receiving guests, something she was unable to do in Washington. Relations between Mary and Betsy Todd reached an acceptable level for both women. Most of all, she was able to spend some quality time with her father, enjoying their political discussions and talking about his campaign to retain his state senate seat. Robert Todd brought her up to date about activities of their friends, such as Cassius M. Clay, who had his anti-slavery newspaper, *The True American*, seized by a mob led by Henry Clay's son, James.

All the political news, Mary passed on to her husband, but few of her letters remain while several of Lincoln's letters to her provided a rare glimpse into their relationship. The affection they held for each other was obvious in the letters. There was also an underlying indication that Mary was disappointed in her Washington sojourn. Most Congressmen's wives, unless they were wealthy or lived in nearby states, remained at home while their husbands represented their constituents. Without a doubt, Mary Lincoln insisted on accompanying her husband. With two small children and a limited budget, it was naive of her to expect to be part of the Washington's busy social life.

Lincoln's April 16, 1849, letter to his wife indicated Mary had been gone for some time, as he received three letters from her. He made it quite clear that he was lonely. "Dear Mary," he wrote, "in this troublesome world, we are never quite satisfied, When you were here, I thought you hindered me some in attending to business; but now having nothing but business—no variety—it has grown exceedingly tasteless to me. I hate to sit down and direct documents, and I hate to stay in this old room by myself."[1]

Lincoln expressed concern about the burglary into the Widow Parker's residence and suggested she should not be alone. Items stolen included a gold watch and a quantity of monogramed silver. Most likely the silver pieces were crafted by Asa Blanchard, Lexington's famed silversmith. Elizabeth Parker offered a $100 reward for their return.[2]

Unable to find the plaid stocking Mary wanted for Eddy, Lincoln said he would continue looking. "If I can get them," he wrote, "I have an excellent chance of sending them. Mr. Warrick Tunstall, of St. Louis is here. He is to leave early this week and to go by Lexington. He says he knows you, and will call to see you; and he voluntarily asked, if I had not some package to send you."[3]

Mary, in her letters, had told him about socializing with friends from her youth, Margaret and Mary Wickliffe, who still lived in Lexington. "I wish you to enjoy yourself in every way possible; but is there no danger of wounding the feelings of your good father, by being so openly intimate with the Wickliffe family?"[4]

Lincoln was referring to Robert Wickliffe's two daughters—Margaret, who married Robert Preston, and Mary, the wife of John Preston, Jr. Wickliffe had been Robert S. Todd's arch political and personal enemy for decades. Todd was, at the time of Mary's visit, serving in the Kentucky Senate and planned to seek re-election. Wickliffe had mounted opposition to his re-election. In addition, Todd had filed suit against Wickliffe in an effort to gain title to the land holdings of Col. John Todd, which the slaveholder obtained through his marriage to the former Mary Owen Todd Russell, the colonel's only heir and Robert Todd's first cousin.

Much of Mary's sharp rhetoric was inherited from her father. Todd's responses to Wickliffe's charges against him in the bitter state senate campaign of 1845 were excellent example his power of the pen. Wickliffe specialized in grasping onto the slightest innuendo, or falsehood, and attempting to turn it into truth. Todd, in a pamphlet replying to Wickliffe's charges concerning his association with the Northern Bank of Kentucky, wrote, "Mr. Wickliffe has never being willing to tell more than half the truth, even when the whole is fairly presented, has in the presence instance only presented the mangled half."[5]

Robert Todd, speaking of Wickliffe's hatred of abolitions and emancipationists, said, "He has, as I have heard, indulged in the belief that Queen Victoria and her Ministers, at their leisure moments, are plotting to steal away his 300 slaves." Todd closed his pamphlet by saying, "Fellow Citizens, with all the loathing, which an upright man can feel toward an habitual and notorious falsifier an unscrupulous and indiscriminate calumniator, reckless alike of fame, of honor and of truth, I must now take my present leave of this miserable old man, and express to you my regret that to justify myself, against his unprovoked assaults, unfounded charges and illiberal insinuations, I have been reluctantly compelled in this manner and at this time to trespass on your patience."[6]

Mary, however, lacked her father's talent and skill to know when to tread lightly and when to exert pressure. She often just plowed ahead regardless of the situation.

In a rather off-handed manner, Lincoln indicated there had been some friction at the Washington boarding house before Mary left. "All in the house—or rather, all with whom you were on decided good terms—send their love to you. The others say nothing."[7]

He asked her not to use the prefix, "Honorable" in addressing her letters to him. Lincoln was delighted that Mary was free from her headaches. "That is good—good—considering it is the first spring you have been free from it since we were acquainted. I am afraid you will get so well, and fat, and young, as to be wanting to marry again. Tell Louisa I want her to watch you a little for me. Get weighed and write me how much you weigh." Lincoln signed the letter, "Most affectionately, A. Lincoln."[8]

In May, Mary wrote Lincoln a rambling but newsy letter from Lexington apologizing for not posting the day on her missive. She talked about asking Frances Wallace to send her some of her son's outgrown clothes for Eddy. Frances, apparently, thought the shipping would be more than the clothes were worth. Mary, while thinking it might save her a few stiches, decided to write Frances to forget the request. She mentioned that her aunt, Maria Bullock, was coming in for her the next day, Sunday.[9]

Mary then launched into a story about little Eddy, a cat and Betsy Todd. "Bobby in his wanderings to day, came across it in a yard, a little kitten, *your hobby*, he says he asked a man for it; he brought it triumphantly to the house; so soon Eddy spied it, his *tenderness*, broke forth, he made them bring it *water*, fed it with bread himself, with his *own dear hands*, he was a delightful little creature over it; in the midst of his happiness Ma came in, she, you must know dislikes the whole cat race. I thought in a very unfeeling manner, she ordered the servant near, to throw it out, which of course was done—Ed—screaming and protesting loudly against the proceedings, she never appeared to mind his screams, which were long and loud I assure you. Tis unusual for her *now a days*, to do any thing quite so striking, she is very obliging and accommodating, but if she thought any of us were on her hands again, I believe she would be *worse* than ever. In the next moment she appeared to be in good humor, I know that she did not intend to offend me. By the way, she has just sent me up a glass of ice cream, for which this warm evening, I am duly grateful."[10]

She told Lincoln that the weather was so delightful that she planned to spend two or three weeks in the country. Mary was referring to the Todds' summer home, Buena Vista, in Franklin County.

> Grandma has received a letter from Uncle James Parker of Miss. saying he and his family would be up by the twenty fifth of June, would remain here some little time and go on to Philadelphia to take their oldest daughter there to school. I believe it would be a good chance for me to pack up and accompany them. You know I am so fond of *sight-seeing* and I did not get to New York or Boston or travel the lake route. But, perhaps, dear husband, like the *irresistible Col. Mc.* cannot do without his wife next winter and must needs take her with him again—I expect you would cry aloud against it. How much, I wish instead of writing, we were together this evening, I feel very sad away from you.[11]

She mentioned going with Betsy Todd to return a call on Henry Bell at his magnificent mansion, Bell House, just off East Main Street. The mansion, a combination of Greek Revival, Queen Ann and Romanesque architecture, was designed by Thomas Lewinski on land originally owned by Col. John Todd. The mansion was built in 1845 for David A. Sayre, who sold it to his business partner Bell. "The house and grounds are magnificent," Mary wrote. "Frances W. [Wallace] would *have died* over their rare exotics."[12]

She told Lincoln if he came down in July or August she would take him to the springs, an obvious reference to Crab Orchard Springs where the Todds spent their summers when she was a young girl. The letter's closure speaks for itself, as Mary mentioned one of her former beaus. "*Patty Webb's* school in S [Shelbyville] closed the first of July. I expect *Mr.*

Webb, will come on for her, I must go down about that time and carry on quite a flirtation, you know *we* always had a penchant that way. ["With love" at this point had been marked through.] I must bid you good night. Do no fear the children, have forgotten you. I was only jesting—even E—eyes brighten at the mention of your name. My love to all-Truly yours M.L."[13]

On May 24, 1848, Lincoln sent Mary a short letter and a fifty-dollar draft for her father to cash so that she would have some money. After returning from the Whig convention in Philadelphia that nominated Zachary Taylor for president over Henry Clay, Lincoln wrote Mary on June 12, 1848, addressing her request to leave Lexington. The letter opened with, "My dear wife. The leading matter in your letter is your wish to return to this side of the Mountains. Will you be a *good girl* in all things if I consent? Then come along, and that as *soon* as possible. Having got the idea in my head, I shall be impatient till I see you. You will not have enough money to bring you; but I presume your uncle will supply you and I will refund him here."[14]

He assumed she received the fifty-dollar draft he sent earlier. "I do not much fear but that you got it; because the want of it would have induced you [to] say something in relations to it." Lincoln was so anxious to see Mary and the boys that he suggested, "If your uncle is already in Lexington you might induce him to start earlier than the first of July; he could stay longer on his return and make up for the lost time."[15]

Lincoln closed the letter saying, "Come on just as soon as you can. I want to see you, and our dear—*dear* boys very much every body here wants to see our dear Bobby. Affectingly A. Lincoln."[16]

By July 2, 1848, arrangements had been made for Mary, Robert and Eddy to travel with James Parker and family to meet Lincoln in Washington. In a letter of that date, Lincoln was concerned that the $100 draft he sent would arrive in Lexington after they left and asked her if she made arrangements for her mail to be forwarded. It seemed wherever Lincoln was, he ran into an acquaintance of Mary's. Like his earlier encounter in Washington with Warrick Tunstall, from St. Louis, Lincoln said he met Thomas W. Newton, an Arkansas delegate to the Whig convention in Philadelphia, who also knew Mary. Lincoln mention receiving two bills from local merchants totaling $13.88 and said he thought Mary cleared all their bills before leaving Washington, and asked her to let him know.[17]

The remainder of Lincoln's letter brought Mary up to date on the Washington gossip. "Mrs. Richardson (William A.) is still here; and what is more, has a baby—so Richardson says, and he ought to know. I believe Mary Hewett has left here and gone to Boston. I met her on the street about fifteen or twenty days ago, and she told me she was going soon. I have seen nothing of her since."[18]

Lincoln had gone to a musical on the Capitol grounds and told Mary about seeing some members of the Ethiopian Serenaders with a congressman. "Our two girls, whom you remember seeing first at Carusis [the old Washington Theatre] at the exhibition of the Ethiopian Serenaders, and whose peculiarities were the wearing of black fur bonnets and never being seen in the close company with other ladies, were at the musical yesterday. One of them was attended by her brother, and the other had a member of Congress in tow. He went home with her; and if I were to guess, I would say, he went away a somewhat altered man—most likely in his pockets, and in some other particular. The fellow looked conscious of guilt, although I believe he was unconscious that every body around knew who it was that had caught him."[19]

The girl Mary had hired to help with the boys had left and Lincoln urged her to find someone else as soon as possible. "Father expected to see you all sooner," he wrote in closing, "but let it pass; stay as long as you please, and come when you please. Kiss and love the dear rascals. Affectionately A. Lincoln."[20]

It did not please Mary to remain away from her husband any longer. By the third week in July, they were a complete family once more, even if it was back to the boarding house.[21]

Then, they embarked on Mary's long awaited trip to New England, New York and Canada. During the August Congressional recess, Lincoln was asked to campaign for Taylor in New England along with others, including Gen. Leslie Combs, a staunch Whig supporter and thoroughbred horseman from Lexington, who served with Taylor in the War of 1812. Mary knew that Combs, the former president of the Kentucky Association Track, had been an ardent supporter of Henry Clay for the nomination. However, he was more than willing to support the nominee for the good of the party. Taylor needed all the help he could muster from the New England anti-slavery Whigs to defeat Democrat nominee Lewis Cass, who had been Jackson's secretary of war and territorial governor of Michigan. His running mate, William O. Butler, was a former Lexington lawyer and Congressman, whom Mary also knew.[22]

In addition to Cass and Butler, Taylor and his vice-presidential candidate Millard Fillmore also had competition from disgruntled northern Democrats who broke with their colleagues over Cass' selection and established the Free Soil Party. The Free Soilers fielded a presidential ticket of former President Martin Van Buren and Charles F. Adams, the son of former President John Q. Adams.[23]

Mary wanted to see New England and that was what she did as Lincoln spoke in Boston, where he shared the platform with William H. Seward, in Bedford, Lowell, Cambridge and Dorchester as well as in Delaware and New Hampshire. New York was included in the trip as the Lincolns met with Taylor's running mate Millard Fillmore in East Auora. Not only did Mary and the boys enjoy the trip to Niagara Falls; Lincoln was fascinated with the natural phenomena.[24]

The Lincolns returned to Springfield on October 10, 1848. Their house was still rented until November. Lincoln returned to Washington for the final congressional session of his term, which expired in March 1849. "This may well be the occasion when, according to an old-timer's recollection, they stayed temporarily at the Globe Tavern," Randall wrote. "A lady who was boarding there at the time later recalled Congressman Lincoln going up and down the hotel dining room shaking hands with everyone and how kind he was about bringing up wood to the ladies' bedrooms."[25]

When he returned to Washington, Lincoln prepared an amendment to a Congressional resolution calling for abolishing slavery in the District of Columbia and providing compensated emancipation. After his faint-hearted backers deserted him, Lincoln never formally introduced the amendment. On March 7, 1849, Lincoln was admitted to practice before the Supreme Court.[26]

True to his agreement with Whig friends in Illinois, Lincoln did not run for reelection. His first law partner, Stephen T. Logan, ran on Lincoln's record and lost.[27] Lincoln's opposition to the Mexican War had not been well accepted in Illinois.

Lincoln attended Taylor's inauguration, which he helped plan, and then returned to Springfield to resume and rebuild his law practice. He became involved in a squabble over nominations for the commissioner of the General Land Office, whose responsibility was the supervision of public lands sales to private ownership. Lincoln proposed Cyrus Edwards, Ninian Edwards' brother, for the position and Edward D. Baker supported J.L.D. Morrison for the job. Lincoln and Baker, who both worked diligently for Taylor's election, left it to Edwards and Morrison to work out a solution. Edwards and Morrison were unable to reach a decision. Meanwhile, Justin Butterfield, a Chicago lawyer who supported Henry Clay against Taylor, emerged as a candidate. At that time, Lincoln, believing that those who labored to elect Taylor should receive the party patronage, became a candidate for the office. "He [Butterfield] is my personal friend," Lincoln said, "and is qualified to do the duties of the office but of the quite one hundred Illinoisians, equally well qualified, I do not know of one with less claims to it." Butterfield, however, undercut all their efforts and, with Clay's support from Senate colleagues, got the plum patronage job, which paid $3,000 a year. Once Butterfield was appointed, Lincoln supported him.[28]

In June 1849, Lincoln wrote Thomas Ewing, secretary of the interior, about Cyrus Edwards placing on file some not too flattering remarks about him.

> You had the kindness, as I remember, to volunteer the remark, in my defense, that but for my devotion to Mr. Edwards, manifested by withholding my own name for his benefit, I would now in your opinion be the Commissioner. If, in this, my memory serves me correctly, you will greatly oblige me by saying as much on paper, with anything additional to the same point which may occur to you. It will enable me, I think, to remove from the mind of one of my most highly valued friends, a bad impression, which is now the only thing much painful to me personally, in this whole matter.[29]

Lincoln's vigorous defense of awarding patronage to those who helped elect Taylor produced an interesting result. He was offered the governorship of the Oregon Territory in August 1849. Telegraphs flew back and forth between Washington and Springfield concerning the appointment. On August 21, Lincoln declined the offer. Finally, on September 27, he said emphatically he could not consent to accept the appointment. Moving to the Pacific Northwest would have taken Lincoln out of the mainstream of American politics. "Mrs. Lincoln's objections, reinforcing his own doubts, caused him to reject the offer out of hand," Justin Turner wrote. "Her distaste for the prospect of raising her children in a wilderness, far from family, friends and the little luxuries she prized, may have been selfish but it at least succeeded in keeping Lincoln close to the center of political activity." The *Pacific Monthly* agreed: "Lincoln refused the position of governor of the Oregon Territory, offered by Taylor, due to the unwillingness of his wife to undergo the hardship of a journey across the Plains and the privations of life on the western frontier." The position went to another native Kentuckian, John P. Gaines, from Boone County.[30]

Mary resumed housekeeping. For Mary, going back to their home necessitated moving furniture, seeing to repairs, cleaning and re-establishing a routine of child care, cooking and sewing. In addition, she was tutoring Bobby. Emilie Todd Helm recalled that Mary read the novels and poems of Sir Walther Scott to Bobby. She remembered when Bobby and a playmate were engaged in a duel using fence palings as lances. "Mary, bubbling with laughter," she said, "called out, 'Gramercy, brave knights. Pray be more merciful than you are brawny.'"[31]

Those happy days did not continue.

In early June 1849, Robert Todd took his family to Buena Vista for the summer. He commuted by train to Lexington to execute his duties as president of the Branch Bank of Kentucky, check on his manufacturing company and to continue his senate campaign. Residents were leaving the city in droves as another cholera epidemic broke out. "My friends and neighbors," the Reverend Breckinridge wrote, "are sick and dying around me. The cholera continues to prevail very severely and a great many of the people are gone off from the fright." By the middle of July so many local physicians had died that an appeal was made for medical aid. Henry Clay and his wife came down with the disease but survived.[32]

Robert Smith Todd did not.

On July 16, 1849, after being dosed with the recommended treatment for cholera—calomel, rhubarb and opium—by Lexington and Frankfort physicians attempting to save his life, Mary's father died at Buena Vista. A Lexington newspaper reported that he fell ill four days earlier. "Mr. Todd visited Lexington on Monday of last week returning to his country residence the same evening. He complained of being greatly fatigued on Tuesday and had a slight chill, but felt no uneasiness about his situation until Wednesday evening when a physician was sent for. Disease, however, had taken so deep a hold upon him that all efforts to arrest proved fruitless and he died at 1 o'clock Monday morning."[33]

The newspaper's editorial lauded Todd, saying, "He had impressed himself indelibly upon the country for the zeal, fidelity and ability with which he discharged all his various and multiplied public duties. No man more truly and faithfully conformed to all the requisitions of virtue and benevolence and no man occupied a higher position in the society in which he moved than Robert S. Todd. He was emphatically 'the noblest word of God—an honest man.'"[34]

Due to the cholera epidemic and the hot weather, Todd was buried immediately in the Lexington Cemetery. It was possible that Mary learned of her father's death by telegraph, as the service had been available in Springfield since June 1848.[35] Telegraph service was available in Lexington at that time but, with all the anxiety of the cholera epidemic, it was possible that she was not notified until days later.[36]

Her father's death was a hard blow for Mary. There was solace to be found from the months they had spent together during her recent visits to Lexington. Lincoln was busy rebuilding his law practice, which Herndon, his partner, had allowed to lapse while he was serving in Congress. It was her father's estate and the legal action he had filed against Wickliffe that drew them back to Lexington.

Todd left the bulk of his fortune to his wife, Betsy. She was to receive his slaves and then pass them on to her children. The remainder of his property was to be divided equally between his first and second sets of children. Mary's youngest brother, George Rogers Clark Todd, who bore a distinct resemblance to their father and who Betsy Todd had raised from an infant, discovered that his father's will contained the signature of only one witness when two were required by state law. His objection to the validity of their father's will was sustained by the Fayette County court. Although Betsy Todd had qualified as the administratix of her husband's estate, her husband was declared to have died intestate and that meant all his assets had to be converted into cash and divided between his widow and fourteen children.[37]

Sometime in his early years, George and Betsy had an irreparable conflict and he moved out complaining his father treated his first set of children differently. However, Todd convinced him to move back into the family fold and paid for him to attend medical school at Transylvania, where he obtained his degree. Lincoln was selected to represent the interest of the Todd siblings in Illinois regarding their father's estate. But, that was not the only legal action involving the Todds. In 1848, Robert Todd, completely fed up with the verbose antics of Robert Wickliffe, filed suit against him to recover the estate of Col. John Todd, which came to Wickliffe through his second marriage to the colonel's daughter, Mary Owen Todd Russell.[38]

"However, if Wickliffe cherished a hope, as there is reason to believe he did," William Townsend wrote, "that the children of his deceased adversary would drop the case, such a possibility vanished upon the filing of a bill of reviver on October 2, 1849, in behalf of 'Abraham Lincoln and Mary A. Lincoln, his wife; Ninian Edwards and Elizabeth P. Edwards, his wife' and the other heirs of Robert S. Todd—who charge as in the original & cross bills of their ancestor."[39]

After the action against him was revived, Wickliffe began spewing not only his vicious hatred of the Todds but outright falsehoods. Not only did he deny knowing Robert Todd's children but claimed to have no knowledge of their names or relationships. Mary Lincoln and Margaret Wickliffe Preston had been childhood friends and visited in each other's homes for years. Townsend wrote that Wickliffe knew Mary Lincoln as well as he knew his own daughter. Wickliffe claimed, Townsend said, that Todd "did have a daughter he *thinks* they called Mary who he understands married a member of Congress, *his name not recollected.*"[40]

The Lincolns and their two sons once again made the trip to Lexington in October 1849. On the steamboat going down the Mississippi, a fellow passenger played several pranks and was punished at a mock trial presided over by Lincoln as the judge. They experienced a steamboat race up the Ohio. Their boat, running short of wood, managed to latch on a flatboat of wood, which had to reach the boiler to build up steam. Lincoln, according to Randall, jumped on the flatboat, encouraged the workers and began pitching the wood with great enthusiasm. "One can imagine Mary and the little boys on the deck cheering," she wrote.[41]

There was little cheer awaiting the Lincolns in Lexington. Betsy Todd and her children had moved permanently to Buena Vista as their family home and contents were going to be sold to settle her husband's estate. The Lincolns spent most of their time with the aging Widow Parker at her home on Short Street and with Mary's brother, Levi, who then lived next door in the house where she was born. They also visited Betsy in Franklin County.[42]

Settlement of Robert S. Todd's estate was a long, drawn out process with George, and eventually Levi, causing additional problems. The Wickliffe lawsuit was nothing but nasty. If he was not aware of Wickliffe's legal shenanigans and the Milly and Alfred saga, Lincoln certainly learned about it when he read the lawsuit and filed replies. In his answer to Lincoln's reviver, Wickliffe filed a voluminous forty-eight-page reply stating his defense, which unless the Todd heirs miraculously found the long lost will of Col. John Todd, left little room for doubt about how the case would end. Lincoln was a shrewd and able lawyer and why he agreed to continue a lawsuit destined to fail was a mystery. Mary's close relationship with the Wickliffe daughters could have turned cold with their father's ranting. However, that was unlikely, as they later exchanged correspondences. Ninian Edwards, also a lawyer, appeared to have no further involvement in the case. Betsy Todd was too busy figuring out how to live on the one-third dower from her husband's estate to get involved. Neither George nor Levi Todd had an interest in the case unless there would be property and money involved, which was doubtful. The only logical answer was that Lincoln felt a strong obligation to his father-in-law, a man he obviously admired, that he continued what Todd began. Perhaps Todd discussed the idea of filing the lawsuit with Lincoln during the 1847 visit.

An interesting array and large number of witness were deposed. They included Mm. Mentelle, who maintained that Mrs. Wickliffe was entirely satisfied with the disposition of

Top: Mary Lincoln's photograph produced from an 1846 or 1847 daguerreotype taken by Springfield, Illinois, photographer Nicholas Shepherd. *Bottom:* Abraham Lincoln is shown in a matching photograph. Both photographs hung in the Lincoln home in Springfield until they moved to Washington (both photographs, Library of Congress, Prints and Photographs Division).

her property and that theirs was a marriage of love not property. In an attempt to prove the contents of Col. Todd's missing will, the Rev. Robert Stuart, father of Lincoln's first law partner, and Elizabeth Porter Parker were called upon. The ordeal was taxing on the Widow Parker. After three weeks in Lexington, the Lincolns returned to Springfield in November 1849, leaving Judge George Robertson as their local counsel.[43]

Losing her father was certainly a blow to Mary Lincoln, but only six months later—January 26, 1850—she lost the woman who had been her refuge during the first two decades of her life; who guided her through the loss of her mother and always took her part in whatever rows she had with her stepmother. Elizabeth Rittenhouse Porter Parker, who outlived her husband by fifty years, was eighty-one. In her will, she freed her three slaves, Prudence, Ann and Cyrus, and asked that Prudence receive twelve dollars a year as long as she lived. They received their freedom at the next session of court in May. Unlike Mary Humphreys, who entailed her slaves to her daughter, Betsy Todd, to be freed at a later date, the Widow Parker's slaves were freed as soon as possible. The *Lexington Observer and Reporter* referred to her as being universally esteemed and beloved by all who knew her for her many excellent qualities.[44]

Mary was fortunate to have spent time with her grandmother during her last visit to Lexington. The visit gave the Widow Parker a chance to become better acquainted with her great-grandchildren, Bobby and Eddy.

Eddy Lincoln experienced a brief illness during his first visit to Lexington in the spring of 1848. He was never a healthy child regardless of Mary's careful watch over her sons' health. During Eddy's illness, most likely pulmonary tuberculosis—commonly called consumption—the Lincolns' account at Corneau and Diller's Drug Store contained a number of interesting purchases. They bought a bottle of extract of cedar in October 1849, for seventy-five cents. Extract of cedar, an expectorate, was later discovered to have antibacterial properties. Another purchase was a bottle of "Bears oil" for twenty-five-cents. If "Bears" was not a brand name, it most likely an oil extracted from an herb, called bears root, because the animals, after hibernation, sought out the roots. The oil promoted healing, and like the cedar extract, had antibacterial and antiviral properties. Another purchase that month was a box of pain extractor for fifty cents. Dalleys Magic Pain Extractor, if that was the brand Mary purchased, was advertised to cure everything from broken bones, sores, burns, blisters and swelling to constipation.[45]

Randall, in her biography of Mary Lincoln, wrote about how careful she was in administering medicines to her sons. She wrote that Mary's purchase of a bottle of vermifuge "shows that Mary was taking no chances on her children's having worms, though from their point of view that malady was probably preferable to the nasty-tasting medicine. The Lincoln boys were dosed in the good, old-fashioned way." Randall also mentioned a box of ox marrow being included in the Lincolns' pharmacy purchases. It was doubtful that was intended for the boys, as ox marrow was used to rid dogs and cats of fleas.[46]

Few if any of the home remedies or doctors' administrations helped Eddy. He developed dangerous high fevers with coughing fits followed by intense exhaustion. Mary and Lincoln, with the help of her sisters and Huldah B. Stout, a favorite neighbor, nursed little Eddy around the clock. Nothing alleviated Eddy's fifty-two days of suffering except his death on the morning of February 1, 1850. Lincoln and Mary were beside themselves with grief. Mary took to her bed unable to stop weeping; a routine that deepened repeatedly in the future with the loss of her loved ones. Only Lincoln could coax her to stop crying long enough to eat some food.[47]

The new rector of the First Presbyterian Church in Springfield, Dr. James Smith, conducted Eddy's funeral services the next day at the Lincoln home. Eddy was buried in Hutchinson's Cemetery. Dr. Smith continually called on the Lincolns and counseled them as they worked through their grief. Perhaps Justin Turner put it best when he wrote, "Lincoln at least could bury his grief in activity and draw on that well of resignation which enabled him to give tragedy its place in the scheme of things. The man who was by nature melancholy, solitary and self-doubting would from then on gain in assurance and magnetism. The humor and control that had sustained her in the past became increasingly submerged in fearfulness, self-indulgence, and in sudden outbursts or rage, often directed at her husband, a servant and occasionally overheard by neighbors. Lincoln, who knew something of black moods himself, could only cope and commiserate, feeling that she was powerless to help herself and knowing, with it all, that she loved and needed him more than ever."[48]

Five days after Eddy's funeral, an unsigned poem entitled "Little Eddie" appeared in the *Illinois Daily Journal*. The first stanza of the twenty-four line poem contained these words, "Those midnight stars are sadly dimmed, that late so brilliantly shown, and the crimson tinge from chafed lip, with the hearts warm life has flown—the angel death was hovering nigh, and the lovely boy was called to die." The last line of the poem, "For such is the kingdom of God," Lincoln had carved on Eddy's tombstone. Who wrote the poem is a mystery. Some historians credit it to Mary; others to Lincoln. There were problems with those assertions. Mary was prostrate with grief until long after the poem was published. Lincoln had his hands full with looking after his wife. He was the only one who could convince her to eat. In addition, somebody had to look after Bobby. Neither Mary nor Lincoln, in their letters ever spelled their son's name other than Eddy, not Eddie as in the poem.[49]

While there is no proof, it was possible that Edward D. Baker, for whom Eddy was named and who shared an attachment with the Lincolns that eclipsed some family ties, might have had a hand in the composition.

What happened to Eddy's grave marker is a story in itself. After Lincoln's death, a temporary tomb was erected at the Oak Ridge Cemetery in Springfield. His body, along with that of Willie, was placed in the tomb. Mary and Bobby came from Chicago in December 1865 for the interment. John T. Stuart met them and, at that time, Eddy's body was moved from Hutchinson's Cemetery to the tomb. According to Harry E. Pratt, Elizabeth Edwards asked Mary for Eddy's marker and she gave it to her. Elizabeth had the word *Edwards* in large letters carved into the back of the tombstone and used it to mark the entrance to her family's plot at Oak Ridge. The marker had been knocked over and was re-discovered in 1954. When it was turned over, there was Eddy's tombstone. It was removed to the Illinois State Historical Library and a new stone was placed to mark the entrance to the Edwards plot.[50]

In a span of seven months, Mary experienced the death of three people exceedingly close to her. The tie formed in her early childhood with Grandmother Parker was never broken but she realized the woman was elderly and infirm and her time had come. The death of the father, who had bestowed upon his favorite daughter the opportunity, almost unheard of at that time, to develop and nourish her intellect and who believed in her husband's political future, was more difficult to accept. But it was the loss of little Eddy that cut a deep valley in her heart.

Mary and Lincoln were fortunate to have the Reverend Smith in their lives at a time when they desperately needed grief counseling. His ministry to them established a close relationship that lasted until the end of Smith's life in 1871. Considering his relationship with Mary and Lincoln, both pastoral and as a friend, Smith had a special insight into their personalities and their marriage. In later years, Smith recalled Mary's intelligence, her conversational talents and the ability to adapt herself into any social situation. Smith said Lincoln's heart overflowed with love and affection for his wife.[51]

Smith, a truculent Scotsman, had been, like Lincoln, called a deist early in his life. *The Oxford English Dictionary* describes a deist as one who acknowledges the existence of a God but rejects revealed religion. Smith began his ministerial career in the Cumberland Presbyterian Church in Kentucky but left the sect. He bought a newspaper and became the editor. When the paper failed, he turned to mainstream Presbyterianism at a church in Shelbyville, Kentucky, where he published *The Christian's Defense* in 1843. It was Smith's book, in which he outlined his way back to God, the Bible and the Church, that Lincoln found in the Todd Library and began reading. When he returned to Springfield, Lincoln obtained a copy of the book. Smith's guidance of the family through a most difficult time in their lives was something they never forgot. Mary joined the First Presbyterian Church, Lincoln rented a pew and they were active in the church for the next ten years.[52]

In the spring of 1850, a few months after Eddy's death, Mary, Bobby and Lincoln returned to Lexington for the settlements of the Widow Parker's and Robert S. Todd estates. Commissioners were appointed by the court to divide the Widow Parker's property among her heirs. After the land division, there was $1,891 to divide. Mary and her siblings were entitled to their mother's part of one-fifth of that amount.[53]

Mary's younger brother George raised further complaints against Betsy Todd, claiming she was hiding assets from her husband's estate by keeping valuable silverware and not listing all the Todd slaves on the inventory. George demanded his sisters from Illinois join him in legal action to reclaim the property. He had not seen his sister, Mary, for a number of years, but soon discovered she did not respond well to being ordered about. Lincoln had a talk with George, pointing out that the silverware had been a gift to Betsy from an uncle and that the slaves in question had never belonged to Todd but had been inherited from Mary Humphreys. George would not be deterred. He filed a lawsuit not only against Betsy but included Lincoln, his sisters and brother. The legal action went nowhere.[54]

George Todd went after Betsy Todd's dower's rights, one-third of her husband's estate, from the sale of Oldham, Todd and Company for $45,000, and land that Robert Todd sold belonging to Eliza Parker Todd. Oldham, Todd and Company's cotton factory was destroyed by fire in April 1845, or the amount would have been much larger. George won on the land, whose value was appraised at $8,000. Betsy was ordered by the court to pay each of the six children from her husband's first marriage $916.66, two-thirds the appraised price, plus interest from April 10, 1851, less $2,500 in improvements made to the property by Todd. However, the funds Todd advanced the children from his first marriage deducted were as follows: Elizabeth and Ninian Edwards received $40.00; Mary and Lincoln, $475; the Wallaces, $452; C. M. and Ann Smith, nothing; George R. C. Todd, $192, and Levi Todd, nothing. Betsy was ordered by the Court of Appeals, in September 1857, to pay the Edwardses, $876.66; the Lincolns, $441.66; the Wallaces, $916.66; George, $724.66, and Levi, $916.66 from Oldham, Todd and Company's sale of assets.[55]

According to those figures, Todd advanced more money to Elizabeth Edwards than her other siblings, including Mary. It took numerous lawsuits, family estrangements and eight years to settle Robert S. Todd's estate. Mary's portion of the estate, according to Harry E. Pratt, was $1,000.[56]

Mary and Bobby remained for a few weeks with Betsy at Buena Vista while Lincoln returned to Springfield and his law practice.

CHAPTER 8

Laying a Presidential Foundation

The decade of the 1850s saw Mary and Abraham Lincoln both in despair over losing their son, Eddy, and the culmination of years of networking and planning to achieve the Republican nomination for the president of the United States.

Within the decade, two more sons were born to the couple. Lincoln's father died and the estate of Robert S. Todd was finally settled. Mary and Lincoln enlarged their home. Lincoln was again elected to the legislature—for ten days; he lost two United States Senate races and participated in the famous Lincoln-Douglas debates. His law practice expanded to include railroads, and the couple traveled more. The Kansas-Nebraska Act's passage intensified Lincoln's opposition to slavery. The Whig Party's last gasp of political life expired during the nominations and presidential election of 1852, when President Millard Fillmore was not re-nominated due to his support of the Fugitive Slave Act and his public announcement of using the military to enforce the law. The dying Whig organization was replaced by the Republican Party, forever after associated with Lincoln.

When Mary returned to Springfield from Lexington in 1852, she resumed her multitasking role of single parent: housekeeper, cook, tutor, seamstress and caring for a toddler. William "Willie" Wallace Lincoln was born December 21, 1850. Of all their sons, it was said that Willie was the one most like his father in personality and intellect. She also found time to read both for pleasure and to keep her husband informed of the national political trends while he was traveling the circuit.[1]

Willie's birth was difficult for Mary. At the same time, Lincoln's father was critically ill. His step-brother, John D. Johnston, implored Lincoln to come to the bedside of his father in Coles County, Illinois. Lincoln replied on January 12, 1851, that he was unable to come. "You already know I desire that neither Father or Mother shall be in want of any comfort either in health or sickness while they live; and I feel sure you have not failed to use my name, if necessary, to procure a doctor, any thing else, for Father in his present sickness. My business is such that I can hardly leave home now, if it were not, as it is that my own wife in sick-abed (It is a case of baby-sickness and I suppose not dangerous.)" Thomas Lincoln died five days later.[2]

The birth of their last son, Thomas "Tad" Lincoln, named for his paternal grandfather, on April 4, 1853, was even more difficult for Mary. She only referred to the malady as a disease of a womanly nature but it troubled her for the rest of her life.[3]

After Tad's birth, although she had a difficult delivery, Mary Lincoln wet-nursed a neighbor's baby born about the same time. Mrs. Charles Dallman, who lived near the Lincolns, was too ill to nurse her baby. Mary found out about her neighbor's situation and offered a solution. Ruth P. Randall quoted Mrs. Dallman's later recollections when "she told of how the tall, gaunt figure of Abraham Lincoln came across the street from the Lincoln Home, knocked at her door, entered with a gentle step so as not to disturb the sick mother, and then gathered up the little mite of the new-born child into his big brawny hands, formed like a basket for that purpose and carried the infant across the street.[4]

"Soon he would return," Randall wrote, "in that same eloquent silence with a tender expression of profound sympathy ... as he deposited the little child in a cradle." Despite these early efforts, Mrs. Dallman's child died in early childhood. Both the Lincolns knew well the agony of losing a child. Mary prepared food for the wake on her best silver tray and Lincoln carried it across the street.[5]

At age thirty-five, Mary was the mother of three sons, two of them under three, tutoring the ten-year-old, running a household that was outgrowing their home and assisting her husband in his political ambitions. She was still sewing her own clothes but the materials she purchased for her dresses were silk, Irish linen and cashmere instead of calico and cottons. In February 1853, Mary bought what was listed as a Marseille quilt from John Williams' store. The quilt was stamped design which required the most intricate corded French needlework, an art three centuries old that fused design imagery with fine hand-stitching. These bed-coverings were often used as counterpanes in the warm weather when heavy bed-linens and draperies where taken down, cleaned and stored.[6]

During this time, Mary had household help of indeterminate tenures which allowed her more time for needlework, sewing, reading and entertaining. Harriett Hanks, daughter of Lincoln's cousin Dennis Hanks, lived with them for a year and a half while helping with household chores and attending school. Mary had black, Irish and Portuguese servants. Keeping household help was a problem, not just for Mary, but for other Springfield matrons. Mrs. Benjamin S. Edwards, wife of Ninian Edwards' brother, experienced the same problem. "It was almost impossible to get servants," she said. "I had brought a woman [in] from St. Louis, but found her so intemperate that in less than a year I had to discharge her."[7]

Having household help provided Mary with a better use of her time: that of political advisor to her husband. Mary's opposition to President Millard Fillmore's offer to appoint Lincoln as governor of the Oregon Territory in 1849 turned out to be correct, while some of his influential friends, such as John T. Stuart and others, disagreed. They pointed out that Oregon would soon be a state and he could be one of that state's first senators. Had he left Illinois, he would have been isolated from the political mainstream. There would have been no Lincoln-Douglas debates, no "House Divided" or "Cooper Institute" speeches. Lincoln wisely listened to his wife.[8] It turned out to be a smart move.

When Senator Stephen Douglas introduced the Kansas-Nebraska Act in 1854, his intentions were to open the vast Nebraska Territory for settlement and development of railroads with Chicago, of course, being the hub. By the time the bill passed in Congress on May 30, 1854, and was signed into law by President Franklin Pierce, Douglas had made two damaging concessions. The law wiped out the Missouri Comprise of 1820, which prohibited slavery above the latitudinal line of 36° 30'. The latitude ran from the East Coast borders of Virginia and North Carolina (which were already slaves states), Kentucky and Tennessee, Arkansas and Missouri and across unorganized territory to land whose ownership was in dispute with Mexico. In addition, the law split the region into two territories, Kansas and Nebraska. Douglas envisioned two things: the citizens of the two territories would decide for themselves whether to admit slavery, a process he called popular sovereignty, and that such local control would remove slavery from the national political stage.[9]

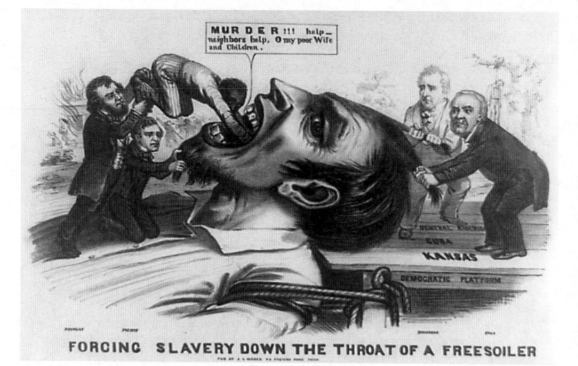

FORCING SLAVERY DOWN THE THROAT OF A FREESOILER

John L. Magee's political cartoon depicts slavery being forced down a Free-soiler's throat as a result of the Kansan-Nebraska Act. The drawing appeared in a Philadelphia publication in 1856 (Library of Congress, Prints and Photographs Division).

People in Illinois and the North were outraged and indignant over Douglas' actions. He was burned in effigy and shouted down when he attempted to speak in Chicago.[10] However, Douglas, a Democrat, continued in office because he had a well-organized political network.

Mary, who had a unique talent for gauging political trends, predicted a big anti-Kansas-Nebraska backlash in the upcoming legislative election, which would be of assistance for her husband in becoming a candidate for the U.S. Senate in 1856. One of Lincoln's friends, Dr. William Jayne, a Springfield physician, and others disagreed and took it upon themselves to announce that Lincoln and Logan would be candidates for the Illinois House of Representatives. Lincoln was out of town at the time.[11] Dr. Jayne was a brother of Mary's friend Julia, who assisted her in composing the poem insulting Shields, and later married Lyman Trumbull.

Mary was most unhappy when she saw the announcement in the *State Journal* that her husband was a candidate for the legislature. A diminutive woman, just over five feet tall, she marched down to the newspaper office and asked the editor, Simeon Francis, to remove Lincoln's name from the list of candidates. Francis and his wife were among the Lincolns' friends responsible for re-uniting the couple after their broken engagement in 1842.[12] The encounter between Mary and Francis could have been a quite pleasant conversation between two old friends.

Events gradually unfolded revealing the Lincolns had other political plans which did not include his being a candidate for the state legislature.

A couple of days later, Lincoln's name again appeared in Francis' newspaper's list of legislative candidates. Mary Lincoln made a second visit to the editor. The tenor of their conversation was not known but one can suspect it was not as pleasant as the earlier visit. She not only asked that her husband's name be removed but secured Francis' word that Lincoln's name would not appear again among the legislative candidates until he returned home.[13]

Jayne persisted, called on Lincoln after he returned home and insisted that he allow his name to be listed as a legislative candidate. Lincoln refused. When Lincoln was again out of town, his name appeared in the newspaper as a candidate just before the election. Both Lincoln and Logan were elected.[14]

A candidate's wife publicly inserting herself into her husband's career and the political process was unheard of in 1855. She would never have pursued such a path unless she and her husband had discussed in depth their plans and both agreed for him to enter the senate race. Mary had no fear where Lincoln's future was concerned, but knew she had to tread the political waters carefully. After all, it would be another sixty-five years before women were allowed to vote. It seems implausible that Mary never considered the inequity of not being allowed to vote because of her gender. After all, she had surely read about the first leaflets being circulated in England in 1843 advocating women's right to vote.[15]

Mary's political acumen was correct. The more anti–Kansas-Nebraska legislators of either party elected, the better Lincoln's chances were of being sent to the Senate. Lincoln's Senate chances improved, not with his election to the legislature, but with another anti-Kansas-Nebraska candidate being selected instead of him. In 1855, U.S. senators were still selected by state legislatures and would be for the next fifty-eight years. The Seventeenth Amendment, ratified on April 8, 1913, called for senators to be elected by direct popular vote.[16]

To help her husband prepare and lobby legislators for their votes in the Senate race, Mary researched and prepared notebooks on the party allegiances of each member of the legislature.[17] As loquacious as Mary was, she probably contributed further notes about the individual legislators as reminders for her husband, if he needed them.

The February 8, 1855, selection of Illinois' junior U.S. senator was filled with political intrigue, vote swapping, a secret candidate and charges of vote buying. Mary was at the legislature with Elizabeth Edwards and Emilie Todd to witness the event.

Douglas, while supposedly supporting James Shields, who was a Catholic, instructed his operatives to make the Know Nothing Party, which was strongly anti-immigrant and anti-Catholic, the issue in the voting instead of the Kansas-Nebraska law, which reflected badly on the Democrats. Lincoln began leading the balloting by three votes over Shields, forty-four to forty-one, with one for Lyman Trumbull, who was also anti–Kansas-Nebraska. As the vote swapping continued for ten more ballots, a new, stealth Democrat candidate, Gov. Joel Matteson, began picking up Shields' supporters, as had been planned. Lincoln realized if something was not done the state would have two Democratic senators. There was no indication that Trumbull, who had gained some votes, made any overture to switch his votes to Lincoln. Rather than see Matteson elected, Lincoln placed his party affiliations and concern for the nation ahead of his personal political advancement and asked his supporters to vote for Trumbull, who was elected.[18]

In a February 9, letter to Elihu B. Washburne, a member of Illinois' Congressional delegation and a Whig lawyer from Galena, Lincoln explained what happened.

The agony is over at last, it was Govr. Matteson's work. He has been secretly a candidate ever since (before even) the fall elections. All the members around the canal were Anti-Nebraska; but were nevertheless nearly all Democrats and old personal friends of his. His plan was to privately impress them with the belief that he was as good Anti-Nebraska as anyone else—at least could be secured to be so by instructions, which could easily be passed. We saw that plan ten days ago; but with every possible effort could not head it off.[19]

Such is the way things are done. I think you would have done the same thing under the circumstances; though Judge Davis, who came down this morning, declares he never would have consented to the forty-seven men being controlled by the five. I regret my defeat moderately, but I am not nervous about it. I could have headed off every combination and had been elected had it not been for Matteson's double game—and his defeat gives me more pleasure than my own gives me pain.[20]

Lincoln's pleasure over Matteson's defeat in the Senate race may have had more to do with the governor's involvement in what was called the "Great Canal Scrip Fraud" than his double-dealing in the Senate race. Lincoln was in the legislature in 1839 when an ambitious program of internal improvements was launched, including the Illinois and Michigan Canal, which would provide a transportation system for the northern portion of the state. Three different sets of scrip were issued as the project experienced financial difficulties. However, the project was saved and the canal was finished in 1848 and became one of the few canals to pay for its operation.[21]

Illinois was a small state in the 1850s, and Springfield was a small town where everybody knew everybody's business, especially if politics was involved. John M. Lamb, in a 1977 article for *The Magazine of Illinois*, chronicled the travels of some of the unredeemed scrip. He wrote that many of the unredeemed notes, in denominations of $50 and $100, had not been hammer cancelled. Canal officials sealed some in a wooden box and others in an old candle box. They remained in the Branch State Bank of Chicago until 1841 when the canal trustees had the boxes removed to their offices, also in Chicago. "There they remained, still sealed, but much battered about evidently, until 1853," Lamb wrote. "In that year the newly appointed state trustee, Josiah McRoberts, asked newly elected Governor Joel Matteson to take them to Springfield so they could be deposited with the state treasurer. McRoberts had to re-pack the scrip that was in the old candle box, which was falling apart. This scrip he unwisely put into a shoebox."[22]

McRoberts met Gov. Matteson in Joliet with a trunk containing the scrip for the transfer to Springfield and its final resting place in the Capitol basement. It would have been unusual if Lincoln was not aware of the scrip movement. "In 1858, it became known that a large amount of the scrip had been redeemed," Lamb wrote. "This had been going on since 1856, and the person redeeming it was none other than Governor Matteson." A hue and cry of fraud began. In order to forestall a legislative investigation, Matteson paid the state $224,182.66.[23]

Whether Matteson used any of his ill-gotten gain from the canal scrip fraud in building his enormous mansion in Springfield is not known. In 1856, Matteson bought an entire city block—three acres—across from the new governor's residence. He spent $100,000 ($2.68 million in 2012 dollars) building a three story, plus basement, edifice which contained fourteen bedrooms, a master suite with bath, floor to ceiling bookcases in the library, specially designed carpet, and walls covered with ceiling-high mirrors or oil murals painted by artists from a Chicago firm.[24] Mary likened the Matteson mansion to a palace. For guests who attended soirees in the palatial home, a life-size statue of Stephen Douglas would have been the first thing they saw when entering the vestibule.[25]

In the fall of 1856, Mary appeared to have kept her social relations with Mary Matteson intact. In a November 23, 1856, letter to Emilie Todd Helm, she wrote about calling on Mary Matteson and of her disappointment that the wedding of their daughter, Lydia, was not going to be public. "Several of us who had a handsome dress for the season, thought it would be in *good taste* for Mrs. Matteson, in consideration of their being about to leave their present habitation, to give a general reception."[26]

Lincoln, two years later, preferred to avoid further social contact with Matteson. Mary, in a letter to Hannah Shearer, wrote: "Gov & Mrs Matteson give a large entertainment on Wednesday evening, Mr L—*gives me* permission to go but declines the honor himself. I should like to go, but *may probably* pass the evening at home."[27]

Matthew Pinsker, in his 1993 article in the *Journal of the Abraham Lincoln Association*, wrote that Mary refused to speak to Julia Trumbull, once her close friend, after the Senate election. "We feared it would be a terrible blow to Mary, but if she was disappointed she kept it strictly to herself," Emilie Todd Helm recalled.[28]

Mary was somewhere in the middle of those assessments. In later letters, she had no kind words for Julia Trumbull.[29] However, Mary Lincoln kept up her social contacts with Mary Matteson when her husband wanted nothing to do with the governor. There was another senatorial election in two years with none other than Stephen Douglas, and the Lincolns had that race in their sights. All those years Lincoln spent on the Eighteenth Judicial Circuit—which covered fourteen counties with a combined population in 1850 of 100,000, when he did not return to Springfield, as other lawyers did, on the weekends—provided a solid political base built on those personal contacts.[30]

Mary, meanwhile, was doing her own networking at social events. She attended as well as held them in their home. In 1854, the Lincolns sold for $1,200 the eighty-acre tract her father gave her in 1844. In 1856, the Lincolns paid Hannan and Ragsdale, Springfield architects and builders, $1,300 to add a second story to their home. The renovation gave Mary a dining room separate from the kitchen, four bedrooms plus a maid's room on the second floor, a main staircase and a smaller one in the rear; front and back parlors on the first floor were joined; a second floor porch with attractive iron grille work was added but the downstairs sitting room remained the same.[31] Mrs. John T. Stuart, on April 3, 1856, wrote her daughter, "Mr. Lincoln has commenced raising his back building two stories high. I think they will have room enough before they are done, particularly as Mary seldom used what she has."[32]

In 1855 and 1856, the Lincolns purchased thirty-three pieces (as was listed on their account) of wallpaper and twelve pieces of border from John Williams and Company. In May 1857, Mary bought thirty-six yards of buff linen, changed her mind, returned the material and selected thirty-six yards of cotton damask, which she probably made into draperies. Undoubtedly, they began adding pieces of better furniture. Lincoln ordered thirty-five yards of carpet from J. C. Louderman and Company in St. Louis and sent a piece of their old carpet by a banker who was traveling to that city. In 1857, Lincoln also purchased a cottage bed for eleven dollars from John Hutchinson, who also operated an undertaking business.[33]

The March 9, 1861, issue of *Leslies Illustrated Weekly Newspaper* described the Lincolns' public reception rooms. "The sitting-room and parlor of Abraham Lincoln, in his house in Springfield, are, as the reader may observe, simply and plainly fitted up, but are not without indications of taste and refinement. They are called 'leisure rooms,' as parlors might properly be called, of the great majority of Americans in comfortable circumstances in county towns and will doubtless suggest to the reader many a pleasant hour passed in such apartments.... The rooms are elegantly and comfortably furnished with strong well-made furniture, made for use and not for show."[34]

A *New York Herald* reporter described the Lincolns' home thusly. "It is like the residence of any American gentleman in easy circumstances, and is furnished in a like manner. It is not near so aristocratic an establishment as the houses of many members of your Common Council. In short, there is no aristocracy about it; but there is a comfortable, cosy home, in which it would seem that a man could enjoy life, surrounded by his family."[35]

In the mid–1850s, Springfield was awash with social activities and Mary and Abraham Lincoln not only attended these events but now had a home where they could entertain. If her husband was out of town, Mary usually accepted invitations to parties.

One of the splashiest parties held in Springfield in 1855 was in the newly built, red brick, Italianate-style, three-story governor's mansion. Gov. Matteson built the structure at a cost of $35,500, which in 2012 dollars is $959,000.[36]

"The good people of Springfield seem to have given themselves up to the spirit of gayety for the last few weeks, parties and entertainment are the order of the day and our ladies intend next week shall be devoted to the same course," Mrs. John T. Stuart wrote her daughter, Elizabeth, on January 28, 1855. "The week is to be opened by a party Monday evening at Mr. Ninian Edwards and also one the same evening at Mr. William Grimsleys. Tuesday evening a dance for the young people at the Governor's. Wednesday, Mrs. William B. Fondey is to give a large party and others to make out the week which I do not remember. Last Friday we dined at Mr. Smith's in company with Dr. and Fanny Wallace, Mr. Lincoln and Mary, Mr. Edwards and Elizabeth."[37]

In February 1855, Mary helped prepare a dinner, served at the Masonic Hall, to raise money to install gas in the First Presbyterian Church. The dinner raised more than $200. John T. Stuart wrote his daughter that the supper was very good, everything went off pleasantly and the event was well attended. "The next evening," he continued, "Mrs. Geo. L. Huntington had a party, not large but very pleasant ... the next evening there was a very large party at Mr. Nicholas Ridgleys. A perfect *squeeze*. The house was brilliantly lit by gas. The company was very gaily dressed, the supper very good and upon the whole everything was very pleasant."[38]

Hopefully Stuart was a better lawyer than social commentator, as his nineteen-page letter to his daughter about the wedding of Caroline Lamb to William J. Black, a Springfield attorney indicated.

> We press through the crowd, we push and they push. We tread on their toes and they tread on ours. See there is Judge [Stephen] Logan with Miss Mary on his arm making toward the bridegroom and bride—look at his forehead—how the sweat rolls down. Would rather argue a case before the Supreme Court than struggle with this. All the world is here.... All the sewing societies broke loose. I reach the passage. I back into a corner and look upon the crowd ... how many old acquaintances seem to be thrown together tonight.... But look they are crowding in to supper. Mother takes my arm and we go in with the crowd. Close by are cousins Mary Lincoln, Lizzie Edwards and Mrs. B. E. Edwards. First oyster salad and then ice cream and cake.[39]

Stuart raved about the parties that Matteson threw in the new governor's mansion a month before the senate election. The first party, Stuart related, topped anything ever seen before in Springfield, especially when the house was taken into consideration. The Lincolns were among the guests, 400 of whom were from out of town. The only flaw Stuart found with the event was that the gas lighting malfunctioned and candles were brought out. "On the second night," he wrote, "the house was full of girls and boys. The gas was in full operation—the band was in attendance—all the rooms were thrown open, and the children danced or at least hopped around. John [his son] danced all evening *his way*. The next day he and Bob Lincoln were hunting up dancing masters."[40]

On the evening of February 5, 1857, the Lincolns invited 500 guests to a party at their newly renovated home. Mary addressed all the invitations. The invitation to Mrs. Henry Remann survived and read, "Mr. and Mrs. Lincoln will be pleased to see you on Thursday evening Feb. 5th at 8 o'clock." Only 300 accepted due to rain and the bridal party Col. William B. Warren gave for his son in Jacksonville the same evening. Justin Turner wrote, "How Mrs. Lincoln managed to squeeze three hundred people (much less than the expected 500) into the downstairs rooms of a modest house in mid–winter, and with women wearing crinolines and hoops, is—to use Lincoln's words on another occasion—'a matter of profound wonder.'"[41]

Mary told Emilie Todd Helm, in her February 16, 1857, letter, there had been a party almost every night and some two or three grand fetes were scheduled for that week. "I may perhaps surprise you, when I mention that I am recovering from the slight fatigue of a very large & I really believe a very handsome & agreeable entertainment, at least our friends flatter us by saying so." She told Emilie that she saw a number of her acquaintances at a very large party, given three days earlier by Gov. William H. Bissell, a Republican who succeeded Matteson.[42]

"For the last six weeks," she wrote her friend Hannah Shearer, who had lived across the street from them before moving with her physician husband and family back to Pennsylvania, "we have had a continual round of *strawberry* parties, this last week, I have spent five evenings out—and you may suppose that this is a day of rest, I am happy to enjoy. You need not suppose with our *pleasures* you are forgotten. I shall *never cease* to long for your dear presence, a cloud always hangs over me, when I think of you. This last week we gave a strawberry party of about seventy."[43]

In the same letter, Mary was unable to resist making a snide remark about Julia Trumbull, wife of Sen. Lyman Trumbull, who defeated Lincoln in the 1855 senate race. "Mrs. Trumbull made her first appearance last evening looking as stately and *ungainly* as ever. Altho, she has been in the city 20 days, this has been about the first notice that has been taken of her, Tis' unfortunate, to be so unpopular."[44]

Mary continued her letter saying that she anticipated a quiet summer at home after Bob left for college. But, a week later she was off on another trip of 1,100 miles over the lines of the Illinois Central Railroad. "Many in the party were of your acquaintance. Mr. and Mrs. [Jesse] Dubois, Mr. and Mrs. Tom Campbell [she was the former Ann E. Todd, Mary's Cousin], Mr. [Ozias] Hatch *of course* and some few others, I believe you knew. *Words* cannot express what a merry time, we all had, the gayest pleasure party I have ever seen." The other members of the party were Mr. and Mrs. Stephen T. Logan, Mr. and Mrs. John Moore and Mr. and Mrs. William Butler.[45]

Henry G. Little, an Illinois legislator, recalled the Lincolns' big party. Little said a long table was stretched nearly the whole length of the room, while above the table was a succession of shelves growing narrower upwards. On these shelves the edibles were placed and the guests were left to help themselves, the waiters serving only coffee. Little said Lincoln joined him at the table and asked, "Do they give you anything to eat here?"[46]

Not all of Mary's parties involved hundreds of guests. In September 1857, she invited Mr. and Mrs. Mason Brayman to their house. Her note to Mrs. Brayman read, "If your health will admit of venturing out, in such damp weather, we would be much pleased to have you, Mr B & the young ladies come round, this eve about seven & pass a social evening also any friend you may have with you." Brayman was a Springfield lawyer with whom Lincoln worked on the Illinois Central Railroad's legal affairs.[47]

If Lincoln was out of town and unable to accompany Mary to a party, he asked his law clerk Gibson Harris to escort her. Harris recalled these events, "As a frequent visitor I was made comfortable at the Lincoln home and, on two occasions, at the insistence of Mr. Lincoln, he being unable to attend, I became Mrs. Lincoln's escort to a ball where I danced with her. I always found her most pleasant-mannered. She was a bright, witty accomplished young woman, naturally fond of fun and frolic, but very staid and proper when it was in order to do so. I was impressed with her brilliant conversational powers and the superior education she constantly evinced."[48]

Social activities for the Lincolns waned in the months prior to the 1858 general election, where Lincoln opposed Stephen Douglas for a seat in the United States Senate. They were bitter political rivals over the issue of slavery. But, so to speak, they appeared to leave the battle in the political arena. There was a collegiality and respect between the candidates that was certainly lacking in Lincoln's previous Senate race against Gov. Joel Matteson. Douglas wrote a recommendation to Harvard for the Lincolns' son, Robert. The grueling campaign contained the famous Lincoln-Douglas debates, which included Ottawa, August 21; Freeport, August 27; Jonesboro, September 15; Charleston, September 18; Galesburg, October 7; Quincy, October 13; and Alton, October 15.[49]

Except for the final debate in Alton, Mary remained behind in Springfield. Henry B. Rankin, Lincoln's law clerk from 1856 to 1861, had an insight into this period of their lives. Rankin wrote that Mary did not neglect her household, domestic or social duties while giving her attention to politics. "None other ever had such faith in Lincoln as hers," he wrote. "He had less faith and hope in himself than she. No denial was too severe or service too hazard, if it promised the goal she had in view for Lincoln. She was more aggressive than her husband. She steadfastly inspired and kept him aimed higher. Until 1858, he needed influences outside himself to push him to the political front and hold him there. She gave

Abraham Lincoln photographed in Pittsfield, Illinois, two weeks before the last Lincoln-Douglas debate at Alton, during the 1858 U.S. Senate race. Mary Todd dated Stephen Douglas before marrying Lincoln in 1842 (Library of Congress, Prints and Photographs Division).

him this unstintingly. Some misunderstood, regarding her officious in this, and said cruel things about her for it. This annoyed her greatly, and her replies were equally stinging, creating life-long enemies."[50]

Given his position as Lincoln's law clerk, Rankin knew Mary through contacts both within and without the office. While going through the law office's collections of periodicals and pamphlets, Rankin found a September 1851 copy of the *Southern Literary Messenger* which included a translation of Victor Hugo's address against capital punishment. Knowing Mary's interest in French, he took the periodical to her home and she was delighted. Mary, after reading the Victor Hugo article, insisted the translation was lacking and asked Rankin to obtain a copy of Hugo's speech in French. Rankin said she compared the original speech with the reporter's translation and found it lacking. "I hoped she would read it aloud, which she did, stopping often to compare the translation and the original. She read with such clearness and dramatic fervor, and translated with such sympathy that, instead of following the English translation, I could only sit entranced by the force and effect of her tones as she translated, or at time, read Hugo's inspiring oration in his native tongue."[51]

Rankin said it was Mary who insisted that Lincoln stay on the debate trail with Douglas to the very end. "With the children and household affairs and Lincoln's personal wants to be provided for, she was the managing partner who kept the expense accounts within limits which their moderate income placed at her disposal," he wrote. Rankin said that Lincoln, both before and after the debates, accorded Mary his "unstinted appreciation of her efficiency in all home and financial affairs, as well as in forecasting the progress of political events."[52]

Mary, with fifteen-year-old Bobby, traveled by train from Springfield to Alton for the last debate. Both candidates booked passage on the steamboat *City of Louisville* after the Quincy debate. They arrived in Alton around five o'clock in the morning and went to their respective hotel rooms.[53]

Gustave Koerner, Gov. Matteson's lieutenant governor, switched sides over the Kansas-Nebraska legislation and traveled to Alton for the debate in support of Lincoln. Koerner, who knew Mary when he was a student at Transylvania, met Lincoln at the hotel. "Let's go up and see Mary," Lincoln said to him. Koerner agreed, saying he had not seen her since attending Lexington parties while at Transylvania. He recalled Lincoln's request, "Now tell Mary what you think of our chances. She is rather dispirited." Koerner said he was fairly certain Lincoln would carry the state but only tolerably of winning in the legislature. "I found Lincoln a little despondent," he added.[54]

Koerner was Lincoln's connection to the German-American population in Illinois, according to a letter Lincoln wrote him on July 15, 1858. Lincoln told Koerner that he had just returned from Chicago and Douglas' rampant endorsement of the Dred Scott decision had cost him some Republican votes. "His tactics just now, in part is, to make it appear that he is having a triumphal entry into; and march through the country; but it is all as bombastic and hollow as Napoleon's bulletins sent back from his campaign in Russia."[55]

His wife, son and others attending the Alton debate and heard Lincoln say, "There are two principles that have stood face to face from the beginning of time; and will ever continue to struggle. The one is the common right of humanity and the other is the divine right of kings. It is the same principle in whatever shape it develops itself. It is the same spirit that says: 'You work and toil and earn bread and I'll eat it.'"[56]

The speeches and debates could sway the popular choice, but the legislature usually voted along party lines. The newly-minted Republican Party in Illinois failed to have the resources to elect enough legislators to insure Lincoln's victory over Davis. On January 5, 1859, the Illinois State Senate voted fourteen to seven for Douglas. In the House, the vote was forty for Douglas and thirty-five for Lincoln.[57]

Rankin said Lincoln was despondent at time during those days filled with political tension. "The stress and turmoil went hard with him," he recalled. "Not so with her. She had a spirit that never tired on the battle line. She was less pleasant on a retreat, and could stand almost anything better than a political dead calm. Lincoln could be more at entire ease on the retreat, or in a calm, for he went into one of his moods of meditative silence that was at such time exasperatingly unintelligible for her and to so many of his friends. To whom would his mood not have been a trial? Yet, she always found a way of getting him out of it and back on the firing line again."[58]

Stephen A. Douglas, Mary's former beau, was Lincoln's opponent in the famous debates. After Lincoln's election and before his death Douglas worked with Lincoln to keep the Union intact (Library of Congress Prints and Photographs Division).

Lincoln told his long-time friend Dr. Anson Henry he was glad he made the race against Douglas. "It gave me a hearing on the great and durable question of the age, which I could have had in no other way; and though I now sink out of view, and shall be forgotten, I believe I have made some marks which will tell the cause of civil liberty long after I am gone."[59] Lincoln ended his letter to Dr. Henry, "Mary joins me in sending you our best wishes to Mrs. Henry and others of your family."[60]

Irving Stone, in the *Lincoln Monographs*, wrote, "She may not have participated in the writing of her husband's speeches for the crucial Lincoln-Douglas debates, she certainly contributed to their thinking and feeling." Stone continued, "Lincoln did not have to leave his problems on the front porch when he entered the house on Eighth Street, he had a wife who was well read in history, who understood the nature of the growing conflict over slavery, as well as the *modus operandi* by which certain men got themselves elected to office, and how American governments were run. She was an equal partner in a growing enterprise."[61]

Being an equal partner, Mary had no intentions of allowing her husband to sink out of view because he lost the race for U.S. senator. In a joint effort, they both reached down into their inner depths and found the wherewithal to make one final election campaign— this time for the office of president of the United States.

CHAPTER 9

"Mary, We Are Elected!"

"Without Mary Todd for his wife, Abraham Lincoln would never have been president," Henry B. Rankin, one of Lincoln's former law clerks, wrote. "Without Abraham Lincoln for her husband, Mary Todd would probably never have been a president's wife."[1]

Rankin was not the only one to voice those sentiments. A century later, Ronald C. White, Jr., in his biography of Lincoln, wrote, "Mary was eager to join her husband's campaign in ways that most previous candidates' wives were not. In past presidential campaigns, the wives of candidates were seldom seen and never heard. But Mary had inherited from her father a passion for politics, and for years she had put that enthusiasm to work encouraging her husband and, in an 'unwomanly' way for her time, offering her counsel on all manner of politics and people."[2]

The male-dominated world of Illinois politics would later extract a heavy price for Mary's ground-breaking participation into their nineteenth century political world after, of course, the death of her husband.

"From the early days of their marriage, when Lincoln was running for state office, again while he served in Congress, and even when he was seemingly exiled to the Eighth Judicial Circuit, Mary always had her eyes on faraway horizons." White added, "She recognized long before others his abilities, which she believed would one day carry him all the way to the presidency."[3]

In the early days of their marriage, Mary and Lincoln had a partnership, in addition to the love and affection they felt for each other. It was, in a manner of speaking, them against the world. From those small rooms in the Globe Hotel, they talked about their dreams for the future and worked in tandem to reach the pinnacle of their success, the presidency. Did either of them ever consider the divergent paths that would come with that success? Lincoln probably did but it was doubtful if the thought ever occurred to Mary. With Mary, it was full speed ahead regardless of the collateral damage. She had shared him with the Springfield Republican operatives—David Davis, Isaac Arnold, Leonard Swett, Stephen Logan, John T. Stuart and others—because it was necessary. But now, she would have to share him with the nation. To make matters even worse, that nation was being torn apart over slavery. Others who considered themselves more qualified to dispense political advice than Mary would compete with her as Lincoln's advisors. Very few of them had his best interests in mind.

After all, in the nineteenth century idiom, Mary Lincoln was just a woman. That is not to say that Lincoln agreed or no longer needed Mary. Actually he needed her support more than ever, just not in the same way as in earlier times when he traveled the circuit or when he and Douglas were holding their debates.

The Lincoln-Douglas debates, one in each of Illinois's seven Congressional districts during the 1858 U.S. Senate campaign, propelled Lincoln to the forefront of the new Republican Party, and requests for speaking engagements poured in to Springfield.[4]

Although he lost the Senate election in the legislature, his statements in the last debate in Alton resonated throughout the country.

> We are now in the fifth year since a policy was initiated with the avowed object and confident promise to putting an end to the slavery agitation. Under the operation of this policy, that agitation has not only not ceased, but has constantly augmented. In my opinion it will not cease until a crisis shall have been reached and passed. 'A house divided against itself cannot stand.' I believe the government cannot endure permanently half slave and half free. I do not expect the house to fall—but I do expect it will cease to be divided. It will become one thing, or the other. Either the opponents of slavery will arrest the further spread of it and place it where the public mind shall rest in the belief that it is in the course of ultimate extinction, or its advocates will push it forward till it shall become alike lawful in all the states—old as well as new, North as well as South.[5]

In September 1859, the Lincolns traveled to Ohio where he was invited to speak in Columbus and Cincinnati, as was Stephen A. Douglas. In Columbus, a publishing firm offered to print a pamphlet of all the Lincoln-Douglas debates. Lincoln had been trying to get them published for some time. While in Cincinnati, Mary and Lincoln visited her cousin, Annie Parker Dickinson, and her family. On October 29, Mary wrote Hannah Shearer about their trip. "We visited Columbus & some beautiful portions of Ohio & made a charming visit to Cincinnati. I am at home again and Mr. L—is in Wisconsin."[6]

It was doubtful that Mary made any contributions or suggestions to the speech Lincoln was invited to give at the Rev. Henry Ward Beecher's Plymouth Congregational Church in Brooklyn. Lincoln did his own extensive research in preparation and it was not finished before he left for New York. The $200 lecturer's fee was indeed welcome as Lincoln had been absent from his law practice during the debates and while making speeches in several states. The location of the speech was moved from Beecher's church to the Great Hall at Cooper Institute and the sponsorship was assumed by the Young Men's Republican Union. Had she gone with him, Mary would have reveled at the Great Hall, with its soaring arches and graceful columns, in the neo-Romanesque-styled building industrialist and philanthropist Peter Cooper built in 1859, to offer a free education in architecture and engineering to poor students. Cooper Institute classes were open to men and women as well as students of all races. A more fitting location for Lincoln's speech than Cooper Institute could not have been found.[7]

Lincoln crafted the speech around the thirty-nine signers of the Declaration of Independence and pointed out that twenty-one of them believed Congress should control slavery in the territories and not allow it to expand. After a rocky start, Lincoln fell into the rhythm of his speech, gradually winning over his audience. When he closed, the Great Hall erupted in prolonged applause. Mary, no doubt, enjoyed hearing the account of the speech from Springfield lawyer Mayson Brayman, who with his wife were guests in the Lincolns' home. Lincoln had asked Brayson to stand in the back of the hall and raise his hat if he could not hear his voice. Brayson, like many others, was amazed at Lincoln's command of his audience. It was somewhat funny, he said, "To see a man who *at home*, talks along in so familiar a way, walking up and down, swaying about, swinging his arms, bobbing forward, telling droll stories and laughing at them himself, *here in New York*, standing up stiff and straight, with his hands quiet, pronouncing sentence after sentence in good telling English."[8]

Lincoln wrote Mary on March 4, 1860, that the Cooper Institute speech, "being within my calculation before I started, went off passably well, and gave me no trouble whatever." He added that he was making a "little" speaking tour and taking Bob and George Latham, another Phillips Exeter Academy student from Springfield, with him as they were caught up on their lessons. He was concerned to find, from a letter Mary had written Bob, that Willie and Tad became ill the Saturday he left. "Having no dispatch from you and having one from Springfield, of Wednesday, from Mr. [Harrison G.] Fitzhugh, saying nothing about our family, I trust the dear little fellows are well again."[9]

He gave her his schedule—speeches in Connecticut and Rhode Island—before returning to New York to catch a train for Springfield. "I have been unable to escape this toil—If I had foreseen it I think I would not have come East at all. If the trains do not lie over Sunday, of which I do not know, I hope to be home to-morrow week. Once started, I shall come as quick as possible."[10] By the time Lincoln reached Springfield, Mary had probably already read the accolades heaped on her husband by the eastern press.

Looming ahead was the Republican presidential nominating convention. Norman B. Judd, in December 1859, had convinced the Republican National Committee to hold it in Chicago in May 1860.[11]

Chicago hastily put together an enormous rectangular, two-story, pine-plank building which could hold 10,000 to 12,000 convention goers. Although the letters over the main entrance read "Republican Headquarters," the building was referred to as the Wigwam. The Chicago History Museum provided the following explanation. "The term originally referred to the lodges or tents of some of the North American Indian tribes, by the early 1800s, American political parties had begun to refer to their campaign headquarters by the same name."[12]

Mary Lincoln was not the first presidential candidate's wife to be a vital part of his campaign as an advisor. Sarah Polk was one of her husband's chief political advisors and researched and wrote his speeches. Like Mary Lincoln, Sarah Childress Polk was far more educated than most women of her day.[13] Where Sarah Polk remained in the political background, Mary Lincoln relished not only the spotlight but getting down into the trenches of rough and tumble world of nineteenth century politics, something women were seldom allowed to do in those times.

Considering her earlier correct readings of the political winds, there was no reason to consider that her husband ceased discussing the presidential race with Mary or taking her advice. When candidates for national political offices neither appeared at the nominating conventions nor campaigned for themselves afterwards, Lincoln would have had problems if his wife came to the forefront as one of his political advisors.

So, it was judges David Davis and Stephen Logan; lawyer friends from the Eighth Circuit such as Leonard Swett, Isaac Arnold, Henry C. Whitney and Ward Hill Lamon; political operatives including Norman Judd, O. H. Browning, Jesse Fell, Jesse Dubois, Ozias Hatch, and newspapermen Joseph Medill and Charles Ray who were the "official advisors" and became the public faces of his campaign.[14]

Davis, who adjourned courts in the Eighth Judicial Circuit, and his crew of lawyers ran their operation for Lincoln's nomination at the national convention like a well-oiled machine. Davis rented the third floor of the Tremont House Hotel for $300. In addition, he spent $34.50 for whiskey, $60 for wine, $77 for brandy and $25 for cigars in entertaining the delegates. An additional expenditure of $125 was for porters and whatever those porters procured. The entire expenditures of $591.50 were paid by Ozias Hatch, who was Illinois secretary of state, and Ward Hill Lamon, the state's attorney. "They doubtless considered this the best investment of their lives," Henry Pratt wrote.[15]

Judd, who was in charge of convention seating, arranged for the New York delegation, backing William H. Seward, and the Pennsylvania delegate, supporting Simon Cameron, to be seated on opposite ends of the Wigwam, where it would be difficult for them to converse. Judd, also a railroad lawyer, arranged for special excursion trains to bring in Lincoln supporters to fill the galleries at the Wigwam.[16]

Lincoln kept in touch with the balloting at the convention by telegraph. He was in the offices of the *Illinois State Journal* when a telegram arrived announcing that Lincoln had won the nomination on the third ballot. A crowd of friends gathered around Lincoln congratulating him, but he excused himself. "Well gentlemen there is a little woman at our house who is probably more interested in this dispatch than I am."[17]

"No wife of a presidential nominee ever received news of her husband's nomination with greater joy than did Mrs. Lincoln," Henry B. Rankin wrote. "She was radiant with joy, and faced the future without the shadow of fear to darken that one most perfect day of her life. She in common with most other Springfieldians, never closed her eyes for sleep that night. The shouting and blazing of bonfires made the whole night luminous and hideous. Thousands of Wide Awakes, clad in capes and bearing torches, marched the streets most of the night singing campaign songs."[18]

The Wide Awakes, started by five young dry goods clerks, in Hartford, Connecticut, in March 1860, after Lincoln spoke there, were a unique political organization. "Young men from Bangor [Maine] to San Francisco and from huge Philadelphia clubs to tiny Iowa troupes donned uniforms, lit torches and 'fell in' to pseudo-military companies," Jon Grinspan wrote in 2009. "They flooded every northern state and trickled into upper South cities like Baltimore, Wheeling and St. Louis." By November 1860, the Wide Awakes had evolved into a grassroots movement with hundreds of thousands of members.[19]

Lincoln, according to the *Hartford Evening Post* editor Daniel D. Bidwell, was responsible for giving the group their name. After Lincoln finished speaking at Hartford, he got in a carriage for the drive to Mayor Timothy M. Allen's home for a reception. A large group of young men marched alongside his carriage singing and cheering. "The boys are wide awake," Lincoln was quoted as saying. "Suppose we call them the wide awakes."[20]

Mary's family was well represented at the convention by her cousin, Stephen T. Logan, who headed the Sangamon County delegation. In public, Logan exhibited a rather stern demeanor and ran a strict courtroom. In private, as when he was teasing Mary about her suitors years earlier, he exhibited a delightful sense of humor.

Logan, Rankin wrote, had purchased the finest new suit he had ever owned for the two-day convention. In addition, he had Springfield's best hat maker craft a tall, shining, silk hat. "He came back [from the two-day convention] with his suit a sight to behold, dusty and wrinkled beyond recognition, for he had not been out of it since he left Springfield. He came back wearing a little Scotch cap, the glossy tall silk hat having been left somewhere in the debris of the Wigwam, near Lake Michigan, after Logan had beaten it into shapeless ruin over the heads and shoulders of his fellow-delegates upon the announcement of the third ballot. No one would credit this report at first, but everybody who had been there said it was true—except the Judge. And he was silent!"[21]

Logan knew that Lincoln would have to leave his law practice during the campaign. "With his nomination Lincoln abandoned his law practice," Pratt wrote, "except for four pending cases in federal court in which he appeared briefly in June 1860. Several unpaid fees were collected but, otherwise, his income ceased."[22]

While Lincoln served his term in Congress his law practice income dwindled considerably and it took him four years to build it back up to 500 cases a year. Even while being away making speeches in 1859, he still maintained a 400-case level. In 1861, after he went to Washington, the law firm's cases fell to less than 200, and the next year dropped by more than one-half.[23]

It was Logan who recognized the need for and who took the lead in raising campaign funds for expenses he felt Lincoln should not be expected to meet. Pratt wrote that he only knew the names of eight or nine—Logan, Jacob Bunn, John W. Bunn, William Butler, Robert Irwin, John Williams, Ozias Hatch, Thomas Condell and probably Jesse K. Dubois—who pledged $500 each for such expenses. They became the Sangamon County Finance Committee and they paid the seventy-five dollars a month salary of John G. Nicolay, who had been a clerk in Hatch's office, to help Lincoln with his correspondence.[24]

The Wide Awakes were not the only ones who marched in Springfield to celebrate Lincoln's nomination.

Mary Lincoln never dreamed a cannon would be named in her honor during the Republican Party rally held in Springfield on August 8. Thousands of supporters came from every part of the state. Sixty years later, William H. Smith recalled being a part of that rally when he was fifteen. Smith said some came by train, others on horseback but most came in wagons. "Many came two, and some even three hundred miles in this way, joyfully, gladly, to show their devotion to the cause they represented, the party they were a part of, and the man they loved. They drove by day and camped by the roadside at night." He said his father, a delegate to the convention, had two hundred acres to till that fall but he fitted out his largest and strongest farm wagon and hitched up his four best horses for the trip.[25] "No sooner were we started on our journey capitalward than we began to be joined at every cross-road by other pilgrims bound for the same goal. This procession grew and grew in length as we progressed until before the second night of our encampment it was more than seven miles long, and it was made up almost exclusively of farm wagons and men on horseback. One would see here and there an 'express wagon' with springs under its bed and there were very few carriages."[26]

When they arrived in Springfield, Smith's father recognized Lincoln walking down the street and stopped the wagon to speak with him. Smith's group, along with banners and musicians, brought a cast-iron cannon, about three feet long with a two-inch bore. They set the cannon up outside Lincoln's gate and fired a thirteen gun salute. "As soon as the salute had been fired the captain of the squad went up to Mr. Lincoln and after shaking hands with him and receiving thanks for the honor conferred, asked him if he would name the gun."[27]

"Mr. Lincoln laughed good naturedly and replied, 'Oh, I never could name anything. Mary had to name all the children.'" The captain asked if they could name the gun after Mary Lincoln. "Mr. Lincoln waved his long right arm and with a hearty laugh said, 'Yes. Let it go that way.'"[28]

Smith said the little gun still worked and was well-neigh worshiped by second and third generations of Rosemond, Illinois, residents. "It bears the name of 'Mary Lincoln' engraved in letters of brass on its own proper person and once a year it is almost reverently fired, a single time, 'For Auld Lang Syne.'" There were other honors and accolades for Mary in Springfield but perhaps none were so touching as the cannon named in her honor.

Mary's cousin, Annie Parker Dickinson, whom they had recently visited in Cincinnati, wrote her after Lincoln's nomination, "You are an ambitious little woman and for many reasons I am delighted with your success."[29]

Leading newspaper and periodical reporters, editors and photographers descended on Springfield to interview Lincoln. Since Lincoln was not out on the campaign hustling, the media interviewed him in his temporary office in the Capitol or at their home, where Mary provided them with gracious hospitality. "Newspapers of the day seldom talked about the wives of politicians," White wrote, "but the *New York Tribune* departed from this tradition to offer a first assessment of Mary Lincoln on May 25, 1860. [Horace] Greeley's newspaper wrote that Mary Lincoln was 'amiable and accomplished ... vivacious and graceful.'"[30]

A reporter from the *New York Evening Post* wrote of Mary Lincoln, "Whatever awkwardness may be ascribed to her husband, there is none in her. She converses with freedom and grace, and is thoroughly *au fait* in all the little amenities of society." The profile described her Kentucky relatives, her education, her speaking French fluently, their son being at Harvard and her Presbyterian Church membership.[31]

In October 1860, Mary wrote Hannah Shearer to thank her for the beautiful collar she sent, and the letter drifted into politics. "You used to be so worried that I took politics so cooly you would not do so, were you to see me now. Whenever I *have time*, to think, my mind is sufficiently exercised for my comfort. Fortunately, the time is rapidly drawing to a close, a little more than two weeks, will decide the contest. I scarcely know, how I would bear up, under defeat. I trust that we will not have that trial. Penn. & Indiana have made us fair promises for Nov. & I trust other doubtless states will follow in their footsteps. You must think of us on election day, our friends will feel quite anxious for us, as we do ourselves."[32] Mary's statement that their operatives in Pennsylvania and Indiana, which voted Republican in the October state elections, promising a victory in those states indicated that she knew exactly what was going on in the campaign.

Due to her social relationship with Mary Fish Matteson, Mary may have discouraged Lincoln from using the canal scrip fraud as a campaign issue against Douglas by connecting him to the former governor. In September 1860, further irregularities arose in connection with Matteson and the canal scrip scandal. *The Illinois State Journal* editorialized numerous times on the scandal. Three weeks before the election, Lincoln prepared a timeline on the subject but never used it.[33]

"With her husband home, Mary acted as a consultant—not about issues, but about people," White wrote. "Mary long believed her husband was too trusting of others. She had strong feelings about his political colleagues. She did not like or trust Norman Judd. She relied on David Davis."[34]

Davis, however, saw no place for women in politics—they were to be seen, only occasionally, and never heard. After the convention, he wrote his wife, "We are all in the highest glee on act of the elections. Mr. Lincoln will evidently be elected the next Pres't." He described traveling to Springfield to celebrate the nomination with the Lincolns, Trumbull and Governor Corwin at a dinner Mary prepared. Although he admitted that he was never better entertained, he told his wife that Mary was still "not to my liking. I am in hopes that she will not give her husband any trouble." He described her as being in high feathers.[35]

If Davis was referring to her gown, it was a garment she either sewed with her fingers or was made by a local dressmaker. If he intended his remarks to be a criticism of her joining the political conversation around the dinner table, that was something she had done practically all her life. Mary was who she was and changing her personality to suit David Davis's idea of a political wife was not going to happen. However, her shrewd political mind recognized that Davis was critical to her husband's election and she knew it would not be wise to pick a fight with him.

"From May through November 1860, Mary was with Abraham nearly every day, expressing her opinions and counting herself as his chief advisor," White wrote. "It was one of their longest periods together."[36]

It may have been one of their happiest times. After dining with Mary, Willie and Tad on election night, Lincoln returned to the statehouse around 7 p.m. Two hours later, along with Davis and other supporters, he went to the telegraph office to await the election results. With the returns in, they walked over to Watson's Confectionery, where Mary and a group of Republican women had prepared a victory supper, and was greeted with "How do you do, Mr. President!" Lincoln exclaimed, "Mary, Mary, we are elected!"[37]

And, elected they were. The popular vote was 1,865,908 for Lincoln; 1,380,202 for Douglas, the Democrat; 848,019 for the Southern Democrat John Breckinridge, and 590,901 for John Bell of the Constitutional Union Party. Lincoln's plurality over Douglas was 485,706.[38]

The Kansas Chief in White Cloud ran a headline that said, "Whoop-ee," over an illustration of an American flag and a cannon being fired. "We have glorious tidings to provide that Lincoln and Hamlin [Hannibal] are out next president and vice-president by an overwhelming majority," the article read.[39]

Mary and Abraham Lincoln were deluged with congratulations from family, friends and political well-wishers as well as those seeking appointments. They were also showered by gifts from well-wishers and those looking for favors. "Well, wife," Lincoln is supposed to have said, "there is one thing likely to come out of this scrape anyhow. We are going to have some new clothes." The *New York Herald* questioned the propriety of Lincoln receiving $200 for the Cooper Institute speech. He explained, in an April 6, 1860, letter to Cornelius F. McNeill, an attorney and editor of the *Middleport Press*, that—due to arrangements being changed—he was not aware before the event that the Cooper Institute charged for his speech. "They took in more than twice $200," Lincoln said. "I have made this explanation to you as a friend; but I wish no explanation made to our enemies. What they want is a squabble and a fuss; and they can have if we explain; and they cannot have it if we don't."[40]

Joshua Speed wrote Lincoln on November 14 to congratulate him and suggested they meet. "I think I can impart to you some valuable information as to men and public sentiment here which may be valuable." Lincoln replied four days later, "I shall be in Chicago Thursday the 22nd. Inst. and one or two succeeding days. Could you not meet me there? Mary thinks of going with me; and therefore I suggest that Mrs. S. accompany you." Lincoln had already planned to meet Hamlin in Chicago.[41] He cautioned Speed, "Please let this be private, as I prefer a very great crowd should not gather in Chicago."[42] That was not going to happen.

Lincoln purchased tickets for the November 21, 1860, trip on the Chicago, Alton and St. Louis Railroad for himself, Mary and Lyman and Julia Trumbull in a regular train car.[43] Mary was speaking to Julia Trumbull because now her husband held the higher office.

Mary and Fannie Speed did a sight-seeing tour of Chicago while Lincoln, Trumbull, Speed and Hamlin held their meetings. A New York newspaper reported Mary had a wonderful time visiting the Wigwam. She also visited the custom house, federal courthouse and post office housed in the recently completed massive five-story stone building the *Chicago Tribune* called the "Granite Octopus."[44]

The trip to Chicago gave Mary a better idea of the current fashions for women. It was one thing to look at patterns in *Goody's* and quite another to see and examine the fabrics as well as the finished product in person. Although she was a clever seamstress and could afford to hire a Springfield dressmaker, those gowns would have certainly been inappropriate for the president's wife in the Executive Mansion and for all the entertaining she was expected to do. In January 1861, Mary along with Bob, New Hampshire Representative Amos Tuck and her brother-in-law, Clark M. Smith, married to her sister, Ann, boarded the train for a shopping excursion to New York City. Smith owned a mercantile establishment in Springfield and regularly made buying trips to the city. She certainly would not have taken the trip without her husband's approval.

But, she did more in New York than just shop. While in the city, she attended teas, receptions, the theater and spoke her mind. Her political statements were most disturbing to men such as Herman Kreisman, editor of the *Illinois Staats Zeitung*. Kreisman, who was in Washington at the time of her trip, was greatly offended not only by Mary's traveling to New York but the fact that she had opinions and expressed them. "Mrs. Lincoln's journey is considered very much out of place, the idea of a president's wife kiting about the country and holding levees at which she indulges in a multitude of silly speeches is looked upon as very shocking," he wrote newsman Charles Ray.[45]

Kreisman's criticism of Mary's New York trip had more to do with what he saw as her audacity to speak out on public issues—something nineteenth women were not supposed to do. Kreisman's censure of Mary was just the beginning of what she could expect in Washington.

Mary knew how to manage money. She had been running her household for nineteen years on a limited budget. Her father was a banker as well as a businessman and not all the after dinner discussions she heard in their home were about politics. Todd entertained his business associates as well as political friends. Mary listened and learned. She held on to the property her father gave her for twelve years before selling it only to pay for enlarging their home. If Mary had been one to squander money, her land would have been sold much earlier.

Lincoln was able to stay on the campaign trail with Douglas due in a large part to Mary's management of their finances. "With the children and household affairs and Lincoln's personal wants to be provided for, she was the managing partner who kept the expense accounts within the limits which their moderate budget placed at her disposal," Henry Rankin wrote.[46] "Lincoln himself accorded her both before and after the Douglas debates unstinted appreciation for her efficiency in all home and financial matters, as well as in forecasting the progress of political affairs."

Considering their previous, and successful, fiscal partnership, it would be irresponsible to assume Mary and Lincoln did not discuss the shopping trip to New York and decide on her allotted expenditures. That is making an assumption of gigantic proportions. To presume that she bought all her purchases on credit is a leap of gargantuan scope. Yet, that is what some historians and authors have done for decades without citing any financial records, receipts or a close examination of the Lincolns' income.

"Little is known of her doings, although a great deal has been written of the shopping trip since 1932, when Dr. W. A. Evans published his astute psychological study, *Mrs. Abraham Lincoln: A Study of Her Personality*," Daniel Mark Epstein wrote in his 2008 book, *The Lincolns: Portrait of a Marriage*:

Dr. Evans argues that "in January 1861 there occurred the first act of Mrs. Lincoln indicating that she might not be mentally 'right.' Taking advantage of her financial credit as the President's wife, under her brother-in-law's guidance, she shopped at the finest stores and at A. T. Stuarts' the 'Marble Palace' on Broadway. She purchased not only the finest clothes and jewelry for herself but also articles for the White House (Executive Mansion) such as lace curtains. Newspapers of the period confirm this fact, including *The Cleveland Herald* of January 10, that Mrs. Lincoln was bound for a 'few days stay to make purchases for the White House.'"[47]

"She took advantage of an unlimited line of credit and overspent; her purchases of silk, jewelry and lace were lavish and inappropriate as if driven by what is now recognized as clinical mania," Epstein continued citing Evans' book.[48]

"In the latter part of January 1861," Evans wrote, "she and a party, of which her merchant brother-in-law, C. M. Smith, was one, went to New York to do some shopping. Mrs. Lincoln had sewed to some extent for herself and family, and she had employed the best dressmakers in Springfield; but she was now about to enter Washington social life and wanted a wardrobe befitting the occasion. A. T. Stewart and the other great New York merchants extended credit and courtesy to her as the president's wife. At this point is recorded her first evidence of poor judgment in money matters; the peculiar direction and bent of this error were later to become a quality of her insanity. She bought dress goods, particularly silks, and ornaments, and jewelry for her neck and ears, and used this newly acquired credit to the breaking point. Her purchase of lace curtains for the White House (Executive Mansion) is not easily understood."[49]

Evans, citing no evidence of examining any receipts, bills or invoices for Mary's purchases, had no knowledge of how she paid for her purchases. Evans' assumptions, without documentation, about how the Lincolns paid for Mary's purchases have been referenced by historians for eight decades. His words were nothing more than a precursor to the principal idea Evans wanted to make—that Mary Lincoln was insane.

Any president-elect's wife would have wanted to make a good impression in Washington, not just for herself but for her husband, and Mary Lincoln was no exception. Dolley Madison, whose first husband, John Todd, was a distant relative of Mary's, certainly subscribed to that theory. She ordered expensive, elegant gowns from Paris during the administration of James Madison, 1804–1817. She bought her wigs, hats and turbans in Philadelphia and New York.[50]

The Lincolns could have afforded for Mary to buy new clothes. In 1860, Lincoln's deposits, not necessarily all his earnings, totaled $4,680. In addition, he had $9,337 lent in notes, at ten percent interest, which he left with John Irwin when they moved to Washington. The 2012 value of the $4,680 in deposits was $133,000 on the basis of the historic standard of living. The economic status value of that amount was $1.69 million and the economic power value of the deposits was $16.9 million. Applying the same 2012 standards to the $9,337 in notes, not including any interest, was: historic standard of living, $266,000; economic status value, $3.38 million; economic power value, $33.7 million.[51]

Returning to Springfield, Mary and Lincoln were faced with the ordeal of not only packing for the family's trip to Washington but deciding which furnishings they wanted to ship, which pieces to sell and what they wanted to store. She was also contending with the continuing media presence and the political guests who came to their home to confer with Lincoln and had to be entertained. While cleaning out the household accumulation of their married life, Mary and Lincoln burned old letters and papers in the alley behind their house.

He gave away some and she kept a few. Lincoln left some of his letters and papers for safe-keeping in Springfield with Elizabeth Grimsley, another Todd Cousin. Mrs. Grimsley's maid mistook the documents for trash and burned most of them.[52]

During the confusion of packing, Lincoln looked for a quiet place to write his inaugural address. Clark M. Smith, his brother-in-law, offered him space on the third floor of his store.

Although Lincoln's inaugural was scheduled for March 4, 1861, the family planned to leave Springfield on February 11. Neither Mary nor Lincoln had much time to get everything done. Which of their furnishings they took to Washington was difficult to determine. That they probably took some furnishings was documented by the National Park Service's historic data on original furnishings of the Lincoln home. Lincoln gave Benjamin Bunch a two-drawer pedestal sewing table for his assistance in crating furniture.[53] It was possible that the furniture was crated for local storage.

The Lincolns hosted their final social event in their Springfield home before moving into the Chenery House. "The first levee given by the president elect took place last evening at his own residence in this city and it was a grand outpouring of citizens and strangers together with the members of the Legislature," Helm wrote, quoting the *Missouri Democrat* of February 6. "Mr. Lincoln threw open his house for a general reception of all the people who felt disposed to give him and his Lady a parting call. The levee lasted from seven until twelve o'clock in the evening and the house was thronged by thousands up to the latest hour."[54]

On February 9, two days before their departure, Lincoln sold the following furnishings to Samuel H. Melvin, a druggist and neighbor of the Lincolns. The items included six chairs for $6; one spring mattress, $26; one wardrobe, $20; one whatnot, $10; one stand, $1.50; nine and one-half yards stair carpeting, four comforters, $8, for a total of $82.20. Lincoln signed the receipt.[55]

Some of the furnishings the Lincolns sold to Lucian Tilton, president of the Wabash Railroad, who rented their home for $350 a year. Included in that sale was the massive secretary which served as Lincoln's desk in the back parlor. That piece of furniture was made famous in a line drawing that appeared in *Frank Leslie's Illustrated Newspaper* after Lincoln was nominated. Apparently, the secretary was destroyed after the Tiltons moved to Chicago and lost their home in the fire of 1871.[56]

A train journey from Springfield to Washington in 1861 was a two day trip. However, Lincoln wanted to broaden his political base by meeting people along the way and gauging the mood of that part of the country. The inaugural train schedule—covering 1,904 miles, through eighty-four cities and towns in eight states on eighteen different railroads over twelve days—was printed in newspapers to attract crowds. While that publicity certainly gathered more people at the train stops, it also presented an increased danger of assassination. For more than two months, Lincoln and his family had been receiving death threats. Before Christmas, Mary received a sketch of Lincoln with a noose around his neck, his feet chained and his body tarred with feathers. Even little Tad was included in the threats.[57]

Lincoln was accompanied on the train—that included an engine, tender, baggage car and three (sometimes four) passenger cars—from Springfield by William M. Wallace, his brother-in-law; John G. Nicolay and John Hay, his secretaries; friends Norman Judge, David Davis, Ward Hill Lamon, O. H. Browning; Bob Lincoln and his friends George C. Latham; J. M. Burgess; Major D. Hunter, U.S. Army, Cols. E. V. Sumner and E. E. Ellsworth, U.S. Army; Capt. G. W. Hazzard; William S. Wood, supervisor of the travel arrangements and a former operative of New York politician Thurlow Weed; and Burnett Forbes, his assistant.[58]

At this stage in the Lincolns' lives, his law partner, William H. Herndon, all but disappeared. Herndon, however, re-appeared in Mary's life with a vengeance after Lincoln was killed in 1865. Herndon apparently was not in the crowd at the station the morning the inaugural train left. Daniel Mark Epstein wrote of the event, "He recalled his bibulous, loquacious law partner, Billy Herndon, whose indiscretions had cost him an invitation to Washington, and whose wounded pride now distanced him from the crowd that stood on the cinder and gravel track in the rain."[59] Epstein did not explain just what those indiscretions were. After the inauguration, there are only two short correspondences from Lincoln to Herndon, which appeared in the eight-volume *Collected Works of Abraham Lincoln.*[60]

Lincoln had not planned to make a speech before leaving Springfield on February 11, but the crowd was composed of people he had known for most of his life. It turned out to be a tearful occasion for both Lincoln and the crowd.

> My friends, no one, not in my situation, can appreciate my feeling of sadness at this parting. To this place and the kindness of these people, I owe every thing. Here I have lived a quarter of a century, and have passed from a young to an old man. Here my children have been born and one is buried. I now leave, not knowing when, or whether ever, I may return, with a task before me greater than that which rested upon Washington. Without the assistance of that Divine Being, who ever attended him, I cannot succeed. With that assistance I cannot fail. Trusting in Him, who can go with me, and remain with you and be every where for good, let us confidently hope that all will yet be well. To His care commending you, as I hope in your prayers you will commend me, I bid you an affectionate farewell.[61]

"Eight o'clock in the morning being an inconvenient hour, Mrs. Lincoln had decided to take a later train and join the presidential party in Indianapolis, where they were to stay the first night," Helm wrote. "As the special train conveying the presidential party pulled out of Springfield, Mary was standing on the platform, in the midst of friends, waving him a farewell." Mary, Willie, Tad and a nurse joined the inaugural train later that day in Indianapolis, where Gov. Oliver Morton, 20,000 state legislators, public employees, soldiers, firemen and citizens staged a procession to greet him.[62]

The next morning, the Lincolns left Indianapolis and boarded their train for Cincinnati for what they were going to find at every stop. Governors and mayors attempted to out-do each other in bringing out the crowds with parades, banquets and receptions and attaching themselves to the president-elect for hopeful political benefits.

In Cincinnati, Lincoln rode through the streets in an open carriage drawn by six white horses caparisoned in the national colors. As the parade went down Vine Street, a large German man, sitting on a huge beer barrel with a glass of lager in his hand, called out to Lincoln, "God be with you, enforce the laws and save our country. Here's your health."[63]

Mary reminded Lincoln that it was his birthday. Wishing him a happy birthday, as she had done each year since they had been married, she said, "I am so glad you have a birthday. I feel so grateful to your mother."[64]

On February 15, at Alliance, Ohio, the celebration of Lincoln's arrival almost got out of control. An elegant dinner was given by John G. McCullough, president of the Chicago and Erie Railroad. During the celebration, cannon salutes were being fired. A piece of shot smashed through the window, near were Mary Lincoln had sat during the dinner.[65]

A crowd of 60,000 greeted Lincoln in Columbus, Ohio. Crowds in Ashtabula, Ohio, called for Mary to make an appearance. Lincoln excused her by saying that he "Should hardly hope to induce her to appear, as he had always found it very difficult to make her do what she did not want to do." Former President Millard Fillmore and 10,000 supporters greeted Lincoln in Buffalo. But, Albany organizers for the inaugural train's stop there were embarrassed when crowd control broke down and Lincoln was forced to wait for a contingent of soldiers, who used their rifle butts to clear the unruly throng. In addition, two groups of state legislators created another ruckus with their public bickering.[66]

Newspaper reporters on the train began to talk about Lincoln's clothes—his overcoat was thin and his hat weather-beaten. Mary prepared for this situation on her January shopping trip to New York a month earlier. When the train arrived in Buffalo, Mary asked William Johnson, who had been acting as Lincoln's valet, to bring some boxes from the baggage car. Inside those boxes were an elegant broadcloth overcoat and a new hat for her husband.[67]

An estimated 250,000 people lined the streets to watch the Lincolns' eleven-carriage procession to the Astor House in New York City, where they were greeted by William Cullen Bryant on February 20. That day, Mary and the boys visited P. T. Barnum's museum. That evening, Mary and Lincoln attended a new Verdi opera, *A Masked Ball*, at the Academy of Music. After the first act, the cast and crowd arose and sang the "Star Spangled Banner" in honor of their guests. Before leaving the next day, Lincoln told Mayor Fernando Wood, "There is nothing that can ever bring me willingly to consent to the destruction of this Union." Before leaving City Hall, Lincoln had a meeting with Joshua Dewey, 94, who had voted in every presidential election since George Washington's.[68]

While in New York, Mary held a reception for 500 at the Astor House Hotel's ladies' parlor on February 20. Astor House, not particularly outstanding from the exterior, or as one observer said, "Only a small temple front on the Broadway side, with two Doric columns and a precisely carved anthemion crest, distinguished Astor's 309 rooms project from a government warehouse." The central courtyard, however, was quite elegant, having been covered by a cast-iron and glass roof. Mary wore a steel-colored gown trimmed with box quilting and fine lace. A neat lace point collar was secured by a fine diamond broach and she wore matching diamond earrings.[69]

In Philadelphia on February 21, 100,000 enthusiastic supporters gathered to hear Lincoln speak from the Continental Hotel. The Lincolns' former neighbors, John and Hannah Shearer, joined the train and rode with them from Philadelphia to Harrisburg. An observer was quoted as saying, "We are confident that not one person in the crowd below heard one word of Lincoln's speech." That evening Frederick W. Seward arrived from Washington with a message from his father, Sen. William Seward that there was a plot to assassinate Lincoln when his train stopped in Baltimore.[70]

Young Seward was carrying intelligence put together by Allen Pinkerton, founder of the Pinkerton National Detective Agency, who had been retained by Philadelphia, Wilmington and Baltimore Railroad president Samuel Morse Felton to investigate rumors that rabid secessionists were planning to burn bridges in Baltimore, sink the Susquehanna River train ferry and attempt to assassinate Lincoln. Lamon urged Lincoln to leave Philadelphia immediately. Lincoln initially refused but eventually agreed to take another route into Washington, but not before he raised a new American flag over Independence Hall. Kansas had been admitted to the Union as the thirty-fourth state three weeks earlier.[71]

Pinkerton was initially convinced that Cipriano Ferrandini, a Baltimore barber of Corsican descent, was putting together a ring of southern sympathizers for the express purpose of assassinating Lincoln in Baltimore. His assessment came from one of his operatives who supposedly infiltrated Ferrandini's group of southern supporters. Ferrandini was never arrested, charged or prosecuted. However, he had appear before the Congressional Committee of Five in late January and asserted his support for the south. The committee was created in early January when Pennsylvania Republican Representative Thaddeus Stevens suggested the House investigate treason against the Union after President James Buchanan confessed the sectional crisis was beyond his control and washed his hands of the problem.[72]

Regardless of the advice given by his security team, Lincoln told Mary of their plan and swore her to secrecy. She was extremely upset. Telegraph service to Baltimore was cut off to prevent any communication about his movements. Lincoln, after making his last scheduled appearance at Harrisburg, boarded a special train to West Philadelphia, where Pinkerton was waiting in a carriage to take Lincoln to the yards of the Philadelphia, Wilmington and Baltimore Railroad, where a sleeping car was waiting for him. When the PWB train arrived in Baltimore, the sleeping car was hooked to another train and Lincoln arrived in Washington around 6:00 a.m.[73]

Lincoln telegraphed Mary in Harrisburg that had he arrived safely in Washington, where he was met by a good friend, Illinois Congressman Eli Washburne, who took him to the Willard.[74] Mary Lincoln and family left Harrisburg on the inaugural train at 9 a.m., as scheduled.[75]

Maryland State Archivist Edward C. Papenfuse wrote that the details surrounding how Mrs. Lincoln and the children were guarded had been overlooked in the partisan debate over the Baltimore plot. He pointed out that Marshall George P. Kane, chief of the Baltimore police force, had a plan for their safety and it was implemented.

> Mrs. Lincoln and the Children did not arrive at the Calvert Street Station to be greeted by a hostile crowd. There was a hostile crowd there all right, as the *New York Times* correspondent pointed out, but Mrs. Lincoln and the children were let out of the train where the tracks crossed Charles Street above the Washington Monument and were whisked to Democrat John Gittings mansion on Mount Vernon Street, where they were treated to a quiet, private dinner, before being taken to Camden Station much later that afternoon. Whether or not they encountered some unpleasantness at Camden Station is a matter of debate, but Lincoln did not abandon his family to an unprotected journey through a raucous Baltimore. Marshall Kane, southern sympathizer and future Confederate businessman who many have met with John Wilkes Booth in Canada in 1864, did his job well on behalf of Mary Todd and the children.[76]

They arrived in Washington around 4 p.m. and were met at the station by Seward and Washburne, who accompanied them to the Willard.[77]

The president-elect on his first day in Washington, February 23, had an full schedule meeting with government officials. He asked to meet with the Illinois delegation, specifically Stephen Douglas, at 4 o'clock at the Willard. "Lincoln was shocked at Douglas' appearance," White wrote. "He did not look well. Lincoln surmised the strain of constant campaigning had taken its toll. He had heard that Douglas was drinking too much. On this afternoon, Lincoln expressed his delight to see his old Illinois competitor. The two men shared more in common than the casual observer might have thought. They both believed in the indivisibility of the Union. A newspaper correspondent reported a 'particularly pleasant' meeting between the two leaders. Later in the day, Adele Douglas, 'with gracious courtesy,' called on Mary Lincoln."[78]

On the evening of February 25, 1861, Mary held her first public reception at the Willard

Hotel. It was, according to one of Lincoln's secretaries, William O. Stoddard, "very promiscuously attended."[79]

Originally, a private home had been rented for the Lincolns and their entourage but they chose to stay at Willard Hotel. Lincoln was familiar with the hotel when he was a member of President Zachery Taylor's inaugural committee. Expanded to ten stories in 1858, the rather non-descript, architecturally speaking, Willard was the gathering place for government officials, lobbyists, reporters and job-seekers. Writer Nathaniel Hawthorn described the Willard as the city's alternative center of power.[80]

The hotel was so overwhelmed with requests for rooms that the 465 mattresses laid out in the corridors and public areas were inadequate. John Nicolay, one of Lincoln's secretaries who came from Springfield, complained that the hotel had sorry accommodations except for the Lincoln's suite. Lincoln was without his house shoes and that created a problem for his perpetually aching feet. Henry Willard could find no house shoes big enough for Lincoln's feet. Then, he remembered his wife had knitted a pair of house shoes for her grandfather, who had big feet. Lincoln gratefully used the house shoes and returned them with a note of thanks.[81]

Three days before the inauguration, Mary, accompanied by Sarah B. McLean, wife of Supreme Court Justice John McLean, called on Harriet Lane, President Buchanan's niece and hostess, at the Executive Mansion.[82]

CHAPTER 10

Inauguration

Inauguration Day, March 4, 1861, dawned gray and gloomy over Washington.

Lincoln, after sharing a draft of his inaugural address with Mary the evening before, added the finishing touches to his speech. Mary looked out the window at the teeming mass of 30,000 there to see and hear her husband, the president. Many of them, like the Lincolns, were from the West, which at that time were states east of the Mississippi River. Mixed with the visitors were soldiers on horseback patrolling intersections, riflemen on rooftops of buildings along Pennsylvania Avenue, snipers stationed at windows in the Capitol and sharpshooters concealed under the inauguration stand. Marching units were assembling, along with 100 parade marshals, to accompany their carriages from the Willard to the Capitol.[1]

It was the day that each, in their own way, had been working toward for decades. Now, it belonged to them and those who worked to help them. Mary and Lincoln were too involved in the details of the day to talk about the long political trail, the victories and the defeats that brought them to Washington. Lincoln, and perhaps Mary, thought of those who, through petty political avariciousness, would attempt to derail their agenda. Circumstances surrounding the occasion were not what they would have chosen: seven states had already seceded; Fort Sumter, in South Carolina, was in danger of being captured; there were more threats on Lincoln's life, and rumors of an attack on Washington.[2]

The nation was on the brink of disaster.

Lincoln had spent most of his time prior to the inauguration selecting his cabinet with the consultation from his Illinois cadre of advisors and others whose character he respected. While desirous of making himself available to the people, he, at times, became bogged down with those seeking only federal jobs. Soon after the election, Lincoln wrote down the name of seven men under consideration for cabinet appointments. His list included William Seward, Salmon Chase, Edward Bates, Gideon Wells, William Dayton, Norman Judd and Montgomery Blair.[3]

Mary was very much aware of the men under consideration for the cabinet. While in New York in January, she wrote David Davis, who was working with Lincoln, to protest Norman Judd's inclusion in the cabinet, although he had been a major player in Lincoln receiving the nomination instead of Seward or Chase.

> Perhaps you think it is no affair of *mine*, yet I see it, almost daily mentioned in the Herald, that *Judd* & some *few* Northern friends, are *urging the former's* claim to a cabinet appointment. *Judd* would cause trouble & distractions, & if Wall Street testifies correctly, his business transactions have not always borne inspection. I heard the report, discussed at the table this morning, by persons who did not know who was near, a party of gentlemen, evidently strong Republicans, they were laughing at the idea of *Judd*, being in any way connected with the Cabinet in *these times*

when honesty in high places is so important. Mr. Lincoln's great attachment for you, is my present reason for writing. I know, a word from you, will have much effect, for the good of the country and Mr. Lincoln's future reputation, I believe you will speak to him on this subject & urge him not to give him so responsible a place. It is strange, how little delicacy these Chicago men have. I know, I can rely on what I have written to you, to be kept private. If you consider me intrusive, please excuse me, our country, just now, is above all.[4]

Judd was not included in the cabinet. Instead, he was appointed minister to Berlin.[5]

Lincoln's final selections were William H. Seward, from New York, secretary of state; Salmon Chase, from Ohio, secretary of the treasury; Simon Cameron, from Pennsylvania, secretary of war; Gideon Wells, from Connecticut, secretary of the Navy; Caleb B. Smith, from Indiana, secretary of the interior; Edward Bates, from Missouri, attorney general, and Montgomery Blair, from Maryland, postmaster general.[6]

Seward and his alter ego, New York political boss and newspaper editor Thurlow Weed, were still reeling from the shock of losing the nomination to Lincoln the previous November. In attempting to recover their loss, they decided Lincoln would not only be a weak president but one they could dominate. Weed came to Washington to assist Seward in, among other things, attempting to sway Lincoln's selection of cabinet members, Chase in particular. Their attempted manipulations were not lost on the president-elect. On Saturday, March 2, before the inauguration, Seward wrote Lincoln asking him to withdraw his name for the position of secretary of state, a position he had accepted in December. Seward wrote, "Circumstances which have occurred since I expressed to you in December last my willingness to accept the office of Secretary of State seem to me to render it my duty to ask leave to withdraw that consent."[7]

Lincoln gave a dinner at the Willard on Sunday, March 3, for Seward, Chase, Wells, Blair, Cameron, Smith and Bates. Whatever conversations that took place at the dinner, Seward got the message. Lincoln wrote Seward on the morning of the inauguration acknowledging receipt of his withdrawal letter. "It is the subject of most painful solicitude with me; and I feel constrained to beg that you will countermand the withdrawal. The public interest I think, demands that you should; and my personal feelings are deeply inlisted in the same direction." Lincoln asked for his answer by 9 a.m., the next day.[8]

When Lincoln left the hotel to ride in the Inaugural parade to the Capitol with Buchanan, he was dressed in a new black suit provided by Titsworth and Brothers of Chicago, white shirt, a tall black hat, black boots and a black cravat. He refused a closed conveyance and chose an open four-seat carriage. Soldiers were grouped so closely around the carriage that Lincoln was hardly visible. Buchanan was quoted as telling Lincoln, "If you are as happy in entering the White House [Executive Mansion] as I shall feel on returning to Wheatland you are a happy man."[9]

The procession for the inaugural parade formed in front of City Hall at 9 a.m., and at 11 a.m., moved up Louisiana Avenue and halted on Pennsylvania Avenue at the Willard Hotel, where Buchanan, Lincoln and his entourage waited. "The entire column will, under orders, left face, and the military will present arms," Marshal-in-chief Benjamin B. French advised in the March 2 issue of the *Washington Star*. Had there been an assassination plot, French laid out a clear path in the newspaper article. "The President and President-elect will then be received into the line and the column will, under orders, right face, and move, escorting them to the Capitol."[10]

The open carriage was protected by marshals for the District of Columbia. Following the carriage was the Senate Committee on Arrangements, Buchanan and Lincoln's private secretaries, former presidents, the judiciary, the Republican Association, the clergy, foreign ministers, the diplomatic corps, members of the House of Representatives past and present, former cabinet members, members of the Peace Congress, heads of bureaus, governors and former governors, Army, Navy, Marine Corps and militia in full uniform, Revolutionary and War of 1812 veterans and then local officials, students and civic groups. As soon as the ceremonies at the Capitol were over, Buchanan, the military, marshals and their aides escorted the president to the Executive Mansion.[11]

French was Clerk of the House of Representatives, 1843–1847, before the Lincolns arrived in Washington. Lincoln knew him as one constantly looking for government jobs. Almost immediately after the Inauguration, French began lobbying Lincoln for the job of Commissioner of Public Buildings, a position he held under President Franklin Pierce.[12]

Mary, their sons, members of her family and friends were in the diplomatic gallery of the Senate as Hannibal Hamlin took his oath as vice-president. They were seated on the platform along with Sen. Stephen A. Douglas, just behind Buchanan, Chief Justice Roger B. Taney, who would administer the presidential oath, and the president-elect. Unable to find a place for his hat, Lincoln accepted Douglas' offer to hold it. "If I cannot be president, I can at least be his hat bearer," Elizabeth Grimsley quoted Douglas as saying. Lincoln chose his close friend and former colleague from the Eighth Circuit, Oregon Senator Edward D. Baker, to introduce him.[13]

As Baker introduced Lincoln, the weather turned bright and clear.

The North was not entirely pleased with Lincoln's inaugural speech, although he made it clear he intended to preserve the Union. There was little in it beyond an olive branch to make the South happy. Montgomery C. Meigs, the supervising engineer in the Capitol expansion and later quartermaster general of the Union Army, wrote his brother, John, of his impression of the speech. "It was a noble speech ... delivered with a serious and solemn emphasis.... No time was wasted in generalities or platitudes ... and no one could doubt that he meant what he said.... The disease of the body politic was analysed [*sic*], its character & its remedy pointed out, & each sentence fell like a sledge hammer driving in the nails which maintain the states."[14]

A *New York Times* reporter, observing Buchanan during Lincoln's speech, wrote, "Mr. Buchanan sighed audibly and frequently but whether from upon reflection of the failures of his administration, I can't say."[15]

Buchanan accompanied the Lincolns and entourage to "a rather dilapidated and wholly unattractive Executive Mansion," former Ohio Congressman Albert G. Riddle wrote. He said a visitor would have been "Struck by the bare, worn, soiled aspect of that part of the house devoted to the office of the executive, an aspect not unlike that presented by 'the breaking up of hard winter' about a desolated farmstead."[16]

Harriet Lane planned a dinner at the Executive Mansion for the Lincolns and their guests, seventeen in all, before they attended the inaugural ball, renamed the Union Ball. Elizabeth Grimsley, Mary's cousin, would have been less complimentary of Harriet Lane if she had known Buchanan's niece's true feelings about the Lincolns and their friends. Her description of the new occupants of the residence was a harbinger of the social attitude Mary Lincoln would receive in Washington. The new president, Harriet Lane wrote Sophie Plitt, was like the awkward Irish doorman they had. "Mrs. Lincoln," she continued, "is awfully *western*, loud and unrefined."[17]

Mary Lincoln was undoubtedly from the West—by way of the South, she could be loud if the occasion called for it, but she certainly was not unrefined. Nobody questioned that after the Union Ball.

However, the Lincolns' first dinner at the Executive Mansion was rudely interrupted by a visiting group of New Yorkers asking to speak with the president. Perhaps it was a coincidence the men from Seward's home state appeared at the dinner hour to lobby for Lincoln to allow the New Yorker to have a part in selecting cabinet members. The *New York Times* estimated the size of the New York delegation at 500. The *Washington Star* said the crowd numbered around 1,000.[18]

"May I hope that the public expression which I have this day given my sentiments, may have contributed in some degree to your happiness," Lincoln told them. "As far as I am concerned, the loyal citizens of every state, and of every section, shall have no cause to feel any other sentiment. As towards the disaffected portion of our fellow-citizens, I will say, as every good man throughout the country must feel, that there will be more rejoicing over one sheep that is lost and is found, than over ninety-nine which have gone not astray. And now, my friends, as I have risen from the dinner-table to see you, you will excuse me for the brevity of my remarks, and permit me again to thank you heartily, and cordially, for this pleasant visit, as I rejoin those who await my return."[19]

"The Mansion was in a perfect state of readiness for the incomers," Elizabeth Grimsley gushed over the dinner. "A competent chef, with efficient butler and waiters, under the direction of the accomplished Miss Lane, had an elegant dinner prepared, and it is needless to say, after the excitement and the fatigue of the day, it was most thoroughly appreciated."[20]

The Union Ball was held in a hastily constructed wood building at the back of City Hall. The temporary pavilion was called "Aladdin's Palace" because the walls were heavily decorated with bunting, muslin, banners and shields. Three enormous gas-lit chandeliers provided illumination. The Marine Corps Band furnished the music. Around 11 p.m. the Lincolns and their guests arrived. The president was accompanied by Vice-President Hamlin and Senator Henry Anthony from Rhode Island. Mary, to everybody's surprise, came in on the arm of Sen. Stephen Douglas. Sen. Edward Baker escorted Mrs. Hamlin. "They walked around the room, receiving the congratulations of the assembly and afterwards took seats at the upper end of the room, where sofas had been placed for them," the *Washington Star* reported.[21]

Mary was indeed elegant in a blue watered silk gown trimmed with Alençon lace. She wore the jewelry that Lincoln had purchased for her from Tiffany and Company while they were in New York: a pearl necklace, earrings, broach and bracelets. He was said to have paid $530 for the set of jewelry. A line drawing of Mary in the dress and jewelry indicated a headpiece of flowers.[22]

Any criticism about Mary's attire was silenced by the description of a New York woman's gown and jewelry. "Mrs. Drake Mills was gorgeously attired in two thousand dollars' worth of lace and twenty thousand dollars' worth of diamonds," the *New York Times* reported.[23] Mrs. Mills had her diamonds but Mary Lincoln was the wife of the president of the United States. She was not a visitor to Washington; she was living out her childhood dream being in the Executive Mansion.

The dancing began with Mary and Douglas dancing the quadrille, as they had done back in Illinois during their younger years. About an hour after the midnight supper, Lincoln returned to the Executive Mansion, where a message awaited him from Major Robert Anderson, commander of Fort Sumter, saying his provisions would be exhausted before any relief could be sent.[24]

Mary remained at the Union Ball for some time after her husband left. "We learn that the ball was a success, fiscally, a fact upon which the committee of arrangements may be congratulated," the *Washington Star* reported.[25]

When Mary and Elizabeth Grimsley took a tour of the Executive Mansion the morning after the Union Ball, they discovered what Riddle was talking about. "And, the tour of observation was a disappointing one," Elizabeth Grimsley wrote, "as the only elegance of the house was concentrated on the East, Blue and Red rooms, while the family apartments were in a deplorably shabby condition as to furniture, (which looked as if it had been brought in by the first president), although succeeding housekeepers had taxed their ingenuity and patience to make it presentable."[26]

George Washington never lived in the Executive Mansion and, if any of the furnishings he bought for the earlier official residences in New York or Philadelphia ever made it to Washington, they were probably gone by the time the Lincolns arrived. Since Washington declined an official salary, Congress granted him an expense allowance of $25,000, some of which he used to buy furniture.[27]

Washington, 1789–1797, was closely associated with the mansion's origins. He selected an architect, Pierre Charles L'Enfant, but Secretary of State Thomas Jefferson suggested a competition be held for architectural designs for the building. James Hoban, an Irish architect, was chosen. The cornerstone of the President's House, as it was then called, was laid in 1792, and construction was not finished for eight years.[28]

John Adams, 1797–1801, who had been Washington's vice-president, was the first to occupy the President's House. Adams and his wife, Abigail, moved in before the residence was finished. Congress appropriated $15,000 to furnish the house. That was the first of the four-year stipends given each president specifically for furnishings. In a pique because he was denied a second term, Adams left the President's House before Jefferson, 1801–1809, was inaugurated, taking his own furnishings and personal servants with him. It was a few weeks before Jefferson could move into the residence.[29]

Regardless of the condition of the Executive Mansion, Mary was not moving into a partially-finished house or one without, for the most part, any furnishings at all. The state rooms, while in better shape than the private quarters, were not adequate considering how much money Harriet Lane had spent on refurbishing during the Buchanan Administration. Congress appropriated $20,000 for furnishings at the beginning of Buchanan's term. Harriett Lane, with the assistance of James B. Blake, who had replaced French as commissioner of public buildings, began a buying spree of carpets and furnishings. Blake, unable to control her expenditures, showed the furnishings accounts to Buchanan. There was $8,396.02 remaining in the fund when the president wrote his niece, "I wish you to consider this sum must serve our purposes until the end of my term." Somehow, Congress found an additional $12,000 for Harriet Lane to spend.[30]

Between Blake and Harriet, in the four years of the Buchanan administration 1856–1860, they managed to spend the Congressional furnishings appropriation of $20,000 plus the additional sum of $12,000, not including what was called annual repairs to the President's House that amounted to $49,905 for a total of $81,905. Also, $38,000 was spent on the stable and conservatory.[31]

In 1861, that was an enormous amount of money expended for a residence that was

Above, left: Mary in a formal gown with pearl jewelry circa 1864 (Brady-Handy Collection, Library of Congress). *Above, right:* Wearing the pearl jewelry her husband purchased for her from Tiffany's in New York in 1861, Mary Lincoln is shown wearing a band of flowers in her hair, which was a common fashion of the times. A congressman poked fun at her for wearing low cut gowns—which were never as revealing as Dolly Madison's—and having "flower pots" on her head (Library of Congress, Prints and Photographs Division). *Left:* Mary Lincoln seated in a chair in one of her earlier Mathew Brady photographs taken in Washington in 1861. Gracefully sitting in a chair wearing hoops was a very difficult task. In other photographs of her in ball gowns she appears to be more comfortable standing (Library of Congress, Prints and Photographs Division).

in deplorable condition, as numerous people described it. In 2012 dollars, the economic value of the $61,905 the Buchanan administration spent on the Executive Mansion was $211,000,000.[32] What happened to all that money? If the accounts of Grimsley and others who examined the building first hand, are accurate, it is difficult to believe that all that money was spent on the residence.

"The East Room had a faded and worn, untidy look in spite of its frescoing and its glittering chandeliers," wrote William Stoddard, one of Lincoln's secretaries who often worked with Mary. "Its paint and furniture require renewal, but so does everything else about the house, within and without." The basement, which contained the kitchen and lumber room, had the odor of a stale and unsuccessful hotel, Stoddard said, and "is perennially overrun with rats, mildew and foul smells."[33]

There was no time for Mary to do much more to the Executive Mansion than attempt to clean and spruce things up before they held their first reception on March 8. Seward, as Lincoln had said, "attempted to take the first trick" in the selection of the cabinet, and suggested that as secretary of state he should be the person to host the administration's first official social function. That was not going to happen with Mary Lincoln in the Executive Mansion. "There was some little discussion," Elizabeth Grimsley wrote, "from which it could perhaps be seen that Mr. Seward had even in so small a matter the same idea of taking precedence which he expressed as to a larger one in his famous letter of the same month." Mary insisted that the first entertainment should be hosted by the president and the matter was settled.[34]

"So dense was the pressure that hundreds, after Herculean efforts to worm their way through the throng, gave it up and went home without seeing the new president," the *Washington Star* reported of the Lincoln's first reception on March 8 at the Executive Mansion. "Captain Goddard was present with his police, regulating the insetting current as far as possible but not much could be done where the assault was so fierce and persistent. It would have facilitated ingress and egress much if the mode of letting out the crowd through one of the large windows in the East Room, sometimes adopted heretofore, had been followed."[35]

James B. Blake, commissioner of public buildings, had his hands full controlling the people who wanted to be presented to Mary Lincoln. Blake remained in his position for a few weeks with the new administration. Apparently, Mary was not as adept as moving people along as her husband but she gave a "smiling welcome to all comers." The newspaper reported that Lincoln, for two hours, "shook hands in right good earnest with all comers at the rate of twenty-five per minute, (as timed by a gentleman in his vicinity) or one thousand five hundred per hour." Mary tried to follow his example but was unsuccessful.[36]

Dressed in a bright crimson watered silk gown with a lace point cape, Mary again wore the pearl jewelry. She had red and white camellias in her hair. In the receiving line with Mary were her sister Elizabeth Edwards, in a brown satin brocade gown; her half-sister, Margaret Kellogg, attired in ashes-of-roses silk brocade; her niece, Elizabeth Edwards, who wore an embroidered needle-work gown; another niece, Julia Edwards Baker, who chose a lemon-colored watered silk gown, and Elizabeth Grimsley, who was dressed in a blue silk embroidered gown.[37]

The newspaper reported cabinet members, military leaders and other high-ranking government officials were in attendance except for Seward, who was "detained at home by illness."[38]

The reception was a grand affair, as described by the newspaper, which "certainly made many friends [for the Lincolns] last night among those not heretofore favorably inclined to them." Some of that good will eroded when no proper arrangements had been made for handling the guests' wraps, coats and hats. "The last scene of the levee was a tragic one. The mob of coats, hats and capes left in the hall had somehow got inextricably mixed up and misappropriated, and perhaps not one in ten of that large assemblage emerged with the same outer garments they wore on entering. Some thieves seem to have taken advantage of the opportunity to make a grand sweep, and a very good business they must have done. Some of the victims utterly refused to don the greasy, kinky apologies for hats left on hand, tied up their heads in handkerchiefs and so wended their way sulkily homeward."[39]

It was Nicolay and Hay's job to take care of the planning aspects and supervising of social events, including the proper management of guests' coats, wraps and hats.[40] Obviously they failed at their first undertaking, but they learned.

Beginning the next day, Mary began receiving guests at the Executive Mansion on Saturday mornings.[41]

During their first week in the Executive Mansion, Mary and Lincoln took separate visits to the Soldiers' Home, about three miles from the residence. Washington banker George Riggs built the "Corn Rigs" cottage as a summer retreat on his 250-acre estate in 1842. "The irregular shape of the house, its many gables, latticed windows and elaborate Gingerbread trim mark it as Gothic Revival," according to the National Park Service. In 1851, the federal government purchased the property as a home for disabled and retired Army veterans. The veterans moved into a large, new stone Gothic building nearby in 1857, and Buchanan used the thirty-four-room cottage his last two summers in office.[42]

Mary tucked the memory of the cottage away for future use as she launched into the busy social season. On March 28, the Lincolns gave their first formal dinner, in the State Dining Room, for his cabinet. It was an occasion marked by both social and political tension. Mary, however, found the time that day to write her friend, Hannah Shearer, whom she had not seen since the Shearers left the inaugural train in Pennsylvania. She apologized for not writing sooner, "If you were aware how much *every moment* is occupied, you would excuse me." Mary only gave a passing mention to the cabinet dinner that evening. "This is certainly a very charming spot & I have formed many delightful acquaintances. Every evening our *blue room* is filled with the elite of the land, last eve, we had about 40 to call in to see us *ladies*, from Vice P. [John] Breckinridge down."[43]

Mary did not mention to her friend any of her husband's personnel problems. Lincoln was assailed as much from within as from without. Thurlow Weed, Seward's mentor from New York, was attempting to gain control of patronage but lacked success due to the efforts of Chase, Wells and Blair. Seward had decided to make himself the premier of the cabinet while interfering with Wells' duties as secretary of the Navy and countermanding some of Lincoln's orders concerning Fort Sumter. At issue was whether to reinforce or evacuate Forts Sumter, in Charleston, South Carolina, and Pickens, built to defend Pensacola Bay, Florida. Seward told Lincoln that just one person in the cabinet should make decisions without any debate and he was available. Lincoln told Seward, without mincing words, that was the president's job and he would handle it. Lincoln was so exhausted in dealing with such subterfuge, while deeply concerned when and if the war would begin, that he keeled over. Mary saw that he was put to bed and she nursed him through one of his migraine headaches.[44]

Lincoln recovered enough to be his usual loquacious self. Before going in to dinner, Attorney General Bates let the president know he was not happy with one of Lincoln's judicial appointments. Irish-born journalist William H. Russell, Washington correspondent for *The Times* of London, was one of the dinner guests. Russell was amazed at the manner in which Lincoln handled Attorney General Bates' displeasure with one of his judicial appointments. "Come now Bates," Russell quoted Lincoln as saying,

> He's not half as bad as you think. Besides that, I must tell you, he did me a good turn long ago. When I took to the law, I was going to court one morning with some ten or twelve miles of bad road before me and I had no horse. The judge overtook me in his wagon. "Hollo, Lincoln! Are

you not going to the courthouse? Come on and I'll give you a seat." Well, I got in, and the judge went on reading his papers. Presently the wagon struck a stump on the side of the road; then it hopped off to the other. I looked out, and I saw the driver was jerking from side to side on his seat; so says I, "Judge, I think your coachman has been taking a little drop too much this morning." "Well I declare, Lincoln," said he, "I should not much wonder if you are right, for he has nearly upset me half-a-dozen times since starting." So, putting his head out of the window, he shouted, "Why you infernal scoundrel, you are drunk!" Upon which, pulling up his horses and turning around with great gravity, the coachman said, "By gorra! That's the first rightful decision you have given in the last twelve months."

With that, Russell observed, Lincoln turned and walked away from the stunned attorney general.[45]

"Every detail was formal, the men in black, the ladies in ball gowns with jewelry and flowers in their hair," White House historian William Seale wrote.

> At seven, they were joined by President and Mrs. Lincoln. John Nicolay made the necessary introductions. The Marine Band played as they marched to the State Dining Room where they took their prescribed places, according to Nicolay's seating chart, composed very carefully in conference with Secretary of State William Seward, showed black ink for men and red ink for women. Flowers and ferns were massed on the great gilded plateau, from the James Monroe administration, on the dining table. Gas and candle light illuminated the textures of mirrors, gilt, silver, crimson and white damask.[46]

The Lincoln seating charts survived, Seale said, and showed forty at a long rectangular table with the President and Mrs. Lincoln facing each other about half way down the table with his secretaries, Nicolay and Hay, at each end. "The president was always served first. No one was to rise from the table before the president, and guests were not free to depart from the house before the president retired."[47]

Elizabeth Grimsley said there were few women at the state dinner: Mrs. Frederick Seward, the secretary of state's daughter-in-law; Kate Chase, daughter of Secretary of the Treasury Salmon Chase; Mrs. Edward Bates, the attorney general's wife, and Mary's relatives, the Kellogs and Mrs. Grimsley.[48]

Elizabeth Grimsley wrote:

> By degrees we ceased to meet at our informal receptions the Maryland and Virginia families who had always held sway, and dominated Washington society. Easy, suave, charming in manner, descended from a long line of aristocratic families, accustomed to wealth and all the amenities of social life, and etiquette, they resented the introduction of these new elements, and withdrew, to go into the Confederacy, where all their sympathies centered. These were, in time, replaced by members of cultivated, refined intellectual and wealthy people from the Northern cities, and officers of the Army and Navy with their wives, these, with several ladies of the legation, notably Russian and Chilean with our many western friends, gave a new life to home parties.[49]

Her assessment of the Maryland and Virginia families and their attitudes toward Mary are enforced by observations Russell gathered from his time in Washington. The Irishman described Mary as being plump, middle-aged, plain and very well dressed. "Mrs. Lincoln struck me as being desirous of making herself agreeable and I own that I was agreeably disappointed as the Secessionists ladies at Washington had been amusing themselves by anecdotes [about Mary] which could have scarcely have been founded on fact."[50]

When Virginia left the Union on April 17, 1861, secessionists in Maryland cut telegraph lines, disrupted railroad traffic between Baltimore and the capital, and sunk ships in Chesapeake Bay, and there were not enough troops to protect the city should the Confederates invade. The majority of Union troops, between 16,000 and 17,000, were stationed west of the Mississippi.[51]

"History cannot tell of the great gloom over the city as we recognized the danger we were in," Elizabeth Grimsley wrote. "All the public buildings were barricaded and guarded by sentinels, no business transacted and no places of amusement were open, all strangers and visitors who could get away, hurried to a place of safety." Lincoln called for 75,000 troops and the most immediate to respond were from New York and Massachusetts, and they had difficulty getting through Baltimore to reach the Capitol. "Most anxiously did General Scott and Mr. Lincoln look for the promised relief, in the coming of the regiments detained in Baltimore, and more than once were heard to exclaim, 'Why don't they come?'"[52]

Mary's childhood friend, Cassius M. Clay, who made campaign speeches for Lincoln in Ohio, Indiana, Illinois, Wisconsin and Minnesota, was in Washington at that time for instructions for his ministerial appointment to Russia. He was appointed a major general by Cameron and Lincoln and gathered up clerks, shop owners and government officials for the Clay Battalion. They were assigned to guard the Navy Yard and the Long Bridge, a wooden span between the city and the Virginia shore. The Navy Yard had been abandoned by Commodore Franklin Buchanan, who deserted to join the Confederacy. Clay's counterpart, Gen. James H. Lane, a U.S. senator-elect, brought nearly 200 men from Kansas. Lane and his Frontier Guard were assigned to the Executive Mansion and bivouacked in the East Room. "When Clay started for the bridge," John Speer wrote, "a great crowd of rebels followed, hooting and yelling and crowding, until the insults became unbearable: when, suddenly, he gave the command: 'Halt! About–face! Ready!' He did not have to give the command to 'aim.' There was nobody to aim at. That voice of Clay's was worth a thousand men."[53]

Lane's Frontier Guard, Clay's Battalion and others miraculously bluffed the Confederates' efforts to seize the city until reinforcements arrived.

Mary, joined by her cousin and sons, cried tears of joy when they heard the Sixth Massachusetts Infantry, with bands playing and flags waving, arriving at the Executive Mansion. The troops were attacked by a mob in Baltimore and four soldiers were killed and several wounded, and nine protestors lost their lives. The injured soldiers were quartered in the Senate Chamber, where Clara Barton and other women cared for their wounds.[54]

Even with soldiers quartered in the Executive Mansion's East Room, Commissioner of Public Buildings James Blake, on April 25, requested six additional Colt pistols for the guards, saying the six they had were insufficient under the present circumstances.[55]

Aside from fearing for her children and herself, Mary was most concerned about her husband. April 1861 was a horrible month for the presidency. The Confederates captured Fort Sumter after a two day battle, April 12–14. Lincoln was working almost day and night. Mary was concerned about his health. If he ate breakfast at all, sometimes it was not until mid–morning. She decided to invite special friends to the Executive Mansion for breakfast and then sent word to Lincoln that they had company. On one occasion, Elizabeth Grimsley wrote, Lincoln came in when the gregarious Samuel Galloway, a former Ohio congressman, was the guest. She said Lincoln came in looking sad and harassed and said, "Mother, I do not think I should have come." Galloway began telling a funny story, engaging Lincoln's participation.[56] "Presently Mr. Lincoln's mouth would relax, his eye[s] brighten, and his whole face, as only those who had seen the transformation would believe, and we would be launched into a sea of laughter—he himself falling in with his oft quoted expression, 'and this reminds me of.'"[57]

In addition, Mary began instituting an afternoon carriage ride and insisting her that husband accompany her. "This was the only way in which she could induce him to take the fresh air, which he so much needed."[58]

Mary, like her husband, knew they needed Democrat supporters as well as Republicans, whether they were elected officials or not. The women she asked to receive with her at the Executive Mansion were from both parties. Adele Cutts Douglas, wife of Stephen A. Douglas, was frequently asked to receive with Mary. Douglas, of course, was a Democrat but he ardently supported Lincoln in holding the Union together. Another was Elizabeth Moss Crittenden, the third wife of John J. Crittenden, who was the best man at the wedding of Mary's father and Betsy Humphreys. Crittenden, a Whig turned Republican, had been governor of Kentucky, the attorney general and secretary of state under Fillmore and was a U.S. senator.[59]

Partisanship within the Washington elite, where Mary was concerned, was never going to work, as was evidenced by William H. Russell's statement about the untruths southern women in and around Washington told about her. She had a brother and half-siblings who were ardent Confederate combatants and supporters and, unfortunately, there were those who chose to paint her with the same brush.

"In some way, the story became current," Elizabeth Grimsley explained, "that Mrs. Lincoln 'was not loyal,' 'was a rebel' 'not in sympathy with her husband,' and for a time it was believed by some that she was in communications with the Confederate Army, as State secrets were leaked out, and it was well known that her brothers and sisters in the South were active Confederates. This exasperated her beyond measure, as she was heart and soul with her husband and the Union."[60]

Without naming anyone as the person suspected of leaking information and accusing Mary, she continued her narrative. "With her quick womanly wit, she set herself to work, to discover, if possible, who the guilty party was, in making these charges. And she did prove, to the satisfaction of those most interested, that a guest in the house was in the habit of listening about the cabinet room doors, when they were in session, and retailing all the information he could thus gather to those only too willing to make use of it. He also reported the visits of a brother and sister of Mrs. Lincoln, who had been most kindly entertained and passed by the president through the lines."[61]

Lincoln was able to temporarily escape the worries of the war and back-biting politics by visiting the Navy Yard. Mary, who was fascinated by ships, often accompanied him. On May 9, 1861, the Lincolns, with other officials, spent the afternoon at the Navy Yard reviewing the dress parade of the 71st New York Regiment, listening to a band concert and aboard the USS *Pensacola* watching target practice. Commandant John Dahlgren put on a show of pomp and circumstance with his artillery demonstrations for the guests. Dahlgren, who invented and developed bronze coat guns, heavy smoothbore shell guns and rifled ordnance, often took Lincoln on cruises down the Potomac during weapon tests. On one occasion, after watching Dahlgren test a machine gun which had a problem with escaping gas, the president remarked, "Well, I believe this really does what it is represented to do. Now have any of you heard of any machine, or invention, for the preventing the escape of 'gas' from newspaper establishments?"[62]

Following the busy afternoon at the Navy Yard, Mary and Lincoln hosted a reception at the Executive Mansion for Army, Navy, Marine Corps, and volunteer militia officers and their families. Major Robert Anderson, under whose command Fort Sumter was surrendered, arrived quietly at the reception. When Lincoln learned Anderson was in the room, he located him and placed him in the receiving line with Mary and himself.[63]

In early May, Elizabeth Grimsley omitted the date that William S. Woods, whom Lincoln had nominated for the position commissioner of public buildings, arranged a trip to New York for Mary to select a carriage. "Our objective point was 'Brewster's' for an open carriage as the weather was growing warm for the coach," she wrote. After Mary selected the carriage, they took a drive to test the vehicle. The next day they spent in Brooklyn touring Green-Wood Cemetery famed for its park-like landscape, carriage paths, marble sculptures, granite monuments, brownstone mausoleums, plants and trees. At that time, Green-Wood had over 500,000 visitors a year, rivaling only Niagara Falls as the nation's favorite tourist attraction.[64]

After dining with Mary's friends in New York, they left for Washington the next day. "The reporters did not hear of us until we had left the city," Grimsley wrote, "but what was our amazement upon taking up the New York papers after our return home, to find that we had been on an extensive shopping trip; that Lord & Taylor, Arnold and Constable and A. T. Stewart had been largely patronized, that Mrs. Lincoln had bought, among other things, a three thousand dollar point lace shawl, and Mrs. Grimsley had also indulged to the extent of one thousand dollars, in a like purchase (this is the nearest I ever came to having one), whereas we had not even driven by the stores."[65]

CHAPTER 11

Furnishing the President's House

In the exuberance of being first lady, Mary Lincoln was determined to turn the Executive Mansion into an elegant setting for national and international social and political events, as well as a home for her family. In her efforts to send a message to the world—that despite the seceded states—the Union, under her husband's leadership, was strong and would persevere, Mary would have been well served to discover how some of her predecessors felt about the constant criticism that came with the position of first lady. Along with the Executive Mansion came a congressional appropriation of $20,000 for furnishings. Those congressional appropriations, which varied from $6,000 to $25,000 over the years, were not only a budgetary nightmare but had a long history of graft, corruption and bureaucratic bungling, which in her case proved to be a pitfall. In achieving her dream, she momentarily forgot the business acumen of keeping her eye on the money that she learned from her father.

All of her married life, Mary Lincoln had been a frugal money manager. That personality trait did not suddenly evaporate when she entered the Executive Mansion. This was the same woman who refused to pay the Irish maid, Margaret Ryan, an extra seventy-five cents until she was overruled by her husband. The days were not too far behind Mary when she sewed all her family's clothes, except for Lincoln's suits, with her fingers. She was the same woman who offered John F. Mendosa ten cents for three pints of blackberries in 1859. Her husband gave Mendosa the requested fifteen cents.[1]

What tripped her up was depending on the wrong person, interim Commissioner of Public Buildings William S. Wood, who not only controlled but was dipping into the furnishings account himself. It was a common failing that had been repeated, more or less with regularity, from the very beginning by those who held that position.

As the struggling federal government began with the election of George Washington in 1789, there was no President's House. When Washington began his first term in a rented house on Cherry Street in New York City, part of the $25,000 Congress granted Washington for his expenses—he accepted no salary—was spent on furnishings. The next year, the president's residence was moved to a larger house on Broadway. "In the summer of 1790, Congress agreed upon a permanent site for the national capitol, somewhere within a ten-mile square federal district established along the Potomac River," former White House Curator Betty G. Monkman wrote. Philadelphia was the interim seat of government until 1800, and the Washingtons lived in a larger house rented from Robert Morris, located on High Street.[2]

As Washington arranged for his return to Mount Vernon, he made two lists—"Furnished by the U. States and purchased by GW." He added notes concerning the condition of the items supplied by the government. "Nothing here has been said relative to the Table

Linens, Sheeting, China and Glassware which was furnished at the expense of the United States, because they have been worn out, broken, stolen and replaced (at private[3] expense) over & over again." The list of furnishings Washington left for the new president, Monkman wrote, was considerable, including dozens of mahogany chairs, ten yellow damask upholstered chairs, three sofas covered with yellow silk, two mahogany dining tables, cabinets, bookcases, bureaus, sideboards and bedsteads.[4]

Abigail and John Adams were the first presidential couple to live in what was then called the President's House. The plastering was half finished when Adams arrived in November 1800. But he assured his wife it was habitable. When she arrived two weeks later, Abigail Adams found the house was not finished, furniture bought by President George Washington was worn and defaced, curtains were too small for the large windows, carpets were lost in the large rooms and there was a lack of china. Abigail wrote:

> If my opinion be taken, it is to take time for furnishing the House, and to send abroad for such furnishings as cannot be procured Here. As there will not be any Lady there the ensuing winter: the furniture which is there, will suffice for the present; with the addition of new carpets, window curtains and looking glasses. It if should be my lot, to go to the House, I would then mention the propriety of a superior sett of Tea, and table china, and an additional quantity of table and Bed Linen will be wanted. It will be thought proper to furnish one Bed Chamber elegantly.[5]

By the time she left Washington in 1801, Abigail compared the position of first lady to being "fastened up hand and foot and tongue to be shot at as our Quincy lads do at the poor geese and turkies." She went on to say, "I have been so used to freedom of sentiment that I know not how to place so many guards about me, as will be indispensable to look at every word before I utter it and to impose silence upon myself when I long to talk."[6]

President Thomas Jefferson, 1801–1809, used Benjamin Latrobe's architectural expertise in an effort to solve the building's roof problems, which was unsuccessful. As Jefferson was working on the interior design of the new residence, Latrobe wrote a friend complaining the president fished his ideas out of some old French books. "But," he added, "it is a small sacrifice to my personal attachment to humor." His mistake was placing his friend's letter in an envelope addressed to Jefferson. Latrobe was gone.[7]

For decades, bureaucrats handled, or rather mishandled, the congressional furnishings appropriations. Latrobe, once again in Washington, was appointed surveyor of public buildings and oversaw the furnishings fund for President James Madison, 1809–1817. In 1810, Latrobe sold some of the President's House furnishings through the Washington firms of Andrews and Jones, Auctioneers. That and future auctions far exceeded that of a rummage sale and held a faint taint of political corruption, although the proceeds were supposed to be used in the next Congressional furnishings appropriation. Latrobe purchased, at the auction, six of the chairs he had designed for the Adamses. That first sale set a precedent for disposing of President's House furnishings between administrations.[8]

While Latrobe and his wife, Mary Elizabeth Latrobe, were in Philadelphia purchasing items—carriages, china, linens, cutlery, curtains—for the residence, they were also buying and shipping Dolley personal items including a guitar, wig, hat and turban.[9]

Madison fired Latrobe in 1812 for meddling in his affairs with Congress, but brought him back to Washington to rebuild the President's House after the British burned the residence, Capitol and other government buildings in 1814, during the War of 1812. Latrobe wanted to not only rebuild the buildings but redesign them. He was sent packing a second time. Madison hired Samuel Lane to succeed Latrobe as commissioner of public buildings.[10]

Lane continued in that post during the administration of President James Monroe with disastrous results. Monroe, Washington's minister to France, developed a taste for expensive French furnishings. Monroe ordered fifty-three pieces of furniture designed by Pierre-Antoine Bellange, one of the foremost cabinetmakers of the era. The Bellange furniture, wallpaper, chandeliers, porcelain, silver candelabra, fireplace implements, clocks and carpets—one of which was designed with the emblem of the United States—cost $19,716, and filled ninety-three crates which the *Resolution* carried to America. There went Monroe's $20,000 furnishing allowance from Congress.[11]

While waiting for his elegant furnishings, Monroe sold the federal government some of his personal furniture on a temporary basis for $9,017, saying it had been independently appraised. Congress very obligingly appropriated an additional $30,000 for his furnishing account. He withdrew $6,000 from the account for a northern tour of the United States.[12]

Mary Lincoln has been pilloried for 152 years for allegedly spending $6,658 more than her congressional furnishings allotment while Monroe's extravagance of an additional $30,000 for furnishings has gone virtually unnoticed.

When Lane died in 1822, the furnishings account fund was $20,000 in arrears. Among Lane's outlandish expenditures were 1,200 bottles of champagne and burgundy charged to the furniture account. He also made $6,500 disbursements from the account in Monroe's name. Congress, outraged over Lane and Monroe's expenditures, demanded an investigation which finally required an inventory be made of the President's House furnishings before the next administration occupied the residence.[13]

According to the inventory, the President's House was fully furnished, noting some card tables, chests, chairs and china were broken and some of the carpets damaged and worn. Yet, when John Q. Adams, 1825–1829, arrived, he was shocked by the condition of the residence and refused to move in for a month.[14] Security at the President's House was nonexistent. Between administrations, when the mansion was unoccupied, scavengers roamed at will through the residence taking whatever they wanted and could carry.

Had it not been for the Civil War and attempting to hold a fragile Union together, Abraham Lincoln would probably have watched over the furnishings money much like Andrew Jackson did. Although Jackson placed Major William B. Lewis in charge of the Congressional furnishing allocation, he closely examined all expenditures and told guests the costs of each of the new furnishings for the East Room. Jackson saw that the money from the sale of old silver, furniture and glassware, $4,300, was used to pay for a 130-piece French silver service costing $4,308.[15]

President Franklin Pierce, 1853–1857, exercised little supervision over his congressional furnishings appropriation of $25,000. Pierce, on the advice of Secretary of the Navy Jefferson Davis, appointed Thomas J. Lee, from the Army Corps of Engineers, to select furnishings for the President's House, which was renamed the Executive Mansion. Apparently, no one questioned what an engineer knew about interior design. Lee, however, acknowledged his lack of expertise and depended on the advice of Architect of the Capitol Thomas U. Walter. Lee's shopping list for A. T. Stewarts, where Mary Lincoln later shopped, read like an order for a new hotel including draperies, lace curtains, monogrammed linens and a 7,000-pound carpet for the East Room.[16] Walter told a friend in June 1853, "We have the President's House turned inside out and will make it look more like a President's House than it has ever done."[17]

The money to pay Stewarts' bill became a tug of war between Pierce and Commissioner of Public Buildings W. M. Easby, who controlled the furnishings monies. When Easby was not forthcoming with the funds, Pierce asked Secretary of the Interior Robert McClelland, in whose cabinet Easby's office was located, for assistance. Easby, like his predecessors and some of those who came later, withdrew large amounts of cash from the fund. In Easby's case, he had the cash stashed in the safe of a physician friend. Easby resigned.[18]

Waiting in the wings for Easby's job was none other than Benjamin B. French, who had been an assistant to Pierce's secretary, Sidney Webster. French went to work with gusto and spent $15,729.13 on repairs and furnishings for the President's House which, six months earlier, was pronounced in fine shape. "Other repairs have been made, such as were represented to me by the inmates of the house to be necessary," French wrote in his apparent disdain for the President's House occupants.[19]

Congress appropriated $1,500 in 1855 to create a Botanic Garden outside the Executive Mansion for the vast number of plants and trees Commodore Matthew C. Perry brought back from his voyage to Japan and China. French attempted to divert some of those funds to extend the mansion's greenhouse. The project was taken away from him and placed under the watchful eye of the Library of Congress. When Pierce's term was over in 1857, so was French's.[20]

French's successor, James B. Blake, remained as commissioner of public buildings in the Lincoln administration until around the end of April 1861. Mary was impressed with the manner in which William S. Wood planned and handled the inaugural train trip to Washington. Apparently she looked no further into his background or his connections to Seward and Weed and their New York cronies. It was a case where her usually astute judgment of people failed her. She wrote Ward Hill Lamon on April 11, 1861, asking him to encourage Lincoln to appoint Wood as commissioner of public buildings. Lamon replied that he would talk with Lincoln at once and regretted that anyone had prejudiced Lincoln against Wood.[21]

Wood was a man on a mission to make money. He was a lobbyist for the American Bank Note Company of New York. Tracy R. Edson, president of the American Bank Note Company, asked Wood to call Lincoln's attention to their company's printing of bonds for the State of Missouri, and to solicit the business of printing of government securities. Wood met with the president to discuss the government's printing business.[22]

Lincoln referred Wood to the secretary of the treasury for an interview. The president appointed Wood commissioner of public buildings and awaited confirmation by the senate. Wood was on an interim basis when he arranged and accompanied Mary Lincoln and Elizabeth Grimsley to New York in May 1861 to select an open carriage. The senate knew more about Wood than Mary and Lincoln and held up his confirmation.[23]

The office of the commissioner of public buildings was a powerful position which involved tremendous responsibilities and the handling of a great deal of public monies. The commissioner was accountable for the conditions of public streets and roads in the district, federal grounds and parks, the Executive Mansion, Capitol, jail, courthouse, infirmary and Patent Office.[24]

"No first lady since Dolley Madison had taken such personal interest in the furnishing and decorating of the house," Betty C. Monkman wrote. "Mrs. Lincoln's interest was less in its historical association than it was to provide a comfortable home for her family, to furnish a showcase for entertaining and to reflect the high status of the presidency. Since 1800, the president or someone to whom he delegated the task assumed responsibility for ordering furnishings and overseeing the interior decorations; in the Lincoln era this was the commissioner of public buildings. However, it was Mrs. Lincoln who made decisions on purchases."[25]

William "Willie" Lincoln, standing, and Thomas "Tad" Lincoln, seated, with their cousin John Lockwood Todd after the Lincolns moved into the Executive Mansion (Library of Congress Prints and Photographs Division).

Benjamin B. French, a perennial federal employee, served as commissioner of public buildings in the Lincoln administration and was responsible for the upkeep of the Executive Mansion. While supposedly admiring Mary, he was quite critical of her in his personal diary (Library of Congress Prints and Photographs Division).

Some of Mary's New York purchases included $1,006 in carpeting from A. T. Stewart for the Red Room, the guest room and Lincoln's office. The porcelain dinner, dessert, breakfast and tea service she purchased from E. V. Haughwout were decorated with gilt and a wide band of purple with the United States coat of arms in the center. The glassware she purchased from Christian Dorflinger also had the coat of arms etched into the crystal. Succeeding administrations reordered Mary's selections of both the china and glassware for their use.[26]

In Philadelphia, Mary shopped at Wm. H. Carryl and Bro., buying drapery material and accessories. It was at Carryl that she purchased a rosewood bed whose massive headboard had carvings of flowers, exotic birds and grapevines. The bed, almost six feet wide and eight feet long, became famous as the "Lincoln bed," although the president never slept in it. Mary purchased chairs, wash stand, bureau and tables to go with the bed. Those expenditures totaled $7,500. She also purchased 1,600 yards of gilt and French wallpaper for the East, Red, Blue and Green Rooms, the president's bedroom and her room, amounting to $3,549.[27]

After those initial purchases for the Executive Mansion in 1861, Monkman wrote, Mary made few purchases for the official residence. Damaged, destroyed or stolen items had to be replaced. In addition to fabric cut from the Green Room draperies, the loops and tassels were also stolen. Expensive gold ornaments were taken from the East Room. By 1863, the scavengers grew bolder and took down and carried away one of the fragile lace curtains from the East Room windows.[28]

Both Blake and Wood had access to the furnishing fund, as the $20,000 was appropriated on February 20, 1861, but Blake, aside from ordering the revolvers for guards at the residence, made few if any other purchases. Wood's bookkeeping, what there was, indicated he probably fell into the practices of previous holders of his office. Cancelled checks and ledgers from the office of the commissioner of public buildings in July and August 1861 indicated questionable practices. On July 13 a check was written to "Self to pay small bills" for $200. A July 31 check was written to "Self to pay small bills and salaries for $3,500." On August 31, a check for $4,000 was written to "Self to pay small bills and salaries." Wood wrote $7,700 in checks to himself from the furnishings fund in just those two months. Other cancelled checks for small amounts were made to various firms and employees.[29]

Wood's actions afforded a new look at what happened to the Lincoln furnishings account monies. Had those funds not been removed, the $6,858 invoice for furniture from Wm. H. Carryl and Brothers would have been paid just as their previous $7,500 statement was in July 1861. Consequently, Mary Lincoln would not have been accused of overspending the furnishings appropriation and would not have been maligned for the past 150 years as a careless spendthrift.[30]

Mary could have saved herself, and the president, much grief had she double checked the amount of her purchases against what remained in the furnishings fund instead of depending on Wood's accounting. When Wood approved her wallpaper order of $3,549, he knew that furnishing funds were not available to pay the bill.[31] It was understandable why Wood lacked funds to even pay all his employees. A direct congressional appropriation of $22.18 was necessary for J. B. Blake to get paid for work he did for Wood. Other direct appropriations were made to make up a $4,500 deficit for papering and painting the President's House and to pay the Carryl bill of $6,858.[32]

In recent decades, a scenario has evolved where Mary Lincoln supposedly directed Wood pay extra money to John Watt, the public gardener, so he could return the funds to

Mary to pay for her furnishing purchases. A number of insurmountable impediments had to be cleared in order for that conclusion to have validity. Bills to be paid from the furnishings appropriation were sent to Lincoln for his approval. Lincoln, if he approved them, forwarded the bills to Salmon Chase, secretary of the treasury, for payment as he did with the $7,500 invoice from Wm. H. Carryl and Brother invoice, dated May 29, 1861. Chase, as treasurer, paid the bills from the Congressional furnishing appropriation fund. There was no way for Mary to insert money from Wood, Watt or anyone, as has been suggested, into the method of payment procedure. Wood's checks to Watt of $614, on July 2, 1861, was for "President's House," and for $600 for "Repairs to President's House," twelve days later, smelled of a kickback scheme between the two.[33]

Mary, accompanied by Elizabeth Grimsley, was besieged by reporters at every stop on her shopping trip, arranged by Wood, regardless of efforts to evade them. While in New York, A. T. Stewart gave a dinner for her. While visiting Bob at Harvard, Sen. Charles Sumner arranged a reception and dinner at the Revere House in Boston.[34]

Upon her return to Washington, Mary was shocked to learn of the death of Stephen A. Douglas, whose relationship with both she and the president had been closer in recent months.[35] Sen. Stephen A. Douglas died of typhoid fever on June 3, 1861, at his home in Chicago. "His death, at this time, may be regarded as a national calamity," the New York Times opined. "For whatever his political faults, or his errors as a statesman may have been (and we are among those who believe they were great) his peculiar relations and exalted position, his firm and manly support of the Union would have made his name a tower of strength."[36]

Social events went on while the Executive Mansion was being refurbished, as Mary and Lincoln not only entertained but occasionally found time for a trip to the theater and even hosted an operatic performance in the Executive Mansion. Mary had invited the great opera singer Meda Blanchard to join a small gathering on July 4. Lincoln heard her singing from his upstairs office, came down and requested an encore. The singer graciously agreed, accompanying herself on the piano. When the Lincolns attended her performance four days later at the Willard, one newspaper reported that the president was wholly absorbed by her siren voice.[37]

The military element was in full array at the July 9 reception. Mary, a newspaper reported, "attracted universal attention by her graceful bearing and high social qualities." A week later the Washington Evening Star reported, "Mrs. Lincoln never looked better and drew around her a large circle of friends and admirers."[38]

The refurbished Executive Mansion was on display with a grand reception held in the East Room signaling the opening of the winter social season on December 17, 1861. William Watts Hart David, a colonel in the 104th Pennsylvania, said the large crowd resulted in "squeezing and pushing, smashing of hoops, and treading on tender dresses, all sorts of people in all sorts of costumes and homely women with sharp shoulder blades and low-necked dresses." David paid Mary and Abraham Lincoln the supreme compliment on the success of the event and her efforts. "There was a marked disregard of form and ceremony," he wrote, "and the etiquette of the occasion was simple enough to satisfy the straightest republican. The most pleasant feature was the Marine Band stationed in the vestibule, which played delightful music. It was apparent to me that the president is the servant of the people and that the house he lives in belongs to them."[39]

The Washington Evening Star observed the reception was unlike the high society of the antebellum days. Several cabinet members and Congressmen were in attendance but the crowd was largely military with a sprinkling of black coats and crinoline. The British minister was absent since his government was contemplating war with the United States over the *Trent* incident. The French and Spanish ministers were also absent but those from Russia, Sweden, Bremen and Nicaragua attended.[40]

The *Baltimore Sun* reporter wrote about the rush of guests to Gen. and Mrs. George B. McClellan when they arrived at the reception. The *New York Herald* observed the apparent cordiality between McClellan and Lincoln and speculated that there was no truth "to the repeated assertion that there is not a perfectly good understanding between them, and that the former does not have confidence in the latter."[41]

The *New York Times* pointed out that the East Room gave little indication that it had recently been occupied by troops and that was about the kindest thing the newspaper had to say. "Mrs. Lincoln, a noted spendthrift, has recently overseen redecorating of the Executive House, which included buying imported drapes, carpets, dishes and furniture while exceeding congressional appropriations by nearly $7,000. The principal apartments of the Executive Mansion have been refitted and refurbished, and this, with the recent artistic decoration, has increased the attraction of the place."[42]

A California newspaper was much more complimentary of Mary's efforts to make the President's House into a residence the nation could be proud of and a place for international diplomacy as well as a home for her family. "Very little new furniture has been introduced," the *Daily Alta California* reported, "as much of the old is yet substantial, having been procured in the time of Monroe and is only valuable on that account, but is really very handsome from its antique style. Much of this old furniture, however, has been re-varnished and the chairs have been cushioned and covered with rich crimson satin brocade, tufted and laid in folds on the back, rendering a modern appearance."[43]

The two new attractions in the East Room, the newspaper pointed out, were the Parisian heavy velvet cloth wallpaper of crimson and gold, and floral carpet, which covered the 100 by 40 foot floor in just one section. The Axminister carpet was woven in Glasgow, Scotland, on the only loom in the world capable of making a rug so large. Another outstanding feature of the East Room were the crimson brocaded draperies, trimmed with heavy gold fringe and tassel work, over delicate wrought lace curtains from Switzerland.[44]

Mary knew beauty and superb workmanship when she saw it and simply had the three enormous chandeliers, purchased by President Andrew Jackson in 1829, cleaned. When the chandeliers were hung their style was described as being "entirely new; the color of glass and cutting perhaps *exceeds any thing of the kind ever seen*." She left the three monumental mahogany center tables, with black and gold marble slabs inserted into their tops, placed below each chandelier. One of the circular tables was slightly larger than the other two. She also left the eight mirrors intact in the room.[45]

The Green Room had been newly papered and had new carpet and draperies. The only new feature of the Blue Room was the carpet. The new sofas and chairs in the Red Room were covered with crimson brocade satin. The guest room, which contained the Lincoln bed with its purple canopy, had all new furniture, according to the newspaper.[46]

The bed was made of rosewood veneers and wood grained to resemble rosewood. A round table with a white marble top was made from layers of laminated rosewood and was similar to the work of the famous New York furniture maker John Henry Belter, said to be without peer in making laminated pieces. Carvings of vines, grape clusters and roses on the table were similar to those on the bed. The two armchairs and four side chairs Mary bought for the room were also thought to be by Belter.[47]

"The private apartments of Mr. and Mrs. Lincoln are more modestly but very beautifully ornamented and furnished," the article continued. "Green is the color that predominates the rooms. The room where cabinet meetings are held and where the president is usually to be found is very neatly papered, but should be better furnished. All the furniture is exceedingly old and too rickety to venerate."[48]

Regarding Mary Lincoln's shopping trips to New York, former White House curator Betty Monkman wrote, "Criticism of Mrs. Lincoln, her shopping trips and purchases in the midst of a terrible war did not abate, and in 1864 New York newspapers continued to report and comment on her shopping." Monkman pointed out that despite such critics as Mary Clemmer Ames, who charged that "the wife of the president of the United States spent her time in rolling to and fro between Washington and New York intent on extravagant purchases for herself and the White House," Mary Lincoln made few purchases for the residence after 1861. One of those exceptions was china, French porcelain with a buff band, she ordered for the Executive Mansion that did not arrive until well into the Johnson administration.[49]

Mary Clemmer Ames was correct in one of her assessments of Mary Lincoln. Reaching the Executive Mansion was the fulfillment of a life-long ambition. That dream was something she worked for and she earned it. Being the president's hostess was not handed to her on a silver platter. But, contrary to Ames' screeching appraisals, the wife of the sixteenth president venerated the Executive Mansion as the house that belonged to the people of the United States and respectfully treated it as such. Many of the furnishings Mary Lincoln purchased for the President's House were used by other occupants for decades and certainly the Lincoln bed, even today, remains the residence's most famous piece of furniture.

Mary's success in refurbishing the Executive Mansion was overshadowed by Washington's bilious gossipmongers. Perhaps the best description of that scene came from Stoddard, Lincoln's secretary who worked with her. "People in great need of something spicy to talk or write about are picking up all sorts of stray gossip relating to asserted occurrences under this roof, and they are making strange work of it," he wrote. "It is a work they will not cease from. They will do it, to the very end, so effectively that a host of excellent people who will one day close their eyes to the wife's robe dabbled with her husband's blood."[50]

CHAPTER 12

Dirty Politics

Refurbishing of the President's House–Executive Mansion over the decades created little attention in Washington's political world with a few exceptions. Mary Lincoln was among those exceptions that also included former presidents.

The so-called excessive purchases made by Mary for the Executive Mansion would have been paid if funds had not been purloined from the congressional furnishings account by William S. Wood, whom Lincoln nominated for the position of commissioner of public buildings, a man trusted by the president's wife. Then, there was Wood's successor, Benjamin B. French, the ultimate bureaucrat who spoke quite well out of both sides of his mouth, especially when it came to Mary and Executive Mansion furnishings.

However, it was not the first time government officials played fast and loose with the furnishings appropriations. Monroe's interest in decorating the President's House appeared to be endless, White House historian William Seale said. "When Congress obliged by appropriating an additional $30,000 for furnishings in the winter of 1818, the president spent it quickly," Seale wrote.[1] Monroe's expenditures occurred while the United States was still paying off debts incurred in the War of 1812, which cost $90 million.[2]

Congress demanded an investigation of Monroe's expenditures from the furnishings appropriation after his commissioner of public buildings, Samuel Lane, died, leaving the account $20,000 in arrears. Little came of the investigation, as congressmen reasoned their way out of it saying Lane was not there to defend himself. An inventory, completed before the next administration came into the President's House, indicated the residence was fully furnished but some card tables, chests, chairs, fire screens, lamps, china, silver and carpets were broken, damaged or worn.[3]

Yet, John Quincy Adams, 1825–1829, who moved in the President's House a month after he took office, was shocked by the conditions he found and asked Congress for more money. Congress appropriated $14,000 for furnishings. A year later, Adams was given an additional $6,000 to finish the interior of the East Room but spent most of it for repairs.[4] Adams, furious over Congress questioning not only his but also Monroe's furnishing expenditures, said such inquiries were like requiring "a blooming virgin to exhibit herself naked before the multitudes."[5]

Mary could relate to that, for she must have felt that every dagger and stiletto in Washington was pointed toward her. According to most national newspapers, if something went wrong in the Executive Mansion, it was most likely Mary's fault.

From 1797 to the Lincolns' arrival in March 1861, the government had spent $346,659 on furnishings for the Executive Mansion. Translated into 2012 dollars, the economic power value of that figure swelled to $1.250 billion. Repairs to the Executive Mansion and grounds from 1807 to 1860 cost the taxpayers $424,601. The 2012 equivalent of that amount was $1.530 billion.[6]

In the 148 years that have passed since Mary purchased some remarkable pieces of furniture for the Executive Mansion, few have questioned furnishing expenditures for the U.S. Senate and House of Representatives. During the just over four years of the Lincoln administration, $79,500 was spent by Congress for their furniture, repairs to furnishings and packing boxes.[7]

In short order, Mary became a lightning rod for criticism and a target for her husband's political opponents. If it was not the furnishings appropriations, it was her being a part of her husband's administration—something nineteenth century women did not do. If women like Mary openly participated in politics, they could expect to be ripped to shreds. If she took an unpopular stand or supported someone she believed in, then as the president's wife, Mary was unbelievably vulnerable.

Mary could hold her own in Illinois politics but getting into the entrenched slime that consumed many Washington politicians and government officials was another venue. Those people had been in the game all their lives and knew when and how to play dirty. However, Mary made the best possible use of the assets at her disposal.

Wood was still writing checks to himself when Rep. John F. Potter, a radical Republican from Wisconsin, asked the House to create a special committee on July 8 "to ascertain and report to the House the number of persons, with names thereof, now employed, in the several departments of the government, who are known to entertain sentiments of hostility to the government of the United States, and those who have refused to take the oath to support the Constitution of the United States."[8]

The committee netted 550 lower level, not those in high office, government employees: some were guilty; others were innocent and tried to clear their names and reputations; some never regained their reputations. The committee's operational criteria sounded much like that of another Wisconsin lawmaker a century later. Their parameters were, under oath, "to entertain and examine into all charges preferred by respectable and responsible citizens against any person employed by the government. These examinations have been made by calling such witnesses as the committee was led to believe, for the best information they could obtain, possessed the most reliable knowledge of the sentiments and views of the parties charged in relation to the present rebellion."[9]

Potter's committee was little more than a "he said; he said" tribunal. Some men were charged whose first names were unknown. The committee, assuming guilt while leaving those they charged to prove innocence, was interested in some employees of the Executive Mansion.

Of particular interest to the committee was John Watt, the public gardener at the residence; Thomas Stackpole, a messenger-watchman; Thomas Burns, doorkeeper, and someone with the last name Edwards, an assistant messenger.[10] Not having an accused's first name did not bother Potter's committee; they just forged ahead.

Watt's appearance before the committee came from a long and twisting route. Watt, the public gardener since the Millard Fillmore administration, knew how the Washington bait and switch worked. If there was an absence of funds, then the goods could be purchased and they would be paid for from the next appropriation. It was the way the government worked in 1861.

Salmon Chase, secretary of the treasury, operated his office the same way. An extra Congressional appropriation was needed to reimburse the contingency fund in the treasurer's office for additional clerks hired. A special appropriation was needed to hire two clerks in the assistant treasurer's office. Then, there was another appropriation for the treasury "to supply deficiencies in the appropriation for the current fiscal year."[11]

Just because Chase juggled his accounts did not make for good government, but it does indicate the methods used by all from the cabinet to the gardener as they conducted the public's business. Watt was supposedly padding his expenses and giving the excess amount to Mary Lincoln to pay on the deficits in the furnishing. However, there was no way for Watt or Mary to insert such monies into the payment process of government bills.

Neither were those unpaid bills—the Carryl invoice and the wallpapering-painting— the largest of the commissioner of public buildings' deficits, nor was their payment hidden in other bills. In *Public Laws of the United States of America Passed at First Session of the Thirty-Seventh Congress*, each amount had its own entry. "Deficiency in account for papering and painting the Presidents House in the fall of 1861, $4,500." The other read, "To enable the Commissioner of Public Buildings to pay Carryl account, $6,858."[12]

There were other special laws passed for covering other deficits in the commissioner of public building's accounts: $2,614 to pay on repairing plate and gas fittings in the President's House; $2,400 for fuel for the President's House; $5,000 for repairs to the President's House; $4,200 for clerks and messengers for the commissioner of public buildings, and $50,000 for lighting the President's House, the Capitol and surrounding area.[13]

A total of $81,444 was needed in additional appropriations to cover the deficits in the office of William S. Wood, the commissioner of public buildings in 1861. In 2012, the equivalent value was $28.5 million.[14] Somewhere along the way Wood and Watt seemingly had a serious disagreement. Watt left the Executive Mansion and joined the Army.

On September 8, 1861, Lincoln and Mary went for an afternoon ride across Long Bridge and along the river. He told her he had countermanded an order given by McClellan to have a soldier shot for falling asleep on guard duty. Lincoln said he told McClellan the decision was by request of the lady president. He also told her he had fired Wood. Inferences to their detailed discussion about Wood and Watt were evident in her letters immediately afterwards.[15]

From the time she was very young, Mary displayed a soft spot in her heart for the disadvantaged and downtrodden and tried to help them. Just as she was so very kind to the vagrant King Solomon after the typhoid epidemic in Lexington, she saw a similar situation with John Watt being made a scapegoat and decided to do something about it.

Mary gathered enough information to convince her that Wood was responsible for Watt losing his position. On September 8, the same day as the carriage ride with Lincoln, she wrote Caleb B. Smith, secretary of the interior (who had been Wood's superior) in defense of Watt. "I much regret that Mr. Wood still pursues the attack and tries to bring charges of dishonesty upon Mr. Watt who in all his accounts with us has been rigidly exact."[16]

Four days later, she sent a letter to Secretary of War Simon Cameron asking him to change Watt's appointment to the cavalry instead of the infantry, as he could still be attached to the Executive Mansion. "This is an especial request & if you would make it out in writing in the morning, the kindness will always be remembered," she wrote. She told Cameron there were strange things coming from Wood and that Watt would explain them the next morning.[17]

Meanwhile, Rep. Potter's committee was taking testimony about Watt being a secessionist. Lewis Clephane, Washington postmaster who appeared to be one of Potter's prime witnesses, testified that Watt "has the reputation of being in league with the secessionists; his associations are such as to lead any one to so regard him." John Plant, an employee at the Capitol, told the committee, "The associations of John Watt, gardener at the President's House, are with known secessionists and very intimately so."

H. W. Gray and Franklin Smith, both from Philadelphia, told the committee they saw Watt in the St. Lawrence Hotel in Philadelphia after the June 21, 1861, Battle of Bull Run praising the Confederates and called Union soldiers cowards. There was no testimony in the committee's report from Watt.[18]

The committee apparently did not inquire—at least in their report—how the public gardener could afford the St. Lawrence Hotel, a celebrated summer resort. The report did question Watt's sudden appointment in the Army. "It is proper to state, in this connection, that more than two weeks before the appointment of Mr. Watt as a lieutenant in the army the chairman informed the president that testimony had been taken before the committee gravely impeaching the loyalty of that person, who was then acting as gardener at the White House."[19]

Potter's note to the president was dated September 12, 1861, and read, "Mr. President: I herewith transmit minutes of the evidence taken before the investigating committee of the House of Representatives against Mr. Watt, the gardener at the White House, and other persons occupying positions at the White House. I do this from a sense of public duty." Potter failed to include in his note to Lincoln this sentence from the committee report. "The committee can only add an expression of surprise that, in the face of such testimony, a man clearly disloyal, instead of being instantly removed, should have been elevated to a higher and more responsible position."[20] Watt, according to Potter, had been found guilty of disloyalty to his country on what appeared to be hearsay testimonies.

On September 13, Mary wrote committee chairman Potter a most revealing letter concerning her surprise that Watt had been charged with being a secessionist.

> I know him to be a Union man & have many opportunities of hearing and judging him. The day after the battle of Manassas [Bull Run] I never saw a more troubled man. The charge [against Watt] originated in a tool of Wood, who is now proved to be a very bad man, to my own knowledge, who does not know what *truth* means, all hands acknowledge Wood to be a most unprincipled man so much so that the President to save his family from disgrace—when the Senate *would not* confirm him, re-nominated him until the 1st of September with a promise he would resign. Knowing Mr. Watt found out much about *him* when he was in office—he supposes Watt was the one means of his removal—and employs men to bring false charges against him—This man, who has brought charges against Watt—brought a piano to this house and is closely allied to Wood—which does not say much for him—The charge is false, any can prove to the contrary—there is no better Union man than Watt & no one who has a greater contempt for Jeff Davis.[21]

Watt was not the only Executive Mansion employee Potter's committee decided was disloyal. "The following employees of the President's House have been reported by the committee as disloyal: Thomas Stackpole, messenger; John Watt, gardener; _____ Edward, assistant messenger, Thomas Burns, doorkeeper." The committee report then listed an extract from the testimony against Stackpole, which again included Lewis Clephane, the Washington postmaster and four others. Clephane told the committee that Stackpole, who had been at the residence since 1853, and Bill Spaulding, who did the painting and wallpapering at the Executive Mansion, were in league with Watt and they kept questionable company.[22]

Not only did Lincoln keep Stackpole in his position, but he lent him $380 in November 1861, one of only two loans he made to residence employees, and promoted him to steward at a salary of $100 a month. Stackpole had not paid the loan back at the time Lincoln was killed and Mary instructed David Davis, administrator of the estate, to forgive both loans.[23]

Lincoln wanted more information on the Watt situation. On November 16, 1861, he wrote Adjutant General Lorenzo Thomas a terse, straightforward letter. "Lieut. John Watt, who I believe, has been detailed to do service about the White House [Executive Mansion], is not needed for that purpose, and you assign him to his proper place in Regiment." Watt's Army appointment was revoked on February 3, 1862.[24]

Clearly there was a power struggle going on about the former gardener, who became a handy foil for Wood and others to blame for their own indiscretions. In the middle of it all was Mary.

In February 1862, Henry Wikoff, a Washington stringer for James G. Bennett's *New York Herald*, obtained and sent to the newspaper parts of Lincoln's annual address to Congress. The newspaper printed it before it was sent to the House and Senate. In those days, the address was printed and distributed to Congress. Wikoff, a gadfly who called himself a diplomat, spent considerable time toadying up to Mary by writing cloying columns about her such as the one that appeared in the August 10, 1862, issue: "The President's Lady received and entertained the most polished diplomats and the most fastidious courtiers of Europe with an ease and an elegance, which made the republican simplicity seem almost regal. Her state dinner for the Prince [Napoleon Joseph] was a model of completeness, taste and geniality; and altogether this Kentucky girl, this western matron, this republican queen put to blush and entirely eclipses the first ladies of Europe—the excellent Victoria, the pensive Eugenie and the brilliant Isabella."[25]

This was not Mary Lincoln's first time on the dance floor. She had seen Wikoff's kind come and go and was much too astute to have her head turned by the slobberings of an influence peddler. It was difficult to call Wikoff a journalist, as he often acted as a go-between for high ranking officials such as Union Gen. Daniel Sickles when they needed sensitive information leaked to the press. Sickles was famous for having killed Francis Scott Key's son, Phillip, in broad daylight in Lafayette Square in 1859. He successfully claimed temporary insanity through a remarkable defense devised by Edwin Stanton. Washington district attorney Phillip Barton Key, Sickles claimed, was having an affair with his young wife.[26]

Certainly the Wikoffs and Sickles of the world flattered Mary Lincoln. However, she was a forty-four-year-old woman who had been striving all her life for the position she held and she was not going to throw it away on a bunch of sniveling, nattering nabobs.

Wikoff was subpoenaed to appear before Rep. John Hickman's House Judiciary Committee to testify on how he obtained parts of Lincoln's annual speech to Congress. Wikoff refused to testify and, on February 12, 1862, he was sent to the Capitol jail for contempt of Congress.[27]

Members of the press were falling all over themselves to accuse Mary of leaking the information from her husband's speech, with no evidence to back their spurious claims. Samuel Wilkerson, Washington bureau chief for the *New York Tribune*, told Hickman's committee he understood the portion of the speech was given Wikoff by Mary. Benjamin Perley Poore, *Boston Journal* correspondent, wrote that it was generally believed that Mrs.

Lincoln allowed Wikoff to copy the speech. The *New York Times* reported that gossip first placed Wikoff's source as being females in the Executive Mansion, but decided later the Wikoff got the information by blackmailing Secretary of War Simon Cameron.[28]

Sickles, rushing to mount a legal defense for his friend Wikoff, was reportedly seen scurrying around Washington, even going to the Executive Mansion. He and Wikoff concocted a defense that was so far-fetched nobody believed it but everybody accepted it. It was not the butler that leaked Lincoln's speech but Watt, the former gardener, whose Army commission had been revoked nine days earlier. Sickles' biographer, W. A. Swanberg, wrote that the senator had evidence of embezzlement and used it to pressure Watt into admitting complicity. Watt told the committee that, while he was in the library on the second floor of the residence, he noticed the speech and perused it, but did not copy it, and being of a literary mind, committed portions to memory. The next day, he repeated it to Wikoff.[29]

Sickles, Wikoff and Watt could have saved their efforts. On February 13, 1862, Lincoln, whose demeanor was stiff and formal, walked to the Capitol and into the House Judiciary Committee while they were meeting. In very measured words, he assured them that no member of his family was involved in leaking the Congressional report to Wikoff.[30]

Case closed.

Collectively, Washington breathed a sigh of relief. Few believed Watt's story, but nobody refuted it. The legislative branch avoided a confrontation with the executive branch. By the time everything was over, everybody just wanted the whole mess to go away, except Mary.

She used her considerable influence and Watt was offered a job on March 14, 1862, with the Agricultural Division of the Patent Office by David P. Holloway. The job entailed going to Europe to select and purchase seeds. The job began July 1, 1862, and paid $1,500 per annum plus travel expenses. The Watt situation continued to bother Lincoln. In January 1863, he wrote Smith, "I wish you would tell me in writing, exactly what did you promise Watt about going to Europe last Spring. If it was in writing send me a copy; if merely verbal, write it as accurately as you can from memory and please send it to me at once." No reply from Smith was found. He did however, endorse and approve Holloway's March 12, 1862, letter to Watt offering him the job in Europe. Watt enlisted as a private in August of 1863 in the Thirteenth New York Artillery and was promoted through the ranks to first lieutenant in January 1866.[31]

Wood's departure left open the position of commissioner of public buildings. The position carried enormous responsibilities: supervision of the construction of public buildings; care and maintenance of the President's House and the Capitol; existing offices and public grounds; direction of the Capitol police and night-watchmen; repairs of roads, streets, bridges, and 'drawkeeper' for the Potomac. The Navy Yard, Upper Bridges, enclosing and improving public reservations, installing statues and selling public lots in the District also came with the job. The commissioner's office was in the Capitol.[32]

Benjamin B. French, a career bureaucrat who had managed the Lincoln inaugural ceremonies, was the commissioner under President Franklin Pierce. The two men knew each other from Lincoln's Congressional term, 1847–1849, when French lost his job as clerk of the House. French had to know that Wood left the office in shambles but, nonetheless, he lobbied Lincoln continuously for the position. If French expected his confirmation to breeze through the Senate, he was mistaken. The past rose up to bite him when two of his former employees showed up to testify against him. French did not take that kindly, as he outlined in his diary where he recorded events as well as elaborating on his aches and pains.[33]

Yesterday, although suffering the most excruciating pain in my head, most important business relative to myself, demanded my presence before the Committee on Public Buildings and Grounds before which my nomination as Commissioner, & to whom the most damnably false charges have been made by two ingrates and liar whom I put in office 7 or 8 years ago, and removed since I entered on the duties of Commissioner under the present appointment— George W. Dant & James H. Upperman. For the past three months these scoundrels have done naught else than go about this city lying about me. They gave their entire budget of falsehoods to a Senator, Mr. Pomeroy of Kansas & he brought the charges before the Senate, which induced a recommitment of the nomination to the Committee, before which I was summoned to appear yesterday, and, notwithstanding one of the most severe headaches I ever had, I went over and heard the lies one after another as detailed by Mr. Pomeroy, with all patience and then answered them in about 1/2 hour's speech as I think effectively.

Dant had been a messenger in French's office and Upperman was a Capitol gatekeeper.[34]

French had previously executed bonds of $20,000 for the position of commissioner of public buildings and $40,000 for disbursing appropriations for the Patent Office building and was confirmed by the Senate.[35]

He was sure he could work with Mary as, he said, she was satisfied with his appointment. "I hope and trust she and I shall get along quietly," he wrote. "I shall do everything in my power to make her comfortable. She is evidently a smart, intelligent woman and likes to have her own way pretty much. I was delighted with her independence and her ladylike reception of me." French was also delighted to be invited to dinners the Lincolns had for their friends. At an October 18, 1861, dinner party Mary had for Gen. Robert Anderson and guests Joseph Holt, Caleb Smith, James Speed and Thomas Clay, "I sat between Mrs. Lincoln and Mr. Holt and we carried on quite an interesting conversation about many things."[36]

When French made his first annual report to Congress on November 11, 1861, he said the entire $6,000 appropriated the preceding March for annual repairs to the President's House had been absorbed and a considerable debt had been incurred on account of the wall-papering and painting. "Of the appropriation of four thousand four hundred and twenty dollars for introducing Potomac water into the President's House," he reported, "so much has been extended as was necessary to do the work designed. At this time the bills of the contractor under my immediate predecessor have not been rendered, and I do not know how much of the appropriation has been consumed." Actually, French's tabular statement which accompanied his report indicated there was $39.85 left in the water account.[37]

Mary also invited him to the residence on November 13, 1861, to see a performance by Monsieur Carl Herrmann, known as the "Great Prestidigator." "Mrs. Lincoln looked remarkably well and would be taken for a younger lady at a short distance," he wrote in his diary. "She is not very old, say 40 to 45. She seems much at ease and strove to be very agreeable and was so."[38]

While enjoying being included in Mary's entertaining at the Executive Mansion, French was, at the same time complaining about her. On October 11, 1861, he wrote his brother, Henry F. French, about "the interviews I have with the 'Republican Queen' who plagues me half to death with wants with which it is impossible to comply, for she has an eye to the dollars."[39]

French's attitude toward Mary continued to change when she requested, on December 8, that he be present at the Tuesday and Saturday receptions to announce their guests. At the January 8, 1862, reception to show off the refurbished residence, French wrote, "I had to officially introduce 'The American Queen' to her numerous and brilliant visitors."

In discussing Mary's gown, French pointed out that she wore "a wrought lace scarf or shawl valued at $2,500!" One had to wonder where he got that information. He made himself at home when he visited the Executive Mansion, snooping around, and would go into the president's office, he claimed, to read.[40]

"My daily life is somewhat monotonous," French wrote after just five months in office. "About 9 I go to my office & remain there, annoyed beyond measure by persons after office, or after *something* constantly. I do not think I have been ten minutes alone in my office for ten days! At about ½ past 2, I come home, dine and have some peace. Every Saturday, from 1 to 3 p.m., & every Tuesday from ½ past 8 to ½ past 10, I am required, as an official duty, to be at the President's to introduce visitors to Mrs. Lincoln. It is a terrible bore, but, as a duty I *must* do it, and it leads to acquaintance with very many celebrities of whom I should otherwise have no personal knowledge."[41]

As he had demonstrated during the Pierce administration, French was unable to stop meddling. Three months into his second term as commissioner of public buildings, French was up to his old tricks. He took it upon himself to have a long talk with Senator David Clark, another New Hampshire resident, and Senator James W. Grimes, former Iowa governor who was also originally from New Hampshire, about the extravagance at the president's house. "Gov. Grimes is peculiarly worked up about it," he said.[42]

However, a day before his meeting with Clark and Grimes, French made the following entry in his diary. "I like Mrs. L. better and better the more I see of her and think she is an admirable woman. She bears herself in every particular, like a lady and, say what they may about her, I will defend her."[43] The longer he remained in office, the bolder French became in his political intrigue. In 1863, he urged Congress to build a new residence for presidents in a healthier part of the city, which was not a bad idea.[44]

The next year he ran afoul of Lincoln in a big way and had to rapidly backpedal to keep his job. French clashed with Smith's successor at the Department of Interior, John Palmer Usher, who took over the supervision of the completion of the Capitol dome construction. French discussed the matter, not with Lincoln, but with Sen. John C. Foote from Mississippi, who introduced a bill that would remove the office of commissioner of public buildings from the interior department. Lincoln, of course, became aware of French's maneuverings and wrote him the following letter. "I understand a Bill is before Congress by your instigation, for taking your office from the control of the Department of the Interior, and considerably enlarging the powers and patronage of your office. The proposed change may be right for aught I know; and it certainly is right for Congress to do as it thinks proper in this case. What I wish to say is that if a change is made, I do not think I can allow you to retain the office; because that would be encouraging officers to be constantly intriguing, to the detriment of the public interest, in order to profit themselves."[45]

"I had no agency whatever in the introduction of the bill by Senator Foote," French replied to the president immediately. Yet, he admitted that he not only drew up the bill, at Sen. Foote's urgings, but had about a dozen copies of the bill printed to pass around.[46]

Lincoln allowed French to continue, albeit in a somewhat reduced capacity, in office. French, still infuriated at having Lincoln call his bluff, wrote his son Frank saying if he should be removed, "We shall see some unexpected developments." French added, "There is an *inside* as well as an *outside* to most things and watches and other delicate movements become injured at much exposure. Abraham is not a fool."[47]

For all his complaints, most of which were correct, about his predecessor's handling of the office, French fell into somewhat of the same trap. After he left the commissioner of public buildings' office in 1870, the secretary of the treasury, in order to close out French's accounts, requested two special Congressional appropriations, in the amount of $3,347, to erase the deficits French himself left.[48]

It is unfortunate that Benjamin Brown French, with his own checkered bureaucratic bungling, political intrigues and fiscal arrears, is the source who characterized Mary as a spendthrift while never mentioning the heinous activities of his predecessor, William S. Wood, who depleted the furnishings account.

French wrote in his diary on Sunday, December 16, 1861, that Mary sent him an urgent message the preceding Friday stating she needed to see him. French said their Saturday interview concerned her furnishing purchases for the residence that exceeded the $20,000 Congressional appropriation and she asked him to intercede with the president without letting him know they had discussed the matter.[49]

French's timing is suspect. The big gala scheduled for displaying the refurbished Executive Mansion on January 1, 1862, was in the final planning stages. Mary had much more to do than deliberately create a confrontation with her husband over these bills. Since that was going to be her crowning moment, it was most unlikely that she would have done anything to mar the occasion. On that Saturday, she had a reception and if Mary had been as upset as French indicated after their alleged conversation, she would have cancelled the reception.[50] Not only did Mary hold the December 14, 1861, afternoon reception, but she also hosted the regular public evening levee on December 18.[51]

French gave a vivid description of the event.

> Last evening I attended, officially, the first public reception at the President's. It was a jam & well might the President exclaim *jam satis!* My particular duty consisted in introducing the guests to Mrs. Lincoln, and I found it no sinecure. For two mortal hours a steady stream of humanity was passing on & there we stood, I saying, "Mr. or Mrs. or General or Col. or Gov. or Judge, so & so, Mrs. Lincoln," and she curtseying and saying, "How do you do," & sometimes to a particular acquaintance, "I am glad to see you," and giving the tips of white-kidded fingers in token of that gladness. She bore herself well and bravely, & looked Queenly. At ½ past ten the Band played "Yankee Doodle" & in 5 minutes the East room was deserted. I arrived home at 11.

In his diary entry, French indicated, from his conversation with Mary about the appropriation overrun, that the president already knew about the overdue bills and refused to approve them.[52] French listed no specific date that he allegedly spoke with Lincoln about the bills. He just wrote, "I accordingly saw him."[53]

French quoted Lincoln in his diary with words and phrasing that did not correspond with the president's normal use of expressions. "He said it would stink in the land to have it said that the appropriation of $20,000 for furnishing the house had been overrun by the president when the poor freezing soldiers could not have blankets, he *swore* he would never approve the bills for *flubs dubs for that damned old house.* It was, he said, furnished well enough when they came—better than any house *they* had ever lived in—and rather than put his name on such a bill he would pay it out of his own pocket!"[54] But Lincoln did not pay the bills out of his own pocket. Special appropriations of $6,858 and $4,500, both dated March 1, 1862, were paid by the federal government.[55]

Mary and Lincoln weathered their first year in Washington but the next would change their lives forever.

CHAPTER 13

Slings and Arrows

Devastating allegations about Mary Lincoln's personal behavior were swirling around Washington in 1861, like she was the vortex of a tumultuous storm. The contentious litany ran the entire gauntlet. By far the most popular speculation: Mary had to be a Confederate spy because she grew up in the border state of Kentucky and her kin were either serving in the rebel army or supporting the Confederacy.

Or, she was having an affair with John Watt, the gardener. There was a liaison with William S. Wood, the Lincolns' first selection for commissioner of public buildings, when they traveled to New York and Philadelphia to purchase furnishings for the Executive Mansion—regardless of the fact that Mary's cousin, Elizabeth Todd Grimsley, and other family members and friends accompanied her. Mary was the national poster woman for a spendthrift, a shopaholic. She was terribly stingy and tried to sell manure from the stables to make money. Of all things, she wanted to buy cows to furnish the residence with milk. Her mode of formal dress was, at the same time, determined to be outrageous and elegant.

Even more amazing is that 152 years later, new, uncomplimentary and questionable narratives about Mary Lincoln are still being unearthed. It has almost become a national pastime to target the wife of the sixteenth president with verbal slings and arrows of the most malicious sort.

The extent to which Mary Lincoln was thought to be a Confederate spy was detailed, tongue-in-cheek, by William O. Stoddard, Lincoln's secretary assigned to read her mail and assist her with the levees and receptions. He painted a word picture of the Red Room, where she held most of her receptions. "It is not large," he wrote, "and it is made smaller by the massive furniture, its heavy curtains, its grand piano, and by the consciousness that it is in the middle corner, so to speak, of an unusually large house."[1]

Put aside the curtains and look out this window, across the White House grounds. You cannot see far, because of the trees and bushes; but, upon a careful study, you will understand, as you shove up the sash, that this is one of the most important windows in the United States. Mrs. Lincoln is in constant communication with the Confederate government, betraying the war-plans of the Union generals, and this must be where she does it, for this is sacredly her own room. Even the president himself has never been seen here. The mails are not a channel for treachery, since every letter to Mrs. Lincoln is opened and read upstairs. The telegraphic wires are under war department censorship, of a peculiarly rigid kind, and there is no private line to the White House. The servants, downstairs, are known to be intensely loyal and would neither carry nor bring a communication of the [Benedict] Arnold-[John] Andre kind. There is, therefore, but one entirely reasonable solution of the problem of how Mr. Jefferson Davis, or his next of kin, can receive army plans from Mrs. Lincoln, after she obtained them from the president, and Halleck, and Stanton, and McClellan, and General Smith. The Confederate spies work their way through the lines easily enough, fort after fort, till they reach the Potomac down yonder. The Long Bridge is closed to them and so is the Georgetown Bridge, but they cross at night in rowboats, or by swimming, and they come up through the grounds, like so many ghosts, and they put a ladder up to this window, and Mrs. Lincoln hands them out the plans.[2]

Stoddard put his finger on the real problem Washington had with Mary Lincoln. "That she should make a success here, under such circumstances, was simply out of the question: but she has done vastly better than her ill-natured critics are at all willing to admit," he continued. "They are a jury empaneled to convict on every count of every indictment which any slanderous tongue may bring against her, and they have already succeeded in so poisoning the popular mind that it will never be able to judge her fairly."[3]

At the time her detractors were accusing her of spying for the Confederacy, Mary was working with her husband to direct arms into Kentucky, where they were both born, to keep the commonwealth in the Union. Kentucky was seen as the key to keeping the southern border states in the Union. The commonwealth's rivers and transportation facilities were an important supply route for federal troops in the South. Mary's friends, such as Col. John Fry, wrote asking for her assistance in obtaining weapons. In June 1861, Lincoln asked Secretary of War Simon Cameron to obtain a pair of Navy revolvers and a saber so Mary could send them to Fry, who lived near Danville, in Boyle County.[4] At the same time, Lincoln was working with Joshua and James Speed on a project to send 18,000 rifles and ammunition into Kentucky to arm Union supporters.[5]

There was so much more that Mary's critics neglected to learn, then and now. Occasionally, a detractor who took the time and effort to know her turned into an avid supporter.

The secretary understood the first lady and knew how to work with her. Stoddard acknowledged she was the absolute mistress of the first floor of the Executive Mansion and of the second floor, east of the folding door where Lincoln's administrative offices were located. "She was never less than a somewhat authoritative ruler of her own affairs, but it was entirely easy, for all that, to meet her with the most positive and strenuous negatives," Stoddard recalled. "She is always ready to listen to argument and to yield plainly put reason for doing or not doing, provided the arguments come from a recognized friend, for her personal antipathies are quick and strong, and at times they find a hasty and resentful form of expression. It was not easy, at first, to understand why a lady who could be one day so kindly, so considerate, so generous, so thoughtful and so hopeful, could, upon another day, appear so unreasonable, so irritable, so despondent, so even niggardly and so prone to see the dark and wrong sides of men and women and events." He understood her better after talking to a medical expert[6] about the illness of depression.[7]

An example of the judge and jury illustration Stoddard used to describe those who disparaged Mary was found in the partisan ranting of author Mary Clemmer Ames. A day of national mourning should have been declared, according to Ames, when Harriet Lane left the Executive Mansion. "She became the supreme lady of the gayest administration which has marked the government of the United States," Ames gushed about Buchanan's niece, who was his hostess. "Societies, ships of war and neck-ties were named after her. Men, gifted and great, from foreign lands and in her own, sought her hand in marriage. Such undulated pleasures and honors were never brought upon any other one young woman of the United States. At White House receptions, and on all state occasions, the sight of this golden beauty, standing beside the grand and gray old man, made a unique and delightful contrast, that thousands flocked to see."[8]

Ames conceded that Mary Lincoln entered the Executive Mansion at the height of national bitterness, but that was about all she accorded her in a book written in 1874. Mary had departed Washington nearly ten years earlier but Ames' venom was as vicious as if she still lived in the Executive Mansion. "To no other woman in America has ever been vouchsafed so full an opportunity for personal benevolence and philanthropy to her own countrymen. To no other woman in America has ever come an equal chance to set a lofty example of self-abnegation to all her countrywomen."[9]

Then, Ames really unloaded.

"But just as if there were no national peril no monstrous national debt no rivers of blood flowing, she seemed chiefly intent upon pleasures, personal flattery and adulation upon extravagant dress and careless self-gratification. Vain, seek admiration, the men who fed her weakness for their own political ends, were sure of her favors. Thus, while daily disgracing the state by her own example, she still sought to meddle in its affairs."[10]

Ames conveniently forgot that former First Lady Julia Gardiner Tyler hired her own publicity agent to tell the world about her activities as the "Lady President." Imagine what would have happened if Mary Lincoln had bought an elaborate carriage drawn by eight matched Arabian horses, as Julia Tyler did? Or, if Mary Lincoln had sashayed around Lafayette Park with an Italian greyhound on a leash as Julia Tyler did. Ames was terribly concerned about Mary Lincoln meddling in affairs of state but ignored Julia Tyler's lobbying Congress for control of federal patronage in New York and for the annexation of Texas. Mary Lincoln lobbied for federal appointments for friends in the first ever Republican presidential administration.[11]

In the game of politics, to the victor goes the patronage. Just as Democrats Buchanan and Tyler dispensed political favors to their supporters, so did the Lincoln administration.

Partisan rancor seeped through the planks of Ames' ship of state. Humanity is flawed by its very nature and that included Mary Clemmer Ames, Julia Gardiner Tyler as well as Mary Lincoln.

If it bothered Mary that Ames and others heaped disparagement on her at every turn, she did not let it show. If she was the weak, vain creature given to her own pleasures, as they alleged, such criticism would have laid her low in a short time. Her detractors underestimated her strength and determination.

Whether it was intentional or not, Mary answered her critics in the best way possible. She spent numerous hours visiting wounded soldiers in the various hospitals in Washington and raised money for their holiday dinners and citrus fruit to enrich their diets. She never visited a hospital empty handed. The first lady brought them fruit and flowers from the residence greenhouse. She wrote letters to their families for them. Enormous amounts of champagne, wines, whiskeys, gin, rum and brandy, gifts to the Executive Mansion, were sent to hospitals where anesthetic was in short supply.[12]

The wounded exceeded the available hospital space. Space in schools, churches and government buildings was converted into hospitals such as the museum in the Patent Office, where the Lincolns, journalist Noah Brooks and Mr. and Mrs. Abner Doubleday visited wounded soldiers in 1862. A sprawling hospital complex was built on the Harewood estate of financier William W. Corcoran.[13]

When Mary visited hospitals without her husband, she took no reporters with her.

Stoddard thought she missed an opportunity to reap some positive publicity. "She rarely takes outside company with her upon these errands and she thereby loses opportunities. If she was worldly wise, she would carry newspaper correspondents, from two to five, of both sexes every time she went out and she would have them take shorthand notes of what she says to the sick soldiers and what the sick soldiers say to her. Then she would bring the writers back to the White House and give them some cake and coffee, as a rule, and show them the conservatory,"[14] he wrote.

"By keeping up such a process until every correspondent that Colonel Baker can find for her has been dealt with, say twice, she could somewhat sweeten the contents of many journals and of the secretary's wastebasket. The direct course, as she pursues it, has not by any means worked well."

Of course, it was much more tantalizing for her enemies to dwell on Mary Lincoln's possible affairs than to acknowledge her good works. Abraham Lincoln's statement at one of the Executive Mansion's social events eliminated any need for further comment. "My wife is as handsome as when she was a girl and I a poor nobody then fell in love with her and what's more I have never fallen out."[15]

Mary Clemmer Ames, *New York Times* and other denigrators, even Benjamin B. French, were so enamored of the amount of money Mary Lincoln supposedly spent on clothes that one would think the funds to pay for them came out of their pockets. Actually, given her official schedule from March 1861 to April 1865, Mary exhibited an enormous amount of frugality. During those dates Mary Lincoln attended 105 events that called for particular apparel: two inaugural balls, thirty-eight formal receptions, twenty-seven less formal receptions, six state and other formal dinners and thirty-two trips to the theater. In addition to those 105 social events, she attended formal affairs as first lady when she traveled to New York, Philadelphia and Boston. In addition, there were scores of visits to hospitals, troop installations and travel on government steamers that required an entirely different wardrobe.[16]

Some found it exceptional that Mary's Washington seamstress, Elizabeth Keckly, made her fifteen or sixteen gowns in the period between inauguration day, on March 4, through July 1861, and cite that as evidence of her excessive spending on clothes. However, during that span of time, Mary Lincoln attended nineteen official functions that included the inaugural ball, receptions, levees, and state and diplomatic dinners.[17]

Her January 1862 social schedule illustrated the need for a variety of proper attire. On New Year's Eve, the Lincolns hosted a big gala at the Executive Mansion. Mary held four public receptions that month. She attended a celebration of the French Regiment in Washington and attended the opera with her husband. A Washington newspaper, reporting on the Saturday, January 28, reception, described Mary Lincoln as never having been more elegantly attired.[18]

Had Mary Lincoln appeared in the same gown twice at any official events, her ever vigilance critics would have accused her of having no fashion sense, of being a frump of a housewife from the West. If she had altered any of her gowns by adding or removing ruffles, flounces, drapes or flowers, the charge of skinflint or cheapskate would have prevailed as when she instructed her New York milliner to make her a headdress costing not more than five dollars. On the other hand, the *New York Times* called her "a well-known spendthrift."[19]

And, that was not even the newspaper's best shot. The publication's spoof of the Lincolns' gala invitation only ball on February 5, 1862, was not quite as sophisticated as they intended. Two reporters, the Worldly Jenkins, who wrote about the pomp and vanities, and the Devil Jenkins, whose concern was the food, agreed that Mary was elegant in a white gown with black lace flounces. Worldly Jenkins said her only jewelry was a simple diamond broach. Devil Jenkins insisted she was loaded down with diamonds and pearls.[20] "It was one of the finest displays of gastronomic acts ever seen in this country. On one of the side tables, by the way, he tells us, was a 'very large fort named Fort Pickens,' the inside of which was filled with quail, which, it is manifest, brought vividly to his mind how delicious the pickin's of that fort would be."[21]

A Washington newspaper called the event "the most superb affair ever held here." It was said there were so many congressmen attending that the House had a forum to conduct business.[22] Stoddard, not exactly an objective observer, wrote, "Seldom, indeed, on this continent have so many men of mark gathered at one time under one roof."[23]

Criticism of Mary, and often her husband, was not limited to the nineteenth and twentieth centuries but has swollen into immense proportions in the twenty-first century. An example was *New York Times* columnist Adam Goodheart writing, in 2011, about the 1861 visit of Prince Napoleon Joseph Charles Paul Bonaparte, the emperor's nephew, when he and his entourage arrived in Washington on August 3. There are two contrasting accounts of the prince's visit: those of Elizabeth Grimsley and assistant Secretary of State Frederick W. Seward, who were there, and Goodheart's 2011 article, "Peevish Prince, A Hairy-handed President, A Disastrous Dinner Party," based on a supposed diary found decades later.[24]

According to Goodheart, when the prince's party arrived at the Executive Mansion no one was at home. "The prince and his companions (various counts, barons and lesser lackeys) had been impressed enough by their first glimpse of the White House: 'a rather nice place,' one of them noted. On ascending the grand steps, they found no valet or butler to greet them; not even a doorman of the sort to be found at any decent American hotel. Finally after being admitted unceremoniously by a passing clerk, they were left standing in the vestibule, wondering when—or if—President Lincoln might deign to emerge and greet them."[25]

Currying favor with the French was critical, Goodheart wrote, since Napoleon III appeared to have private sympathies for the Confederacy.[26]

"All this made it more bizarre that it took more than 15 minutes before Lincoln, preceded by Secretary of State William H. Seward, finally came ambling into the reception room that morning. The infuriated prince, one of the Frenchman later wrote, had been on the verge of turning on his heel and departing." Goodheart said the French party had hoped Lincoln would have the charm of Benjamin Franklin, minister to France 1776–1785. Instead, according to the columnist, they found a tall, awkward man, with large hairy hands, whose beard would make Jupiter himself look vulgar. "After shaking hands with the visitors, the president, who spoke no French, seemed at a total loss for words, even English ones." The prince, unhappy because he had been made to wait, "took a cruel pleasure in remaining silent."[27]

Frederick W. Steward had met the prince's steam yacht in New York and escorted him to Washington. "Secretary (of State) Seward received him and presented him to the president, who gave a state dinner in his honor," the younger Seward wrote in a biography of his father.[28]

The secretary of state obviously had advanced knowledge about the prince's arrival but, according to Grimsley, Seward only informed the Lincolns of his visit in early August. Since the dinner took place August 3, there was not much time for preparations. Seward offered, with Lincoln's consent, to give the dinner for the prince. "Mrs. Lincoln did not fail to make a prompt objection to this suggestion," Grimsley said, "which seemed an echo of an earlier one which I have already mentioned, and she at once caused one of the private secretaries to be summoned and charged with arranging a formal dinner on the day of the prince's presentation to the president. It was at the same time settled that Mr. Seward should give an evening reception in honor of the prince on a subsequent day."[29]

"Saturday, at noon, Prince 'Plon Plon,' as he was widely known, attended by his suite, was presented to the president by Count Mercier, the French Minister," Grimsley wrote.[30]

"Later that day," Goodheart continued, "Lincoln had a second chance to try to impress the Corsican artilleryman's nephew, when he hosted Prince Napoleon and his suite at a state dinner in the White House. Mary Todd Lincoln—who adored French fashions and even prided herself on speaking a few words of the language, albeit in an atrocious Kentucky accent—pulled out all the stops to woo her imperial guests. She personally chose the menu, the flowers and even the vegetables from the White House garden with an eye toward enchanting the Parisian sophisticates."[31]

The prince, the president and their guests went out on the balcony to greet the assembled crowd and then returned to the Blue Room. "Then came the entrance to the dining room," Grimsley wrote, "the president leading, I upon his arm, Mrs. Lincoln with the prince, the other guests following in the usual order of precedence. A beautiful dinner served, gay conversation in which the French predominated, led Prince Napoleon to remark gallantly, that after enjoying the elegant hospitality in Washington, especially of those presiding in the Executive Mansion, he should be forced to confess that 'Paris is not all the world.'"[32]

"Half a century later," Goodheart maintained, "Prince Napoleon's actual feelings were revealed when a French magazine published excerpts from his private diary. 'Mrs. Lincoln,' the guest of honor recorded after the White House dinner, 'was dressed in the French mode without any taste; she had the manner of a petit bourgeois and wears tin jewelry.' Her lovingly prepared meal was 'a bad dinner in the French style.'"[33]

The prince described the president as being "badly put together in a black suit with the appearance of a boot maker," according to Goodheart. "What a difference between this sad representative of the great republic and her founding fathers," he quoted the prince as saying. The prince concluded Lincoln was a good man but one without greatness and not very much knowledge. However, when the Prince's party crossed into Virginia, they poured praise on Confederate Gen. P.G.T. Beauregard: "Everything in him points to a remarkable military aptitude, if not superior intelligence."[34]

While weighing those accounts of the visit, there is something else to consider. After the state dinner for the prince, which his wife Princess Clothide did not attend, Mary, accompanied by Elizabeth Grimsley, Bob and John Hay took a short vacation. She stopped first in Long Branch, New Jersey, where she called on and was received by the Princess Clothide in her hotel suite.[35]

Mary Lincoln's critics were unable to deliver the one jolting wallop that would force her into victimhood. At least not as long as Abraham Lincoln was alive.

CHAPTER 14

In the Blink of an Eye

Their first year in Washington was an eventful one for Mary and Abraham Lincoln, but not necessarily a stellar period. Fort Sumter was captured, the remaining southern states seceded and created their own government, the Civil War began, Mary became a lightning rod for criticism over refurbishing the Executive Mansion as well as daring to enter the political realm and even Lincoln admitted he spent too much time on patronage.

Time was fleeting and their loss of loved ones was enormous.

There were other personal losses in addition to Stephen A. Douglas's death. A law clerk in Lincoln's law office and former drill instructor, Elmer E. Ellsworth, who accompanied them to Washington on the inauguration train, was killed May 24, 1861. When Lincoln asked for 75,000 volunteers, Ellsworth recruited 1,100 New York firemen for a regiment known as the Zouaves, named after his successful drill team. The Zouaves were ordered into northern Virginia to gain control of the port of Alexandria. Meeting no resistance, they headed for the telegraph office when they noticed a Confederate flag flying over the Marshall House Inn. Ellsworth went inside, removed the flag and, on his way back down the stairs, was shot through the heart by innkeeper James W. Jackson, who was then killed by one of the Zouaves.[1]

Mary and Abraham Lincoln went to the Navy Yard the next day to view Ellsworth's body. "My boy! My boy! Was it necessary this sacrifice should be made?" Lincoln mourned. Later, the president returned to the Navy Yard to make arrangements for Ellsworth's body to be taken to the Executive Mansion, where a funeral service was held in the East Room. Mary placed a picture of Ellsworth and flowers on the casket, Willie and Tad cried and Lincoln held his head in his hands during the service. The president, and members of the Cabinet, accompanied Ellsworth's body to the train that would carry him back to his parents in Mechanicsville, New York.[2]

The president wrote Ellsworth's parents a most touching letter saying, "In the untimely loss of your noble son, our affliction here, is scarcely less than your own. So much of promised usefulness to one's country, and of bright hopes for one's self and friends, have rarely been so suddenly dashed, as in his fall. In size, in years, and in youthful appearance, a boy only, his power to command men, was surpassingly great. This power combined with a fine intellect, an indomitable energy, and a taste altogether military, constitute in him, as seemed to me, the best natural talent, in that department, I ever knew."[3]

Lincoln closed by saying, "In the hope that it may be no intrusion upon the sacredness of your sorrow, I have ventured to address this tribute to the memory of my young friend and your brave and early fallen child. May God give you that consolation which is beyond all earthly power. Sincerely your friend in common affliction, A. Lincoln."[4]

Five months later, the Lincolns lost a dear friend from their days in Illinois, Sen. Edward D. Baker. Lincoln and Baker had been close friends for more than twenty-five years and they enfolded Mary, who named their second son for him, into that close relationship. Baker was credited with swinging the Pacific states' support to Lincoln in the 1860 election. It was Baker, a former representative, current Oregon senator and brilliant orator, not any of his other associates from Illinois, whom Lincoln chose to introduce him at his inauguration.

After Baker raised a militia unit, Lincoln wanted to raise him in rank from colonel to brigadier general. Baker refused, saying he would be forced to give up his Senate seat if he accepted. With Congress out of session, Baker and his troops were called into battle as Confederate forces were advancing on Washington. On October 19, Baker spent the warm autumn afternoon sitting on the lawn of the Executive Mansion with Mary and Lincoln reminiscing about their days in Illinois and talking about current political problems as Willie and Tad played in the leaves scattered about the lawn. The boys were always enthralled with the stories Baker told them, as his first memories were of the pageantry surrounding the funeral of Lord Nelson.[5]

Before Baker left, Mary gave him a bouquet of autumn flowers. He picked up Willie and gave him a hug and a kiss. Baker, who had a premonition that he would die in combat and made his will the previous month, had a mournful parting with his dear friends. The next day Baker was killed in the Battle of Ball's Bluff. Baker's Senate biography gave the following account of the battle. "Lightly schooled in military tactics, Baker gamely led his 1,700 brigade across the Potomac River 40 miles north of the capital, up the steep ridge known as Ball's Bluff, and into the range of waiting enemy guns. He died quickly—too soon to witness the stampede of his troops over the 70-foot cliffs in to the rock-studded river below. Nearly 1,000 were killed, wounded or captured." Lincoln was in the War Department telegraph office, monitoring the battle, when he heard the news. He walked out the door with head bowed, looking pale, with tears streaming down his cheeks. Baker's death and the results of the battle led to the creation of the Joint Committee on the Conduct of the War. Baker remains the only sitting Senator to die in battle.[6]

Baker left instruction that his funeral be held at the residence of Major J. W. Webb. Prior to the funeral, Lincoln and some of Baker's other friends went to the mortuary to view his body for the last time. Mary and Lincoln attended the funeral services before Baker's body was placed in a temporary vault in the Congressional Cemetery prior to being shipped to California and its final resting place in the San Francisco National Cemetery.[7]

Mary's decision to wear a silk lilac dress, bonnet and gloves to Baker's funeral struck her Washington critics as a social error of such enormous proportions that it was the equivalent of her having climbed astride one of the horses pulling the caisson. "This evoked so much ridicule and outrage in society that her associates sent a delegate to scold her in case she was unaware of her impropriety," Daniel Mark Epstein wrote.[8]

Mary understood the social mourning requirements and had from the time she was six years old experiencing the death of her mother. She had gone through the mourning process when their son, Edward "Eddy" Baker Lincoln died. Within a span of two years, 1849–1850, she not only lost her son but her father, Robert S. Todd, and her beloved grandmother, Elizabeth Porter Parker. Mary needed no one to advise her about mourning wear. Mary and Lincoln loved the man like a brother, and she would have done nothing to dishonor Baker's name. Obviously, Lincoln approved of her choice of dress; otherwise she would have worn black. She simply chose not to share the reason for her attire with the world.

Ten-year-old Willie Lincoln and his brother, Tad, were devastated by Baker's death and could not be consoled. Willie, in his grief, wrote a tribute to the man he so admired and sent it to the *Washington National Republican*, which printed it. The first four lines read, "There was no patriot like Baker, So noble and so true, He fell as a soldier on the field, His face to the sky of blue."[9]

The Lincolns, with a heavy heart, closed out the year by inviting their friends Joshua and Fannie Speed from Louisville as holiday house guests and to have dinner with them. Their Christmas was a quiet celebration with family and friends.[10]

One of their Springfield friends, the Rev. Noyes W. Miner, who was Hannah Shearer's brother, came to visit early in 1862. The Reverend Miner and his family had lived near the Lincolns. In his discussion with Mary, the subject of her brother and half-brothers fighting for the Confederacy came up. She bluntly told the minister she hoped they would all either be killed or captured. When the Reverend Miner expressed surprise, she said, "They would kill my husband if they could and destroy our government—the dearest of all things to us."[11]

Also dear to Mary's heart were the Executive Mansion's state rooms, which she had elegantly refurbished as an indication that the government was strong and would survive. Willie and Tad had settled into what, for them, was a routine of rowdiness and pranks. Mary started the new year with a busy social schedule. The Lincolns' reception on January 1, 1862, opened the year's social season. Benjamin B. French, still the commissioner of public buildings, wrote that the crowd was immense. Mary held four public receptions that month and joined her husband in the celebration of the French regiment at Tennalytown, in the District. The Lincolns accepted a portrait of Baker from the California congressional delegation. Later that month, they went to the Washington Theatre for the New York Academy of Music's performance of selections from Verdi and Bellini operas.[12]

In January, Mary came up with an innovative idea for entertaining in the residence. She convinced Lincoln that instead of having expensive state dinners, they should give a ball for invited guests only. More than 500 invitations were mailed; some said as many as 800.[13] The ball was going to be Mary Lincoln's reply to all her Washington critics.

If Mary's social plans were going well, Lincoln's attempts to deal with his recalcitrant Army leader, Gen. George McClellan, were unsuccessful. After accompanying Lincoln to a February meeting with McClellan, Stoddard wrote the general told the president, "That the army cannot move, and that the plan of the winter campaign is frustrated by the mud." In his own opinion, Stoddard added, "The Confederate commanders have some wonderful secret of their own by means of which they overcome the mud."[14]

Another of Lincoln's commanders was having success, despite the mud. Brig. Gen. U.S. Grant captured two Tennessee forts, Henry and Donelson, on the Cumberland River, in an eight-day span in February.[15]

Mary cancelled her first weekly reception for February because Willie became ill the last of January. She had frequently stayed up with her son all night doing her best to nurse him back to health. She wanted to cancel the ball they had scheduled for February 5. Lincoln, concerned about the already issued invitations, asked Dr. Robert Stone to examine Willie. The physician assured the parents they could expect an early recovery, so they decided to hold the event.[16]

Had Mary engaged Washington caterers for the ball, she might have scored a few points with the city's elites. By then, however, she was beyond attempting to please the city's self-appointed social arbitrators. In earlier trips to New York, she became familiar with the work of Henri Maillard, who immigrated from Paris in the 1840s and began as a chocolatier before going into the catering business. Undoubtedly, Maillard reminded Mary of the pleasant experiences she had as a girl in the Lexington shop of confectionarie Mathurin Giron. She ordered wine and champagne from another New York firm, that of Clement Heerdt.[17]

Nicolay and Hay made sure there were no further gaffes with guests' coats, hats and wraps. Containers, carefully numbered, were provided. Everything went smoothly until it came time to move from the East Room into the State Dining Room as Lincoln gave his arm to Mrs. Orville Browning and Mary followed with Sen. Browning and they were unable to get into the room. The State Dining Room doors were locked and guests had to wait until the steward was located with the key. One of the guests remarked that regardless they could expect a forward movement once the doors were open, an apparent reference to Gen. McClellan's reluctance to move his men into battle.[18]

Mary and Lincoln took turns leaving the ball to check on Willie, who was being cared for by Elizabeth Keckly, the seamstress. Dorthea Dix, superintendent of women nurses, wrote Lincoln offering the services of one of her nurses to care for Willie, who took turns improving and then digressing. At the time Lincoln replied to her offer, Willie appeared to be improving, and he felt they needed no additional assistance.[19]

Willie was moved from his room into the larger guest room with the ornate bed his mother purchased. Along with Keckly, Mary Jane Wells, wife of the secretary of the Navy, and Eliza Browning, wife of Illinois Senator Oliver Browning, assisted the Lincolns in caring for the young boy.[20]

Willie did not get better and Tad became ill. The source of their illness, which most now think was typhoid fever, was probably contracted through the polluted water from the Potomac that was pumped into the residence. Mary cancelled all her social engagements and receptions after the ball. Both she and Lincoln spent as much time as possible with the boys. Willie, the light of their lives, died on the afternoon of February 20. Mary was desolate, exhausted from caring for the boys and was unable to function. Lincoln asked Dorthea Dix to send a nurse to care for Tad and help with Mary. She sent Rebecca Pomeroy, the daughter of a New England sea captain, who had lost her husband and two of her three children to illnesses.[21]

On the day Willie died, Attorney General Edward Bates made the following entry in his diary. "Feb. 20. Thursday. This day at 5 p. m. the Prest's son Wm. Wallace Lincoln died. A fine boy of 11 yrs, too much idolized by his parents."[22]

An apt description of Willie Lincoln was written by Nathaniel Parker Willis, an editor with the *Home Journal*.

This little fellow had his acquaintances among his father's friends, and I chanced to be one of them. He never failed to seek me out in a crowd, shake hands and make some pleasant remark; and this in a boy of ten years of age was, to say the least, endearing to a stranger. But he had more than mere affectionateness. His self-possession—aplomb as the French call it—was extraordinary. I was one day passing the White House when he was outside with a play-fellow on the side walk. Mr. Seward drove in with Prince Napoleon and two of his suite in a carriage, and in a mock-heroic way—terms of amusing intimacy evidently existing between the boy and the secretary—the official gentleman took off his hat, and the Napoleon party did the same—all making the young prince president a ceremonious salute. Not a bit staggered with the homage, Willie drew himself up to his full height, took off his little cap with graceful self-possession, and bowed down formally to the ground, like a little ambassador. They drove past and he went on unconcerned with his play; the impromptu readiness and good judgment being clearly a part of his nature. His genial and open expression of countenance was none the less ingenuous and fearless for a certain tincture of fun, and it was in this mingling of qualities that he so faithfully resembled his father.[23]

Both parents were devastated by Willie's death. Losing Eddy at age four was a terrible blow. The Lincolns had Willie for eleven years and could see a most remarkable future for him. One might say he was their shining light. Lincoln pulled himself together and began making the necessary arrangements.

Lincoln sent for his friend, Sen. Orville Browning, according to Benjamin B. French, to ask him to handle the funeral arrangements at the Executive Mansion. However, it was Browning, along with Mary's friend, Isaac Newton, the commissioner of the agricultural bureau in the Patent Office, who witnessed, along with Willie's physicians, the embalming done in the Executive Mansion. William Carroll, Supreme Court clerk, offered Lincoln space in his family vault at Oak Hill Cemetery as a temporary receptacle for his son. Browning, accompanied by Carroll, visited the cemetery to inspect the vault.[24]

French saw that the interior of the Executive Mansion was draped in black and the great mirrors were also covered. Willie, in repose in a rosewood casket trimmed in silver and covered with flowers, was placed in the Green Room, where Mary, Lincoln and Bob spent a half an hour alone with him before the services in the East Room. Tad was still ill. Mary, collapsed with grief, and was unable to attend the funeral or burial. Two white horses pulled the hearse carrying Willie to Oak Hill Cemetery followed by his father's carriage pulled by black horses in a long line of mourners.[25]

Pomeroy nursed Tad well into March until he was able to walk a few steps before she returned to her hospital duties. Elizabeth Edwards, at Lincoln's request, came from Springfield to help care for Mary with assistance from Keckly, Eliza Browning and Mary Jane Wells. Mary did not just collapse; her entire body appeared to shut down. It was as if all the life had been sucked out of her. Elizabeth, after two months, was called back to Springfield and appeared anxious to depart. "She feels since her trouble that she cannot be alone," Elizabeth wrote to her daughter, Julia Edwards Baker. In another letter, Elizabeth wrote, "Aunt Mary is nervous and dependent upon the companionship of someone." Elizabeth was annoyed with Mary, but not to the point of refusing to answer the president's request for assistance, because Lincoln's administration had been in office for six months before a plum appointment came for her husband, Ninian Edwards, who was still paying off a loan from Lincoln.[26]

Lincoln, deeply concerned about Mary, requested Dix to send Pomeroy back to the residence to help his wife. "Mrs. Lincoln secludes herself from society," the nurse wrote, "and I was alone with her most of the day in her room. When I told her of my trials and afflictions, and above all, of God's dealings with me, she could not understand how I could be so happy under it all, and bursting into tears, said she wished she could feel so too." Pomeroy nursed Mary's physical, emotional and mental infirmities and was so successful that Mary asked her to stay with her during the summer. The nurse told Mary that her duty was with the wounded in the hospital at Columbia College. "She suffers from depression of the spirits, but I do think if she would only come here and look at the poor soldiers occasionally it would be better for her." When her strength returned, Mary did just that with renewed vigor.[27]

Mary owed her recovery not just to the nurse but also to her husband. Lincoln, unbelievably busy as he was, found time to spend with her and include her in his local visits. On

Above: **Mary in mourning wear after Willie's death in 1862.** *Right:* **Lincoln and Tad after Willie's death (both photographs, Library of Congress, Prints and Photographs Division).**

March 20, 1862, a Washington newspaper reported that Mary, confined to her room since Willie's death, was almost back to normal.[28]

At that time, Pomeroy was still with Mary. On March 22, Pomeroy wrote that Mary gave her pictures of Willie and Tad, potted plants for her bay window, fruit for the wounded and other luxuries for the boys. Those were parting gifts and the president ordered horses and a carriage to take her back to the college hospital.[29]

In addition, Mary asked New York milliner Ruth Harris to make "a *very fine* black straw—trimmed stylishly with colors—I want it got up with great haste & make the price as reasonable as possible—I want it very pretty, I am in need of a mourning bonnet—which must be exceedingly plain & genteel." Justin Turner thought the fine black bonnet with colors she ordered was a gift to the nurse. Harris rushed the order back to Mary and she wrote the milliner how pleased she was with the bonnet intended for a gift and ordered another plain black straw bonnet along with short and long veils made from fine black silk.[30]

Mary found outlets for her grief by writing her friends back in Springfield and describing her emotions. One such letter was to Julia Ann Sprigg, who had written her after Willie's death. Mary apologized for two weeks having lapsed before she answered her letter.

We have met with so overwhelming an affliction in the death of our beloved Willie a being too precious for earth, that I am so completely unnerved, that I can scarcely command myself to write. What would I give to see you & talk to you, in our crushing bereavement, if any one's presence could afford comfort—it would be yours. You were always such a good friend & dearly have I loved you. All that human skill could do, was done for our sainted boy, I believe that the severe illness (scarlet fever), he passed through, now, almost two years since, was but a warning to us, that one so pure, was not to remain long here and at the same time, he was *lent* us a little longer—to try us & wean us from a world whose chains were fastening around us when the blow came, it found us so unprepared to meet it.[31]

Admitting that she found little pleasure in the refurbished Executive Mansion, Mary continued,

Our home is very beautiful, the grounds around us are enchanting, the world still smiles & pays homage, yet the charm is dispelled—everything appears to be a mockery, the idolized one is not with us, he has fulfilled his mission and we are left desolate. When I think over his short but happy childhood, how much comfort, he always was to me and how fearfully, I always found my hopes concentrating on so good a boy as he was—when I can bring myself to realize that he has indeed passed away, my question to myself is, "can life be endured?" Dear little Taddie who was so devoted to his darling brother, although as deeply afflicted as ourselves, bears up and teaches us a lesson, in enduring the stroke, to which *we must submit.*[32]

A month after Pomeroy left, Lincoln, knowing how much Mary loved ships, took her, along with Seward and others, to the Navy Yard to meet Commander John A. Dahlgren. Mary stayed in the carriage while the others took a cutter to visit a French warship. The next week, Lincoln took her back to the Navy Yard to see a new breech-loading cannon demonstrated. Several members of congress were present and Lincoln was in the middle of one of his famous stories when the first discharge occurred. On May 28, Mary and Lincoln attended a concert at Ford's Theatre by the opera singer Clara Louise Kellogg.[33]

In June, Mary resumed her visits to the wounded in hospitals and the Lincolns moved to the Soldiers' Home for the summer. A decision was made in July 1862 that a change of scenery might be good for Mary. In a June 26, 1862, letter to Mrs. Charles Eames, whose husband was a former newspaper editor and admiralty lawyer for the government, Mary thanked her daughter for calling and leaving her card. "*At the time*, I was making a short and unexpected visit to the North (New York and Boston), undertaken with much reluctance, yet found to be more pleasant, than I could have hoped, with spirits so depressed—In the loss of our idolized boy, we naturally have suffered such intense grief, that a removal from the scene of our misery was found necessary."[34]

She spent a few days in New York at the grand Metropolitan Hotel, on Broadway. The brownstone building accommodated 600 guests in rooms and family apartments with private drawing rooms. While there she bought some books. In a July 26 letter to French, Mary wrote, "Happening to be in N.Y & having a day of leisure—in accordance with your letter, which mentioned there was an appropriation of $250—I selected some books for the library—$75 worth were selected in W. and the remaining $150—in N.Y. There is a very poor set of Waverly—also Shakespeare in the home library, so I replaced each with a fine new edition."[35]

"I presume, with your usual kindness, you are willing to leave such things to my judgment. No one has the interest of the place, more to heart than myself." Mary added that she was sorry that she missed French and Amos Tuck, a former New Hampshire congressman who was a friend of both the Lincolns, when they called at the Soldiers' Home.[36]

Three days later, Mary and Robert left New York City and went to West Point, where she remained for a week before returning to Washington. She was accompanied by Lt. S. Long and Thomas W. Sweney, revenue collector for Philadelphia.[37]

The next two months, Mary spent some time in Boston, where she collected $1,000 for wounded soldiers. The amount was deposited with Lincoln by Gen. Michael Corcoran, who led the Irish Legion and had been captured at First Bull Run. Lincoln helped her spend part of it. On August 16, he telegraphed Hiram P. Barney, collector for the Port of New York, to send Mary $200 of good lemons and $100 of good oranges and she would pay him. She was back in Washington on August 28, 1862, when she visited wounded soldiers in the Odd Fellows Hall hospital. A month later, she returned to New York for a short stay at the Metropolitan Hotel. Mary, along with Gen. Winfield Scott, visited the Brooklyn Naval Yards and went aboard the USS *North Carolina*.[38]

While in New York, she wrote Lincoln asking him to take $200 out of the $1,000 funds for soldiers and send her a check for $200 to buy bedding for the former slaves in Washington through the Contraband Association that Elizabeth Keckly was working with in collecting money. An immense number, she told Lincoln, was suffering intensely without any bedding and using pieces of carpeting to cover themselves.[39]

Memories of Willie in the residence and at the Soldiers' Home enveloped Mary in a cocoon of melancholy, which she found difficult to escape. She sought closure by traveling but there were always the nights and the haunting memories of the bright, sunny, intelligent child. Mary had not reached the point in the grieving process, if she ever did, where she could relish her recollections of Willie.

Mary, even four years later, wondered if her involvement in politics was a factor in their losing Willie. "I had become, so wrapped up in the world, so devoted to our political advancement," she wrote Hannah Shearer after her son, Edward, died, "that I thought of little else besides. Our Heavenly Father sees fit, oftentimes to visit us at such times for our worldliness, how small and insignificant all worldly honors are, when we are *thus* so severely tried." Mary told Hannah that she was far better prepared "than I was to pass through the fiery furnace of affliction."[40]

Lincoln did everything he could think of to help her. In the fall of 1862, Lincoln went to Madame Patti's operatic performance in Washington where she appeared with pianist Maurice Strakosch, another prodigy. He had seen her in Illinois when Adelina Patti, a ten-year-old child prodigy, appeared with the Norwegian violinist and composer Ole Boremann Bull. The child made such an impression on him that he told Mary that she had a bright future. He was correct; she became one of the great coloraturas of the nineteenth century. The president sent word backstage that he would like to speak to her and invited the two of them to come to the Executive Mansion the next afternoon and play for his wife.[41]

When Patti and Strakosch called the next afternoon, Mary received them and told her of the many compliments the president used in his descriptions of her talents. "My dear," Mary told her, "it is very kind of you to come to see us. I have wanted to see you, to see the young girl who has done so much, who has set the whole world talking of her wonderful singing." Patti described Mary as a handsome woman, almost regal in her deep black and expansive crinoline, only an outline of white at the wrists and throat." Her manner, the singer said, was most gracious without a particle of reserve or stiffness.[42]

Patti said the president joined them and again mentioned how much she had changed since he saw her perform with Ole Bull. After playing a couple of pieces of music, Patti said she accompanied herself singing "The Last Rose of Summer," which she would sing a few hours later in the title role of Martha.[43] The sad song, adapted from Thomas Moore's poem, ended with these lines: "So soon may I follow, when friendships decay and from Love's shining circle, the gems drop away. When true hearts lie wither'd and fond ones are flown, Oh, who would inhabit this bleak world alone."[44]

"When I finished the last long-drawn-out note of the song," Patti said, "I turned to look at my audience. Mrs. Lincoln had risen from her seat and was standing in the back part of the room with her back toward me. Of course, I couldn't see her face but I knew she was weeping.... I reproached myself that I had made such an awkward choice and was about to remedy my mistake by ending the performance with a rollicking bolero when Mr. Lincoln, who had been sitting motionless on a sofa nearby, his eyes shaded by his left hand, asked, without removing his fingers from his face, 'Will you please play Home Sweet Home?'"[45]

Patti said Strakosch did not know the song and she had never sung the words. She said Lincoln rose from the sofa, went to a nearby music stand, removed a music book, opened it to the song and placed it on the piano rack. "Well, I sang the song the very best I could do it," she said, "and when Mr. Lincoln thanked me his voice was husky and his eyes were full of tears. By that time, I was so wrought up over the situation myself that I was actually blubbering when we were taking our leave of the recently bereaved parents."[46]

Holding out hope that she might once again contact Willie, Mary turned to mediums.

Elizabeth S. Brownstein, in her book *Lincoln's Other White House*, wrote that Keckly had been able to reach her only son, who been killed early in the war, through mediums. Brownstein mentioned others—Secretary of the Navy Gideon Wells and his wife, Mary Jane; Harriett Beecher Stowe; Horace Greeley; Queen Victoria and the Empress Eugenie—who engaged mediums in efforts to reach departed loved ones.[47]

Keckly's actions might have been well intended, but she did Mary no favor by encouraging her to consult a spiritual medium, Charles J. Colchester, who claimed to be the illegitimate son of an English duke. "The poor lady at time was well-nigh distraught with grief at the death of her son, Willie," the journalist Noah Brooks wrote. "By playing on her motherly sorrows, Colchester actually succeeded in inducing Mrs. Lincoln to receive him in the family residence at the Soldiers' Home, where, in a darkened room, he pretended to produce messages from the lost boy by means of scratches on the wainscoting and taps on the walls and furniture."[48]

Mary was not the first president's wife to attempt to reach a dead son through a medium. President Franklin Pierce, 1853–1857, and his wife, Jane, lost one son in infancy, another at age four, and their third son, Benjamin, was killed in a train accident two months after Pierce's election. Jane Pierce took to her bed and was weeks finally arriving in Washington, missing her husband's inauguration. She first had to leave the train in Boston and spend time with friends. Then, she made it as far as Baltimore and refused to go farther. Pierce made several trips to Baltimore before he convinced her to accompany him to the Executive Mansion, where she held séances in efforts to reach her son, Benny.[49]

Unlike Mary, Jane Pierce never wanted to be in the Executive Mansion. When informed that her husband, a senator, was nominated for the presidency, she fainted. For the most part, her widowed aunt, Abigail Means, served as the president's official hostess. Jane emerged only to attend official dinners. Most of her séances were held in the state rooms.[50]

Brooks said Mary told him about Colchester's alleged manifestations and asked him to the Executive Mansion when the Englishman appeared. Brooks declined the invitation

The Soldiers' Home, the Lincolns' summer retreat, sat on a hilltop outside Washington. The Lincolns were in residence here from June to November of 1862, 1863 and 1864 (Library of Congress, Prints and Photographs Division).

Journalist Noah Brooks traveled with the Lincolns and was to be the president's new secretary at the time of the assassination. Brooks chronicled Mary Lincoln's move from the Executive Mansion to Chicago in May 1865 (courtesy Wilson Museum, Castine, Maine).

but did pay a dollar to attend a séance of Colchester's at a friend's home. Brooks caught Colchester in the act of manipulating the drums, banjo and bells and, before his friend could light a match, the medium had banged him over the head with the drum, cutting his forehead. The meeting broke up in disorder, Brooks wrote, with Colchester slipping out of the room during the confusion claiming he had been insulted.[51]

A couple of days later, Brooks said, he received a note from Mary asking him to come to the residence without a moment's delay. Colchester sent Mary a note requesting that, unless she obtained a pass from the War Department for him to New York, he would have some unpleasant things to say about her. Mary and Brooks concocted a plan where she again invited him to the residence. After introducing Brooks to Colchester, Mary left the room. "Going up to Colchester," Brooks wrote, "I lifted my hair from the scar on my forehead, yet unhealed, and said, 'Do you recognize this?' The man muttered something about his having been insulted, and then I said: 'You know that I know you are a swindler and a humbug. Get out of this house and out of this city at once. If you are in Washington tomorrow afternoon at this time, you will be in the old Capitol prison.'" Brooks said Colchester scampered out of the room.[52]

Mary spent much of the remainder of 1862 traveling to New York, Boston and Philadelphia. She took Tad, Elizabeth Keckly, and perhaps others with her to Boston in November. Mary wrote Lincoln on November 2, 1862, complaining that she had not heard from him. "I have waited in vain to hear from you, yet as you are not *given* to letter writing, will be charitable enough to impute your silence, to the right cause. Strangers come from W & tell me you are well—which satisfies me very much—Your name is on every lip and many prayers and good wishes are hourly sent up for your welfare—and McClellan & his slowness are as vehemently discussed. Allowing this beautiful weather, to pass away, is disheartening to the North."[53]

She said Tad was well, enjoying himself, and she had two suits of clothes made for him, which cost twenty-six dollars. "Have to get some fur outside wrappings for the Coachman's Carriage trappings—Lizzie Keckly wants me to loan her thirty dollars—so I will have to ask you for a check of $100—which will soon be made use of, for these articles. I want to leave here for Boston on Thursday & if you will send the check by Tuesday, will be much obliged." Mary told him that she accompanied Gen. and Mrs. Robert Anderson to call on Gen. Winfield Scott. "He looks well," she wrote, "although complaining of rheumatism. A day or two since, I had one of my severe attacks, if it had not been for Lizzie Keckly, I do not know what I should have done—some of these periods will launch me away."[54]

Returning again to the subject of McClellan, Mary wrote, "Many here say, they would almost worship you, if you would put a fighting general, in the place of McClellan—This would be splendid weather for an engagement." She ended the letter saying, "One line, to say that we are occasionally remembered, will be gratefully received—by yours truly, M.L."[55]

In the late summer and autumn of 1862, Mary appeared to be breaking through her cocoon of grief over Willie's passing. She assisted a childhood friend and encouraged an old acquaintance to call. Margaret Wickliffe Preston, daughter of Robert S. Todd's perennial personal and political enemy Robert Wickliffe, asked Mary to provide her with a pass to go through the Union lines to see her husband William Preston, a Confederate general. Mary did not reply directly since Lincoln intercepted her message. He replied, "Your dispatch to Mrs. L. received yesterday. She is not well. Owing to her early and strong friendship for you, I would gladly oblige you, but I can not absolutely do it. If Gen. Boyle and Hon. James Guthrie, one or both, in their discretion, see fit to give you the passes, this is my authority to them for doing so." Obviously, Lincoln told his wife about the request. Mary telegraphed Boyle, "I presume you have received a dispatch from Mrs. Preston, If you can consistently, will you not grant her request?"[56]

Mary was delighted that Oziah M. Hatch, Illinois secretary of state and a close friend of both the Lincolns, was coming to Washington in September 1862 to join the president on a five-day tour of battlefields. She wanted to spend some time with him and, on September 28, invited him to tea at the Executive Mansion and to share some fresh raspberries with them. The next day Mary asked Hatch to accompany her and two other ladies to the insane asylum—St. Elizabeth's Hospital which had been turned into a rehabilitation facility—to visit Gen. John Hooker, who had been wounded. The red brick, fortress-like building sat on a hill in southeast Washington overlooking the Anacostia and Potomac rivers.[57]

Hatch was better received in Washington than some of Mary's Springfield relatives would have been. Weary from all that was swirling around her, a lot of which she created, Mary wrote Elizabeth Grimsley a long letter on September 29, telling her about having the chills, being far from well and striking out at her sisters.

I received a letter from *Elizabeth* E. the other day—very kind and aff yet very *characteristic*—said if *rents* and means permitted, she would like to make us a visit I believe for a season—I am weary of *intrigue*, when she is by herself she can be very agreeable, especially when her mind is not dwelling on the merits of fair daughters & a talented son in law, such personages always *speak for themselves*. I often regret E.P.E. little *weaknesses*, after all, since the election she is the only one of my sisters who has appeared to be pleased with our advancement—you know this to be so—Notwithstanding Dr W—who has received his portion, in life, from the Administration, yet Frances always remains *quiet*. E. in her letter said—Frances spoke often of *Mr. L's* kindness—in giving him his place. She little knows, what a hard battle, I had for it—and how near he came to getting *nothing*. Poor *unfortunate* Ann, inasmuch as she possesses such a miserable disposition & so false a tongue—How far dear Lizzie, are we removed from such a person. Even if Smith, succeeds in being a rich man, what advantage will it be to him, who has gained it in *some cases* most unjustly, and with such a woman whom no one respects, whose tongue for so many years has been considered "so slander"—and as a child & young girl, could not be outdone in falsehood—"Truly the Leopard cannot change his spots." *She* is so seldom in my thoughts I have so much more, that is attractive, both in *bodily* presence, & my mind's eye, to interest me. I grieve for those who come in contact with her malice, yet even *that* is so well understood, the object of her *wrath*, generally rises, with good people, in proportion to her *vindictiveness*. What *will you name*, the hill on which I must be placed. *Her* putting it on *that* ground with Mrs Brown, was only to hide her envious feeling toward you. Tell Ann for me, to quote her own expression, *She* is becoming still further removed from "Queen Victoria's Court." How foolish between us to be discussing such a person, Yet, really it is amusing, in how many forms, human nature can appear before us—Nicolay told me, that Caleb Smith, said to him a few days since that he had just received a letter from Kellogg-of Cin. That he did not know why he had *not* received his appointment as *Counsel*—Is not the idea preposterous?[58]

Undoubtedly, Mary felt much better when she finished that portion of her letter, as she went on to say, "I know I have no cause to grieve over my lot—If the country, was only peaceful, all would be well. If I thought sending your Father, a pass, would bring him here, I would do so with pleasure. Give my best love to them both."[59]

In late September, Mary also wrote Gen. Daniel Sickles, from the Soldiers' Home, that she would like to have a chat with him about conditions in Virginia. "We always have so many evening callers, that our conversations, necessarily are general," she wrote. "When we are within hearing, as we are on this elevation, we can but pause & think. Yet, as to Washington yielding to the Rebels, a just Heaven would prevent that! If you are in on Monday, and, if you have leisure & of course, are so disposed, can you not drive out about 11 o'clock in the morning. Mr. L. has so much to excite his mind, with fears for the Army, that I am quite considerate in expressing my doubts and *fears* to him concerning passing events."[60]

In addition to problems with the war, Lincoln was busy that fall creating his Emancipation Proclamation. He spent a great deal of time working on the document at the Soldiers' Home in September.[61]

In her haste leaving Washington, Mary neglected to leave instructions for closing the Soldier's Home. Lincoln telegraphed her on November 9 saying Mary Ann Cuthbert, the housekeeper, and Aunt Many Dines, their nurse, wanted to move back to the Executive Mansion since it had grown cold at the Soldiers' Home. "Shall they?" he asked.[62]

Moving from the Executive Mansion to the Soldiers' Home was no easy task. It required moving nineteen or twenty carts of the family's belongings to the thirty-four-room Gothic Revival-styled cottage and back again to the Executive Mansion.[63]

Mary got her wish about McClellan being dismissed three days after she wrote Lincoln. The president, having already named Henry Halleck general-in-chief in July 1862, replaced Gen. McClellan with Maj. Gen. Ambrose Burnsides, when McClellan allowed Gen. Robert E. Lee to escape his grasp after winning the battle of Antietam.[64]

Bad weather in November curtailed Mary's activities in Boston while she was staying at the Parker House, where she received Sen. Charles Sumner, Gov. and Mrs. John Andrew and Julia Ward Howe. However, she was able to take a drive with Robert. After a short stay back in New York she returned to Washington. *The Washington Chronicle* reported Mary was apparently much improved after her visit to the north.[65]

On Christmas Day 1862, Mary and Abraham Lincoln visited a number of hospitals in the Washington area. Which hospitals they visited is not known since there were eighty-six different facilities, in and around the district, housed in government buildings—including the Capitol for a short while—hotels, schools, colleges, synagogues, churches, the Odd Fellows' Hall and private residences, including the former home of Sen. Stephen A. Douglas.[66]

Despite her activities, such as visiting the wounded soldiers and bringing them gifts, Mary remained unable to overcome her grief from Willie's death and turned more and more to spiritualists and séances. There were some bright spots, however, where she appeared to be emerging from her grief.

While in New York, she took up the appeal of Mary Read, a twenty-six-year-old woman who shot her husband when she discovered he had a mistress. The trial jury found her guilty of manslaughter in the third degree with mitigating circumstances. She was sentenced to thirty months of hard labor at Sing Sing State Prison. Mary could have been thinking of Gen. Daniel Sickles being found not guilty by reason of insanity in the Lafayette Square murder of Phillip Barton Key, who supposedly had an affair with his wife, when she wrote the governor on the woman's behalf. "I think, *her*, entitled to your clemency—She must have acted under the influence of a mind, distrait, besides there is but little evidence that she contemplated or committed the deed, she is punished for," Mary wrote Gov. Edwin D. Morgan. "Pray, let me know if my signature, to a petition for mercy, with other names of respectability, will induce you to remit her sentence?" Mary would have been well served to end the letter there, but she plowed ahead as was her wont. "I am confident, the District Attorney, will readily recommend her pardon—An early answer will oblige me, & I shall feel grateful if you think proper to signalize your retirement from office, by an act of grace, which I cannot but feel, is well deserved."[67]

The woman who wrote that 1862 letter to the New York governor pleading for clemency for a woman she never knew was a century ahead of her time in demanding equal rights for women.

CHAPTER 15

Pivotal Year of 1863

The Lincolns' New Year's Day reception in 1863 at the Executive Mansion was a historical one that remains unmatched in American history. The evening before, he and others discussed the Emancipation Proclamation Lincoln had been working on since July. The day before, he presented the document to his cabinet for their ideas. Most had suggestions. Mary asked him what he intended to do. He accepted only Chase's request, which was to invoke both the Constitution and God.

By the time a final handwritten copy was prepared, it was time for the reception. At 11 a.m., Mary and Lincoln greeted the diplomatic corps, Supreme Court judges, congressmen and military officers in the Blue Room. Among the invited guests were the "Old Defenders," veterans of the War of 1812. "The prest looked rather cheerful," War Department telegrapher Edward Rosewater wrote in his diary. "[He] stood in the center of Room & shook hands with every one remarked to me How do you do sir, to a lady going by before me How's the baby?" It was Rosewater who later that day telegraphed Lincoln's Emancipation Proclamation to the nation.[1]

An hour later, the Executive Mansion doors were opened to a vast crowd that had been lined up two and three abreast along Pennsylvania Avenue back to Seventeenth Street. The crowd was so vast that a small detachment of police and members of the Pennsylvania regiment attempted to keep order by admitting groups in intervals. Or, as Benjamin French put it, "After the above named dignitaries, the officers of the Army and Navy came, and then *the people en masse*."[2]

The Lincolns had been steadily shaking hands for three hours. Mary, dressed in a black velvet gown trimmed with thread lace, left the reception for a brief period to refresh herself and then returned. Lincoln's right hand was visibly swollen when he returned to his office to sign the Emancipation Proclamation, which freed slaves in all seceded states, with a few exceptions.

The document, covering five pages, was tied with narrow red and blue ribbons and had the seal of the United States of America. When he signed his name, Abraham Lincoln, with a careful but painful hand, the president said, "I never, in my life, felt more certain that I was doing right, than I do in signing this paper." The last paragraph of the document read, "And upon this act, sincerely believed to be an act of justice, warranted by the Constitution upon military necessity, I invoke the considerable judgment of mankind and the gracious favor of Almighty God."[3]

It was as if the fire and brimstone Mary experienced the previous year had given her a steely resolve to simply be herself regardless of the political critics and social harpies; to devote herself to the causes that were important to her; to utilize her ingrained sense of social justice whenever possible. She reached down and reinvigorated her Scottish roots.

While Lincoln had evolved into a strong emancipationist, Mary joined him while expanding her own horizons. Her hospital visits with wounded soldiers increased and she shared gifts sent to the Executive Mansion with them. She became a one-woman reference bureau finding jobs for diplomats, clerks, night-watchmen, lamplighters and former slaves. She asked Edwin M. Stanton, secretary of war, to look into a situation with a West Point cadet who was a Quaker. Frank Jones had a roommate who attempted to disturb his studies and advancement. Mary took Quartermaster Montgomery Meigs to task for a man not being paid for his boat. She recommended Elizabeth Keckly, her seamstress, for a job in the office of George Harrington, assistant secretary of the treasury. She managed to have Lt. George Butler, Jr., who lost an arm, discharged from the service. He began a successful career as a painter. One of her more curious requests was asking George Harrington to hire Nettie Colburn and her friend Parthenia Hannam. Colburn was a spiritualist whose séances Mary apparently attended in Georgetown.[4]

Mary read about the February 11, 1862, wedding of Charles S. Stratton and Lavina Warren Bumpus in the *New York Herald*. Stratton was better known as the performer Tom Thumb in P. T. Barnum's American Museum. The couple came to Washington on their wedding trip.[5] After discussing it with Lincoln, she decided to give them a reception, on February 13, in the Executive Mansion's East Room.

Bob Lincoln, home from Harvard, was appalled by his mother's plans. "I do not propose to assist you in entertaining Tom Thumb," he told Mary. "My notions of duty, perhaps are somewhat different from yours." The uptight young man's opinion might have changed had he known the cream of New York society—the Astors, Vanderbilts and others—attended the couple's wedding at Grace Episcopal Church and their reception at the Metropolitan Hotel.[6]

Lincoln, however, enjoyed trading puns with Stratton. Mary, dressed in a pink gown instead of her usual black, greeted them warmly. Tad was intrigued by the couple who sat on the sofa with his parents. "Mother," he later commented, "if you were a little woman like Mrs. Stratton, you would look just like her."[7]

Mary was glad the reception provided a distraction for Lincoln, who was becoming more and more despondent about the war. She knew there was one person who had helped her husband in the past and could probably be of assistance in their current situation.

Dr. Anson Henry, who helped reunite the Lincolns during their courtship and whom the President appointed surveyor general of the Washington Territory, suddenly showed up in the capital. He came, apparently, to lobby for funding for better roads and military posts in his part of the country. Though that may have been the official line, it was more likely that Mary instigated his trip out of her concern for Lincoln's health.

While waiting to see the Lincolns, Henry spent some time with Julia Trumbull, from whom Mary had been estranged since the 1856 Illinois senatorial election. She told him Mary's distinguished position had turned her head. Reconciliation between the two women, he decided, was not going to work. Henry spent time talking with Mary about her family's expectation that Lincoln would provide lucrative jobs for all of them and, when that did not happen, they blamed her. Mary deeply resented their reactions, as evidenced by the venom in her letter to Elizabeth Grimsley. Henry lived in Springfield and knew the interactive relations between Mary and the Edwardses, the Wallaces and the Smiths. He found no fault with Mary's attitude toward them.[8]

Henry finally managed to spend some time with Lincoln. He completed his business and was ready to return to the Washington Territory. Lincoln would not hear of Henry leaving during the winter to make the long trip back to the West and ordered him to stay with them at the Executive Mansion.[9]

Mary insisted that Henry must attend their last levee of the season on March 2, which the *New York Herald* called the best attended and most brilliant of the season. Benjamin B. French wrote, "I think I never saw such a stream of humanity for 2½ hours of all sorts of people. Ladies in magnificent toilets and in the plainest imaginable garb. The major general in his dress coat & the common soldier in his patched great coat and boots covered with mud halfway up the leg. Every grade of every arm of the service seemed to be there, from Gen. Hallech, comm. in chief down to the private. Epaulettes & shoulder straps, chevrons & scales were as thick a leaves in valambrosa. Citizens in all sorts of dress, from the finished and perfumed dandy down to the shabbiest of the shabby."[10]

Henry accompanied the Lincolns on an unusual trip. Mary had an idea for lifting their spirits, which were somewhat sagging from the war news, while inspiring the Army of the Potomac after Lincoln had relieved Gen. McClellan. They took a trip down to the Aquia Creek Landing. Aquia Creek was a 27.6-mile tributary of the tidal section of the Potomac in Northern Virginia. The steamer *Carrie Martin* took them to review Gen. Joseph Hooker's headquarters troops. The party included Mary, Lincoln, Tad, Henry, Noah Brooks, Attorney General Bates and Captain Medorum Crawford.[11]

Mary knew what she could expect: cramped quarters on the steamer, living in a tent during cold nights and bumping over rough ground in an ambulance with plank seats. She gladly endured the hardships because the excursion took Lincoln out of Washington. The war was extracting a heavy toll on him. A couple of weeks earlier, French described a breakfast meeting with the president. "I was with him for about an hour," he wrote. "He certainly is growing feeble. He wrote a note while I was present and his hand trembled as I never saw before and he looked lean & haggard. I remarked that I should think he would be feeling glad when he could get some rest. He replied that it was a pretty hard life for him."[12]

Unfavorable weather, Noah Brooks said, postponed the trip several days. The Lincolns and their party left the Washington Navy Yard on the afternoon of April 4, 1863. Soon after departing the Navy Yard, snow became so thick it was difficult to navigate and the steamer put into a cove on the Potomac, opposite Indian Head, Maryland. "I could not help but thinking," Brooks wrote, "that if the rebels had made a raid on the Potomac at that time, the capture of the chief magistrate of the United States would have been a very simple matter. As far as I could see, there were no guards on board the boat and no precautions were taken against a surprise." Brooks said Hooker, expecting their party to arrive the same day, sent scouts out looking for them. The scouts heard Confederate sentries discussing if "Abe and his wife" had come yet.[13]

Brooks said the snow was still falling when they reached their landing place at Aquia Creek, a village of hastily constructed warehouses whose waterfront was lined with transports and government steamers. There were enormous freight trains running from it to the army encamped among the hills of Virginia lying between the Rappahannock and Potomac rivers. "The president and his party were provided with a freight-car fitted up with rough plank benches and profusely decorated with flags and bunting. A great crowd of army people saluted the president with cheers when he landed from the steamer and with 'three times three' when his unpretentious railway carriage rolled away."[14] At the Falmouth Station, two ambulances and a cavalry escort received the guests and took them to Hooker's headquarters, where three large hospital tents, with floors, had been prepared for them. The tents were furnished, Brooks said, with camp bedsteads and rude appliances for nightly occupation which were within reach.[15]

The cavalry was for the first time massed as one corps instead of being scattered among the various army corps, Brooks said. "The cavalry force was rated at 17,000 men and horses and Hooker said that it was the biggest army of men and horses ever seen in the world, bigger even than the famous body of cavalry commanded by Marshal (Joachim) Murat."[16] Murat was Napoleon's brother-in-law.

Mary was bursting with pride as she watched from the reviewing stand as Lincoln, riding like a veteran, and Hooker led the column followed by several major-generals, a host of brigadiers, colonels, staff officers and those of lesser rank, the Philadelphia Lancers and there was Tad, in charge of a mounted orderly, his gray cloak flying in the wind. "It was a grand sight to look upon," Brooks wrote, "this immense body of cavalry, with banners waving, music crashing and horses prancing as the vast column came winding like a huge serpent over the hills past the reviewing party and then stretching far away out of sight."[17] The infantry reviews were held on different days for the four corps of some 60,000 men. There was another parade of eighty pieces of artillery. "It was noticeable that the president merely touched his hat in return salutes to officers but uncovered (his head) to the men in the ranks," Brooks said.

Tad, Brooks said, expressed a consuming desire to see how the "graybacks" looked. One of Gen. Hooker's aides and an orderly escorted Tad and Brooks down to the picket lines opposite Fredericksburg. There were two Confederate pickets, across the river, warming themselves before a tall chimney near the river bank. "Noting our appearance, these cheerful sentinels bawled to us that our forces had been 'licked' in the recent attack on Fort Sumter. And, a rebel officer, hearing the shouting, came down to the riverbank and closely examined our party through a field-glass." The officer, Brooks continued, failing to see Lincoln, took off his hat, made a sweeping bow, and disappeared.[18]

While driving around the encampment on what Brooks described as corduroy roads, the Lincolns came upon a settlement of colored refugees, who shouted, "Hurrah for Massa Linkum." Mary smiled and waved at the children, who Brooks said were innumerable. She asked Lincoln how many of those little children he supposed were named for him. Mr. Lincoln said, 'Let's see; this is April 1863. I should say that of all those babies under two years of age, perhaps two-thirds have been named for me."[19]

Lincoln was uplifted by their trip but it appeared to have been hard on Mary, especially when spring brought about her most debilitating headaches. Lincoln was attempting to pull Mary out of her doldrums. On April 22, he invited Sen. Charles Sumner to go to the opera with them. "Mrs. L. is embarrassed a little. She would be pleased to have your company again this evening at the opera, but she fears she may be taxing you. I have undertaken to clear up the little difficulty. If, for any reason, it will tax you, decline, without any hesitation; but if it will not, consider yourself already invited and drop me a note." Lincoln's elation with Gen. Hooker faded rapidly after the battle of Chancellorsville, on May 6, 1863, when 30,000 men were lost; two-thirds of them Union soldiers. Noah Brooks said he had never seen Lincoln so broken and so dispirited.[20]

On June 8, Confederate Gen. Robert E. Lee reached Culpeper, Virginia, on his march to the north. The next day, Lincoln took Mary and Tad to the railroad station, kissed them goodbye and sent them on their way to Philadelphia. That same day, Lincoln sent Mary, who was staying at the Continental Hotel, a telegram saying, "Think you had better put Tad's pistol away. I had an ugly dream about him."[21] It was probably Lincoln who gave his ten-year-old son a pistol but the bigger question was his traveling with the weapon, especially in wartime.

Mary remained quite concerned about her husband and sent him three telegrams the next couple of days. Lincoln replied on June 11, "Your three dispatches received. I am very well and am glad to know that you and Tad are so." Dr. Henry was still in Washington with Lincoln but that did not relieve her worries, and those concerns were supported by the president's June 15 telegraph. Lincoln told her he was "Tolerably well. Have not rode out much yet, but have at last got new tires on the carriage wheels and perhaps shall ride out soon."[22]

After receiving that telegram, Mary decided she wanted to return to Washington. Lincoln replied on June 16, "It is a matter of choice with yourself whether you come home. There is no reason why you should not that did not exist when you went away. As bearing on the question of your coming home, I do not think the raid into Pennsylvania amounts to anything at all." She returned to Washington and shortly thereafter she supervised their move from the Executive Mansion to the Soldiers' Home on June 22.[23]

Both Lincolns loved the Soldiers' Home, where there was quiet and they could read to each other in the cool airy house. There was another side to the Soldiers' Home—the location almost took both their lives. As Lincoln was riding out alone to their summer home one evening, someone shot his hat off his head. A soldier found the hat and returned it to the president. Lincoln asked him not to say anything about the incident.[24]

On the morning of July 2, Lincoln left the Soldiers' Home early, riding with his mounted body guards, to go the War Department telegraph office to read the wire dispatches on the battle at Gettysburg. He left the carriage for Mary to take to the Executive Mansion later. When the driver took a turn in the road, the seat where he sat pulled away from its moorings and he pitched to the ground dropping the reins. The unusual activity spooked the horses and they broke into a wild gallop. Mary had a choice: she could stay with the carriage and risk being injured or killed when it overturned, or she could take a chance on leaping from the runaway vehicle. She jumped from the carriage and hit the back of her head on a rock. Her momentum was eventually stopped by the heavy underbrush along the road. The *New York Times* reported she was treated by an Army surgeon who decided no bones were broken and that her injuries were superficial, and who bandaged her wounds.[25] However, it is unlikely he knew how to assess for a concussion, which was surely induced when her head slammed against the rock.

Mary, when she regained consciousness, refused to go to the hospital, and a passing carriage took her to the residence. Lincoln, still in the War Department, saw her limping, clothes torn, a bloody bandage on her head and scratches and abrasions on her face and hands. He was not only flabbergasted but felt guilty he had left her to return to the city alone. Bad as it was, the accident could have been worse. An investigation revealed that the bolts on the driver's seat had been unscrewed to accomplish exactly what happened. No culprit was ever located. It was a deliberate effort to injure or even kill the president. Mary did her best to reassure him that she was not badly hurt.[26] Lincoln, perhaps wanting to believe Mary was okay, telegraphed their oldest son. "Don't be uneasy. Your mother very slightly hurt by her fall."[27]

To illustrate that point, she continued working with Stoddard on their plans for a big

Fourth of July celebration. The Fourth of July Committee suggested that the annual celebration should be canceled because of the war. "Sir, there will be a Fourth of July celebration
in Washington, this year, if we can hear Lee's cannons all the while, and if we adjourn from
the speaker's stand to the trenches," Stoddard quoted Lincoln as telling the committee. Stoddard arranged for the Marine Band to play on the residence lawn, and the speakers' platform
was set up in the Mall below the Executive Mansion. "The White House seems a furnace,"
Stoddard wrote. "And, the entire city takes on more perfectly than ever before the air belonging to its real character of a frontier post in peril of capture by the enemy."[28]

Mary helped all she could depleting the greenhouse and conservatory of their flowers
and plants for the celebration. She asked Stoddard if there was anything else she could do.
"No," he replied, "unless you can speak to Grant and [Gen. George] Meade [who replaced
Gen. Hooker] and have them win their victories on the third so we can have a bigger fourth."[29]

"The assemblage on the president's grounds today, attending the celebration ceremonies,
was composed in part of the military, corporate authorities, and Masonic and Odd Fellows
fraternities," the New York Times reported on July 4. Former New York Congressman Hiram
Walbridge delivered the oration.

> National salutes were fired by order of the government and generally the day was celebrated with
> much enthusiasm and at night there were in all directions profuse displays of fireworks. Seces-
> sion sympathizers early in the day endeavored to cast a gloom over the community by extrava-
> gant falsehoods concerning disasters to our army, but the light of the truth soon diffused general
> joy and dissipated their dishonest purposes. The reception of an official dispatch of Gen. Meade
> (from Gettysburg) and President Lincoln's congratulatory address, created a furore which soon
> extended throughout the city raising intense enthusiasm among the masses, which found vent in
> cheer after cheer.[30]

Mary was unable to enjoy the news of the victory at Gettysburg as the noise and the
booming fireworks sent her to bed with probably the worst headache she had ever experienced. Lincoln, quite concerned about her, arranged for Rebecca Pomeroy to come to the
Soldiers' Home. Her condition worsened. The nurse discovered the wound, created by her
head striking a rock when she hit the ground, was infected and began to fester, discharging
pus. A surgeon was called to lance the wound and drain it. With no exploratory medical
technology available in those days, physicians were hampered in not only being unable to
diagnose but in their treatment of interior head wounds. Mary required Pomeroy's attention
day and night for three weeks.[31]

"I think mother has never quite recovered from the effects of her fall," Bob Lincoln
later told his aunt, Emilie Todd Helm. "It is really astonishing what a brave front she manages
to keep when we know she is suffering.... She just straightens herself up a little more and
says, 'It is better to laugh than to be sighing.' Tad would go all to pieces if she reversed the
words of that opera, and so would my father."[32]

As she recovered, Lincoln decided it was best for her to leave the steamy heat and
humidity of Washington. Mary, Tad and Bob left in early August for the Tip Top House on
Mount Washington, in New Hampshire's White Mountains, elevation 6,288 feet. The Tip
Top House was built in 1853 by Samuel Spaulding with walls six inches thick to withstand
the fierce winds on the mountain. The facility featured fine dining, beds filled with moss
and four-hour carriage trips to the top of the mountain. Mary took the carriage trip twice.[33]

While she was in New Hampshire, Lincoln wrote Mary an interesting and revealing
letter, dated August 8, that she never received.

My dear Wife. All as well as usual, and no particular trouble any way. I put money into the treasury at five percent, with the privilege of withdrawing it any time upon thirty day's notice. I suppose you are glad to learn this. Tell dear Tad, poor "Nanny Goat" is lost; Mrs. Cuthbert & I are in distress about it. The day you left Nanny was found resting herself and chewing her little cud in the middle of Tad's bed. But now she's gone! The gardener kept complaining that she destroyed the flowers, till it was concluded to bring her down to the White House. This was done, and the second day she had disappeared, and has not been heard of since. This is the last we know of poor Nanny.[34]

After discussing the weather, Lincoln continued telling Mary about the political climate in Kentucky, which they had obviously discussed. "The election in Kentucky has gone very strongly right. Old Mr. Wickliffe got ugly, as you know, ran for governor and is terrible beaten. Upon Mr. Crittenden's death, Brutus Clay, Cassius' brother, was put on track for Congress and is largely elected. Mr. Menzies, who, as we thought, behaved very badly last session of Congress, is largely beaten in the district opposite Cincinnati by Green Clay Smith, Cassius' nephew. But enough. Affectionately, A. Lincoln."[35] Lincoln's words in that letter unmistakably illustrated just how much Mary was a part of his political world.

The August 8, 1863, letter came into the hands of D. P. Bacon, postmaster at LeRoy, Genesee County, New York, from a young man who had apparently served in the Army of the Potomac and received the letter. Bacon returned the letter, in somewhat soiled condition, to Lincoln in April 1864, saying he had been to one of the receptions but had no opportunity to give it to him then.[36]

After Mary's carriage accident, Lincoln's security traveling to and from the Soldiers' Home was increased. The Lincolns' travel route took them past the residence of Walt Whitman, who worked in the Army paymaster's office. Whitman said he and Lincoln had a nodding acquaintance as they passed each other. On August 23, 1863, Whitman said the president went by accompanied by twenty-five or thirty soldiers, with sabers drawn, at a slow trot. On other occasions he saw both Lincolns but Mary was usually wearing a long crepe veil. "They passed me (in a barouche) once very close and I saw the president in the face fully as they were moving slowly and his look, though abstracted, happened to be directly steady in my eye. He bowed and smiled but far beneath his smile I noticed well the expression I allude to. None of the artists or pictures has caught the deep, though subtle or indirect expression of this man's face. There is something else there. One of the great portrait painters of two or three centuries ago is needed."[37]

Knowing Lincoln had increased security enabled Mary to extend her time away from Washington. When she left the White Mountains, Mary spent some time in Manchester, New Hampshire. While there she received a short message from Lincoln dated August 29, 1863. "All quite well. Fort Sumter is *certainly* battered down, and utterly useless to the enemy, and it is *believed* here, but not entirely certain, that both Sumter and Fort Wagner, are occupied by our forces. It is also certain that Gen. [Quincy] Gilmore has thrown some shot into the City of Charleston."[38]

From New Hampshire, Mary and her sons went to the Equinox Hotel in Manchester, Vermont, where Robert would later build his mansion, Hildene. The Equinox, built in 1768, was famous for serving four meals a day plus a tea and gingerbread snacks. The hotel had scales that guests, if they chose, could weigh themselves on at the end of their visits. On September 3, Lincoln wrote her that Gen. Abner Doubleday, who had been relieved by Gen. Meade, had been informed by Secretary of War Stanton to await further orders. "We are all well and have nothing new," he wrote. Apparently Mary had interceded for Doubleday in the matter. Three days later, he wrote, "All well and no news except that Gen. Burnsides has Knoxville, Tennessee." Lincoln wrote her again on September 21 at the Fifth Avenue Hotel in New York asking her to come home. "The air is so clear and cool, and apparently healthy that I would be glad for you to come. Nothing very particular but I would be glad to see you and Tad." Mary immediately telegraphed the residence doorman Edward McManus, "Go to Col. [Daniel] McCullum [director of military railroads] and ask him to send the green car to Philadelphia for me and make arrangements for a special car from New York to Philadelphia."[39]

Lincoln dictated a telegraph, which was missing, to Mary Ann Cuthbert to send and she sent a confused message. He telegraphed Mary again on September 22, correcting the mistake. "Did you receive my despatch of yesterday? Mrs. Cuthbert did not correctly understand me. I directed her to tell you to use your own pleasure whether to stay or come; and I did not say it is sickly & that you should on no account come. So far as I see or know it was never healthier, and I really wish to see you. Answer this on receipt." Mary replied immediately, "Your telegram received. Did you receive my reply? I telegraphed Col. McCullum to have the car ready at the earliest possible moment. Have a very bad cold and am anxious to return home as you may suppose. Taddie is well."[40]

Lincoln wanted to see his wife and son. But, two days later he had another reason for her to be at home when she received the bad news that Emilie Todd Helm's husband Brig. Gen. Benjamin Hardin Helm had been killed at Chickamauga. He did not want her to read about it in the newspapers. On September 24, Mary was still in New York, and he sent her, at the Fifth Avenue Hotel, a very straightforward military-type telegraph about the battle of Chickamauga.[41]

"We now have a tolerable accurate summing up of the late battle between [Gen. William S.] Rosecrans and [Confederate Gen. Braxton] Bragg," Lincoln told Mary.

> The result is that we are worsted, if at all, only in the fact that we, after the main fighting was over, yielded the ground, thus leaving considerable of our artillery and wounded to fall into the enemies' hands for which we got nothing in turn. We lost, in general officers, one killed, and three or four wounded, all brigadiers; while according to rebel accounts, which we have, they lost six killed and eight wounded one of the killed, one major genl. And five brigadiers, including your brother-in-law, Helm; and of the wounded, three major generals and five brigadiers. This list may be reduced two in number, by correction of confusion of names. At 11/40 A.M. yesterday Gen. Rosecrans telegraphed from Chattanooga "We hold this point, and I can not be dislodged, except by superior numbers, and after a great battle." A despatch leaving there after night yesterday said, "No fight tonight." A. Lincoln."[42]

David Davis, according to Katherine Helm, found Lincoln grief stricken over Helm's death. "Davis," he said, "I feel as David of old did when told of the death of Absalom."[43]

It should be kept in mind that the source of the above quote was the daughter of Gen. Helm, which accounts for her contention that Mary wept profusely for her half-brothers when they were killed or wounded. However, Mary's strong statement to the Reverend Miner about her brother George and her half-brothers Samuel, David and Alexander, who were in the Confederate Army, contradicts Helm's depiction: "They would kill my husband if they could, and destroy our government—the dearest of all things to us."[44] Some of her half-brothers, Mary saw two, perhaps three, times in her life. David, she may have never seen.

It was five more days, September 29, after receiving Lincoln's telegram about Helm's death, before Mary and Tad returned to Washington.[45]

Mary was certainly fond of Emilie and her reaction to Helm's death is difficult to decipher. She continued her social schedule. On October 6, Mary, Lincoln and the Seward family attended the performance of Shakespeare's *Othello* at Grover's Theatre. Lincoln had intended to stay only an hour but remained for the entire performance.[46]

Grover's Theatre was one of Tad's, as well as Lincoln's, favorite places and the lad often slipped away from the residence to visit, got to know the stage hands and watched rehearsals. Lincoln took him to the theater to see *The Seven Sisters*, into which the lead actor John McDonough had worked a "Rally A'Round the Flag," segment. Intent on the play, Lincoln failed to notice Tad's absence from the box. The boy crept from the box, went to wardrobe, put on an ill-fitting uniform and went on stage at the end of a line of soldiers. "The president had a bad quarter of a minute shock at the sight," theater manager Leonard Grover recalled, "but the humor of the situation quickly restored him and he laughed immoderately." But, Tad had more in mind than just to make an appearance. "McDonough caught the spirit of the opportunity, walked over to the end and placed the American flag he had been waving in Tad's hands," Grover said. "Tad promptly rose to the occasion, took the initiative, stepped a little in front of the line, and waving the flag to the music, began to sing with all the might of his childish treble the refrain: 'We are coming, Father Abraham, Three hundred thousand more, Shouting the battle-cry of Freedom.'"[47]

Mary and Lincoln, whenever they were able to escape their official duties, had little time to enjoy their respites because the Todds began descending on them for assistance. The president was asked to help Emilie Helm, who had gone to Atlanta for her husband's funeral. E. M. Bruce, from Madison, Georgia, wrote Lincoln on October 6, 1863, that Emilie was staying at his home. Bruce opened his letter by telling Lincoln of Helm's death, assuming the president had not been informed. That was not Bruce's only mistake and he compounded it further. "Mrs. Helm is crushed by the blow—almost brokenhearted—and desires to return to her mother and friends in Kentucky—indeed this is a necessity as you must be aware that her means are very small and the expense of living in the South much more than in the United States—she is now at my home in this place—and will afford me the pleasure to minister to her wants and comfort so long as it may be agreeable for her to remain under my roof; meantime she asks that you order the War Department to send her a pass to enter the Federal truce boat at City Point [Virginia]."[48]

Bruce wanted a pass not only for Emilie but for his own family. "Would suggest that you send *triplicates*, say, one to me here, one to care Col Wm. Preston Johnson [son of fallen Confederate Gen. Albert Sidney Johnston], Richmond and one to Mrs. Helm here by different Boats. Would also be obliged if you would send at the same time a pass for Mrs. Bruce and her sister—Mrs. Hutchinson—to accompany Mrs. Helm to Kentucky, their father having recently died leaving mother in a very desolate condition."[49]

Lincoln saw that one coming.

The president telegraphed Mary' cousin, Lyman B. Todd, in Lexington, on October 15, that he was sending the following pass to his care. "Washington, D.C., to Whom it may concern, Oct. 15th. 63 Allow Mrs. Robert S. Todd, widow to go south and bring her daughter, Mrs. Gen. B. Hardin Helm, with her children, North to Kentucky. A. Lincoln."[50]

Four days earlier Gen. Helm's father, former Kentucky governor John L. Helm, wrote Betsy Todd asking if she could get a pass for Emilie to get to Nashville and he would meet her there, if permitted. "I am totally at a loss to know how to begin," he wrote. "Could you or one of your daughters write to Mrs. Lincoln and through her secure a pass?"[51]

Meanwhile, Lyman B. Todd telegraphed Lincoln on October 31, that he had not received Betsy Todd's pass. Lincoln telegraphed him back the same day saying, 'I sent the pass by telegraph more than ten days ago. Did you not receive it?"[52]

While Emilie Helm was making her way out of Georgia, Mary and Lincoln were attending the theater. On October 16, along with Tad and Stoddard, they went to Grover's Theatre to see James Wallack and Charlotte Cushman in *Macbeth*. The performance raised more than $2,000 for the Sanitary Commission, charged with caring for wounded Union soldiers.[53]

Mary supervised the family's move back to the Executive Mansion from the Soldiers' Home and planned to accompany Lincoln to Gettysburg, Pennsylvania, for the dedication of the military cemetery. The president invited Judge Stephen T. Logan, Mary's cousin and his former law partner, to the event and to accompany him back to Washington and remain for the meeting of Congress. Ward Hill Lamon, who was married to Logan's daughter, was the marshal for the event had planned to travel to Illinois to bring his wife back to Washington, but was unable to leave. Lincoln suggested Logan accompany his daughter to the capital. There was no recorded reply from Logan. On the morning they planned to leave, November 18, Tad became ill. Mary was too concerned to leave him with what later turned out to be scarlet fever.[54]

The official party on the four-car special Baltimore and Ohio Railroad train was made up of Lincoln, his valet William H. Johnson, Nicolay, Hay, Seward, John P. Usher, who had succeeded Caleb B. Smith as secretary of the interior, Postmaster Blair, members of the diplomatic corps, military guards from the Invalid Corps and the Marine Band. While at Gettysburg, Lincoln was a guest in the home of Judge David Willis, where he completed his famous speech. Stanton telegraphed Lincoln in Gettysburg that Tad was better.[55]

Lincoln was not the main speaker at the event. That slot was filled by Edward Everett, a former governor of Massachusetts, minister to England, secretary of state, United States senator and president of Harvard University.[56] Everett spoke for two hours, Lincoln for three minutes, and nobody remembers what the orator said. Lincoln's "Four score and seven years ago" speech, containing 272 words, will be forever remembered by free men and women.

Everett wrote Lincoln, "Permit me to express my great admiration of the thoughts expressed by you, with such eloquent simplicity & appropriateness, at the concentration of the cemetery. I should be glad, if I could flatter myself that I came as near to the central idea of the occasion in two hours as you did in two minutes." Everett added that he hoped Lincoln's anxiety for his child was relieved on his return home. Lincoln replied on November 20, "Your kind note of to-day is received. In our respective parts yesterday, you could not have been excused to make a short address, nor I a long one." Lincoln thanked him for asking about Tad, "Our sick boy, for whom you kindly inquire, we hope is past the worst."[57]

The worst was past for Tad but not for Lincoln. The president was not so fortunate, he had varioloid, a mild case of smallpox. Writing in the *Journal of Medical Biography*, Dr. Armond Goldman, professor emeritus of pediatrics at the University of Texas Medical College, Galveston, and Dr. E. J. Schmalsteig, a neurologist at Mainland Medical Center, Texas City, Texas, wrote, "When Abraham Lincoln delivered the Gettysburg Address, he was weak and dizzy; his face had a ghastly color. That evening on the train to Washington, DC, he was febrile and weak and suffered severe headaches. The symptoms continued: back pain developed. On the fourth day of the illness, a widespread scarlet rash appeared that soon became vesicular. By the tenth day, the lesions itched and peeled. The illness lasted three weeks. The final diagnosis, a touch of varioloid, was an old name for smallpox that was later used in the 20th century to denote mild smallpox in a partially immune individual. It is unclear whether Lincoln had been immunized against smallpox. In that regard, this review suggests that Lincoln had unmodified smallpox and that his physicians tried to reassure the public that Lincoln was not seriously ill. Indeed, the successful conclusion of the Civil War and the reunification of the country depended upon Lincoln's presidency."[58]

There was also the possibility he contracted whatever Tad had, scarlet fever, or something else. Lincoln's confinement, according to newspaper reports, was the better part of a month. During that time the president was under a partial quarantine. There was a December 5 reception for Russian naval officers aboard the frigate *Oslialia*, planned in New York. Russia was an important ally in keeping England and France from supporting the Confederacy in the Civil War. Obviously, Lincoln was unable to travel. The president's representative at the reception was not Secretary of State Seward but his wife Mary. Mary arrived at the Metropolitan Hotel in New York on December 3. On December 5, Gen. John A. Dix escorted Mary to the reception aboard the frigate anchored in Flushing Bay. Mary toasted the health of the Russian czar and the *Oslialia*'s captain toasted the health of the president of the United States.[59]

Lincoln, according to Washington newspapers, returned to a partial schedule of work on December 11 and was able to return to his office four days later. The Lincolns celebrated his recovery by going to Ford's Theatre on December 15 to see *Henry IV* with James Hackett as Falstaff.[60]

Meanwhile, Emilie Todd Helm had made her way north as far as Fort Monroe, Virginia, a Union military installation in Hampton Roads, where she refused to take the Oath of Allegiance. She brought her daughter, Katherine, with her but it was no familial visit. Emilie was another Todd who wanted Lincoln's help and apparently gave no consideration to the predicament her presence created for Mary and Lincoln. She had some cotton that she wanted a protection order for from the president. Orville Browning placed the date she arrived at the Executive Mansion as being December 14, which was the date an Oath of Allegiance, under her name, was prepared. There are questions about whether she signed the oath or Lincoln signed her name. According to Lincoln's Proclamation of Amnesty and Reconstruction, persons seeking amnesty "shall take and subscribe an oath and thenceforward keep and maintain said oath inviolate; and which oath shall be registered for permanent preservation, and shall be of the tenor and effect following, to wit:" and the amnesty followed. The December 14, 1863, amnesty to Emilie T. Helm read, "Mrs. Emily T. Helm, not being excepted from the benefits of the proclamation by the president of the United States issued on the 8th day of December, 1863, and having this day taken and subscribed to said proclamation, she is fully relieved of all penalties and forfeitures and remitted to her rights, all according to said proclamation, and not otherwise; and, in regard to said restored rights of person and property, she is to be protected and afforded facilities as a loyal person. Abraham Lincoln."[61]

Lincoln added a postscript to the amnesty. "Mrs. Helm claims to own some cotton at Jackson, Mississippi, and also some in Georgia; and I shall be glad, upon either place being brought within our lines, for her to be afforded the proper facilities to show her ownership, and take her property."[62]

How Emilie Helm came in possession of the cotton was never clear. Her husband had been in and around Mississippi for a couple of years. Had he confiscated or purchased the

Mississippi cotton in question? Lincoln also referred to cotton Emilie told him she owned in Georgia. The Georgia cotton could have belonged to E. M. Bruce, from Madison, Georgia, who gave Emilie shelter and who asked Lincoln for passes for her as well as his family.

If either Mary or Lincoln thought getting Emilie safely back to Kentucky in December 1863 was the end of problems with her family, they were mistaken. They were besieged with all kinds of requests from four of her five step-sisters and her older brother.

Martha "Mattie" Todd White had accompanied her sister, Emilie Todd Helm, and her daughter, Katherine, to Washington in December 1863. Apparently, she was not invited to the Executive Mansion along with Emilie, although she and her husband, C. B. White, from Selma, Alabama, were among the Lincoln's guests at the inauguration. From all indications she was still in Washington when she wrote Lincoln on December 19, 1863.

> Finding Mother obliged to retrace her steps this route after a long and fatiguing trip after Emilie and the children, and both Emilie and herself being sadly out of condition and unable to cope with difficulties so numerous the season advancing and the children with a new nurse. I took advantage of these fortuitous circumstances to assist them together with my own needs for medical advice from a former physician, & relying on your friendly relations toward us to extend the encounter necessary to enable me to remain a sufficient length of time to recruit my health I also request permission to replenish my wardrobe, take for my own use articles not now obtained in the South.[63]

Martha carefully did not elaborate on what the articles were that she needed. "My husband being a non combatant though living south there can be no restrictions in my case and by granting this you will oblige me & it not allowed to remain a pass to return south unmolested will be acceptable."[64] Lincoln granted her the pass, and articles began appearing in newspapers that charged Martha with using the pass to smuggle contraband to the Confederacy.[65]

The situation involving Martha's pass became so serious that Lincoln dispatched his secretary, John G. Nicolay, to investigate the matter. Nicolay wrote Gen. Benjamin F. Butler, commander of Fort Monroe, to find out exactly what happened. Butler obfuscated in his reply to Nicolay but it was obvious that he did not search her trunk(s) and said he had no problem with her at the checkpoint. Martha claimed she was harassed at the checkpoint. "I did understand that there were in Mrs. White['s] trunks some bridal presents to a young relative about to become a bride, and as I knew it must have taken so much Southern gold to buy them, as they could not have been bought with their currency and could be of no possible use to the Southern army, I concluded it was a fair exchange or at least one in which we got the better bargain." Butler, who said he could not believe the president was annoyed by such a foolish story, told Nicolay that Martha had the pass that Lincoln usually gave out to ladies passing through the lines.[66]

Nicolay, based on his interview with Gen. Butler, wrote a rebuttal to Martha White's charges, picked up by various newspapers, which Horace Greeley printed in the *New York Tribune*. Butler, one of the more controversial Union generals, was not the best source for Nicolay to use. The general, from Lowell, Massachusetts, had commanded Fort Monroe earlier in the war, bungled the Battle of Big Bertha and was sent to New Orleans as the city's military governor. That did not work out too well. When a New Orleans woman emptied her chamber pot on the head of Admiral David Farragut, Butler wrote out his famous Woman Order. Any woman disrespecting Union military personnel would be treated and punished as a prostitute—a night in jail and a small fine. The furor over the Woman Order and allegations that Butler was looting banks of gold and other valuables resulted in him being removed from command there. Sen. Charles Sumner, also from Lowell, intervened and Butler was sent back to Fort Monroe, where he encountered Martha White.[67]

A week after Butler's reply to Nicolay, Lincoln received a letter from O. Stewart, Company D, 3rd Michigan, inquiring about the newspaper articles. "I enclose a piece of the paper taken from the Detroit Free Press stating that you gave Mrs. Todd (White) Mrs. Lincoln sister a pass through our lines with a trunk of medicines and Contraband goods and valuable Papers now if this is so will you please have the 4 Ed of the chronicle confirm it or Condemn it and oblige for I don't believe our President would do that please Answer."[68]

Elizabeth Grimsley said Martha White was almost carrying her weight in quinine, a veritable bonanza to the Southern Army, through the lines.[69]

Katherine Helm, Emilie Todd Helm's daughter, called the quinine charge ridiculous and said her aunt only had a small one-ounce package for her own use. What was actually in the trunks, Helm said, was a splendid sword and uniform for Gen. Robert E. Lee. Helm gave a far-fetched explanation. Martha left one of her trunks with Baltimore friends at the hotel but it contained wearing apparel that she might need at the Executive Mansion. She gave the trunk key to her friends and asked them to send her a blue brocade gown, if needed, that was on the top tray. The friends, Helm said, went back to Baltimore leaving the trunk and key in the hotel office.[70]

Helm's explanation up to that point was plausible with one exception. Martha White was not invited to the Executive Mansion. A Union officer followed her aunt, according to Martha's claim. "What was her amazement and mortification," Helm wrote, "on opening her trunk later to find a splendid sword and uniform for General Robert E. Lee, which her Baltimore friends, without asking her permission, had stored in her trunk. Her first impulse was to return immediately to Washington and explain the whole matter to President Lincoln; her second thought was a fear that she might imperil her friends who often visited Washington. She decided she had better seek wise council in this dilemma." A Baltimore woman, Mrs. S. B. French, wrote Lincoln on April 20 offering to swear that the newspapers' accounts of Martha carrying contraband were false. "Mrs. White was too feeble to go out of the house for ten days before she left this city—she strictly avoided public notoriety—If it would be of any consequence of medicine and other articles could be sworn to but we hope she will not suffer in your kindly estimation and that this statement will disabuse your mind of false representations made against your connection and friend."[71]

Helm's next explanations defied logic. She stated that Martha, who was supposedly ill, went to Richmond, Virginia, although she lived in Selma, Alabama.

> She at once consulted President Davis, whom she knew as well as she did her brother-in-law—should she carry the sword and uniform back to Washington and deliver them to President Lincoln? Of course, he need never know, but she would feel dishonest not to tell him about it. President Davis decided that General Lee should have the sword and uniform but Mrs. White was so mortified and worried over the matter, that President Davis, who had for many years been on pleasant terms with Mrs. White's brother-in-law, wrote a personal letter, with his own hand to President Lincoln explaining the position of Mrs. White. Mrs. White went with this letter to Washington and the Great Man in the White House took the incident good-naturedly, twitting Mattie about the indignant lie to the inspector.[72]

Helm failed to address Martha's bragging about how she duped the president and boasted the buttons on the uniform were solid gold. "Details varied," Ruth P. Randall wrote, "and of course grew in the telling: those gold buttons were worth from four to forty thousand dollars depending upon the newspaper or gossiper."[73]

The Lincolns had not heard the last of Martha. Nearly a year later, she wrote another rather tenacious letter that came close to demanding he give her a permit to remove her cotton from Mobile and be quick about it. "The permit will have to be irrespective of all military authority as Gen [Edward R. S.] Camby, only a few weeks threw aside a permit of that kind & rendered null the trade, 'protection to all Neutral Vessels bearing upon Mobile fully guaranteed.'" Martha tried to absolve herself of any blame at Fort Monroe, saying that she was harassed and her temper got the better of her. "Officers in the hotel all thought I was badly treated by this man [Butler] & *he published* me."[74]

Lincoln said that if Martha "did not leave forthwith she might expect to find herself within twenty-four hours in the Old Capitol Prison." Lincoln was so concerned about Martha Todd White, who was obviously a loose cannon, that he made an official statement to Secretary of the Navy Gideon Wells to get it on the record. Both Mary and Lincoln refused to allow her to enter the Executive Mansion.[75]

Levi Owen Todd, Mary's oldest brother, wrote Lincoln on September 12, 1864, under the guise of talking about all he could do to help him carry Fayette County and the commonwealth in the election that year. He actually wanted to borrow $150 to $200, which he promised to pay back by December 1. "I stand in need of things—that are necessary for the Winter—I have been in bad health for some time and am improving fast and in a short time with the kind assistance of those who ought to be my friends." He closed his letter by saying, "hopeing you and Mary and all others are well and that in your kindness of heart that you will give me the aid and comfort *asked* & *desired* in actual necessity for means and sustenance & clothing as I am out of means on account of my bad health."[76] It was Levi, with the help of his brother George, who created so many problems for Mary and Lincoln in settling the estate of their father, Robert S. Todd. No reply from the Lincolns was found. Levi Todd died a month later, causing Emilie to write an accusing, vicious letter to Lincoln blaming him for all the family's problems.

Emilie Helm had made another unsuccessful trip to Washington in October 1864, in an effort to get permits to move her cotton. On her return to Kentucky she wrote the president such an abrasive, accusatory letter that her relationship with Mary and Lincoln was forever severed. But, she later cultivated a relationship with their son, Robert, that was financially lucrative for her.

"Upon arriving in Lexington, after my long tedious unproductive and sorrowful visit to you," Emilie wrote,

> I found my Mother stretched upon a sick bed, made sick by the harrowing and shocking death of your Brother-in-law and my half-brother Levi Todd—He died from utter want and destitution as a letter sent to sister Mary by Kitty [Katherine Todd Herr] give particulars, another sad victim to the powers of more favored relations—My petition to be permitted to ship my cotton & be allowed a pass South to attend to it—My necessities are such that I am compelled to urge it—The last money I had in the world I used to make the unfruitful Appeal to you. You cannot urge that you do not *know them* for I have told you of them. I have been a quiet citizen and request only the right which humanity and Justice always give Widows and Orphans. I also would remind you that your *Minnie bullets* have made us what we are & I feel I have that additional claim upon you.[77]

If Betsy Humphreys Todd was so disturbed by Levi's situation, where was her assistance? Levi was not her child, he had not joined the Confederacy and he had caused problems in the settlement of his father' estate. Betsy was probably suffering more from peer embarrassment.

Emilie asked about a letter her sister Kitty had written Lincoln and another letter in which Kitty had asked Bishop John B. Purcell, from Cincinnati, to write him on behalf of Confederate Gen. W.N.R. Beall. Emilie closed her letter saying, "If you think I give way to excessive feeling, I beg you will make some excuse for a woman almost crazed with misfortune."[78]

Kitty wrote Lincoln on September 5, 1864, asking for Gen. Beall to be exchanged for a Union officer of equal rank. Beall, she told Lincoln, was a friend of her father's. When nothing happened, she wrote him again two weeks later and enclosed a letter from Bishop Purcell asking Lincoln for an answer. "Should you grant my favor, a letter to Lexington, Ky, will reach me. Hoping you will pardon my troubling you and much love to sister Mary."[79]

Beall was paroled in November 1864 and placed in charge of selling southern cotton to provide clothing and supplies for Confederate prisoners in Union prison camps. Evidently, Beall was involved in some shady dealings because Secretary of War Stanton suspended his parole and placed him in Fort Lafayette Prison in New York Harbor until the cotton arrived from Mobile, Alabama. He was not released until August 21, 1865.[80]

Emilie attempted later to use the pass for something other than safe conduct through the lines. "I hear a rumor to-day," Lincoln wrote Maj. Gen. Stephen G. Burbridge on August 18 1864, "that you recently sought to arrest her, but was prevented by her presenting the paper from me. I do not intend to protect her against the consequence of disloyal words or acts, spoken or done by her since her return to Kentucky, and if the paper given her by me can be construed to give her protections for such words or acts, it is hereby revoked *pro tanto* [only to that extent]. Deal with her for her current conduct, just as you would with *any other*."[81] Emilie later denied she had ever been arrested.

Another of Mary's half-sisters, Margaret Todd Kellogg, wrote Lincoln on September 5, 1864, for assistance in obtaining the release of Tennessee Judge T. Nixon Van Dyke. She said the Van Dykes were kind and helpful to Emilie before and after Helm's death and reminded Lincoln her appeals to him had not been numerous. In February 1863, Lincoln, through the insistence of Secretary of the Interior Caleb B. Smith, had appointed her husband, Charles R. Kellogg, a captain in the commissary. Kellogg, however, was such a bungler that he ended up in a Confederate prison in Richmond, Virginia.[82]

The silence from Elodie Beck Todd Dawson, another half-sister, must have been gratifying to Mary. It seems that neither Elodie nor her husband, Nathaniel H. R. Dawson, begged any favors from the Lincoln. Dawson was a successful attorney who became a United States commissioner of education and a trustee of the University of Alabama and the University of the South.[83]

Mary and Lincoln had survived attempts on their lives and cabinet members who wanted his position. The scurrilous rumor mill about Mary continued and the next year was a presidential election. There was a chance, if these familiar follies and claims continued, the Todd relatives just might lead to the end of Mary's ambitions for her husband.

CHAPTER 16

Election Time, Again

Mary and Lincoln opened the election year of 1864 with their grand New Year's Day reception at the Executive Mansion. There was the usual protocol of greeting members of Congress, the military, diplomats and other government officials before the doors were thrown open to the public, who came by the thousands.

Noah Brooks described the holiday event, noting that Mary had left off her mourning wear and was most attractive in a purple velvet dress with white satin flutings.

> Uncle Abraham stands by the door into the Blue Room flanked by Marshal Lamon and his private secretary [John Nicolay] who introduce the new arrivals, each gives his name and that of the lady who accompanies him. The president shakes hands, say 'How-do,' and the visitor is passed on where Mrs. Lincoln stands, flanked by another private secretary and B. B. French, the commissioner of public buildings, who introduce the party; then all press on to the next room, where they admire each other's good clothes, criticize Mrs. Lincoln's new gown, gossip a little, flirt a little, yawn and go home and say "What a bore!" Such is our Republican Court and the most bored man in it is Old Abe, who hates white kid gloves and a crowd.[1]

That New Year's reception at the Executive Mansion also made history. "Years ago had any colored man presented himself at the White House, at the president's levee, seeking an introduction to the chief magistrate of the nation, he would, in all probability, have been roughly handled for his impudence," the *New York Times* reported. "Yesterday, four colored men, of genteel exterior and with the manners of gentlemen, joined in the throng that crowded the Executive Mansion, and were presented to the president of the United States."[2]

"The White House has never , during my forty years' service, been so entirely given over to the public as during Mr. Lincoln's administration," William H. Crook, the president's bodyguard, wrote. "The times were too anxious to make social affairs anything other than an aid to more serious matters. It was necessary, of course; but it made it difficult for a first-lady-in-the-land with any preferences or prejudices not to make enemies on every hand."[3]

Mary's first reception of the year, on January 9, was also well attended. She wore a white silk gown trimmed in black lace with a pearl necklace. "The spectacle awed me at first," Crook wrote of the reception. "I had never seen anything like it before. The reception, or 'levee' as the name was then, was crowded. It was generally considered a brilliant affair." Crook said the guests left their wraps in the cloak room, which was in the corridor, assembled in the Red Room, made their way into the Blue Room—where they were received—exited through the Green Room into the great East Room.[4]

Crook said he was told not to allow anyone with a greatcoat or wrap of any kind to pass into the Blue Room. He said no one resisted that order until an attractive young woman arrived. Crook told her she could not enter the room with her wrap. "She wore a wrap that completely hid her dress. She could have brought in a whole arsenal of weapons under its folds." When Crook asked for her wrap, she became belligerent. "Do you know who I am?" the woman demanded. Crook told her he was sorry but she had to leave her wrap. "I am Mrs. Senator Sprague [Kate Chase]," she announced. Crook was unrelenting, she surrendered her wrap and went into the Blue Room to look for her father.[5]

The New Year's day event and that first reception set off a whirlwind of social activities for the Lincolns for the first four months of the year. During that period, Mary and Lincoln hosted twenty-nine levees, receptions and dinners, made eleven trips to theaters and appeared at numerous other events outside the Executive Mansion.[6] At January's last reception, on the 29th, an estimated 8,000 people came to pay their respects to Mary and Lincoln.[7]

Such a frantic social schedule demanded clothes, and the elaborate gowns of the nineteenth century were not inexpensive. Mary spent money on clothes; she had no choice considering her position. It was said that she ordered from fifteen to sixteen dresses or gowns each year and they took three months to make since each garment had to be fitted to her small frame.[8] That number did not even cover her forty social events, not including other appearances, she made during the first four months of 1864.

The howl and cry over the years about her expensive purchases of clothes lack any documentation or substantiation of bills and receipts. No other president's wife—not even Dolley Madison with her expensive French gowns—was subjected to such intense scrutiny about her clothes. Mary's apparel critics did not pay her clothing bills but they had plenty to say about them. Their criticism was another way to attempt denigrate a woman they did not like; a woman who had the absolute audacity to insert herself into political affairs.

Much has been made of her alleged purchase of 300 pairs of kid gloves by critics who assumed the gloves were for Mary.[9] Both the Lincolns wore white kid gloves at all the levees and receptions, as Noah Brooks described in his article about their New Year's event. Shaking hands with thousands of people at each event required several hundred pairs of gloves be changed with regularity. The president would have never offended a lady by shaking hands with her wearing dirty gloves.[10] Mary was actually being practical when she purchased their gloves by the hundreds of pairs.

The recollections her seamstress, Elizabeth Keckly, used to exaggerate her debts are questionable since she appeared to have been moved from her position of seamstress to personal maid. Mary had seamstresses other than Keckly; one of them was Mary Ann Cuthbert from the Executive Mansion staff. Stoddard indicated that some of Mary's gowns were "made for her by one of the best dress artists in New York." Despite Keckly's supposed knowledge of Mary's not paying her debts, there is evidence otherwise. On April 1, 1864, Mary asked Emmanuel Uhlfelder, a New York fabrics dealer, to send her a receipt for a bill she had paid. On the same day she asked Edwin A. Brooks, an importer and manufacturer of shoes and boots, to send her a receipt for a bill she had already paid.[11] That bill could have included boots for Lincoln or shoes for Tad. That date was the first of the month, when people usually reconciled their financial records, and indicate Mary kept track of her bills. Again, on August 1, 1864, Mary telegraphed George A. Hearn, a New York merchant, that she would send him a check that day.[12]

Later that month, Mary wrote, presumably, to A. T. Steward in reply about an overdue bill. "I write to thank you, for your patience and soliciting as an especial favor to me (having been a punctual customer & always hoping to be so) a delay of the settlement of my account with you until the 1st of June—when I promise, that without fail, *then* the whole account shall be settled. I deeply regret, that I am so unusually situated & trust hereafter, to settle as I purchase." Some have taken her next request as an indication she was just continuing to buy in order to stave off a settlement. "I desire to order, a black India Camel's Hair shawl, yet in sufficient time, will see you to give directions."[13]

While entertaining in an election year was important, Mary had other duties. Aside from managing the Executive Mansion household and planning meals to include Lincoln's favorite foods, Mary continued visiting the wounded in the hospitals around Washington. In May, Mary wrote Mary Jane Wells that she had been suffering from a severe headache that had left her weak. "I fear that I shall be prevented from visiting the Hospitals today," she wrote. "I cannot venture to promise about *tomorrow*, yet, will say Monday morning if you are disengaged at 11 o'clock." She added that she would have the gardener pick the first few strawberries of the season and send them to her.[14]

Mary perked up some when the Lincolns' oldest son, Bob, came home from Harvard. Bob accompanied his parents to the Patent Office's fair for the benefit of the Christian Commission and volunteers. Lincoln was not on the program but was asked to say a few words. The president said he had not been informed that he would speak and was not prepared. Lincoln said, "I am at a great disadvantage after the eloquent speech of Mr. [Lucius] Chittenden and the poem of Mr. [B.B.] French." He said in consequence of his position, anything he said went into print and any mistake he made might do both himself and the nation harm. He told the audience he hoped they would excuse him and hope the charitable enterprise they were supporting would be abundantly successful."[15]

"That was the worst speech I ever listened to in my life," Mary told him in the carriage taking them and Maj. Gen. Richard Oglesby, who was from Illinois, back to the Executive Mansion. "How any man could get up and deliver such remarks to an audience is more than I can understand. I wanted the earth to sink and let me go through." Neither man said a word.[16]

Everybody was talking the next month about Lincoln naming Ulysses S. Grant lieutenant general in charge of the Union armies. Mary held her last public reception of the spring on March 8, and the crowd was so immense that several women fainted. The rush was increased when Gen. Grant arrived at 9:30. Lincoln greeted him with a big smile and jaunty handshake. Everybody wanted to see the man whom the president thought could win the war. The crowd demanded a look at Grant and he climbed on one of the sofas. Mary cringed at what was happening to the upholstered furniture and sent a messenger to ask Grant to join she and Lincoln as they made a tour of the East Room.[17]

With Grant in command, the war news eventually became more optimistic. In May, the Marine Band, whose concerts had been halted when Willie died, was again performing on the Executive Mansion lawn. Not a bad move in an election year.

Secretary of the Treasury Salmon Chase, with the backing of his son-in-law's (Sen. William Sprague) fortune, began mounting a campaign against Lincoln for the Republican presidential nomination. A carefully scripted, scurrilous attack on Lincoln by a committee headed by Sen. Samuel Pomeroy, from Kansas, failed to get the traction Chase's backers expected. Whether Chase was aware of it or not, the president had a solid, non-partisan base in New York. William B. Astor, son of John Jacob Astor and a Republican real estate magnate, and Robert B. Roosevelt, a Democrat civic leader who helped begin a national conservation movement, asked to meet with Lincoln as representatives of merchants and citizens of New York. Lincoln was more than happy to give them an interview.[18]

Mary, Dr. Henry and others warned Lincoln about Chase's plans to undercut him for the Republic presidential nomination. Dr. Henry was particularly concerned about some of Chase's questionable appointments. One of those appointments was that of Henry Cooke, brother of Philadelphia financier Jay Cooke. Through his brokerage house, Jay Cooke was the sole American financial agent for the sale of government bonds to pay for war expenses. Those bond sales, by the end of the war, exceeded $1 billion and, from those sales, Cooke made a considerable amount of money.[19]

Chase and his daughter, Kate, reaped numerous rewards from his official relations with Cooke. Chase's salary as secretary of the treasury, which was $8,000 a year, did not come near covering the expensive Kate's elegant wardrobe, which rivaled or exceeded that of Mary's. They shopped at some of the same New York stores. Neither could his salary begin to cover the extensive entertaining which included Kate's own levees and receptions, some of which she deliberately scheduled to conflict with Mary's, nor the expensive furnishings in his Washington mansion.[20] None of this escaped Mary's attention.

Kate's bills were dooming Chase, three times a widower, to the point where he had to sell some of his farmland in Ohio and eventually the entire farm. Jay Cooke helped Chase by providing gifts of furniture and a carriage for his daughter, but that was not enough for him to get a handle on Kate's spiraling bills. Chase began borrowing money from Cooke: first it was $2,000 to pay off other loans and then Cooke opened an account for Chase at his brokerage firm, and the secretary of the treasury's finances profited.[21]

Secretary of the Navy Gideon Wells was after Chase to investigate the illegal trade of arms and ammunition for Confederate cotton in Texas and other states. Chase refused. Seems his then son-in-law, Senator William Sprague, was involved in the illegal arms for cotton deal that returned him sixty percent on his investment. Secretary of War Stanton was not too interested either, as he was partially indebted to Chase for his appointment after Cameron left the cabinet. Chase's problems multiplied when Henry Cooke, the financier's brother, was caught attempting to defraud the government by misappropriations of quartermaster supplies in Ohio.[22]

Chase became exceedingly angry when Lincoln refused to approve one of his New York patronage appointments and submitted his fourth resignation. Lincoln surprised Chase by accepting it. In describing Chase's character, Lincoln told Hay he was "like the blue-bottle fly, he lays his eggs in every rotten spot he can find." Lincoln dangled a Supreme Court nomination before Chase, insuring he did not split the Republican Party before the election. The president waited until December 6, 1864, before submitting Chase's name to the Senate for confirmation.[23]

Infuriated at Lincoln's actions and prior to Chase's withdrawal, Kate Chase Sprague and her father's campaign released continuous, merciless guerrilla warfare attacks against both the Lincolns. A friend of Lincoln traced the slanderous, whispering allegations against Mary to the Chase campaign.[24]

Congressman Frank Blair, whose brother, Montgomery Blair, was postmaster general, began a withering attack on Chase and Sprague, demanding a House investigation into how Chase ran the department of the treasury and the senator's association with the arms for cotton trade.[25]

The tactics Chase was using in his primary election campaign brought into question exactly how the precise amount, $6,858, of Mary's allegedly exceeding the $20,000 Congressional furnishing appropriation for the Executive Mansion, was made public. The secretary of treasury, of course, had that figure. Chase may have had access to others of her private purchases since she and Kate Chase shopped at some of the same stores in New York. While Mary was allegedly being dunned by A. T. Stewart for not paying her account, the department store owner had been carrying a long overdue bill for Chase for some of Kate's purchases. In fact, the bill was so old that Stewart had been collecting interest on it for several years.[26]

Newspapers, such as the *New York Times* which called Mary a well-known spendthrift, failed to look at Kate Chase's expenditures. Kate, of course, was not a president's wife but she wanted the office for her father so badly she married a millionaire who had the money to underwrite her efforts. A newspaper from Ohio where Chase had been governor made just that argument. The dollar figures were used to make a point: "The Lincoln-Chase contest has extended into the women's department," the article read. "Mrs. Lincoln has got a new French rig with all the poses costing $4,000. Miss Chase sees her and goes one better by ordering a nice little $6,000 arrangement, including a $3,000 love of a shawl."[27]

Mary, earlier in the year, had taken the names of Chase, Kate and Sprague off the invitation list for a dinner they were giving for members of the Cabinet and the Supreme Court. Nicolay took the problem to Lincoln, who, considering the nature of the event, was unable to allow his wife's decision to stand. Mary's temper got the better of her, leading to a row with her husband, which she lost.[28]

It appeared to be a mutual decision of the Lincolns that it would be best for Mary to spend the summer outside of Washington. The

Top: Kate Chase, daughter of Lincoln's Secretary of the Treasury Salmon P. Chase, was determined to see her father elected president even if she had to marry a millionaire, Sen. William Sprague from Rhode Island. In 1864, the Chase campaign for the presidential nomination targeted Mary with vicious attacks. *Bottom:* Lincoln's Secretary of the Treasury Salmon P. Chase, who wanted to be president. Lincoln outmaneuvered him for the presidential nomination in 1864 and appointed him to the Supreme Court (both photographs, Library of Congress Prints and Photographs Division).

Chase campaign eventually collapsed; Kate took to her bed in tears, Sprague closed his checkbook and in their wake Mary's reputation was damaged almost beyond redemption. But their actions were costly. Chase never made it to the presidency. Kate allegedly had a rip-roaring affair in 1879 with New York Senator Roscoe Conkling, whom Sprague supposedly ran out of their residence with a shotgun. Sprague divorced Kate three years later.[29]

Kate Chase Sprague, who bragged she was the most intelligent, successful Washington hostess, temporarily faded from the scene, much to Mary's relief. Mary later suffered more fallout from the Chases' dirty tactics during the general election campaign.

Mary, Lincoln and Tad attended the Philadelphia Sanitary Fair on June 17 and were almost mobbed. Lincoln contributed forty signed copies of the Emancipation Proclamation, which sold for ten dollars each. The fair, which raised over $1 million for the United States Sanitary Commission for assisting wounded Union soldiers, was enclosed in an enormous 200,000-square-foot complex featuring a 540-foot-long flag-festooned Union Avenue under Gothic arches.[30]

Such fairs were a great place for the president to campaign against the expected Democrat nominee Gen. McClellan. Lincoln was again nominated for president at the Republican Convention in June at Baltimore. One of Lincoln's biggest supporters was former New York governor Edwin D. Morgan, then a U.S. senator and chair of the Republican National Committee. It was to Morgan that Mary wrote her sassy letter in defense of Mary Read and suggested the governor resign. Read, upon learning of her husband's mistress, killed him and was sentenced to thirty months of hard labor in Sing Sing while Gen. Sickles killed his wife's lover and was acquitted.[31]

Mary and Tad went from Philadelphia to New York and Lincoln went back to Washington. Tad later returned to the Executive Mansion and Mary traveled to Boston. Lincoln telegraphed Mary on June 24 that Tad arrived safely and they had just returned from a visit to Gen. Grant's army.[32]

While Mary was in New York, Lincoln telegraphed her that they were all well and Tom (Cross or Stackpole) was making the summer transfer of their personal effects to the Soldiers' Home on June 29. Included in the move were Tad's menagerie, which—at one time or another—included goats, ponies and cats. On one occasion, Tad refused to leave the Executive Mansion until all his pets were accounted for, and his father once helped search for his cat.[33]

On July 8, 1864, Secretary of War Edwin Stanton strongly suggested the Lincolns evacuate the Soldiers' Home and return to the Executive Mansion due to the danger of Washington being captured by Lt. General Jubal Early. Grant's advancements to the south had left the Shenandoah Valley and the road to the capital open. Gen. Lee, seeing one last chance to capture Washington, sent Early and 15,000 troops through the valley. Agents of the Baltimore and Ohio Railroad heard about the Confederate advance and notified B&O president John Garrett, who alerted Gen. Lew Wallace, commander of the Middle Department at Baltimore. Wallace hastily gathered 6,550 men and was able to delay Early for a day, which allowed the Union to move in reinforcements. Early came as close to Washington as Silver Springs, Maryland, where he burned Postmaster General Montgomery Blair's home. The Lincoln's Soldiers' Home household was displaced for only four days.[34]

Mary had returned from New York and accompanied Lincoln, along with some members of Congress, to Fort Stevens to watch the battle on July 12. As Lincoln looked over a parapet, a sniper's bullet came terrifyingly close. A young Army captain, Oliver Wendell

Holmes, Jr., reportedly yelled, "Get down you damn fool before you get shot," not realizing who he was addressing. Mary and Lincoln took a trip that evening along the city's defenses greeting the troops and thanking them for defending the capital.[35]

The cleaning, painting, wallpapering and restoration work Mary began on the Soldiers' Home in May was probably incomplete by the time they made their first move to the pastoral setting. They returned on July 14. Cocoa matting was laid on the pine floors. Chair covers were repaired and cleaned; mirrors and paintings were re-hung. The staff at the Soldiers' Home was small, a housekeeper, manservant and a cook. Lincoln liked to serve their guests himself. If Tad was ever inhibited by the Executive Mansion, which was doubtful, he not only enjoyed but learned from the uninhibited atmosphere of the Soldiers' Home.[36]

For a child who did not learn to read or write until later, Tad was quite creative. He found the mechanism in the Executive Mansion's attic that controlled the bell system and rigged them all to go off at the same time, sending servants and secretaries scurrying about the building. He drove his goat and cart through one of the state rooms during a reception, brought homeless children in for dinner and waved a Confederate flag from one of the building's windows. Tad, Noah Brooks wrote, comprehended the realities of life far beyond the grasp of most boys his age, being a shrewd judge of character, imaginative, compassionate and devoted to his parents. "He knew much about the cost of things, the details of trade, the principals of mechanics, and the habits of animals." Brooks added that Lincoln believed Tad would grow up to be what all women doted on—a good provider.[37]

When Lincoln was at the Soldiers' Home without Mary and Tad, he often shared mess with the soldiers. Mary and Tad spent most of the summer of 1864 in Manchester, Vermont. Lincoln telegraphed her in August saying, "All reasonably well here. Bob not here yet. How is dear Tad?" A record of all the telegrams the Lincolns exchanged is far from complete. On September 8, Lincoln wrote, "All well, including Tad's pony and goats. Mrs. Col. Dimmick died night before last. Bob left Sunday afternoon. Said he did not know whether he should see you." Mrs. Dimmick was the wife of retired Gen. Justin Dimmick, governor of the Soldiers' Home.[38]

The Lincolns' telegrams apparently missed each other. Three days later, Lincoln telegraphed Mary in New York asking what day she would be home since he sent a dispatch four days earlier to Vermont.[39]

The Chase political machine exertions to degrade Mary sowed seeds of smear and defamation that were picked up by the McClellan Democrats. On October 30, 1864, a week before the presidential election, the *Illinois State Register*, the Democrat Party newspaper in Springfield, ran a scalding article about the First Lady. They vilified her about her acquisitions, renovations, personal extravagances, for purchasing Brussels carpets and Inverness tapestries, point lace garments and $1,000 shawls and called her a vain, coarse, unamiable woman completely without taste, dignity or direction who allowed scoundrels like Wikoff to become an advisor. "She introduced sensationalism into the White House economy; courting low company in her innocence of what was superior and forgetting her husband's rank made her head of her sex, desired more tangible tokens that this was so."[40]

But, there was more to come. Mary's appearance on Pennsylvania Avenue seven days a week, the writer groused, was an offense to the public. Describing her as "a sallow, fleshy, uninteresting woman in white laces & wearing a band of white flowers about her forehead like some overgrown Ophelia" indicated the writer's lack of any concept of nineteenth century day attire for women. If she was so uninteresting, why did the newspaper bother to print the article? Then came the unkindest cut of all—Willie's death was the judgment of an angry God, the writer affirmed, for the sins of her frivolous adventures. "Only the death of her little boy could bring this vain and foolish woman to her senses; for a time she scandalized the nation no longer."[41]

Perhaps it was articles of this sort which led New York political boss Thurlow Weed and Illinois lawyer Leonard Swett to predict Lincoln would lose the election to McClellan. Even Mary had some doubts but Lincoln had made all the right calls. The popular vote was 2,211,317 for Lincoln and Sen. Andrew Johnson, a former five-term Congressman and governor from Tennessee, and 1,806,227 for McClellan and Ohio Congressman George Pendleton. The electoral count was 212 to 21. The only states McClellan carried were Kentucky, New Jersey and Delaware.[42]

Mary possessed an inner fiber of toughness that sustained her when scurrilous attacks ran unimpeded against her. Since she could not answer them, Mary did the next best thing— continued with her life, caring for her husband and son, visiting the wounded in hospitals around Washington and scheduling trips to the theater. On December 5, the Lincolns and Seward attended the German Opera Company's production of *Faust*. On Christmas Day, they held a reception in the Executive Mansion.[43]

Had the reception been a day later, the Lincolns could have shared firsthand the good news from Gen. William T. Sherman with their guests. "I beg to present you as a Christmas gift the city of Savannah with 150 heavy guns & plenty of ammunition & also about 25,000 bales of cotton," Sherman wired. Lincoln immediately replied, "Many, many thanks for your Christmas gift—the capture of Savannah."[44]

Neither Mary nor her husband were prepared, health-wise, for the strenuous social schedule that January 1865 brought about. Now the elections were over, more and more people flooded the Executive Mansion for the levees and receptions. A severe snowstorm hit Washington on New Year's Day and the annual reception was held a day later. Canvas coverings were placed over Executive Mansion carpets to keep down the damage from snow and mud. There was such a mass of humanity that it was doubtful the canvas helped. "Many pressed so determinedly to gain admittance that several women and children were nearly suffocated and in some instances ladies and children were raised above the crowd," the Washington Evening Star reported.[45]

The Lincolns had hardly recovered from the New Year's reception than it was time for the first evening levee of the year, on January 9, with the usual crowded attendance. Mary wore a pearl-colored grown trimmed with black lace and a pearl necklace.[46] She possibly used the same lace on a number of other gowns.

After receiving their guests, the president, with Mrs. William Dennison on his arm, and Mary, escorted by the new Postmaster General Dennison, entered the East Room and talked with their guests. The reception was supposed to end at eleven but some remained until twelve. William H. Crook, the president's body guard, said the Lincolns then retired upstairs. "The statesmen who came to consult him, those who had it in their power to influence the policy of the party which had chosen him, never had the consideration from Mr. Lincoln that he gave the humblest of those who served him," Crook observed. After leaving the reception, Lincoln wrapped a rough gray shawl around his shoulders, put on his tall beaver hat and left the residence through the basement for the War Department since there was no telegraph in the Executive Mansion.[47]

"I'm glad it is over," the president said.[48]

Crook asked him if he was tired. "Yes," Lincoln said, "it does tire me to shake hands with so many people. Especially now when there is so much other work to do. And most of the guests come out of mere curiosity."[49]

The pace of the levees and receptions became so hectic with the inauguration looming that Lincoln temporarily suspended the Tuesday receptions on February 19.[50]

Mary accompanied Lincoln to the Capitol, complete with dome the president insisted be finished two years earlier, where he signed legislation passed by the Thirty-Eighth Congress. One of the bills Lincoln signed into law on March 3 created the Freedman's Bureau and Bank. The Freedman's Bureau provided food, clothing, medicine, education, legal services and a bank which helped 70,000 former slaves invest their money. While they were there Grant telegraphed Stanton that Lee had sent him a letter regarding ending hostilities.[51]

The next day Lincoln was inaugurated for his second term as president. Vice-President Hamlin escorted Lincoln to the Senate Chamber for Johnson's swearing into office. Mary was escorted by Sen. James Harlan. Chief Justice Chase administered the oath of office to Lincoln's, who kissed the Bible he held. Chase gave the Bible to Mary. The sun began to shine and Lincoln address was moved outside the Capitol where—with Mary looking on—gave his last great oration, the "Malice toward none; with charity for all" speech. He delivered those 701 words in six or seven minutes. In the audience were a great number of former slaves, freedmen and black Union soldiers.[52]

A public reception was held at the Executive Mansion and the inaugural ball was scheduled for March 6. Frederick Douglass, who had attended the inaugural speech, came to the reception along with more than 6,000 others. Two policemen refused his entrance but Douglass told them he was sure that order did not come from the president. Another officer offered to escort him. He did, through a window set up as a short term exit. As he was shown through the window, Douglass asked a guest to tell the president what had happened. "All handshaking ceased as Frederick Douglass entered the East Room," White wrote. "As he walked in, Lincoln called out, 'Here comes my friend Douglass.' Lincoln's greeting was said in such a loud voice that all around could hear him. Taking Douglass by the hand the president said, 'I am glad to see you. I saw you in the crowd today, listening to my inaugural address; how did you like it?'"[53]

"Mr. Lincoln, I must not detain you with my poor opinion when there are thousand waiting to shake hands with you," Douglass replied.[54]

"No, no, you must stop a little Douglass, there is no man in the country whose opinion I value more than yours," Lincoln replied. "I want to know what you think of it."[55]

"Mr. Lincoln, that was a sacred effort."[56]

Mary must have been so proud.

"Mrs. Lincoln was present through the reception and avowed her intention to remain till morning rather than have the doors closed on a single visitor," Benjamin B. French wrote in his diary. "She appeared very gracious and well. She certainly is a woman of endurance, having been all morning at the Capitol."[57]

The reception continued and the Lincolns went through scores of white kid gloves. Crook said the residence, after the reception was over, looked like a regiments of rebel troops had been quartered there, with permission to forage.[58]

Crook said there were some rough people there and the fever of vandalism seemed to seize them. "They wanted to get mementos while they could," Crook wrote. "A great piece of red brocade, a yard square almost was cut from the window-hangings in the East Room, and another piece, not quite so large, from a curtain in the Green Room. Besides this, flowers from the floral design in the lace curtains was cut out, evidently for an ornament for the tops of pincushions or something of the sort. Some arrests were made, after the reception, of persons concerned in the disgraceful business."[59]

Crook said Lincoln was usually calm after such events but the destruction of the state rooms was painful to him, the senseless violence puzzled him. "Why should they do it," he said Lincoln asked, "How can they?"[60]

Foraging at the residence was nothing compared to that at the inaugural ball. A ten-dollar ticket allowed one gentleman and two ladies admittance to the ball held on the third floor of the Patent Office. Proceeds from the ball, if any, were to go to a fund for war widows and orphans. Between 4,000 and 6,000 attended. There were orchestras in each of the third floor galleries: inaugural music in the North Hall, promenade music in the East Gallery and dance music in the West Wing. The Model rooms were decorated with patriotic bunting draped over the tall windows collected up with flags on the wall between each of the casements. The Lincolns arrived around 10:30 and remained for three hours.[61]

The president wore Brooks Brothers black evening attire with the requisite white kid gloves. Mary was supremely elegant in a white silk dress with an overskirt of pointe applique lace. The bodice had short sleeves ornamented by a bertha and she had a double shawl of the same pointe applique lace. Her jewelry was the pearl set Lincoln had given her four years earlier. Even the *New York Times* complimented her. "She looked exceedingly well with her soft white complexion and her toilet was faultless. Her manners were easy and affable."[62]

There were twenty-one dances—quadrilles, waltzes, schottisches, polkas, and the Virginia reel—to work up the crowd's appetite and certainly enough food to satisfy their cravings.

The food, catered by G. A. Balzer in Washington, is worth describing considering what happened later. Noticeably absent were any vegetables. On the 250-foot table, there was oyster and terrapin stew and pickled oysters. Meats included four selections of beef, three of veal, four of poultry, three of wild game, two patetes and three varieties of ham. Lobster and chicken salads were served. There were ornamental pyramids of nougat, orange and caramel with fancy cream candy, coconut and, the Lincolns' favorite, macaroon. Twelve varieties of cakes and tarts were available. For desserts there were ten selections of jellies and creams and six flavors of ice cream. Beverages included coffee and chocolate.[63]

On the stroke of midnight the elaborate buffet was served. There was such a crush of the crowd toward the long table one would think they were starved. "In less than an hour the table was a wreck positively frightening to behold," the *New York Times* reported. Men, when they hoisted trays of food to take back to their guests, spilled stews, jellies and desserts, not only on the floor, but on the suits and gowns of other guests. "The floor of the supper room was soon sticky, pasty and oily with wasted confections, mashed cake and debris of fowl and meat," the *Washington Evening Star* reported. While the Lincolns left after three hours, the party continued until daylight regardless of the mess.[64]

Mary's last reception of the season was held at the Executive Mansion on March 11. Exhausted as he was, Lincoln made an appearance.[65]

Gen. Grant invited Lincoln to City Point, Virginia, on March 22, during the closing days of the war. Mary and Tad, along with her maid, Crook and Captain Charles Penrose—detailed by Stanton—accompanied Lincoln on the 181-foot long, side-wheel steamboat, the

USS *River Queen*. The *River Queen* was rather well appointed if G.P.A. Healy's 1868 painting of Lincoln, Grant, Sherman and Admiral David D. Porter is accurate. The after cabin was carpeted, had curtained windows, and built-in sofas and chairs. Lincoln telegraphed Grant they were leaving around mid-day on March 23 and might lay over during the night.[66]

Lincoln kept in touch with Stanton during the trip. Stanton telegraphed Lincoln, on March 25, that the weather in Washington was cold and windy and that he was glad he had gone south. "I would be glad to receive a telegram from you dated Richmond before you return. Compliments to Mrs. Lincoln."[67]

After the Lincolns arrived at City Point, Virginia, the president was asked to review the troops. By some happenstance, Mary Mercer Ord, wife of Maj. Gen. Edward Ord, found herself riding next to the president. Mary took exception to that, although it was only for a few minutes. Descriptions vary about what happened next. Some historians chose to believe the precise quotes that emanated from Col. Adam Badeau, an officer on Gen. Grant's staff, who was present during the incident, and reported Mary threw a fit about Mrs. Ord riding beside her husband. Others depend on the eyewitness account of Capt. John S. Barnes, who said that Mary was mad that she was in the coach and Mrs. Ord was not. The behavior of both men after the war lead one to believe that Barnes, who did not go into particulars, was the more creditable source for the incident.[68]

Crook, who was also there, made no mention of an altercation but he did talk about the Lincolns visiting the sick and wounded while at City Point. They also made a close inspection of the hospital facilities.[69]

There is no doubt that Mary behaved badly in losing her temper because Mrs. Ord was riding with the president. She embarrassed herself, the president and those in attendance. Since Barnes was riding with Mrs. Ord, she asked to have him removed from the *River Queen* and he was transferred to Gen. Sherman's staff. When the *River Queen* docked at Point of Rocks, Barnes left and Mary and Lincoln went for a walk in the forest which overlooked the Appomattox River. Barnes wrote about them walking through the forest arm-in-arm in an article in a 1907 issue of *Appleton's Magazine*.[70]

Whatever the Lincolns talked about on their walk remains unknown. Mary returned to Washington and Tad remained with his father. Lincoln kept Mary informed on progress made in the war's waning days. He sent her the following telegram, which was to be forwarded to Secretary of War Stanton.

> Last night Gen. Grant telegraphed that Sheridan with his cavalry and the 5th. Corps had captured three brigades of infantry, a train of wagons, and several batteries, prisoners amount to several thousands. This morning (April 2) Gen. Grant having ordered an attack along the whole line telegraphs as follows "Both Wright and Parke got through enemies lines. The battle rages furiously. Sheridan with his Cavalry, the 5th. Corps & Miles Division of the 2 ne. Corps, which was sent to him since 1. this A.M. is now sweeping down from the West. All now looks highly favorable. Ord is engaged, but have not yet heard the result from his front." Robert yesterday wrote a cheerful note to Capt. Penrose, which is all I have heard of him since you left.[71]

Lincoln, later that same day, telegraphed Mary the following message. "At 4:30 p.m. to-day General Grant telegraphs that he has Petersburg completely enveloped from river below to river above, and has captured, since he started last Wednesday, about 12,000 prisoners and 50 guns. He suggests that I shall go out and see him in the morning, which I think I will do. Tad and I are both well, and will be glad to see you and your party here at the time you name."[72] Mary and her party, Sen. Sumner and Sen. and Mrs. James Harlan, rejoined Lincoln and Tad. They toured Richmond after the president's visit.[73]

After the Lincolns returned to Washington, Crook said he thought the president looked pale and depressed and spoke to his wife about it on April 14. Mary told Crook that, on their drive out to the Soldiers' Home that afternoon, they talked about their life after Lincoln's term was over, how much they would welcome the calm and ease of being out of public life and plans to return to Illinois.[74]

Mary and Lincoln had an early dinner that evening because their attendance had been announced for a play, *Our American Cousin*, at Ford's Theatre. Neither really wanted to go but the president felt they should since their plans had been announced in the newspapers. Crook said Lincoln appeared tired as he accompanied him on the usual evening trip from the Executive Mansion to the War Department and back. As they returned to the residence, Lincoln told Crook he expected to be assassinated. "I have perfect confidence in those who are around me—in every one of you men. I know no one could do it and escape alive. But if it is to be done, it is impossible to prevent it."[75]

When they reached the steps of the residence, Lincoln, who usually bade Crook good night when they parted, paused and turn to his guard and said, "Good-by, Crook."[76]

CHAPTER 17

Love Is Eternal

A shot rang out.

After twenty-three years of marriage to the love of her life, after spending the afternoon planning for their future after the presidency, after whispering and holding hands in their box at Ford's Theatre, Mary saw her husband slump down in his chair never to regain consciousness, never to smile at her again with his twinkling blue-gray eyes, never again to say, "Now, that reminds me...."

Lincoln was carried across the street from Ford's Theatre to a small back bedroom in the modest boarding house of William and Anna Petersen. Physicians, among them Dr. Lyman Beecher Todd, Mary's cousin, were helpless as they watched the president die. Dozens of people were in and out of the Petersen House, which was surrounded by Army guards. Some of the Petersens' boarders had to spend the night in the basement.[1]

William Crook heard about Lincoln early the next morning and rushed to the house on Tenth Street. "They would not let me in," he said. "The little room where he lay was crowded with the men who had been associated with the president during the war. They were gathered around the bed watching, while, long after the great spirit was quenched, life, little by little, loosened its hold on the long gaunt body. Among them, I knew, were men who had contended with him during his life or who had laughed at him. Charles Sumner stood at the very head of the bed. I know that it was to him that Robert Lincoln, who was only a boy for all his shoulder straps, turned to in the long strain of watching. And on Charles Sumner's shoulder the son sobbed out his grief. But the room was full and they would not let me in."[2]

The men Crook talked about, including cabinet members, did not have the decency or graciousness to remove themselves from the small bedroom and give Mary a chance to tell her husband a last goodbye. She whispered out private thoughts to him, kissed him and sobbed out her agony before their censorious, disapproving looks.[3]

Mary Lincoln's life also ended, April 15, 1865, at 7:22 a.m., but she existed for seventeen more years.[4]

"After the president died," Crook said, "They took him back to the White House. It was to the guest room, with its old four-poster bed that they carried him. I was in the room while the men prepared his body to be seen by his people when they came to take their leave. It was hard for me to be there. It seemed fitting that the body should be there, where he had never been in his life. I am glad that his own room could be left to the memory of his living present."[5]

Mary Jane Wells, wife of Secretary of the Navy Gideon Wells, immediately came to

The President's Box at Ford's Theatre (Library of Congress, Prints and Photographs Division).

assist Mary and remained on a daily basis. During the few hours a day when Mrs. Wells was not there, Elizabeth Keckly either called for spiritualists or suggested they be brought in to allow Mary to reach her dead husband. William Crook described what happened. "Women spiritualists in some way gained access to her. They poured into her ears pretended messages from her dead husband. Mrs. Lincoln was so weakened that she had not force enough to resist the cruel cheat. These women nearly crazed her. Mr. Robert Lincoln, who had to take his place at the head of the family, finally ordered them out of the house."[6]

But, twenty-one-year-old Robert was not equipped to be the head of the family after his father was killed, his mother beside herself with grief and his brother Tad seeking comfort anywhere he could find it. Robert deferred to his father's friends, like David Davis, and Secretary of War Stanton since Seward was bedridden. As part of John Wilkes Booth's

One of the last photographs of Lincoln before his death (Library of Congress, Prints and Photographs Division).

conspiracy to kill Lincoln, Johnson and Cabinet members Secretary of State William Seward was also targeted. Lewis Payne (aka Lewis T. Powell), a former Confederate soldier, entered Seward's home in Lafayette Square, pistol-whipped his son, Frederick, almost crushing his skull and attacked Seward, who was bed-ridden from a recent carriage accident. Payne attempted to slash Seward's throat but was preventing from doing so due to physicians having wrapped a wire netting around his neck to keep his dislocated jaw from moving. With Seward unavailable, Stanton took over the arrangements for the state funeral. Stanton never liked Mary and had no intentions of allowing her to be a part of Lincoln's funeral plans. Ellen Stanton, his wife, shared his opinion and refused to call on the president's wife. Stanton delegated much of the actual planning to assistant Treasury Secretary George Harrington and Benjamin B. French. Lincoln's body was in repose in the residence's second floor guest room, which was directly across the hall from his bedroom. Stanton selected the black Brooks Brothers suit Lincoln wore to his inauguration the previous month for the president's burial outfit.[7]

French designed the elaborate catafalque to hold Lincoln's casket in the East Room. The funeral planners did not notice or did not care that the frantic hammering and sawing in the East Room could be heard upstairs by the president's widow. French's design became very elaborate—the catafalque, which sat on two bases, was sixteen feet long and ten feet wide, and the posts at each corner, which held a canopy, were eleven feet high. In order to place the catafalque in the center of the East Room, the enormous Jackson chandelier in the middle of the room was temporarily removed.[8]

On Monday after Lincoln was killed, his body was placed in an ornate, solid walnut, lead-lined casket covered with black material and decorated with sterling silver studs, handles and his name plate. In eight hours, more than 25,000 mourners filed past Lincoln's bier in the East Room and thousands of others had to wait and pay their respects when he lay in state in the Capitol rotunda for the next three days. After the Executive Mansion doors were closed to the public, 400 of Lincoln's Illinois friends and associates paid their respects.[9]

Mary, incapacitated by her grief, was unable to leave her bed. Dr. Henry rushed back from Richmond to lend her his support. He sat with her for hours at a time, counseling her as he did after Eddy died.[10] Hopefully, she was sedated and did not hear, as Margaret Taylor had to endure fifteen years earlier, the hammering on the catafalque to hold her husband's casket in the East Room.

On the second floor of the Executive Mansion, Mary received a few members of the Illinois delegation and agreed to return her husband's body to Springfield. Recalling Lincoln's request to be buried in a country cemetery, Mary decided Oak Ridge Cemetery, outside of Springfield, was an ideal location. The Illinoisans had a different plan and Robert Lincoln agreed without consulting his mother. They organized a National Lincoln Monument Association that called for Lincoln to be buried in downtown Springfield, in what was called the Mathers Block, with a proper monument to mark the spot. There would be no room for Mary or their sons to be interred with him at that site. The committee assumed, since they had Robert's approval, Mary would also agree.[11]

Members of Congress wanted Lincoln to be buried in the empty vault prepared for George Washington under the Capitol dome. Washington chose to be buried on his Virginia plantation, Mount Vernon.[12]

While these decisions, both firm and assumed, were being made, carpenters and workmen descended on the East Room, turning it into an auditorium that would seat 600 for the private funeral service the next day, conducted by the Lincolns' Washington minister, the Rev. Phineas Gurley.

Mary could not overcome her grief, thus leaving Robert and possibly Tad to represent the family. Robert sat at the foot of his father's coffin flanked by Mary's sisters, Elizabeth Edwards and Ann Smith, both of whom traveled from Springfield. Other Todd relatives included Dr. Lyman B. Todd and Gen. John B. Todd. Gen. Grant sat alone at the head of the casket. After the service, Lincoln's casket was loaded on a caisson pulled by six white horses and taken to the Capitol Rotunda where he lay in state April 19, 20, and 21. Cannons were fired each minute as the horses traveled the 1.6 miles down Pennsylvania Avenue. Benjamin French wrote it was likely the short trip took two hours. An estimated 40,000 to 50,000 people filed past Lincoln's casket in the Rotunda.[13]

The chills that must have shook Mary's frail body, and her even more fragile psyche, were intense as those cannons were being fired.

Robert escorted the bodies of his father and brother, Willie, on the funeral train that basically backtracked the Lincolns' 1861 journey to Washington. While the funeral train was en route, Mary discovered the plans for Lincoln's final burial place in downtown Springfield, which were not of her choice. Members of the committee organized for that purpose included some of Lincoln's closest personal and political friends—Gov. Richard Oglesby, who had visited them recently in the Executive Mansion; John Todd Stuart, Mary's cousin and Lincoln's first law partner; James C. Conkling, who was married to Mary's girlhood friend Mercy Levering; Ozias M. Hatch, a close and longtime political ally as was Jesse K. Dubois, and banker Jacob Bunn, later Mary's conservator.[14]

Secretary of War Edwin Stanton assumed responsibility for planning Lincoln's funeral after an attempt on Seward's life. *Right:* Secretary of State William Seward, former governor of New York, was attacked and seriously injured by one of John Wilkes Booth's co-conspirators the night President Lincoln was shot (both photographs, Library of Congress, Prints and Photographs Division).

She telegraphed them that Lincoln was to be buried at Oak Ridge. The committee asked Robert to get her to change her mind; she refused. Lincoln and Willie's bodies were interred in a temporary receiving vault at Oak Ridge on May 4, 1865. But the committee continued with their plans. After she left Washington and moved to Chicago, a representative of the committee called on her and Mary declined to receive him. The committee members appeared to have no regard for the additional stress and harassment they were heaping upon Lincoln's widow when she was the most vulnerable.[15]

After the funeral, the Executive Mansion was left with little or no security for the five weeks Mary was in residence. Before she departed on May 23, people plundered and carried away furniture, silver, china, cut up draperies and carpets and anything else they wanted. After all the carpentry, dust and dirt, the East Room was probably in such shambles there was little left of the lovely carpet Mary was so careful to protect.[16]

The Executive Mansion was the responsibility of the commissioner of public buildings, Benjamin B. French, and he was answerable for what happened to the furnishings and the residence while she was still living there. Being the ultimate bureaucrat that he was, French was too busy beguiling the new president and his family in order to secure his position.

Newly-sworn President Andrew Johnson never bothered to call on Mary or even send his card. Mary remained under the care of the Lincolns' physician, Dr. Robert K. Stone, who refused to allow her to be moved until she was somewhat restored. Mary Jane Wells was with Mary almost daily after the assassination until she left for Chicago. Crook credited her with getting Mary in condition to leave the residence.[17]

Noah Brooks, who was slated to replace John Nicolay as Lincoln's secretary, described Mary, during her remaining time at the Executive Mansion, as being more dead than alive. Though seemingly oblivious to her surroundings and circumstances, once again, she sought to help others. In late April and early May, she wrote Johnson asking him to find an appointment for Alexander Williamson, who had been Willie and Tad's tutor, to make the West Point appointment Lincoln had promised Albert F. Pike and to retain the residence principal doorkeeper Thomas F. Pendel.[18]

By May 17, Brooks wrote, nearly all the preparations had been made for Mary's departure from the Executive Mansion. Mary packed more than two car loads of boxes containing gifts made to the presidential couple, not including their personal belongings. That included a single set of china, a gift from a gentleman in Philadelphia, inscribed with the Lincolns' initials. Brooks said it took three hogsheads, wooden barrels normally used to transport sixty-three gallons of whiskey, to pack the china. Other gifts included paintings, photographs, statuary and other works of art. "Mrs. Lincoln intends to have a sort of museum attached to her future residence so that all people may see these gifts under proper restrictions and regulations," Brooks wrote.[19]

Her oldest son and the former president's friends, including David Davis, the administrator of Lincoln's estate, assumed when she left the Executive Mansion she would return to their home in Springfield.

Crook accompanied Mary, Robert, Tad, and in her capacity as a maid, Keckly, on a private railroad car taking them from Washington to Chicago. "During most of the fifty-four hours that we were on the way she was in a daze; it seemed almost a stupor," Crook wrote. "She hardly spoke. No one could get near enough to her grief to comfort her. But I could be of some use to Taddie. Being a child, he had been able to cry away some of his grief, and he could be distracted with the sights out of the car-window. There was an observation car at the end of our coach. Taddie and I spent a good deal of the time there, looking at the scenes flying past. He began to ask questions."[20]

Her penetrating grief, and she was a woman whose intense feelings ran the entire emotional scale, left Mary searching for answers about her children, how she would support them and what she would do with the rest of her life. She could not bear to return to their Springfield home. While she tenaciously and stridently clung to her internal memories of Lincoln and her lost children, she gave away, as she had done with Eddy and Willie, his clothes, canes and other memorabilia. Those things, like the house, simply lacerated her deep wounds and ripped open new ones. Stanton and others in Lincoln's administration had made enough decisions concerning her deceased husband without consulting her.

One item she did not have to worry about was the cost of her husband's funeral. A year after his death, Congress appropriated $30,000 "for defraying the expenses incident to the death and burial of Abraham Lincoln, late president of the United States."[21]

Mary discovered that the Springfield group planned to erect a monument to Lincoln at the downtown site regardless of the fact that he was buried at Oak Ridge. "I feel that it is due to candor and fairness that I should notify your monument association, that unless I receive within the next ten days, an official assurance that the monument will be erected over the tomb in Oak Ridge Cemetery, I shall yield my consent, to the requests of the National Monument association in Washington & that of numerous other friends in the Eastern States & have the sacred remains deposited in the vault, prepared for Washington, under the Dome of the National Capitol, at as early period as practicable," Mary wrote Gov. Oglesby on June 5. "I remain, your deeply afflicted friend, Mary Lincoln."[22]

Five days later Mary sent Oglesby another letter saying, "I perceive by the paper of to day, that notwithstanding, the note, I recently addressed you, yourself & Mr. Hatch are en route to Chicago, to *consult*, with me, on the subject. My determination is unalterable, and if you will allow me again to add, that without I receive the 15th of this month a formal & written agreement that *the* Monument shall be placed over the remains of my Beloved Husband, in *Oak Ridge* Cemetery, with the *written* promise that no other bodies, save the president, his wife, his sons & sons families, shall ever be deposited within the enclosure; in the event of my *not* receiving a *written* declaration to that effect, I shall rigidly comply with my resolution."[23]

The powerful people she had crossed on her trip up the mountain of success were still there not to restrain her fall but to accelerate it. For nineteenth century women who dared to be active in a man's realm of politics, she paid a dear price. Mary was alone in an unfriendly world with few friends. Her assumption of entitlement after Lincoln's death made that environment more antagonistic.

That she even endured was a near miracle. There was that special something in her inner being that kept her struggling to survive, that refused to let herself be beaten down, that caused her to dig her heels in for the fight of her life. She made mistakes as many heartbroken widows often do. Mary was not forgiven for the miscalculations she made which were, unfortunately, played out in national and international newspapers. Mary became her own worst enemy because of her tendency to exhibit no subtleness in attacking her problems—she met them head-on, full force scattering those who could have helped her.

Yet, she had a few, very few, close friends—Mary Jane Wells, Sen. Charles Sumner, Abram Wakeman, Rep. Elihu Washburne, Elizabeth Blair Lee, Sally Orne, Noah Brooks and, before his drowning in July 1865, Dr. Anson Henry—who really did try to help her.

Assassination of President Abraham Lincoln by John Wilkes Booth at Ford's Theatre on April 14, 1865. Booth is shown holding the dagger with which he wounded Major Henry Rathbone, standing beside Clara Harris. Mary Lincoln is shown sitting to her husband's right (Library of Congress, Prints and Photographs Division).

Alexander Williamson, Willie and Tad's Scot tutor and a clerk in the Treasury Department, was the unfortunate friend Mary selected to help her raise money to pay off her debts, or have them reduced, as well as solicit funds from Lincoln's friends and supporters. From the time of Lincoln's death until the end of 1865, Mary sent twenty letters of instruction to Williamson about whom to talk about raising money for her and about consolidating her debts.[24] The intense letters continued for years without success.

"It had been expected that Mrs. Lincoln would go back to her old home in Illinois. But she did not seem to be able to make up her mind to go there," Crook said. "She remained for some time in Chicago at the old Palmer House." Crook said he lived with a friend for the week he was in Chicago with the Lincolns. "I went to the hotel every day. Mrs. Lincoln I rarely saw. Taddie I took out for a walk every day and tried to interest him in the sights we saw. But he was a sad little fellow, and mourned for his father."[25]

John Wilkes Booth's .44-caliber Derringer destroyed Mary Lincoln's life and forever changed the course of American history (Ford's Theatre National Historic Site, National Park Service, Library of Congress).

The hotel proved to be too expensive for Mary, Tad and Robert. They moved into an apartment in Hyde Park, seven miles south of the city, on the lake shore. Mary often drowned herself in mourning. Robert, bitter at having to leave Harvard Law School and grieving for his father, could be of little assistance. He was commuting daily from Hyde Park into Chicago to read the law at the offices of Scammon, McCagg and Fuller. Tad was the saddest of the trio and apparently no one was helping him with his grief. Robert allegedly said he would almost as soon be dead as to remain three months in the Hyde Park apartment.[26]

After nearly three months at Hyde Park, the Lincolns moved into the less expensive and plainer Clifton House, a boarding establishment, in downtown Chicago. At the end of the year, Robert moved out of Clifton House into his own apartment.[27]

Mary was living on the interest from investments the estate administrator David Davis had made for the family. Davis was no admirer of Mary's and, if he felt he had a score to settle with her for involving herself in politics, he was in the perfect position to do just that. The money Davis was doling out to Mary, Robert and Tad, prior to his final settlement of Lincoln's estate of $110,974.62, in November 1867, was not exactly equitable. Mary had received $4,048.83, Tad, who was under Davis's guardianship, $1,586, and Robert, $7,586.54.[28]

"While her requests for money were refused when she hoped to stay in her home, Robert's had been granted," Jean Baker wrote. "Without his mother's knowledge he had asked Davis for $3,000 to invest and had received the extra money to fix up his bachelor quarters."[29]

For an uncomplicated estate—the majority of which was in government bonds—Davis waited two years and seven months before a final settlement was made. "The law of Illinois provided that upon granting letters of administration," Harry E. Pratt, an expert on Lincoln's finances, wrote, "a warrant should be issued under the seal of the probate court authorizing three persons to appraise the goods, chattel, and personal estate of the deceased. No such appraisal was made in the Lincoln estate."[30]

Newspapers announced that Lincoln had left his family a $75,000 estate. Mary was furious as it undermined her own efforts to raise money to help pay off debts she assumed after Lincoln was killed and wrote Davis about it. "Robert, explains, that the reason, the definite sum was given, or any mention made, that it was owing to it having to be drawn from Mr. Harrington [assistant secretary of the treasury] previous to his leaving for Europe." When David filed his petition for administration in Springfield, he had to list the estimated amount of the estate.[31]

"Of course," Mary continued, "*no less* than the true amount, should be given, yet when it comes to be explained, as I am sure, it will be in your letters, in reply to those written you, on the subject, that one third, as it belongs to a son under age, cannot be invested in a *house, for us to live in*—and the ⅔ thirds—Robert's & my own portion, is all that is left us—Of course, we will be unable to secure a home, with this suitable, to our Station & as to keeping it up, it would be impossible—Coming from you, any explanation, would be well received and have much weight."[32]

Mary's anger in that letter was nothing compared to the rage emanating from a letter to Davis two months later. She told Davis about being informed by one of her callers that he had said their income was ample and that she needed no assistance, as they were living very comfortably. "I replied to her, that there *must* be, some mistake, that it was impossible, you could have said this, or overrated an income, which enabled us to board, in the plainest manner *only*. I further added, what I *Know*, to be correct, that the greater portion of those in Ill, who had received the highest favors, from my noble & generous husband, were, very evidently, the most indifferent, about our having a home, or the wherewithal to keep it up."[33]

This was the Mary of old; fighting for what she believed should be hers. She knew the game Davis was playing and, knowing she had to deal with him, was unable to keep the contempt from seeping into her rhetoric. "Yet I assured, the lady, that I could not realize that you, whom my husband so much respected & loved & knew the exactly the small & limited state of our finances, could have made such an assertion. I told her, that when the time came for action, when Congress met & persons came to you for information, I felt assured, you would insist upon a liberal allowance, which the position, we had *held*, would justify, and that we should be enabled to live, in a manner not disgraceful, to the American Nation."[34]

In the same letter, Mary told Davis not to reply to two creditors, Harper & Mitchell for bills of $817.14, and May & Company for $628.01, that she would attend to it.[35] She did just that, as she had been handling the Lincolns' household fiscal affairs since the 1840s.

The footnote regarding that item in the Turners' book, on page 275, stated the May & Company bill included an item for eighty-four pairs of gloves. The Turners gave the date of the purchase receipt as March 5, 1866. That date had to be in error because March 5, 1866, was six months in the future. If the date was a year in the future, then that meant the gloves were purchased on March 5, 1865, while the Lincolns were still in the Executive Mansion, conducting official entertaining and needing the gloves for the thousands of people they greeted.[36]

Horace Greeley started a campaign for Mary and her son to raise $100,000 through one dollar donations in May 1865. Later that month, Josiah G. Holland, editor of the *Springfield* (Massachusetts) *Republican*, went to Springfield, Illinois, to search for material on a biography of Lincoln. Davis was not in Springfield so Holland spent two days with William H. Herndon, Lincoln's last law partner. Holland returned home and wrote a news story for his paper, saying, "The scheme for a popular subscription to raise $100,000 for Mrs. Lincoln has been abandoned. It has been ascertained that the late president left an ample fortune—very much larger than at first appeared."[37] Greeley was infuriated. "No part of the above mischievous paragraph is true," he insisted, "It is a cruel fabrication. It is not true, far from it that the late president left an ample fortune."[38]

Mary reiterated her belief that Davis was punishing her for her past political actions and for demanding her husband be buried at Oak Ridge Cemetery instead of in downtown Springfield. "*Judge* Davis has been here holding court in Chicago," Mary wrote Dr. Henry, "called out, & said *very complacently*, I am glad to see you are so well situated out *here* & remarked, that there was not the least *indication* that C[hicago] or *any other place,* would *bestow* a house & we would have to *content* ourselves, with boarding. I replied, 'I board *no longer*, than next spring in Ill, *after that*, if we are to be *vagrants*, I prefer being so, in any other *state* rather than where, *every man* in the State owes my husband a deep debt of gratitude.'"[39]

Dr. Henry never received Mary's letter because two weeks after she wrote of her feelings about Davis, the ship he was traveling on, *Brother Jonathan*, sunk off the coast off California. Mary, with her limited financial resources, wanted to help Dr. Henry's wife, who also needed assistance. She had some mining stock that she asked Noah Brooks to help sell and give the money to the doctor's wife.[40]

Mary, with her limited financial resources, did not forget Lincoln's stepmother, Sarah

Bush Lincoln. "In memory of the dearly loved one, who always remembered you with so much affection, will you not do me the favor of accepting these few trifles?" Mary wrote her in December 1867. "My husband a few weeks before his death mentioned to me, that he intended *that* summer, paying proper respects to *his* father's grave, by a head & foot stone, with his name, age && and I propose very soon carrying out his intentions. It was not from want of affection for his father, as you are well aware, that this was not done, but *his* time was so greatly occupied always."[41] Mary had sent Sarah Bush Lincoln some dress fabric, among other items. The following day she mailed her another letter with ten dollars to pay for making a dress.[42]

Another example of her generosity to her children was evident. She took none of the rent from the house in Springfield, allowing her portion to be divided between Robert and Tad.[43]

Mary desperately wanted to make a home for her young son, whom she was home-schooling. On August 3, 1865, she wrote her good friend Sally Orne and discussed their having to live off the interest of Lincoln's investments, bringing in about $1,500 a year. Mary said she brought up their financial problem because she needed her friend's help.

> A friend of my husband's & myself, presented me last February, a *very* elegant lace dress, very fine & beautiful—lace flounce about 6 inches, in width, for the bottom of the skirt—same pattern as dress—a double lace shawl, very fine, exactly similar pattern with the request that I would wear it on the night of the inauguration—for two hours, that evening, I did so, over a while silk dress, next morning, most carefully, the *gathers* were drawn from the skirt—and it was folded *tenderly* away, the flounce was not used. I wore the article reluctantly, as it was too elaborate for my style & too expensive, for my means—My desire is, to dispose of these articles, it cost in New York, to import them $3,500—of course—if I can get $2,500 for them, it will be a great consideration to me.[44]

Sally Orne either did not reply or failed to realize the extent of Mary's financial problems at that time. Mary was unable to sell the lace dress but had more luck selling her carriage through a Chicago sales brokerage firm, Leeds and Miner.[45]

There was, however, a bright spot for Mary in 1866, when the French people, through the efforts of Edouard Rene Lefebvre de Laboulays, a history professor at College de France, collected enough money from 40,000 Frenchmen to present her with a gold medal honoring her husband's dedication to freedom, and liberty and saving the Republic for all people. One side of the medal depicted figures guarding the plaque of liberty and the other side's imagery showed a black soldier and the ballot box.[46]

Davis could have used some of the money, $17,098.64, the estate received from Lincoln's notes and loans he left with Robert Irwin in 1861, to help defray the expenses of allowing Mary to buy or even rent a house for herself and Tad. Instead, he invested it in more government bonds, out of her reach.[47]

Mary's debts were incorrectly estimated to be anywhere from $27,000 to $70,000. Willard L. King, Davis' biographer, wrote that they were closer to about $6,000. Davis was certainly the more creditable source. Galt and Brothers, Washington jewelers, sent Davis a bill for $3,201.50 on August 8, 1865. The jewelers, in a September 2, 1865, letter to Davis, withdrew the bill. Apparently Mary worked out an arrangement with them. On January 3, 1866, Mary wrote Williamson that the jewelers were allowing her to return eighteen nut picks and spoons, as well as an itemized list of thirty-three pieces of jewelry amounting to $2,152. "As a matter of course—they were never taken out of their cases—never worn—scarcely looked at & never shown to anyone."[48]

Mary's anger went up a notch when she discovered that Benjamin B. French not only had accused her of removing furnishings from the Executive Mansion that did not belong to her but was persuading Congress to spend an outrageous amount of money on the residence for the Johnsons. Before the end of 1865, French had spent $30,000 on furnishing for the Executive Mansion, $10,000 more than the Lincolns received four years earlier. In 1866, he spent $66,000 more, and In January 1867 another $30,000. All told, French spent $130,000 on the residence before Johnson left office.[49] Mary wrote referring to French's accusations:

> That villainous & criminal falsehood was gotten up, by the *party*—who wished to have *all* the spoils to themselves—and in consequence was rewarded, in *truly American* style, by quite a $100,000 to fit up the W.H. We will see, how much of it will be used for *that purpose*—His *Yankee* pockets are capacious, perhaps his love for gain, will be discovered ere long. I am receiving letters, *now* constantly on *this* subject and it is being traced to the smooth faced Comm—all those barbarous stories of W.H. depredation The New York World did not *lose*, I imagine, by its correspondence. *He* was kicked out of *that place* [commissioner of public buildings] in Pierce's time—and if Johnson, knows what he is about, he will not long remain where he is.[50]

Having lobbied Rep. Elihu Washburne in the House and others to pay her the remaining salary from Lincoln's second term, which would have been for the remainder of 1865, and $25,000 for each of the next three years. Mary had to settle on December 21, 1865, for the remainder of Lincoln's 1865 salary, $22,025.34.[51]

Simon Cameron, Lincoln's first secretary of war, generously assisted Mary with a $5,000 donation (Library of Congress Prints and Photographs).

That money could have been used for Mary to purchase a home for herself and Tad, but Davis saw that it was invested in government bonds.[52] Davis had his boot firmly placed on Mary's neck and he had no intentions of helping her. That the wife and young son, adored by the man he claimed as his friend, were homeless bothered him not at all.

Not all of Mary's acquaintances were as insensitive as Davis. Noah Brooks solicited a contribution of $400 in gold for her. Mary wrote Brooks on December 18, 1865, that it had arrived. In May 1866, the Boston "Dollar Fund" raised $10,750 for her. Even Simon Cameron, attempting a political comeback, raised $5,000 for Mary.[53]

There appeared to be enough money for her to finally buy a home in 1866, on Chicago's West Washington Street, a row house, despite Davis's dragging his feet in settling the estate. She had to buy furnishings and all that was involved maintaining a house. The Lincolns lived there, rather frugally, for about eighteen months.[54]

Davis, whom Mary informed on February 24, 1867, that she would have to give up the house in Chicago, refused to make a final settlement of Lincoln's estate until November 13, 1867. "The severe winter & and very high prices of every thing, with the utter inability to meet expenses on so small an income & no apparent prospects of a remedy, has determined me, to end this folly of keeping house on a clerk's salary—and there is no other resource but giving up this house," Mary said in her letter to Davis.[55]

On next Friday (first of March) I shall place every thing, in the hands of a house agent to either sell or rent—If I can dispose of my furniture for what I have paid for it, I must be satisfied. To be homeless & a wanderer in the future, is to me, pressed down with care and sorrow—a very great additional grief. My income is barely sufficient, with the most rigid economy, to produce the plainest table fare & my coal bill & living this winter, has completely exhausted, the half-year's sum—which is my portion until 1st of July—I can no longer struggle thus—and must remedy it, with the painful resort of giving all up—With apologies for troubling you with this recital—I remain very respectfully, Mary Lincoln.[56]

Mary appeared to be finally giving up the long fight to make a home for her family, which Davis could have certainly assisted her with by settling the estate earlier. The $36,991.54 Mary received as her one-third portion of Lincoln's $110,974 estate on November 13, 1867, could have saved her home had she received it earlier.[57]

Davis successfully sabotaged Mary's fund raising efforts to keep her home by telling his friends and having it printed in newspaper articles that Lincoln had left his family financially well endowed. He was also successful in beating down a woman he despised. It took a certain kind of person to make sure his good friend's widow was homeless when, a few years later, he built himself a three-story, Mid-Victorian-styled brick mansion with thirty-six rooms, indoor plumbing, central heating, updated gas lighting and two communications systems.[58]

The decision to have to sell or rent her home was difficult enough after the previous year in which she suffered an emotional outrage that left her thunderstruck.

The president's former law partner, William H. Herndon, who was unable to keep their practice going without Lincoln, decided to write a book about him. Herndon most likely saw it as a way to make money for himself. He asked Mary for an interview. Unfortunately, she agreed and met Herndon in Springfield on September 5, 1866, at the St. Nicholas Hotel. Herndon, informed Mary in a letter, that he wanted to get a complete history of the wife of Abraham Lincoln. At their meeting, however, most of his questions were about Lincoln's religion. Mary told him her husband had never joined an organized church but he was still a very religious man, a Christian.[59]

Herndon was not ready to talk about Lincoln's religion, that would come later. He had found a juicier subject, Lincoln's supposed romance with Ann Rutledge in New Salem, Illinois. Somebody gave Herndon a clipping from a small newspaper in Menard County, Illinois, which talked about Lincoln and Ann being lovers. Herndon was off and running with in his efforts to make money, disparage his successful partner and get even for the supposed slights he received from Mary. On November 16, 1866, Herndon told a Springfield audience he was there to tell them a "Long, thrilling and eloquent story." It was long all right, 15,000 words—under his copyright—and he made sure the 500 copies he had printed were well distributed.[60]

Ann Rutledge was the true love of Lincoln's life, Herndon maintained, she was the woman he should have married and Lincoln's life with Mary was a domestic hell. "For the last twenty-three years [the length of the Lincolns' marriage] of his life, Mr. Lincoln had no joy." Herndon expected his ninety-minute lecture would produce some publicity for the book he planned to write but he apparently did not expect the abuse heaped on him. The *Illinois State Journal* found it scandalous and refused to write about it the next day. Isaac Arnold, one of Lincoln's old friends, wrote Herndon had sullied "the greatest & best man our country has produced." A Chicago lawyer wrote him, "You are the last man who ought to attempt to write a life of Abraham Lincoln." The Lincolns' former Springfield pastor, the Rev. James Smith, then American counsel to Dundee, Scotland, wrote a scathing condemnation of Herndon's actions for the *Dundee Advertiser* and sent it to the *Chicago Tribune*.[61]

Robert asked Davis to do something about Herndon. In the meantime, Robert managed to keep the content of Herndon's lecture from his mother for several months. Davis said he advised Herndon against publishing his yarn. "Each and every one of us had had a little romance in his early days," Davis told Robert rather smugly, giving the impression that he was not concerned about Herndon's lecture, especially where Mary was concerned.[62]

Mary, although she had the high road in the situation, could not let Herndon's attack pass unchallenged. On March 4, 1867, she wrote Davis calling his attention to a remark particularly wounding to her. "*He* pointedly says, 'for the last *twenty-three* years, Mr. Lincoln has known no joy,'—it was evidently framed, for the *amiable* latitude he was breathing and was intended to convey a false impression. There is certainly 'method in his madness.' Will you please direct his *wandering* mind to *that* particularly offensive & truthless sentence— he will find, if he has no sensibility, himself, *he will be taught it*—I rely on you for *this*. This is the return for all my husband's kindness to this miserable man!"[63]

"His life is not worth living," Mary told Davis in reference to Herndon two days later. "In the future, he may well say, *his prayers*—Revenge is sweet, especially to womankind but there are some of mankind left, who will wreak it upon him—He is a dirty dog & I [do not] regret the article was sent to the papers—it shows him forth in his proper colors—& I think he will rue the day he did not take your advice."[64]

Mary, by some happenstance, got her wish for Herndon's future. "Herndon gave up the practice of law to focus full-time on researching his Lincoln book," Charles Lachman wrote. "He moved his family to a farm six miles north of Springfield that his father deeded him in 1867. It was 600 acres of fertile bottomland, ideal for corn, but Herndon had the notion of planting fancy fruits. In his first year of managing the farm, which he renamed Fairview, Herndon planted grape vines, apple, peach, plum and pear trees, and exhausted his savings with the purchase of new livestock—a herd of sixty cattle, twelve horses and sixty hogs."[65]

The plagues that afflicted Herndon, Lachman wrote, became very nearly biblical in breadth. The fruit trees died, his potatoes were eaten by beetles, his hogs had cholera, the bank foreclosed on his house in Springfield and Herndon climbed further into the bottle.[66]

Herndon's fiscal downfall may have been satisfying to Mary but she had more pressing problems her own. In a last ditch effort to raise some money, Mary, with the help of Elizabeth Keckly, brought trunks of her clothes and some jewelry, from Chicago to sell in New York in the fall of 1867. Mary contracted with the firm of W.H. Brady & Company to sell her possessions. She let Brady, who turned out to be a shyster, talk her into writing some letters about the contents of the trunks and why she needed the money. The entire scam, known as the Old Clothes Scandal, blew up in her face when the letters were published and caused public condemnation.[67] Any sympathy she accumulated from Herndon's lecture quickly dissipated with the publication of the Brady letters. It was possibly the worst decision Lincoln's widow ever made.

"A notice that you sold articles of value on commission, prompts me to write to you," was the opening of Mary's first letter to Brady backdated in September 1887 in Chicago. "The articles I am sending you to dispose of were gifts of dear friends, which only *urgent necessity* compels me to part with and I am especially anxious that they not be sacrificed."[68]

That letter was bad enough but Mary compounded her problems by claiming, in a second letter, that she had a hand in naming Abram Wakeman as postmaster of New York and later surveyor of the Port of New York. "He will assist me in my painful and humiliating situation, scarcely removed from want. He would scarcely hesitate to return, in a small manner, the many favors my husband and myself always showered upon him. Mr. Wakeman many times excited my sympathies in his urgent appeals for office, as well for himself as others. Therefore he will only be too happy to relieve me by purchasing one of more of the articles you will place before him."[69]

Mary, in her dazed state of grief and the real and immediate concern of how she was going to provide for her family, had just violated the first rule of politics—keep your mouth shut.

The *New York World* pounced on Mary's letter of September 14, saying in an editorial, "Let Mr. Wakeman instantly take the whole lot and send his check for the amount. The sum will be but a drop in the ocean of his reputed wealth."[70] Wakeman, however, did not turn against her.

On September 18 she wrote Brady again saying, "I have this day sent to you my personal property, which I am compelled to part with, which you will find of considerable value. The articles consist of four camels' hair shawls, lace dress and shawls, a parasol cover, a diamond ring, two dress patterns, some furs &c."[71]

In her next letter, September 22, to Brady, Mary appears to attempt to undo some of the damage of her previous correspondence about Wakeman.

> You write me that reporters are after you concerning my goods deposited with you—which, in consideration of my urgent wants, I assure you I am compelled to relinquish—and also that there is a fear that these newsmen will seize upon the painful circumstances of your having these articles placed in your hands to injure the Republican party politically. In the cause of this party, and for universal freedom, my beloved husband's precious life was sacrificed, Not for the world would I do anything to injure the cause, My heart is anxious for its success, notwithstanding the very men for whom my husband did so much unhesitatingly deprive me of all means of support and left me in a pitiless condition. The necessities of life are upon me, urgent and imperative, and I am scarcely removed from want—so different from the lot my loving and devoted husband would have assigned me—and I find myself left to struggle to pursue the only course left me—immediately within the next week to sell these goods, and if not wholly disposed of by Wednesday, October 30th, on that day please sell at auction, after advertising *very largely* that they are my goods.[72]

Three days later, in a letter marked private, Mary told Brady that items she valued at $24,000, could be reduced by $8,000. "If this is not accomplished," she wrote, "I will continue to advertise largely until every article is sold. I must have means to live, at least in a *medium* comfortable state."[73]

The entire episode resulted in only a few of Mary's items selling and tons of negative newspaper publicity, and she had to pay Brady and his partner $824.[74]

The only good aspect of the Old Clothes Scandal was that it apparently forced David Davis into finally settling Lincoln's estate. He did not, however, have the grace to notify Mary of the settlement. She read about it in the newspapers.[75]

While Mary was trying to raise money by selling her clothes, Robert was on vacation in Cheyenne, Wyoming, with some of his friends. When he returned and found out about the Old Clothes Scandal in the newspapers, he demonstrated a temper that would have done any of his earlier Todd ancestors proud. In berating his mother, who was then living with friends, he used an abundance of foul language and threatened to kill himself.[76]

Mary decided it was time to take Tad and set out for Europe. She planned to visit the Reverend Smith in Scotland, find a good school for Tad and settle herself in a warm climate. She postponed her scheduled sailing departure, which coincided with that of Reverdy Johnson, who was just appointed minister to Great Britain. Johnson had planned to look after Mary and Tad during the crossing but, due to health issues, she opted for a later sailing date. Also, she did not want to miss Robert's wedding to Mary Harlan on September 26, 1868, even if she had to return to Washington.[77]

CHAPTER 18

Europe Beckons

Events following Lincoln's assassination two years earlier destroyed some preconceived ideas about Mary. She was honest as she struggled to pay their debts and, in the process, made herself homeless. Some of those debts were Lincoln's. He required clothes, shoes, socks and other necessities of life, which had to be purchased—not everything was given to him. Tad also required clothing and shoes. Department stores, such as A. T. Stewart's, where Mary shopped in New York, carried mercantile goods for the entire family. Consequently, unless all the items on the Stewart bills and others have been itemized, assuming all the charges were made by Mary for herself raises questions.

Those two years again emphasized her frugality as she struggled to manage her financial affairs while David Davis was strangling the fiscal life out of her. Management of business affairs was something she learned from her father. Henry R. Rankin's statement about Mary in that respect bears repeating. "With the children and household affairs and Lincoln's personal wants to be provided for, she was the managing partner who kept the expense accounts within the limits which their moderate income placed at her disposal." Rankin lived in Springfield and knew how frugally she managed on her restricted income.[1]

Not only did Mary manage but she did so under one of the most unrelenting conditions imaginable: seeing her husband killed. Fortunately, there were other influential men, close to Lincoln, who did not share Davis' macabre mirth at Mary's misfortunes, and they helped her. She still had some secrets, which she did not write about.

"It is my comfort to know," Mary wrote Rhoda White with pride, "that I do not owe a dollar in the world—but what little I have, I intend enjoying—and can make myself more comfortable in Europe, than I can for the same amount of means in Chicago, which if possible, surpasses N.Y. in high prices."[2]

Mary had to work her way through more problems before she finally embarked in October 1868 on her first trip to Europe.

While helping Mary with what turned out to be the Old Clothes Scandal, Elizabeth Keckly had been quietly writing a book about the Lincolns and her four years with them in the Executive Mansion. *Behind the Scenes: Thirty Years a Slave and Four Years in the White House*, according to the publisher, Carleton and Company, would appear in the spring of 1868, with startling revelations about the sixteenth president's family. Private exchanges between the Lincolns suddenly became public and the book's appendix included the emotional letters Mary had written her before, during and after the Old Clothes debacle.[3]

Mary once again had carelessly placed her trust in a person she thought was dependable.

She was distraught. It seemed everything she did in attempting to have enough money to support herself and Tad was a failure.

Robert, already terribly angry with his mother, managed to convince the publishers to withdraw the book and Keckly made less than $500, which was certainly more than Mary received from the Old Clothes idea. But, like the fallout Mary suffered from the Old Clothes Scandal, Keckly was, for the most part, lambasted for her literary efforts and requests for her dressmaking skills also disappeared.

It was time to allow the nation to pick on somebody else besides the president's widow. Mary, being who she was, would never admit that she created some of her problems herself. Many of them, however, were perpetrated by her husband's so-called friends who appeared to enjoy her misery and could revel in their political old boys' club once again being sacrosanct. Hence, Europe beckoned for Mary and Tad.

Robert married his long-time love, Mary Eunice Harlan, daughter of Sen. James Harlan, from Iowa, who was Lincoln's last secretary of the interior, on September 24, 1886, in her parents' H Street home. Harlan, disgusted with President Andrew Johnson, resigned, ran for the Iowa Senate seat and won. Ann Harlan, her mother, belonged to the Ladies Relief Association of Baltimore whose mission was to minister to wounded soldiers on the battlefield and see that they were transported to the nearest hospitals. Ann Harlan was said to be one of the first women to reach the wounded after Shiloh. It must have been an interesting wedding since Harlan was among senators who did not publicly support financial assistance for Mary. Attending her son's wedding would be Mary's first trip to Washington since she left the Executive Mansion.[4]

When the newlyweds left the next day on their wedding trip to New York on a private railroad car, Mary accompanied them as far as Baltimore where she got off and stayed at the Barnum Hotel. While eating dinner at the hotel, Mary became disorientated, attempted to stand up and collapsed. She was helped to her room, where she seemed to recover. Tad, wanting to stay in Washington for a few days, remained with the Harlans. Ann Harlan, who did not think very much of Mary, brought Tad to join his mother in Baltimore, and immediately returned to Washington. Tad, a gangly lad of fifteen, wanted to remain in America with his brother and new sister-in-law, who asked him to live with them.[5]

Mary knew he needed more education than her home schooling had provided and he needed discipline. She had been investigating German boarding schools. Without Tad, she would have been truly alone in the world. Mary came to depend more and more on the young boy and, in doing so, appeared to be unaware she was robbing him of his youth.

Mary and Tad sailed from Baltimore on October 1 aboard the *City of Baltimore*, a ship from the Inman Line. One of the faster of the company's liners, *City of Baltimore* set a record one day run of 390 miles with its two horizontal trunk engines and three masts. Had Mary investigated, she would have discovered the liner was built in 1855 in the Glasgow shipyards of Tod and MacGregor. David Tod, a partner in the firm and a distant relative, still spelled his name like her Scot ancestors.[6]

Mary and Tad had first-class tickets which cost $100 in gold, but they did not pay for them. A close family friend did. Joseph Seligman, a German immigrant who became one of the nation's principal financiers, was a close friend of Abraham Lincoln. Early in the war when the nation's credit rating was low, Seligman, at the president's request, arranged to sell United States government bonds in Frankfurt and Amsterdam. The banker, who had met Grant before the war began, advised Lincoln of his leadership skills. Seligman was in Frankfurt when Lincoln was assassinated. When he heard the news, he dissolved in tears and told his family the South had lost its best friend.[7]

While Seligman, like some other associates of Lincoln, assisted Mary with her money problems after the president was killed, he also went above what others had done for her. After Grant succeeded Johnson as president, Seligman appealed to him to take action to provide for presidential widows.[8]

On October 15, the *City of Baltimore* docked at Southampton after a stormy crossing. Mary and Tad continued on and arrived at the German port of Bremen two weeks later. From there, they accompanied their trunks to Frankfurt, where they would share a room at the Hotel d'Angleterre for thirty dollars a week. Mary enrolled Tad in Dr. Johann H. Hohagen's Institute and requested the headmaster to instruct Tad in both English and German.[9]

Mary spent her first few months in Germany finding a physician and banker and sightseeing. "I came to Frankfort [Frankfurt], expecting to remain a week, and now Christmas, is almost upon us. When I was reading *John Rose Bean's* description of a winter & very especially a 'Christmas' in Frankfort, I then scarcely expected to be here, to witness & pass through similar scenes. I was in the famous Alleghenies, last summer, that his account was read. Certainly I expect in no place on the habitable globe, do they make greater preparations for these holy days, than in F. There appears more to tempt on here than elsewhere—the shops are very beautiful and the [visit?]ing Americans [are] said to have increased the prices," Mary wrote Eliza Slataper on December 13, 1868.[10]

Mary had met Eliza Slataper, wife of a prominent engineer from Pittsburgh, when she and Tad were staying at a Cresson Springs, Pennsylvania, resort the previous summer. Tad and young Daniel Slataper had a wonderful time while there.[11] Mary's letter continued:

> We have quite a little colony, at our hotel—which is considered the aristocratic one, in F. All the nobility stop here, counts, dukes & dutchesses abound in the house, and on my table, their cards are frequently laid. Yet in consideration of poor health & deep mourning, I have of course, accepted no dinner invitation & have kept very quiet. Popp, the most charming of *all* dress makers, who received many orders from America, and makes for the royal family of Prussia & all the nobility, has just made me up some heavy mourning silks, richly trimmed with crape. The *heaviest* blk English Crape here, is only in our money $1.50 cts per yard. Think of it! when in *war* times—I once gave, *ten* dollars per yard for the *heaviest!*[12]

Mary appeared to be enjoying herself and talked about how humble the dressmaker was. "He is a very modest man & never speaks of himself. How different *some* of our boastful Americans would be! I like Frankfort exceedingly, the true secret is, I suppose I am enjoying *peace*, which in my deepest, heart rending sorrow, I was not allowed, in my native land! I find it quite expensive here as in America & as I am urged by my physicians to proceed to Italy very soon—at least I expect to start about the 33d of January & remain until 1st April. *That* fearful, sorrowful month will be spent very quietly here on my return."[13]

In one of her more descriptive letters, Mary wrote about other Americans, some of which she knew, in Frankfurt. "My rooms are on the same floor with Consul Murphy & wife, Mrs. [Henry] Mason of N.Y. & Mrs. General Robert Allen & daughter of the U.S. Army. Mrs. M[ason] is the wife of the Organ Mason [Mason and Hamlin Organ Company], a very superior woman, we are much together—yet the attraction is so different—from what I feel for you. Her children have been so long going to school here & she has been in Germany, so much herself, that she has imbibed many of their philosophical ideas, which are often startling to me. She requires that softness of character, without which no woman, can be lovely. Notwithstanding I like her."[14]

While Mary does not elaborate about Murphy in her letter, Charles Lachman wrote in his book, *The Last Lincolns: The Rise and Fall of a Great American Family*, the American Counsel-general Walton Murphy and his wife Ellen, resided on the same floor as Mary, and Murphy took special care of the former first lady. An appointee of the Lincoln administration, the Michigan-raised Murphy was a "rough diamond ... one of the most uncouth mortals that ever lived," according to the memoirs of American diplomat Andrew Dickson White. But Murphy had also been a shrewd and effective promoter of the Union cause during the Civil War and had excellent relationships with Frankfurt's two leading banking families, the Rothschilds and the Seligmans. Murphy was a protégé of William Seward, and in regular dispatches kept the secretary of state informed about the 378 American citizens residing in Frankfurt, including Mary Lincoln and Tad.[15]

At long last Mary appeared to be, as much as she could or as much as she would allow herself, enjoying life. She wrote about visiting a thousand-year-old building housing the portraits of about fifty German emperors. "The chairs on which these men sat, the stone floors, on which they trod, every thing, of course, possesses a great charm for me as I advance in my travels."[16]

Undoubtedly, Mary visited the Städel, a great German museum, in Frankfurt, established in 1815 by Johann F. Städel. However, she missed the simplest of American pleasures, ice water. She talked about wine being the universal drink and yet pondered why she had never seen anybody intoxicated from its consumption.[17]

A passenger on the *City of Baltimore*, the Rev. F. W. Bogen, from Boston and fluent in German, had assisted Mary and Tad in removing their trunks from the liner. Bogen, a former Union chaplain and a good friend of Sen. Charles Sumner, came to the hotel often to check on Mary. "She lives very retiredly in the Hotel d'Angleterre, occupies only one room and sees few friends," Bogen wrote Sumner, "in order not to be exposed to the gaze of the curious," she had room service, which added about four dollars a day to her bill. Bogen agreed with Mary's suspicions that she was charged more by the hotel, merchants and others on the assumption she was rich because she had been married to the great American hero Abraham Lincoln. It was about this time that Sen. Sumner drafted a bill for a pension for her to be presented to Congress in January 1869.[18]

When Mary's physicians suggested she spend the winter in Italy, she was unable to do so because the prices were exorbitant, as she told David Davis in a December 15, 1868, letter. She mentioned that Robert wanted to borrow $30,000 from her.

Sen. Charles Sumner introduced legislation for Mary's congressional pension (Library of Congress Prints and Photographs Division).

Although Davis had incredulously allowed Robert $3,000 from his father's estate to invest and fix up his bachelor quarters over the Opera House in Chicago while Mary was losing her home, she did not appear to hold that against her son when she discovered the judge's duplicity. Supposedly, the amount Davis advanced Robert was to be taken out at final settlement. It was not according to Pratt—Mary, Robert and Tad each received the same amount, $36, 991.54.[19]

She asked Davis to remind Robert that Tad's quarterly tuition, around $96, was due.

> On the subject of Robert, I wish to write you, Please consider all I say as perfectly private. About three weeks since I received a letter from Robert, in which he requested the loan of my 1881 bonds [bonds Lincoln had purchased in 1865, which were then worth around $50,000], to be converted into money—and to be used—in connections with John Forsythe of C [Dr. James Smith's son-in-law] in building 28 houses on the North Side—thereby of course increasing his money & he offered me 10 percent on the money, for four years. R. has been a noble & devoted son to me & I love his sweet little wife very dearly, & their advancement is my first desire—With the thought of this before me—soon after I received the letter, without much reflection, I wrote him that I would consent. But the thought of parting with *those* bonds—which were *so* placed by my dear husband, has made me unhappy—so, on yesterday after consultation with Consul Murphy & a banker, who could be relied on—they, greatly disapproving of my giving them up—I sent R. a telegram, saying that I could not part with them. The telegram cost me 56 *florins*, & of *course* I made it as short as possible. I was compelled to send the Telegram, for fear—the poor fellow, he would receive my letter & make arrangements which might involve him in a difficulty. With my great love for my good son, the necessity for refusing his request, has made me quite ill.[20]

Mary learned a hard lesson—without Lincoln by her side—the field of battle was unevenly tilted toward Davis and his ilk. She was not humbled by that fact; she just learned to live with it.

Mary left the first of February for Nice, France, not Italy. "I find the weather as sunny and balmy as June with us," she wrote Eliza Slataper. "Flowers growing in the gardens, oranges on the trees, my windows open all day, looking out upon the calm, blue Mediterranean. The contrast is inconceivable. I live out in the open air & am gradually finding myself, growing stronger day by day, for I had been very sick in Frankfort." Mary was gradually beginning to make an effort to see friends. En route to Nice, she stopped in Baden for a couple of days to visit a friend she knew in America.[21]

Mary and her friend visited a castle near Baden, which was said to be haunted by the White Lady. That was the Hohenzollern Castle, atop a low mountain range in Baden. The first castle on the site was built in the first decade of the eleventh century, destroyed in 1423, rebuilt after 1454, fell into ruins by the early nineteenth century, and Crown Prince Frederick William of Prussia began to rebuild it in 1819. Mary talked with the guides about the "White Lady," a ghost which allegedly appeared before a member of the family died. In roaming over this immense building, "I said to our two attendants, 'Have you ever seen her'—to which of course, they both replied—'We often do.' As you know, the Germans are very superstitious, and from the King of Prussia, down to his humblest subjects, believe in *her* frequent appearance."[22]

Mary typified herself as humble while she continued writing to Congress about a pension. Sen. Oliver P. Morton, from Indiana, introduced a bill that whenever a commander-in-chief was killed in wartime his widow was entitled to a pension, "upon the same principles and for the like reasons with any other officer who fell in war." The amount was left blank but Sen. Sumner suggested the amount be fixed at $5,000 a year, which was roughly equivalent to the interest on Lincoln's $75,000 salary for his three unexpired years. The Senate voted it down.[23]

Mary made her own official request to the Senate. She must have clinched her jaws as she wrote the undated missive on black-bordered stationary. Lincoln's name was never used until her signature.

> I herewith most respectfully present to the honorable Senate of the United States an application for a pension. I am the widow of a president of the United States whose life was sacrificed to his country's service. This sad calamity has greatly impaired my health and by the advice of my physician I have come over to Germany to try the mineral waters and during the winters to go to Italy. But my financial means do not permit me to take advantage of the advice given me, nor can I live in a style becoming to the widow of the chief magistrate of a great nation, although I live as economically as I can. In consideration of the great service my deeply lamented husband has rendered to the United States, and of the fearful loss I have sustained by his untimely death—his martyrdom, I may say—I respectfully submit to your honorable body this petition, hoping that a yearly pension can be granted me, so that I may have less pecuniary care. I remain, most respectfully, Mrs. A. Lincoln.[24]

The endorsement on the back of the last page indicated it was referred to the Committee on Invalid Persons, which handled pension requests, on January 26, 1869, the same day Sen. Morton read it to an unconcerned Senate.[25]

Mary, back in Frankfurt, wrote Charles Sumner on March 27, 1869, to express her appreciation for all he had done to arrange a pension. "It is a satisfaction for me," she wrote, "whatever the result may be, to remember, that those who most urgently pressed the pension and its justice, even the whole souled men whom my husband, most highly regarded and loved as if they were brothers.[26]

The summer of 1869 was an absolute balm for Mary and Tad, who stopped in Paris and London en route the country of her ancestors. They spent the long summer in Scotland visiting the Rev. James Smith, the consul to Dundee and their Springfield pastor; her cousin, Annie Parker Dickson, who had moved there from Cincinnati; sampled most of the sightseeing treasures the nation had to offer, including those of Robert Burns in particular, and Mary was said to be so enthralled she forgot to feel sorry for herself. Mary and Lincoln were devoted to the poetry of Robert Burns; their sons were taught to recite his verses. Alexander Williamson, Willie and Tad's tutor who was also president of the Washington Scottish-American club, once asked Lincoln to give a toast to Burns. "I cannot frame a toast to Burns," Lincoln replied, "I can say nothing worthy of his generous heart and transcendent genius. Thinking of what he said, I cannot say anything worth saying."[27] The thatched cottage where Robert Burns was born in Alloway had not yet been restored; when the Lincolns were there it was still an ale house. They also visited the grave of "Highland Mary" Campbell, Burns' lover, in the West Highland Churchyard at Greenock.[28]

Mary and Tad saw the castle and small keep on an island in the middle of Loch Leven where Mary, Queen of the Scots, was imprisoned, forced to abdicate and from which she eventually escaped. They walked through the remains of Dryburgh Abby, beside the Tweed River, built in 1150 by Premonstratensian cannons.[29]

Mary was in relatively good physical condition to do all the walking their tour required. Fingal's Cave, on the volcanic Staffa Island, could only be reached by boat, hiking to the opening and walking over a row of fractured columns just above the water line. A considerable amount of walking was required if they visited the Isle of Iona, where King Duncan was buried.[30]

During the four days they spent in Edinburgh, Mary surely visited Greyfriars Church Yard in Old Town, where her ancestors were held prisoners before being shipped to the Colonies to be sold as slaves.[31]

In returning through Brussels, Mary wanted Tad to see where the Battle of Waterloo was fought between Napoleon Bonaparte and the combined forces of the Duke of Wellington and Prussian Gen. Gebhard L. von Bluëcher. Mary was ten days late in returning her son to boarding school.[32] Touring that battlefield must have been a thrilling experience for young Tad, who so enjoyed playing soldier in the Executive Mansion.

Mary's trip to Scotland was expensive and, upon her return to Frankfurt, she moved from the Hotel de Angleterre to the less expensive Hotel de Holland. In her mail, Mary found a note from Sally Orne saying she was in Hamburg with her family on a three-year tour of the continent and was coming to Frankfurt. When she arrived in Frankfurt, she found the Hotel de Angleterre was full and was referred to the Hotel de Holland, where Mary was living. Enraged, Sally Orne wrote Charles Sumner how she found Mary, "I followed the waiter to the *fourth story* and the back part of it too. There is a small cheerless desolate looking room with but one window—two chairs and a wooden table with a solitary candle—I found *the petted indulged wife of my noble* hearted just murdered President Abraham Lincoln."[33]

"It would be hard to say which overcame me the most—the painful meeting or *the place*—My very blood boiled within my veins and I almost *cried out—shame on my countrymen*—Mrs. Lincoln was completely overwhelmed with grief—her sobs and tears wrung my own heart and I thought at the moment if her *tormentors and slanderers* could see her—they surely *might be satisfied*."[34]

No doubt Sally Orne was also blaming herself for not paying enough attention to her old friend. Mary had tried to tell her of the plight she was suffering when she asked for help in selling the dress she wore to the second inaugural. The appeal was inferred but apparently was not forceful enough to get Sally Orne's attention. The full force of Mary's circumstances · in Frankfurt hit her in the face.

"I sat by her side listening to the tales of her sorrow until the night was far spent," she told Sumner. "Through the long night as her tears flowed unceasingly, I would ask myself can this be the once so justly proud wife of Abraham Lincoln ... in a far distant land—*alone and unprotected and impoverished by circumstances best known to herself* that she cannot afford to even keep a *maid to be with her*.... To say she lives retired does not express the manner of her life—she lives *alone*. I never knew what the word *Alone* meant before."[35]

She told Sumner the rumors in Europe that Mary had been an accomplice in Lincoln's assassination were so widespread they had even reached the staff at the Hotel de Holland, who treated her accordingly. "It seems to me Abraham Lincoln might call for vengeance from the ground—and *yet his* loving gentle *big heart*—with all his *sensitiveness*—while breaking over the cruelties practiced upon his wife of his bosom—would in his agony cry out 'Father forgive them.'"[36]

Along with accusations of being a co-conspirator to her husband's murder, rumors were also floating around America as well as in Europe that Mary was insane. Sally Orne addressed that bluntly in her letter to Sumner. "As it has been suggested by some that Mrs. Lincoln is partially deranged, having seen her so closely by day and night for weeks and failed to discover any evidence of aberration of mind in her, and I believe her mind to be as clear now as it was in the days of her greatest prosperity and I do believe it is unusually prolonged grief that has given rise to such a report."[37]

The time spent with Sally Orne gave Mary new hope that Congress would approve her pension request. The visit also improved her spirits; here at last was someone who cared and would to try to help her. Mary's letters to Dr. James Smith, Rhoda White and Eliza Slataper are full of her delightful visits with Sally Orne and her hopes of Congress approving her pension.[38]

Sally Orne certainly had the resources to help Mary. Her brother, Charles O'Neil, who was traveling with her in Europe, was a congressman from Philadelphia. Her husband, James H. Orne, was an exceedingly wealthy carpet manufacturer and was even closer to Grant than he had been to Lincoln. Sally Orne also had entrees to Julia Dent Grant, now the first lady.

Mary was outraged when she discovered that, upon the death of Stanton, a number of prominent Republicans raised $110,000 for his family who needed assistance. Horace Greeley used his *New York Tribune* in another effort to shame the Congress into giving her a pension. Some of her acquaintances, Mary told Sally Orne, must have advanced the idea she would make ill use of any pension they gave her. "If living in garrets—nearly—not far removed from bread & water as my daily food—is proof of extravagance *then* I must be throwing away my money."[39]

Mary had begun to haunt the English Reading Room in Frankfurt in hope of obtaining information about her pension requests. In a British newspaper she found a story relating that the Senate Committee on Pensions had voted to indefinitely table her pension bill. Their reasons: she had a net worth of $58,765, plus the $22,000 she received for the remainder of Lincoln's first year in his second term. Of course, there was no explanation that the $22,000 was invested and later split three ways in the final estate settlement.[40] The most likely source of her supposed net worth was David Davis.

The article insinuated that Mary was living royally and beyond her means and indicated there were other alarming facts about her that probably needed no reference but were generally known.[41]

Mary collapsed on the spot and her doctors sent her to a mineral spa in Marienbad, Bohemia. Before she left Frankfurt, Mary had a conference with Joseph Seligman's brother, George, who urged that "the Committee should hear the truth and not listen to lying reports perhaps from some one who doubtless got punished for disloyalty during the war & now wants to get even."[42]

While at Marienbad, where the mineral baths eventually helped her, Mary wrote a heart-rending, revealing letter to James H. Orne, Sally's husband.

If I could possibly live, otherwise than to be a mortification to myself—I would not make the least request—at the hands of those—who could so ameliorate my sad condition. I am almost helpless. There are days when I cannot walk straight. I am unable to wait upon myself from very frequent illnesses—as in the only *plainest & most obscure* way, I can keep myself—assuredly with my small means I cannot keep a servant. I wrote you, dear Mr. Orne, a hurried but sincere statement of facts, a week since from Egėr, en route here. Then I told you, what my oldest son and myself, have always kept to ourselves—that so soon—as my senses could be regained—I had every Wash. & every other indebtedness—sent to me & out of every dollar—I could command—I paid to the uttermost farthing. In some cases, known by me & my administrator—but in a very few—it was all done by ourselves my son & myself out of my money so that it could be said—that President Lincoln—was not in debt. This is one of the causes, why I am so straightened now—for living as we *were compelled to*, my husband not being a rich man and we had to pay enormous prices for everything—those war times. When I now hear, from cruel wicked reckless assertions—*how rich I am*—often wanting *for a meal*—that I would daily offer a hungry wayfarer—If I could. My broken heart cries aloud and I sigh more than ever to be at rest by my darling husband's side. Under any circumstances, I believe I should have hastened to settle any indebtedness against the estate, but being often told—that the remaining salary of the four years, would be given to the family. All I wished *then* was to die, if it had been Our Heavenly Fathers will—and the great sorrow & oftentimes cruelty—I have endured since, does not soften the aspect of life—or deprive it of its bitterness. Please write me on receipt of this a candid statement and your just views of the situation of affairs.[43]

Mary's proudest accomplishment was Tad. He had grown into a towering young man, much like his father, well-mannered and handsome. After Mary hired an English professor to tutor him, his speech impediment, probably from a cleft palate, improved and he spoke with perfect articulation but with a slight Teutonic accent. With his friends, he learned to skate on frozen Frankfurt lakes, toured the zoo and the Black Forest and accompanied his mother on a trip to Heidelberg. With his mechanical mind, Tad was fascinated with the cycloramas a colossal 360-degree paintings often depicting great historic battles, which encircled the viewer.[44]

Tad was homesick to see his brother and sister-in-law and new niece and wanted to go home. Mary probably wanted the same. Just before the 1870 August congressional recess, Mary's pension bill came up in the Senate. The House had already approved a pension of $3,000 a year.

The insidious language and accusations used to describe a president's wife have never, before or since, been heard as were those used on the Senate floor in discussion of the bill. Sen. Richard Yates, from Illinois, said Mary Lincoln and her family, the Todds, were in sympathy with the rebels all through the Civil War. Yates was just getting wound up. "There are recollections and memories, sad and silent and deep, that I will not recall publicly, which induce me to vote against this bill." Then, he really got nasty saying, "A woman should be true to her husband.... Mr. President, the occasion does not require, and I shall not, so far as I am concerned, go into details. Mr. Lincoln's memory is sweet to me. God almighty bless the name and the fame of Abraham Lincoln."[45]

Even Sen. Lyman Trumbull objected to that scathing description of Lincoln's wife saying there was no need to bring the fitness of Mrs. Lincoln's character into the discussion. One senator brought up the Old Clothes Scandal; another said she did not need the money. Sen. Justin Morrill, of Vermont, objected to the pension on the grounds that Lincoln had not been killed in battle but in Ford's Theatre. Only soldiers' families, he maintained, should receive pensions. He asked, "Did not Mrs. Madison win fame by staying at home?" Dolley Madison remained in America because her friends provided for her when she was penniless after being swindled out of all she owned by her son.[46]

Dolley Madison did not have a David Davis in her life, but Mary Lincoln did.

It was not Sumner nor James Harlan who rose to Mary's defense but Simon Cameron from Pennsylvania, who was Lincoln's first secretary of war. Cameron recalled for the Senate the events of 1861 when the Lincolns arrived in Washington. "The ladies, and even the gentlemen, the gossips of the town, did everything they could to make a bad reputation for Mrs. Lincoln and tried to do so for the president," Cameron said. "They could not destroy him, but they did ... destroy the social position of his wife. I do not want to talk, and I say, let us vote." When the votes were counted it was twenty-eight in favor of granting Mary the $3,000 pension and twenty opposed; twenty-four Senators were absent or did not vote. President Grant signed the bill that very day, July 14, 1870.[47]

James H. Orne telegraphed Mary the good news. In case she had difficulty obtaining funds, Orne had placed a check at her disposal in Frankfurt, which she used until her funds were available.[48]

Mary needed those funds to get out of Frankfurt as the Franco-Prussian War began on July 19, 1870. A month later, Mary wrote Sally Orne that they were leaving Frankfurt and on arriving in London, Tad would contact her banker for her city address. "The sum, that was voted me, will greatly assist me and not a murmuring word shall be heard from me, as to the amount—I feel assured that if a larger sum had been insisted upon, it would have fallen through altogether," Mary told her.[49]

Mary and Tad left Frankfurt in September 1870 and settled in Leamington, England, which was three hours from London and was famous for its salt baths. Tad settled into studies with a new tutor. Perhaps it was because they were back in England, Tad studied diligently seven hours a day, six days a week. Or, he knew if he completed his studies they could return to America sooner and he could see his brother.[50]

Mary and Tad moved to No. 9 Woburn Place, on Russell Street, in London, in the early winter of 1870. "One especial family with whom I have been very intimate for years, has been with me all the time," Mary wrote to Mrs. Paul R. Shipman, wife of a Louisville newspaper editor and a friend of the Speeds. Mary could have been referring to Col. John Evans, former territorial governor of Wyoming who helped establish the Union Pacific Railroad and his family. He was a longtime associate of her late husband. Mary also had other friends in England from her days in the Executive Mansion. Prince Philippe d'Orleans, the Comte de Paris, along with his younger brother Prince Robert, Duc de Chartres, came to the United States in 1861 to serve in the Union army on Gen. McClellan's staff. They were accompanied by their uncle, the Prince of Joinville and his son, the Duc de Penthievre who entered the naval academy. The three elder Frenchmen were often guests of the Lincolns in the Executive Mansion.[51]

The Comte de Paris, an heir to the French throne, and his family were living in York House, in Twickenham, at that time. Mary made mention of the Comte de Paris in a January 1871 letter to her daughter-in-law. "Count de Paris came in about a week since, twelve miles from Truckenham [Twickenham], to see me, having only heard the day before that I was in town. He then wished me to name a day when I would drive with them, and on my table this morning I find a most urgent note to come out to visit them. I will do so, on my return in the spring."[52]

Mary, now with the funds to hire a maid to travel with her, left Tad in the cold, damp London winter and sought the warmer climate of Florence, Italy, for herself. Tad was attending the same school as the Evans' son. In a February letter, again to Mary Harlan, she talked about the sightseeing, especially the Pitti Palace (Palazzo Pitti), with her friend Mrs. Matthew Simpson, who had been in Florence for three weeks. The stark, vast Renascence building was begun by Florentine banker Luca Pitti in the second half of the fifteenth century and finally completed in the nineteenth century. Mary planned to return to England by way of Frankfurt. However, while she was in Florence, Mary visited the studio of sculptor Larkin Mead to see the progress he was making on the statue of Lincoln that was to stand at the foot of the obelisk above his tomb.[53]

On April 29, 1871, Mary and Tad finally set sail for the United States on the Cunard liner *Russia*, a sleek vessel with 235 first class cabins. The *Russia*, built in 1867 in Glasgow, was powered by steam engines with one propeller and three masts and could reach a speed of 12.5 knots (14.38 mph). On board with the Lincolns was Gen. Phillip Sheridan, whom they had seen previously in Frankfurt, and the Earl and Countess of Ellesmere, on their way to Canada. Reuniting with Gen. Sheridan must have been exhilarating for Tad, as he was one of his favorite officers. Tad could talk to him about his father and discuss the battle site he had seen in Europe. In the middle of the Atlantic, the *Russia* encountered such a rough storm passengers were confined to their cabins for three days and their arrival time was extended two days. "We certainly thought we were doomed for destruction," Mary said. "When we did get out on deck we were almost frightened to death, for the waves were actually mountains high and the swell was so tremendous. We were tossed about like a leaf."[54]

Robert was anxiously waiting for them in Chicago and was concerned they were overdue. "I have not thought much as to what I shall advise Tad to do," he confided to David Davis. "He is now past eighteen & entitled to be consulted. I have no fears about him as he is as good a boy as I am told." Unfortunately, Tad was ill with a cold when they reached New York.[55]

A Marine cutter, *Bronx*, was sent out to meet Gen. Sheridan and bring him and his staff to the port, bypassing quarantine restrictions. Gen. Sheridan insisted Mary and Tad join them. They took rooms at the Everett House and remained in New York for five days. Among their guests were Mary's friend Rhoda White, who wanted her to make her home there. John Hay, Lincoln's former secretary and then an editorial writer for the *New York Tribune*, was astounded at the changes in Tad. The lawless, fun-loving youngster who used to tear the residence decorum apart, was gone. In his place was a fine and gracious young man who was cordial, frank and warm-hearted. Hay thought he was greatly improved by his time in Europe.[56]

After Mary agreed to give a reporter from the *New York World* a brief interview, she began to experience a migraine headache. She told the reporter that they were on their way to Chicago to live with her son temporarily. In answer to her returning to Europe, Mary replied, "I cannot tell you. I may, and I may not. I have enjoyed my journey abroad exceedingly and like the European style of living very much, but home seems very pleasant and I was very glad when I landed in America." She excused herself and left Tad to finish the interview.[57]

Tad told the reporter that he did not care for getting into the newspapers. That was emphasized when the reporter asked about his mother remarrying. "That's all nonsense," he replied in a way that was almost reminiscent of his father, "I wish folks wouldn't talk so much about my mother. There's no truth to that report. People say pretty near what they like nowadays." He called the war over his mother's pension an abominable shame. "Such a fuss as she has had is enough to discourage any woman." He answered a few more questions and firmly but politely ended the interview.[58]

When Mary and Tad reached Chicago, they initially stayed with Robert and Mary Harlan and little Mamie. Tad fell in love with his little niece. All went well in the small three bedroom house for a while. But, Mary was Mary and apparently dispensed too much advice to her daughter-in-law. When she wrote Rhoda White, on May 21, Mary said she was going to be looking for lodgings. Tad's cough worsened and, in a few days, Mary was back boarding at Clifton House. Mary Harlan Lincoln visited Tad at least once at Clifton House before receiving a telegram that her mother, in Washington, was gravely ill, and her father was campaigning in Iowa. She left immediately.[59]

By May 22, Tad was confined to his bed; two weeks later he was dangerously ill. The best specialists in Chicago were called to treat him. The young man probably had been tubercular for quite some time. The physicians determined, in addition to that disease, he was suffering from pleurisy. In the nineteenth century there was no cure for either one; all they could do was treat the symptoms. For ten days and nights, Mary—although there were two nurses—sat by his bed. He seemed to rally and was able to eat, but it did not last. Tad's condition worsened and the only way he could sleep was sitting upright in a chair, with a bar across the front to keep him from falling.[60]

David Davis, still Tad's guardian, made a trip to Chicago to see about Tad's condition at Clifton House. "Tadd Lincoln is dangerously ill," he wrote Ward Hill Lamon. "If he recovers, it will almost be a miracle. The disease is dropsy of the chest. He has been compelled to sit upright in a chair for a month. His mother is in great affliction. I saw him and her on Saturday—it made me feel very sad. He seems a warm hearted youth."[61]

The warm-hearted youth, who was so caring of not just his mother but other people experiencing misfortunes, died a painful death on July 15, 1871, at Clifton House. His funeral was held the next day at Robert's home. Mary attended the services and received the guests in the living room. James Harlan left his campaigning in Iowa to attend the services, but his daughter remained in Washington with her mother. The same afternoon, Robert, Davis and other friends, in a special railroad car, accompanied Tad's body to Springfield. The casket was first taken to Elizabeth Edwards' home and then to the First Presbyterian Church. Pallbearers were six friends of Tad from the time he lived in Springfield. All three of Mary's sisters, Elizabeth Edwards, Frances Wallace and Ann Smith, attended the services. His body was placed in the tomb alongside his father and two brothers.[62]

John Hay, in Tad's obituary in the *New York Tribune*, wrote about how the young boy's pranks, so full of life, vigor and enterprise, gave the sad and solemn residence its only comic relief during the Civil War. "The Tad Lincoln of our history ceased to exist a long time ago," Hay wrote. "The modest and cordial young fellow who passed through New York a few weeks ago with his mother will never be known outside his circle of his mourning friends. In his loss the already fearfully bereaved family will suffer a new and deep affliction, and the world, which never did and never will know him, will not withhold a tribute of regret for the child whose gayety and affection cheered more than anything else the worn and weary heart of a great president through the toilsome years of the war."[63]

Robert Lincoln's July 18, 1871, letter to his wife described Tad's last days. Part of that letter was used in Katherine Helm's book. The remaining part, marked "Not published," was rather telling.

> We came back from Springfield this morning all well. I will not attempt to tell you all that has happened in the last few days, for I am a good deal used up. Last Tuesday, Wednesday and Thursday morning Tad appeared a great deal better. He was stronger and looking well and the water was reduced a good deal in his chest. Thursday was very close and oppressive [the heat] and it pulled him back very much. Friday afternoon he seemed to rally again and at eleven P.M. was sleeping nicely with the prospects of having a good night and so I left him with mother and his two nurses and went to the house. I was aroused at half past four and went to the hotel and saw at once that he was failing fast. He was in great distress and laboring for breath and ease but I do not think he was in acute pain. He lingered on so until between half past seven and eight, when he suddenly threw himself forward on his bar and was gone. Poor mother was almost dis-

tracted but Mrs. _____ devoted herself to her and we took her to the house. During the day Mrs. _____, Mrs. Farlin and Mrs. Wm. Brown were with her. The next morning Mrs. Dr. Brown [Elizabeth Grimsely] and your father came.[64]

We had services in the house in the afternoon and at night I went down to Springfield—with a car full of friends. Mother was utterly exhausted and could not go but Mrs. Dr. Brown stayed with her until I got back. I have a nurse with her and she is doing very well—better than I expected. I hope and expect that in a few days I will get her to go down to Springfield to my aunt, Mrs. Edwards, and if so I will think I have done a good deal. Norman and the other boys took everything off my hands and were as good friends as any man ever had. I am very glad the picture of the baby came in Friday for Tad was delighted with it and it was really the last pleasure he had on earth.[65]

In the part of Robert's letter that Helm left out he discussed mourning clothing with his wife.

Now as to practical matters, I want you to do just as you feel is right about your dress. You and I are no better and no worse than other people, and if it were not that we have to be recognized the fact that any slip in the wrong direction on our part is sure to be more commented on in our case than in that of most persons. I would say make no change. As I had to decide the matter for myself here, I have concluded that for the present I will wear black except as to pants. Those I will have of the dark tone but of grey or black and white stripes. I am now wearing a pair I had which you have seen. It does not seem to me necessary that you should wear what is called deep mourning, but for the present avoid any noticeable colors. In a few days I will send you some money for what you want. Dr. Smith advises me to leave town at once, but it is easier said than done.[66]

"Agnes has acted splendidly," Robert told her, "and I have had no trouble running the house. Your father is very well. He went Iowa from S. yesterday afternoon. I would give a great deal to be with you for I want to see you very much. You must not feel at all badly about not being here. My telegraph on Saturday was more curt than I intended, but I hope you did not notice it. It was written when I was confused. Write to me when you can. Affectionately yours, B."

Tad Lincoln's estate "consisted of $1,315.16 in cash and bonds totaling $35,750," Harry E. Pratt wrote. "Mrs. Lincoln was entitled, under law, to two-thirds of the estate, but, at her request, it was divided equally between herself and Robert."[67]

Mary had so many "what ifs" in her life. And, one of them had to be her decision to leave Tad in London while she spent most of the previous winter in southern Italy. More alone than ever before, with all of her "what ifs," Mary had eleven more years before she joined Tad, Willie, Eddy and her beloved husband in their Springfield tomb.

CHAPTER 19

Fire and Brimstone

For the next eleven years being alone was the major component of Mary's life but it was, by no means, an existence without headlines. In the interim, she endured another of Herndon's insulting lectures about her husband, she experienced the great Chicago fire, searched for spas here and in Canada to ease the pain of her aching bones, continued to consult with spiritualists, again lived in Springfield and once more returned to Europe.

In the midst of these sufferings, the worst blow of all came when her surviving son, along with some of Lincoln's supposedly closest friends, subjected her to insanity trial—a trial that appeared to be fixed—in which her attorney failed to tender any kind of defense on her behalf.

Mary, after Tad's funeral, found herself alone in Robert's house on Wabash Avenue in Chicago, with only their boarder. Robert, either exhausted from Tad's illness or his domestic problems, decided he needed a vacation. He told friends he was exhausted and his doctor had prescribed a vacation. He went to the Rocky Mountains for two weeks and stayed a month. Mary Harlan was still in Washington with her mother and remained there as long as Mary was living in their house. Robert mailed his mother a letter informing her of his departure.

In two letters to Eliza Slataper, one written on July 27 and the other on August 13, 1871, Mary begged the woman to come visit her. The content of the letters is similar: her deep grief over Tad, Robert was away, his wife was in Washington and she was terribly lonely. "I have been prostrated by illness & by *grief*," Mary wrote, "that the grave alone can soften. Could you not pass the *15th* with me."[1]

Mary was still at Robert's home on October 4, 1871, when she again wrote Eliza Slataper that she was utterly prostrated and her health had completely given away. "As anxious as I am to see you, I feel that *it is best*. At present if we do not meet. Bleeding wounds would only be opened afresh, in God's Own Time—I MAY grow calmer, yet I very much doubt it. As grievous as other bereavements have been, not one great sorrow, ever approached the agony of *this*. My idolized & devoted son, torn from me, when he had bloomed into such a noble promising youth. I will write you again, in the *meantime*—DO write."[2]

John Hay was visiting Mary and Robert when the great Chicago fire broke out on Sunday, October 8, 1871. "At 653 Wabash Avenue," Charles Lachman wrote, "Robert Lincoln, his mother Mary and their houseguest John Hay watched with mounting panic as the city around them became a raging inferno. The Lincoln house was soon in real danger of going up in flames. They all fled for their lives into the streets of Chicago. What they encountered was sheer terror, and the end of law and order." The wooden structures blazed quickly out of control, taking with them commercial and industrial buildings as well as elegant mansions.[3]

Robert and Hay crossed the Chicago River to help the wife of his mentor and lawyer, Jonathan Young Scammon. When they arrived, Mrs. Scammon was directing the loading of their belongings on wagons. Robert told her removing the furnishings from their mansion would complicate potential insurance claims and her home was not in any immediate danger. She went up to the house's top floor, took a look at the flames consuming the city and continued loading the wagons. Her home was also lost.[4]

When or where Robert and Hay found Mary was not clear. She probably spent that first night among the thousands who lined the shores of Lake Michigan. Not only was Robert's home destroyed by the fire but so was his law office. Some of Lincoln's papers were lost when Robert's home burned but the bulk of them were at Davis' home in Bloomington. More than likely, the letters from Lincoln that Mary treasured were also gone. If Mary was sewing her money and bonds into her petticoats at that time, it was a safer place than the banks. After two days, rain began to fall but 300 people were dead, 100,000 were homeless and $200 million worth of property was destroyed.[5]

Mary left Chicago for St. Charles, forty miles west of Chicago, after the fire. According to local St. Charles historian Jeanne Schultz-Angel, Mary checked into the Howard House Hotel, owned by the famous spiritualist Caroline Howard, as "Mrs. May." Schultz-Angel cited 1936 interviews with eyewitnesses in the *St. Charles Chronicle* who saw her in St. Charles. The articles stated she was accompanied to St. Charles by Robert. Caroline Howard recognized Mary and invited her to séances at her home.[6]

Details of Mary's whereabouts in late 1871 and 1872 are rather limited. She wrote David Davis about Tad's estate on November 9, 1871, but she did not designate a location. On the same date she wrote C. L. Farrington, who requested a Lincoln signature, and headed the letter Chicago.[7]

Mary's generosity of spirit was still evident when, on May 20, 1872, she wrote Mrs. George Eastman, the Chicago postmaster's wife, sending her ten dollars "for the purpose of flowers for 'Decoration Day,'" to strew over the graves of our brave and honored soldiers. I am so much of an invalid at present that I cannot participate in this sacred duty otherwise than by advancing this small mite."[8]

The summer of 1872 Mary spent in Wisconsin and New York. She left Chicago for a number of reasons. Robert and Mary Harlan Lincoln were in Europe for six months, living in another boarding house was not attractive, she revived her interest—if it ever waned—in spiritualism and she wanted to avoid publicity fallout from Ward Hill Lamon's new, unflattering biography of her husband. Lamon's book, based on Herndon's material which he had purchased, was actually written by Chauncey F. Black, a Pennsylvania Democrat who was no admirer of Abraham Lincoln.[9]

Mary, who had been consulting Chicago lawyer James H. Knowlton about some private business, replied to the attorney on August 3, 1872, from Waukesha, Wisconsin, concerning his mention of Lamon's book. "I have not seen it, nor should not allow it, to be brought into my presence. This man, Lamon, thrust himself, upon my *too* good natured husband, through his kindness, had a lucrative office, the proceeds of which he squandered in debauchery." She predicted, "Severe retribution will yet visit this wretch."[10]

Lamon's book, using Herndon's material, was said to be the first to question whether Lincoln's parents were married.[11] That Robert went looking for the page that Dennis Hanks, a cousin, had torn out of the family bible is puzzling. He was a lawyer and surely knew marriages were registered in the county clerk's office. There seemed to be some confusion that people were looking in the Larue County records, which was where Lincoln was born, instead of those in Washington County where Thomas Lincoln and Nancy Hanks were married on June 12, 1806.[12]

For six weeks, local newspapers followed Mary as she took the waters at Waukesha, Wisconsin, spa that summer. While Robert and Mary Harlan were in Europe, Norman Williams, an attorney friend of Bob's, was handling mail for both herself and the younger Lincolns. "I am going up to a *wild* part of the country, North-in Wis," Mary wrote Williams. "I am trying as you will perceive to make the most of *this fearfully* wearisome summer—Gov (Ruben) Fenton & daughter, have just left Waukesha, and I have seen them almost every day. Scarcely a day has passed, without he called, we met in Europe & were together some weeks. The remainder of my stay, I shall miss them very much—They are charmingly agreeable. I live in such a retired manner in a private house, in the outskirts of the town where there are *no other* boarders & have all the advantages of the country Gov F. said on his arrival that he understood that I saw no one—but he was determined to penetrate the solitude." From Waukesha, Mary told Williams she was going to Madison, Wisconsin, and would pick up her mail there from the postmaster.[13]

It was said that Mary's February 22, 1872, trip to Moravia, New York, for a visit with the well-known medium Mary Meehan Andrews helped fan the flames of the spiritualist movement in that area. "After his [Lincoln's] assassination in 1865, it was most likely Millard Fillmore who made Mary Todd Lincoln aware of Miss Andrews," Joyce Hackett Smith-Moore wrote in *The Citizen*. Smith-Moore wrote that, at one time, as many as eight trains belonging to the Southern Central Railroad rolled into Moravia daily. "It was the medium Mary Meehan Andrews whose reputation helped make it happen," she added.[14]

Mary Meehan Andrews appeared to be an early but obscure materialization medium. Her séances were usually held in the home of a farmer named Keeler. Described as a plain, uneducated woman, she held two types of séances, light and dark, beginning in 1871. In the light séances, the medium sat in a cabinet and busts, arms and hands materialized, the lips of phantom faces were seen in motion and, despite the dim light, many departed ones were recognized. In the dark séances, questions were answered by spirit lights, the piano played, participants felt water on their faces and were touched by phantom hands, and spirit voices were heard.[15]

"On her return trip to Auburn from Moravia, she stayed at the National Hotel. It was at this hotel that she visited Dr. [John] Hotaling, a well-known clairvoyant physician who resided there. It was reported in the *Auburn Daily Bulletin* of Feb. 17, 1872 that Mrs. Lincoln told the press that the doctor had given her the best diagnosis of her case ever given."[16]

Mary's friends in the spiritualist community led her to the New York studio of William Mumler, known for photographing a living subject and superimposing a dead relative on the negative to produce the desired printed product. Mumler maintained that his spirit photography opened channels of communications with the dead. In 1872, Mary went to his studio, as Mrs. Tyall, to have her photograph made. Mumler was not fooled and recognized her when she took off her veil. The result was the famous print of Mary sitting in a chair with the shadowy Lincoln standing behind her with his hands on her shoulders.[17]

Little is known of Mary's activities for the remainder of 1872 and early 1873. Somewhere in those years, Mary began using a nurse hired by Robert. Ellen Fitzgerald and her husband

Richard immigrated from Ireland in 1850, and, after his death, she moved to Chicago to be near a brother. One of Elizabeth Fitzgerald's sons was the comedic actor Eddie Foy, who remembered his mother leaving the position twice and being convinced each time by Robert to return.[18]

She spent the summer of 1873 in Canada at St. Catherines an Ontario town famous for its salt and mineral baths. "St. Catherines, situated twelve miles across the border from Niagara Falls, was the terminus of the Underground Railroad," Lachman wrote. "Mary encountered many of the escaped slaves who had remained there after the Civil War to work at the Stephenson House. Invalids, arthritic patients, and women with undiagnosed nervous disorders flocked there to the purported healing powers of the mineral baths. Curiously, Stephenson House also became a favorite of several leaders of the old Confederacy, including Robert E. Lee and Jefferson Davis."[19]

When Mary returned to Chicago, she had a grandson, Abraham Lincoln II, to be called Jack, born on August 13, 1873. Mary moved in with the younger Lincolns and their family in their rebuilt home on Wabash Avenue. Soon the same problems of having two Marys— one young and stubborn and the other hardheaded and set in her ways—presented irresolvable issues. Mary Harlan told Robert if Mary ever lived with them again she would take the children, leave and never return.[20]

On her previous visits to the Lincoln home to see Mamie and Jack, Mary Harlan refused to speak to her mother-in-law. In 1873, Mary Harlan refused her admittance to their home. She did allow the children's nanny to take them to visit their grandmother in her hotel room until one day Mary gave her daughter-in-law a severe reprimand. The nanny reported it to Mary Harlan.[21]

Mary Harlan was, from all indications, a haughty, controlling and domineering individual who had her way regardless. She appeared to be the dominant partner in the marriage. When their son Jack died in 1890, Robert had him buried in the Lincoln Tomb in Springfield, saying that arrangements had been made for him and his wife to also be buried there. Mary Harlan said "she would be damned if she had to be next to her mother-in-law for eternity." After Robert died in 1926 at his Hildene estate, his body remained in a vault at Dellwood Cemetery in Manchester, Vermont, for almost two years. The daughter of a U.S. senator and daughter-in-law of a president, Mary Harlan knew how to use influence and arranged to have her husband re-interred at Arlington National Cemetery, Special Section 31, on March 14, 1928. The next year, she had the remains of their son removed from the Lincoln Tomb and had them reinterred at Arlington, where a site was reserved for her. The three Lincolns' sarcophagi are in a pastoral setting.[22]

There were circuitous references to Mary Harlan being a closet drinker. Lachman, in his volume on the Lincoln family, cited Jean Baker in her biography of Mary Lincoln. "The evidence for Mary Harlan Lincoln's alcoholism is circumstantial, though strong," Baker wrote in her end note. "Her husband never specifically names it, though he does refer obliquely to it in a number of ways. The stories about Mary Lincoln wanting to kidnap her granddaughter, Mamie, were partly the result of the grandmother's desire to get her away from a drunken mother."[23]

The rupture with Robert's family was beyond Mary's ability to repair but she could possibly do something about Herndon's latest attack on her husband. In another Springfield lecture, On December 12, 1873, Herndon assured his audience that Lincoln was an infidel. Three days later, Mary wrote John Todd Stuart, her cousin, that it was with very great sorrow & natural indignation have I read of Mr Herndon, placing words in my mouth—*never once* uttered. I remember the *call* he made on me for a few minutes at the [St. Nicholas] hotel as he mentions, *your* welcome entrance a quarter of an hour afterwards, naturally prevented a further interview with him. Mr Herndon has always been an utter stranger to me, he was not considered a habitué at our house. The office was more, in his line. Very soon after his entrance, I remember well, he branched off to Mr Lincoln's religious beliefs—I told him in positive words, that my husband's heart, was naturally religious—he had often described to me, his noble Mother, reading to him at a very early age from her Bible, the prayers she offered up for him, that he should become a pious boy & man—and then I told Mr Herndon, what an acceptable book, *that* Great Book, was always to him. In our family bereavements, it was *there*, he first turned for comfort—Sabbath mornings he accompanied me to hear dear good old Dr. Smith preach & moreover, I reminded Mr. Herndon that his last words to his dear friends on leaving, for Washington, with an impending Rebellion before the country were words uttered in great anxiety & sadness "Pray for me."[24]

If Herndon intended his words to cut Mary to the core, he exceeded beyond his expectations with his closing words, "*Now let it be written in history and on Mr. Lincoln's tomb he died an unbeliever.*" B. F. Irwin, from Pleasant Plains, Illinois, wrote a reply in the May 16, 1874, *Illinois State Journal* to Herndon's infidel lecture, resourcefully, succulently and successfully refuting his argument point by point. Irwin closed by saying, "When my friend W. H. Herndon dies, if he wishes a monument on a small scale placed over his grave, with this inscription, 'Here lies W. H. Herndon, a man who in life held that the New Testament Scriptures were no more inspired than Homer's songs, Milton's Paradise lost or Shakespeare,' of if he desires add 'Munchausen's Travels,' I will not, for one, object to the inscription."[25]

Mary maintained that Herndon twisted her words, which he did. In another letter to Stuart on January 21, 1874, she wrote that she had no such interview with Herndon in which she uttered the words he attributed to her. However, she gave him an opening to accuse her of being a liar by insisting she meant there was no interview. She closed her letter by saying Dr. David Swing, minister at Chicago's Westminister Presbyterian Church, advised her to rise above such small barking dogs as Herndon and Lamon. Dr. Swing, she wrote, told her "that at a dinner of 15 gentlemen recently, he [Herndon] was denounced at the table by Swett & others as a drunkard, an outrageous story-teller—to use a mild term and as he stole my husband's law books & our own private library, *we* may *safely* call him thief."[26]

A month before Herndon's infidel lecture in December 1873, Dr. Willis Danforth, one of the Chicago physicians who had treated Tad, began prescribing chloral hydrate for Mary. In describing her headaches, Mary told him it felt like someone (he says she said a dead Indian while in a self-induced trance) was pulling bones out of her cheeks and wires out of her eyes. Mary was given to dramatic explanations and had been since a young girl, but that description would come back to haunt her. She said she used to tell Lincoln that her headaches felt like those rails he was supposed to have split.[27]

What strength of chloral hydrate Danforth was prescribing is not known. A nineteenth century scientific publication, *The Encyclopedia Britannica: A Dictionary of Arts, Science and General Literature*, advised that a dose of twenty grains of chloral hydrate was a normal dose for a healthy person. "Taken in large quantities Chloral Hydrate is a powerful soporific; it perceptibly lowers the temperature of the body and diminishes the frequency and force of the heart's action, probably from paralysis of its intrinsic motor-ganglia; whist the rate of respiration is lessened, apparently through the affectations of the medulla oblongata. Excessive doses produce complete insensibility and diminish and at least abolish reflex excitability;

pallor and coldness of the extremities, lividity and muscular relaxation ensures and death may result from cardiac syncope."[28]

On one of his house calls to see Mary, Danforth left her five packets of chloral hydrate in the powdered form. She took all five and the next day asked him for four more packets since she had experienced a miserable night.[29]

Over medication with chloral hydrate produced complete insensibility and could have easily been the cause of what led Robert, Danforth and a trio of Lincoln's so-called friends—Davis, Leonard Swett, and Stuart—to concluded that Mary was insane. Neither the considerable amount of money involved nor the rancor Davis and Swett exhibited toward her can be overlooked as factors in their collective decision. The amount of the dosage Danforth prescribed for Mary and the frequency of its use appeared to be missing from the record.

There was no doubt that she was not feeling well. Mary told Danforth September 6, 1874 that she expected to die soon. A month earlier, she made her will. "Being fully impressed with the idea that my stay on Earth, is growing very short, I think it best to commit my last wishes to writing, knowing full well that my dear son will carry them out." The only haze Mary was in was assuming she could trust her son.

> I wish my remains to be clothed in the white silk dress, which will be found in the lower drawer of the bureau in my room. I desire that my body, shall remain for two days (48 hours), with the *lid* of my coffin being screwed down. On the *3rd* day, after my death, Professor Swing [the Rev. David Swing, minister of the Presbyterian Church] acceding, I wish the coffin taken to the latter's church, he preaching the funeral sermon from the 23rd Psalm. Yea, though I walk through the valley of the shadow of death, I will fear no evil; for thou art with me; they rod and thy staff they comfort me. My coffin I wish to be of *solid* rosewood, but massive silver plate with this inscription. *He, giveth his beloved sheep.* On the *fourth* day of my decease, I wish my remains placed beside my dear husband & Taddies' on one side of me.[30]

Mary, who did not attend the Springfield dedication of the Lincoln Tomb on October 15, 1874, wrote Isaac N. Arnold five days later approving a statement he drafted to newspaper regarding the proposed downtown burial location. "I believe I will ask you, without you *absolutely* consider it necessary *not* to change *the least word*—I hope you will have it appear in the same words *as soon* as possible, in a prominent place in the Tribune and Evening Journal—& [Chicago] Inter Ocean."[31] Arnold wrote:

> It is a great pleasure to state that there is not a word of truth relative to the assertions made, by newspaper reports that unpleasant feelings ever existed between Mrs A. Lincoln and Mrs [Thomas] Mather—On the contrary, Mrs Mather, at least 28 years in advance of Mrs Lincoln in years of age, has always *ever* been an ardent admirer devotedly attached to the later lady, whist Mrs L. has always *ever* been an ardent admirer & continual visitor of Mrs Mather, even when she has herself been in her deepest affliction. It is cruel indeed that such interpretations should be placed on Mrs Lincoln selecting Oak Ridge, as the final resting place of her dearly beloved & lamented husband. Such selection was made, on account of her absolute knowledge—that the beauty & retirement of the spot would have been her husband's choice.[32]

Arnold later joined Davis and Swett in their denigration of Lincoln's widow.

Mary's refusal to accept the downtown Springfield location for Lincoln's burial site was still a sore spot with David Davis, Leonard Swett, Robert, Gov. Richard Oglesby and others. The formal dedication of the tomb in Oak Ridge gave them another chance to pick at the scab of Mary's grief. These were the political wheeler dealers in Illinois politics and they had been put down by a widow, not out of spite, but in simply carrying out her husband's wishes.

Mary, following Danforth's orders, was confined to her hotel for twelve weeks. The estrangement from Robert's family appeared permanent. So, instead of looking at four walls during a cold and dreary Chicago winter, she decided to spend the winter of 1874 in Florida, along with her nurse, Ellen Fitzgerald. They took the train to Jacksonville, boarded a steamer down the St. John's River and arrived at Green Cove Springs, famous for its warm, therapeutic sulfur springs. Some vacationers, such as Henry Flagler and his new bride, Lily Kenan, the Astors and Vanderbilts, were regular visitors at the resort, which boasted four hotels.[33]

Mary was most likely still taking chloral hydrate while she was at Green Cove Springs and she caught a fever, which lasted three weeks, by spending too much time out of the balcony of her room. On February 20, 1975, she wrote her Chicago friend, Myra Bradwell from St. Augustine, talking about the wonderful weather and the fever she was fighting. Wherever Mary traveled, it seemed she met people she knew or knew of and that was the case on the steamer healed for St. Augustine. "I met three or four choice Philadelphia friends, ladies and gentlemen and they insisted on my joining them and instead of a modest journey of five hours to St. A. it proved four days and nights on the boat." She waxed poetically about the St. John's River scenery and said she spent her first three days in St. Augustine in bed.[34]

In mid–March, she decided that Robert was ill, possibly dying. In her preparations to leave the Florida, she sent two telegrams the evening of March 12: one to Robert and the other to his law partner, Edward Isham. The next morning, Mary sent Robert another telegram saying she was starting for Chicago that evening.[35]

When Mary arrived back in Chicago, Robert, who was all right, met her at the train station and they went to the Grand Pacific Hotel, the first of the great hotels to open after the fire. The palazzo hotel, with an elaborate domed inner courtyard, cost $2.5 million to build the 500-rooms with all the accoutrements. Mary previously had a single room there and, from all descriptions, she again chose paying forty-five dollars weekly. They dined in the hotel dining room with its immense frescoed ceiling and red and black marble floors. Mary, not fatigued from her trip, told Robert an attempt had been made on her life in Jacksonville, where somebody gave her coffee laced with poison. Robert, in possession of information unknown to his mother, resurrected the idea that his mother was unbalanced, even insane. He checked into an adjoining room.[36] Mary's son should not have been disturbed about her story of Jacksonville and the coffee since he had a Pinkerton detective on the train watching her as they returned from Florida.

Robert spending that night, and several more, in the hotel while Mary Harlan, pregnant with their third child was at their Wabash Avenue home, exhibited an abundance of concern for Mary which had been missing previously. After all, Robert and John Hay had left her to fend for herself during the Chicago fire while he rushed to help his mentor's wife. Their having dinner together alone was an anomaly.

While Robert was spending the nights at the Grand Pacific on into the month of April, Mary came to his room several times asking him to sleep on the sofa in her room where she feared being alone. He found her one night in her room half-dressed saying that a wandering Jew was waiting downstairs to return the purse that had been stolen. When she attempted to go downstairs, Robert caught her, got on the elevator and attempted to return her to her room. She accused him of trying to murder her.[37]

No accounts of Robert's actions suggested he ever considered that she might be over-medicated or was consuming the wrong combination of medicines. The former president's son set into action a series of events that would forever scar both he and his mother. After all, she was buying lace curtains when she lived in a hotel room.

Robert knew this because of Pinkerton's detectives who were following her in Florida and later in Chicago. When Mary asked hotel employees if they noticed men following her, they replied that they saw no one. Just as he presumed there could be no other reason for Mary's actions than she was mentally deranged, he took the purchase of a large number of fine lace curtains she bought at face value as another sign of her insanity. Mary was lonely and saw very few people in Chicago. That was possibly one reason she shopped for things she did not need—it was a method of social intercourse. She became friends with a young clerk named Beatrice at Charles Gossage and Company and she could afford the purchases. Beatrice, articulate with excellent manners, always had time to talk to her about fine linens and what was going to be on sale or even discuss the weather. Mary knew sales were slow and Beatrice stood in danger of losing her job and, while the nation was in a depression, jobs were hard to find, especially for women. So, she had been buying curtains from her in order to help her keep her job. On May 19, Mary stopped at Matson and Company Jewelers to pick up a watch similar to the one she wore as a surprise gift for Beatrice because she had admired Mary's. Of course, she bought eight pairs of lace curtains, paid for them and had the package delivered at her hotel. It was not the first gift Mary had given Beatrice—the week before it had been perfume—but it would be the last.[38]

For weeks, the Pinkerton detectives had been reporting back to Robert about the places she went and what she bought. Robert, in turn, had been consulting with some of his father's old friends, David Davis, John Todd Stuart and Leonard Swett, about his mother's actions. Swett was among the lawyers who traveled the Eighth Judicial Circuit with his father and had worked for Lincoln's 1860 nomination. Yet, Lincoln never appointed him to a government post as he did with Davis to the Supreme Court. Robert consulted his partner's nephew, Dr. Robert Ismal, who was Robert's private physician, about his mother. Ismal suggested they have a consultation about Mary's symptoms with Dr. Richard J. Patterson, owner of Bellevue Place, a private asylum for women in Batavia, on April 10, 1875.[39]

While Davis and Swett encouraged Robert, Stuart, then mayor of Springfield, appeared to be lukewarm about joining them his proving his cousin insane. In the process of bringing charges against Mary, Davis appeared to have the final word. Robert consulted him often. Swett exchanged letters with him on every aspect of the case. Stuart refused to agree with that Mary should be placed in an institution. Robert hired the Chicago legal firm of Ayer and Kales. They, in turn, hired one of Illinois' best trial lawyers. Ayer decided Swett, a former political associate of Lincoln's, would be an advantage in the field of public perception. Swett began to assemble a medical team regardless of whether or not they had ever seen Mary. He brought in Tad's physicians, Drs. Charles G. Smith and Hosmer A. Johnson; Dr. Nathan S. Davis, who later became editor of *The Journal of the American Medical Association*; Dr. James S. Jewell, founder and editor of the *Chicago Journal of Nervous and Mental Diseases*; Dr. Andrew McFarland, one of the state's leading experts on mental diseases, and Drs. Danforth and Isham, who were the only physicians who had examined Mary.[40]

"Robert was well on his way to mustering perhaps the greatest team of experts on medical jurisprudence of insanity brought together for a trial before the famous trial of [President James] Garfield's assassin [Charles J.] Guiteau," historians Mark E. Neely, Jr., and R. Gerald McMurtry wrote in their book, *The Insanity File: The Case of Mary Todd Lincoln.*[41]

While Robert, Davis and Swett were plotting and planning, Danforth paid Mary a surprise visit on May 8, 1875, at her hotel that would seal her fate. Danforth asked about her Florida trip and Mary described her visit, the scenery and the southern customs. Then she repeated her story about the attempted poisoning at Jacksonville. Danforth decided that, although she was insane, on general subjects she was rational.[42]

After meeting with Danforth and consulting with Robert, Davis and the other attorneys, Swett began his legal strategy. Robert sent a Stuart a telegram asking for a meeting with him but Lincoln's first law partner shied away, saying his wife was ill and he had pressing business in Springfield. Stuart sent Robert a letter agreeing that Mary needed a conservator but he was not sure she needed personal restraint. "There seemed to be plenty of time," Neely and McMurtry wrote, "Mrs. Lincoln 'had been buying expensive lace curtains, perfumery and watches but she paid for very little' ... arrangement having been made with the traders to return the goods at a future date. There was little 'danger of serious loss,' therefore, and Pinkerton agents were watching her movements." Then, Mary threw her antagonists a real scare. The Pinkerton men heard her talking about going to California or Europe. Swett immediately sought Davis' opinion and followed his advice to have his team of doctors to write formal letters attesting to Mary's insanity. For that service, Robert paid each of them fifty dollars, which was charged to Mary. The Grand Pacific Hotel staff's testimonies were assessed, as were those of Pinkerton's men.[43]

Davis was in Indianapolis and was unable to be in Chicago for the trial or preferred not to be there. Regardless, it appeared that Robert, Ayer and Swett were following Davis' instructions. On the morning of May 19, 1875, he sent Swett a letter by a special messenger on the early train.

> Your communication of May 16th in relation to Mrs. Lincoln was received a few moments ago and I hasten to reply. As you are aware, Robert, Mr. Stuart & I have had a protracted consultation on the subject—Your letter has in no wise changed the opinion which I entertained at the time of this consultation—On the contrary, the statement of the eminent physicians named by you 'that Mrs. Lincoln is insane and ought to be confined' has confirmed it—I believe her to be a fit subject for personal restraint and fear the consequences unless action is taken soon— Indeed, my fears are greatly increased by your statement that she now talks of leaving for California or Europe—A separation from Chicago at all in her present condition would be very embarrassing and it seems to me should not be permitted—I trust that you may see your way clear to prevent it—If the physicians affirm in writing what they have verbally stated to you and Mr. Ayer, that Mrs. Lincoln is insane and ought to be confined, you would be justified in taking immediate action. If you and Mr. Ayer as lawyers are satisfied there is evidence enough to warrant you in expecting a favorable verdict from a jury, then proceedings should be commenced at once.[44]

Davis cautioned Swett that his team of six physicians and at least six lawyers could possibly lose the case.

> I am aware that an unfavorable verdict would be disastrous in the extreme, but this must be risked if after maturely considering the subject your fixed opinion is that you ought to succeed— I do not see how Robert can get along at all, unless he has authority to subject his mother to treatment. The appointment of a conservator, without the confinement, will not answer the purpose. It might do with persons of different temperament from Mrs. Lincoln but with her it would not do at all. Like you I have been satisfied for years that her unsoundness of mind affords the proper explanation for all vagaries she has developed.[45]

You and I were devoted friends of her husband and in this crisis it is our duty to give Robert the support which he so much needs. And I doubt not that he will receive this support from his relatives in Springfield. I know that he has the support of Mr. Stuart. I do not see the propriety of waiting until the commission of some act which [would] arrest public attention. It may be that medical attention, in a Retreat for Insane Persons, would operate favorably upon her. This chance should not be lost. After all the whole case turns on the sufficiency of the evidence to procure a favorable verdict. If you are satisfied on this point, believing as I do that Mrs. Lincoln is insane and should be placed under treatment, I see no other course than judicial action. Of course this is painful to all of us and especially so to Robert but like all other painful duties it must be met and discharged. Thoughtful and right-minded men will approve and under the circumstances, it is to be hope newspapers will forbear to criticize. Robert has my deepest sympathy in this terrible ordeal. That he may have the strength given him to bear it, is my earnest prayer. Although I do not wish anything I write to be published yet I wish it distinctly understood that Robert has my support and approval. I sincerely hope that Mr. Stuart will think it advisable to be with Robert during the trial. Be pleased to let me know what is done.[46]

Swett made arrangements with Judge Marion Wallace to interrupt an estate trial for the hearing and suggested the type of jury they would prefer. Wallace told Swett that he wanted no taint of political vindictiveness in a proceeding that would likely result in putting Abraham Lincoln's widow away since he personally had been a political enemy of the late president.[47]

Wallace's jury selection for Mary's insanity hearing was no group of courthouse regulars. The foreman was a banker, Lyman Gage, who would later be secretary of the treasury for Presidents William McKinley and Theodore Roosevelt. Other jurors included Rep. Charles B. Farwell, later an Illinois senator; Thomas Cogswell, a jeweler; J. McGregor Adams, partner in the largest railway supply company in the Midwest; real estate developer Silas Moore; factory owner James A. Mason; grocery-chain owner Henry Durand; leather manufacturer

David Davis, a sitting associate justice of the Supreme Court, was the behind the scenes manipulator in Mary Lincoln's insanity trial. *Right:* Robert Lincoln, Mary's only surviving son, was convinced his mother belonged and should remain in an insane asylum (both photographs, Library of Congress, Prints and Photographs Division).

Isaac Arnold, an Illinois lawyer who claimed friendship with Abraham Lincoln, was Mary Lincoln's attorney at her insanity hearing and offered no defense. After the hearing, and at the instigation of Robert Lincoln's lead attorney, Leonard Swett, Arnold ripped Mary Lincoln's bonds and money from one of her petticoats in what was the equivalent of a nineteenth century body search (Library of Congress, Prints and Photographs Division).

David Davis' thirty-six room mid–Victorian mansion that he built in Bloomington, Illinois (American Historic Buildings Survey, Library of Congress, Prints and Photographs Division).

C. N. Henderson; D. R. Cameron, an unemployed bookkeeper; and Dr. Samuel Blake, who had treated Tad in his last illness.[48] They were a jury of Robert's peers, not Mary's.

Then it was up to Robert sign a petition asking the court to declare his mother insane, send her to a mental institution and name him as her conservator.

If Robert had any idea of the Pandora's box he was opening as he signed his name to the Application to Try the Question of Insanity, County Court of Cook County, no record exists of his hesitancy. The clerk filled out the form that stated: "The petitioner's mother, Mary Lincoln, widow of Abraham Lincoln, deceased, a resident of Cook County is insane, and that it would be for her benefit and for the safety of the community that she should be confined to the Cook County Hospital or the Illinois State Hospital for the Insane." Robert produced the names of the witnesses, who were waiting to be subpoenaed for the form. "That the said Mary Lincoln has property and effects consisting of negotiable securities and other personal property the value which does not exceed the sum of Seventy-five thousand Dollars, and that the said Mary Lincoln is absolutely non compos mentis and incapable of managing her estate, wherefore your petitioner prays that a warrant be issued for a jury of twelve good and lawful men to determine the truth of the allegations in the foregoing petition contained."[49]

The woman in question was neither an average Illinois housewife nor an ordinary widow. She was a historic icon in her own right as the wife, companion and widow of the greatest president since George Washington. Mary Lincoln stood stalwartly beside her husband as he gradually managed to end a war that threatened to rip the nation apart. The lady who greeted, entertained and conversed with heads of state, captains of industry, cabinet members, senators and representatives was also the compassionate woman who constantly visited, wrote letters for, read to and sent fruit and gifts to wounded soldiers. It appeared none of this had any impact on Robert's actions; he seemed to be operating in his own isolated sphere populated by Davis and Swett.

Once the application was signed, a warrant was issued for Mary's arrest. Swett grabbed the warrant and two deputies and headed for the Grand Pacific Hotel, where he gathered Samuel M. Turner, the manager, to go up to Mary's room. On the elevator with them was the delivery boy with her curtains. Mary opened the door to Swett's knock and admitted them. She asked Swett and Turner to wait while she tipped the delivery boy, who put the curtains away and left. She asked Swett and Turner to sit down. Both men declined.[50]

The following exchanges between Mary and the lawyer are based on Swett's own words to Davis in a letter dated May 24, 1875, five days after the trial.

> The writ having been issued, I took two reliable, courageous young officers and went to the [Grand] Pacific hotel. The jury had been summoned for two o'clock and at this time it was about one. I had in the morning tried [Isaac] Arnold to get him to go with me, but he thought it unwise. Ben Ayer went to the Hotel but waited outside. I finally got Sam Turner to enter the room with me, following a bundle boy who was bringing her eight pairs of lace curtains bought that day. As I entered the room, she seemed cheerful and glad to see me—apologized for her undressed appearance and seemed in no way different from what she has always been. I said never mind your hair, Mrs. Lincoln, I have some bad news for you. She seemed startled, as a person ordinarily would be by such an announcement and sat down. About this time, Turner left and I was alone.[51]
>
> "Mrs. Lincoln," said I, "your friends have with great unanimity, have come to the conclusion that the troubles you have been called to pass through have been too much and have produced mental disease."[52]

"You mean to say, I am crazy, then, do you?"[53]

"Yes, said I, I regret to say that is what all your friends think."[54]

"I am much obliged to you," said she, "but I am abundantly able to take care of myself, and I don't need any aid from any such friends. Where is my son, Robert?" said she. "I want him to come here."[55]

I told her she would see him in the court.[56]

"The court," says she, "what court do you mean, who says I am insane?"[57]

"Judge Davis said so," said I, "and your cousin, John T. Stuart; Robert says so and as I do not want to throw the responsibility of this upon others, I say so." I then pulled from my pocket the letters from four of the five physicians names and submitted them to her as opinions establishing her insanity.[58]

"I haven't seen these physicians," said she, "they do not come to see me, they know nothing about me, what does this mean."[59]

I then explained to her that when a person was believed to be insane that an affidavit had to be filed in the county court, whereupon a writ was issued and the sheriff taking the writ ordinarily went and arrested the party and took him or her to court. In this case, I told her that Robert had made the affidavit and the two officers that came along with me having the writ, but I could not submit to having her seised [seized] by the officers and forcibly taken to court and there I had come in lieu of an officer, and requested her to go along with me.[60]

She flatly refused and grew pretty wild. I then explained to her that nothing in her case remained but to go with me or have me turn her over to the officers and let them take her. I told her there were two carriages downstairs—one of them was mine and the other belonged to the officers, and unless she yielded to me, I either had to seize her forcibly myself or turn her over to the officers, who might handcuff her if necessary and certainly would take her to court. How much better, says I, you put on your bonnet and go along with me as you ordinarily would.[61]

The contest on this point lasted from twenty minutes past one until half past two. It was accomplished with no violence or any unladylike expression but with bitterness and sarcasm such as wounded me worse than bullets should.[62]

After the subject became serious she said, "And you are attending to insane people, are you, Mr. Swett, allow me to suggest that you go home and take care of your wife. I have heard some stories on that subject about her—and you, my husband's friend, you would take me and lock me up in an asylum, would you?" And then she threw up her hands, and the tears were streaming down her cheeks, prayed to the Lord and called upon her husband to release her and drive me away.[63]

Finally contemplating going, she said, "See my dress, Mr. Swett, it is all muddy from shopping. I must change me dress and certainly you would not humiliate me and compel me to undress myself in your presence?"[64]

I replied that I regretted that she would throw the necessity upon me, that there was no necessity for a change in her dress, and that whatever might come it might as well be understood that I was not going to leave her, that she must go with me.[65]

"And why won't you leave me alone for a moment," she said.[66]

"Because if I do, Mrs. Lincoln, I am afraid you will jump out of this window." Finally she stepped in a closet at the side of the room some eight or ten feet square and changed her dress and at least she went.[67]

"Will you take my arm, Mrs. Lincoln," I said as we stepped out the door.[68]

"No, thank you," said she, "I can walk yet."[69]

As we got into the elevator for which we had to wait for a moment, she asked me if we had any accidents over at the Palmer House, and then commenced to chat glibly about foreign matters. Thus we reached the carriage. The street not being graded, there was a steep step down and I offered to help her.[70]

"Mr. Swett, I ride with you from compulsion, but I beg you not to touch me."[71]

For a woman, supposedly insane, who had the audacity to keep up with world events, spend her own money for whatever she pleased and who insisted on presenting a pleasing appearance to the public, the worst—the ultimate humiliation for a nineteenth century lady—was yet to come.

"Reaching the court room, as I opened the door she saw the men standing inside and shrank back," Swett continued in his letter to Davis. "I said come right along, Mrs. Lincoln, Robert is in here and I will sit by the side of you. Thus assured, she came in quietly without speaking.[72]

"Giving her a seat, I immediately went to Robert, who hesitated. I told him she had denounced him bitterly for the course he was taking in the proceedings. Said I, 'We must act as though we were her friends. Come sit beside her and do everything as though she was sane.' He came and she received him kindly, and then turning to Mrs. Lincoln I said, 'You are entitled to counsel. Your old friend, Mr. Arnold, is here he was your husband's friend, and maybe you would rather have him and Robert sit by you than any stranger brought in here.' Yes, she said, she would, whereupon in a moment, I had Mr. Arnold by her side. Where upon stepping I then stepped over to Mr. Ayer at the other side and telling him I was too much used up to do anything more, asked him to take care of the case.[73]

"That remark was scarcely made, when Mr. Arnold came over saying that believing Mrs. Lincoln insane, he doubted the propriety of his defending her. That means, said I, 'that you will have put into her head that she can get some mischievous lawyer to make us trouble, go and defend her and do your duty.'"[74]

Arnold did as he was told and failed miserably to provide Mary with proper representation. Mary, hauled into court under threats of handcuffs and arrest, was not allowed any time to prepare a proper defense with an attorney of her own choosing; jury members were installed without her knowledge; her attorney not only refused to cross-examine plaintiff's witnesses, but put on no defense for her.

Hopefully, whenever Arnold looked at Mary, he remembered the set of Shakespeare she recently gave him inscribed, "To Isaac Arnold from your friend Mrs. A. Lincoln." On the other hand, Arnold badly wanted to write the definitive biography of Abraham Lincoln. To accomplish that feat, he needed Robert's permission and access to the late president's papers which Davis had locked in his vault in Bloomington.[75]

"Thereupon immediately the proceedings commenced," Swett continued in his report to Davis.

The trial lasted three hours in which the evidence of insanity was so overwhelming, and so conclusive that we do not put in the whole case, no one entertained the slightest doubt. As an argument at the end, I simply stated to the jury that Mrs. Lincoln in the opinion of her most intimate friends, had been insane ever since the assassination, that the weight of her woes had been too great for her, and as the recent developments were made, yourself, John T. Stuart, and the physicians had been consulted, whereupon the present action had been taken, that I had no doubt it was, through, then that and all Mrs. Lincoln's friends so far as we knew approved the course, and asked them without delay to render their verdict. They stepped aside for a moment and did so.[76]

One item missing from Swett's lengthy missive was Robert's testimony under the expert guidance of Ayers. While Robert was talking about Tad's death, Mary burst into tears and buried her face in her hands. Robert explained his determination to go to court and have his mother declared insane was upsetting but necessary and in her best interests. "She has been of unsound mind since the death of Father; has been irresponsible for the past ten years." Then he recited her behavior after returning from Florida, buying lace curtains when she had no home in which to use them and buying watches for him. While she continued in deep mourning, he said she never wore jewelry yet continued to purchase expensive bracelets and rings.[77]

He was mistaken. Mary did wear mourning jewelry. One such piece of her jewelry is in the Smithsonian—a beautiful lapel watch.[78]

Robert told the jury, as well as the journalists in the courtroom, that his mother could no longer remain unrestrained, as she was eccentric and unmanageable.[79]

When the jury returned their verdict, it read, "We, the undersigned jurors in the case of Mary Lincoln alleged to be insane, having heard the evidence in the case, we are satisfied that the said Mary Lincoln is insane and is a fit person to be sent to a State Hospital for the Insane; that she is a resident of the State of Illinois, and the county of Cook; that her age is fifty-six years; that the disease is of unknown duration; that the cause is unknown; that the disease is not hereditary; that she is not subject to epilepsy; that she does not manifest homicidal or suicidal tendencies, and that she is not a pauper."[80]

Mary may not have been a pauper when the verdict was read but she was soon afterwards.

Robert then came to me and said I must get her bonds away. Believing that to be indispensable, I said to her in the court room, "Mrs. Lincoln you have $56,000 of money or bonds on your person and one of the unpleasant necessities of this case is that you must surrender them." I said that I could get an order of the court or have the sheriff take it forcibly from her, but I hoped she would not impose that necessity on me, and asked if she would not give it proper [to Robert]. No, she said Robert never could have anything that belonged to her. I then said, "here is Mr. Arnold, won't you surrender them to him?" She then told me that she could not because they were upon her underclothing and certainly, said she, would not be indelicate to me in the presence of these people. "Please," said she, "take me to my room it is so hot here." I replied, "Yes, Mrs. Lincoln I would be glad to take you to your room and nothing remains but those bonds. Now if you will promise me after you get there that you will give them to Mr. Arnold, we will go there." She made the promise and we at once started.[81]

Going through the tunnel she said, "Mr. Arnold, I have always been very careful about my money matters, there is no danger that anything will happen to them, and as I am very much fatigued and need rest, suppose you come down tomorrow and we will talk the matter over." He made no comment, neither did I.[82]

As soon as we entered the room at her hotel, as I shut the door, I said, "Mrs. Lincoln you promised as a lady at the court if I would not permit those sheriffs to be rude to you, that you would give your bonds to Mr. Arnold as soon as we came to the room, now I am compelled to extract the performance of that promise. We ought to give you a receipt, said I, and I will go downstairs to get some paper." As soon as I could get the papers, I returned and wrote out the receipt. "Let me read you the receipt," I said, "Mrs. Lincoln, received of Mary Lincoln $50,000."[83]

"Fifty-six thousand dollars," she spoke up immediately.[84]

"I beg your pardon," said I, and wrote out a new receipt. Having read that over to her, I said, "Now Mrs. Lincoln the receipt is all right but we haven't got any bonds." She rose up, the tears streaming from her eyes, and said, and you are not satisfied with locking me up in an insane asylum but now you are going to rob me of all I have on earth. My husband is dead, and my children are dead and these bonds I have saved for my necessities in my old age. Now you are going to rob me of them."[85]

And to her it was such, and although I tried to explain, it had no effect and when she did yield, and although she yielded peacefully, she yielded to force. Stepping to the side of the room, she pulled up her outer skirt and weary and worn out, she called to Mr. Arnold to come and help her to tear out from her pocket that she had made there $56,000 in government bonds. I arranged for her care during the night, and left.[86]

That was Swett's explanation to Davis of what amounted to their nineteenth century strip search of Abraham Lincoln's widow. There was, however, another description of the moment.

"Suddenly she simply wanted nothing more than to have these men out of her room," Samuel A. Schreiner, Jr., wrote. "She turned and went half behind the curtain, pulled up her skirts, tugged at the pocket on her petticoat. She couldn't see for the blur of her tears, couldn't make her shaking fingers behave. She called for Mr. Arnold to help her. She was beyond shame at having her underclothes plundered. Arnold had to get down on his hands and knees. He couldn't open the pockets, containing the bonds, either and she said, 'Rip it away, Rip it away.' She could hear the (petticoat) tearing as he did, could hear his mumble, 'Mrs. Lincoln, I am so sorry, so sorry.'"[87]

That night, although Swett left a woman guard in her room and two men outside her door, Mary was so insane she convinced them to allow her to go down the drug store in the hotel lobby and get something for the pain in her shoulder. The druggist knew she wanted laudanum and asked her to wait before he mixed her a fake prescription. Mary left then and the druggist followed her to two more drug stores warning the pharmacists she might be attempting suicide. He sent a clerk to tell Robert what he suspected. Meanwhile, Mary returned to the hotel drug store and asked for something stronger, an ounce of plain laudanum. He made an excuse that he kept laudanum in the basement and returned with another vial of burnt sugar and water.[88]

The attempt at poison did not work and Robert and Swett thought themselves fortunate. Mary made sure the next day she lulled them into believing that she was accepting her fate, behaved quite politely and went along with their plans.

"While Robert and I remained with her after this and until she departed," Swett told Davis, "she appeared to be cheerful and kind, apologized for many things she said to me the day before, and urged upon me at the train to visit her, which I promised to do. Going over with me to the depot, she took my arm and in every regard was kind and uncomplaining. From the beginning to the end of this ordeal, which was painful beyond parallel, she conducted herself like a lady in every regard. She believed she was sane. She believed that I, who ought to be her friend, was conspiring with Robert and you to lock her up and rob her of her money. Everything she did and said coincided with the condition of unsanity assuring these facts to have been true, excepting there was a conscious weakness in her, and a yielding to me which would not be found in a sane person. In the court room, she never spoke, and from the beginning to the end, her conduct was ladylike and as much above criticism as possible."[89]

Being ladylike, as Swett put it, while being persecuted without a chance to defend herself was Mary's only option. She would continue, seemingly docile, to fight another day when she had marshaled her forces, although she had no funds. Robert immediately took possession of her bonds and cash after the hearing. He just happened to have an inventory of Mary's real and personal property already prepared and dated May 19, 1875, the day of her trial. The inventory was not submitted for court filing until August 10, 1875. It was September 29, 1875, before Judge Wallace approved the inventory; that was eight days after she left Bellevue to live with Elizabeth. Robert labeled the accounting, "Inventory of real and personal estate property of Mrs. Mary Lincoln, of Cook County in the state of Illinois, an insane person." He attested that "the foregoing is a full and perfect inventory of all the real and personal estate, or the proceeds thereof, belonging to the said Mrs. Mary Lincoln that has come to my hands, possessions or knowledge."[90]

The bonds he listed at $58,000 were undoubtedly correct and the cash of $1,029 matches the money Mary had on her person. Robert paid her $125 per month on the Washington Street house. Her pension was paid quarterly on the fourth day of March, June, September and December. Robert devoted an entire section of the inventory to the lace curtains. *"Personal Property.* A lot of lace curtains and curtain material of which the cost price is ascertained to be $549.83."* He knew to the exact cent the value of the curtains and material, but was extremely hazy about the value of the next inventory entry, *"Personal Property of ~~which the value is not satisfied~~.* A tin box containing personal jewelry, and also nine trunks containing wearing apparel and other articles. All stored in the name of the conservator for safe keeping in the Fidelity Safety Depository in Chicago, having been locked and the keys retained by Mrs. Lincoln. Probable value, $5,000."[91]

Mary had some very expensive pieces of jewelry Lincoln had given her. He paid about $530 ($14,200 in 2012 dollars) for the set of pearl jewelry she wore to the first inauguration. There was the diamond encrusted heart pendant Lincoln gave her, among other pieces of jewelry he had given her. If the tin box contained all her jewelry—and it likely did since she did not wear it in mourning—its contents would probably have far exceeded $5,000. Had her second inaugural lace gown, with flounce and shawl, been in any of the trunks that would have been another $2,500 to $3,000 plus all her other fine clothes. Mary's purchases were never inexpensive and, had the contents of those nine trunks been itemized, they could have equaled or exceeded the amount of her bonds. Had that been the case, the amount of Robert's surety bond as conservator would have increased considerably. Henry Eames and Edward Isham, Robert's law partner, signed his bond for $150,000.[92]

Swett made the mistake of falling for Mary's ruse of being nice and ladylike. Robert's weekly visits would look good to the public and repair his relationship with his mother. Both men, in their big victory, dismissed any thoughts of Mary's retaliatory efforts. They forgot about her great intellect, bull-headedness and tenacity, her talent for rallying influential friends to her cause and the careful orchestration with which she executed her plans. Mary, despite the malfeasance which occurred at her trial, moved carefully, did not complain overmuch and did something that was—for her—extremely difficult, exhibited a profound amount of patience.

She had one of the choice rooms—a private bath, an attendant to bring meals to her room and do her laundry—at Bellevue Place, in Batavia, Illinois, for forty-five dollars a week. There were twenty patients and a dozen nurses and assistants. Dr. Richard J. Patterson, the Bellevue owner, accepted only women of wealth who had unacceptable habits at the substantial brick building surrounded with sixteen acres of flower beds, orchards, vegetable gardens, hammocks, lawn chairs and a greenhouse where one thousand roses bloomed. Robert visited Mary on May 26, heard her complaint about her bed and had a new clean mattress delivered. Mary could go into town whenever she wanted but always with a watchful attendant.[93]

Patterson censored Mary's letters and only mailed those on a list approved by Robert. On a carriage ride into Batavia, she sneaked a letter to a postman and the attendant reported her to Patterson. Not to be outdone, Mary included letters to those on her approved list of correspondents to be mailed by them to other people she wanted to reach. Her ruse was discovered; Patterson had a talk with Mary and decided her efforts to reach friends, not on the list he and Robert agreed upon, was more evidence of lunacy. Mary asked to write her sister Elizabeth Edwards, who never believed she was insane at all. After discussing the matter with Robert, Patterson agreed she could correspond with Elizabeth. In her letter to Elizabeth, she enclosed two letters to be sent to prominent attorneys, John F. Farnsworth who lived in St. Charles and had been a strong supporter of Lincoln, and the Chicago couple of Judge James B. Bradwell and his wife Myra, a staunch advocate of women's rights.[94]

Patterson, anticipating good, free publicity for Bellevue Place, allowed *Chicago Post & Mail* reporter Martha Rayne in July 1875 to interview Mary. The former first lady agreed and discovered they had friends in common such as Noah Brooks. Using the reporter, Mary said she wanted all her friends in Chicago to know how much she missed them, particularly Judge Bradwell and his family, with whom she felt a close attachment.[95] Mary successfully sent out her message to the Bradwells that she needed help.

Farnsworth, who had been at Lincoln's bedside when he died, arrived at Bellevue the next day after receiving Mary's letter forwarded by Elizabeth. Mary asked Farnsworth to help her leave Bellevue, which he told Patterson after he spoke with her. Farnsworth told Patterson that Mary had been on the border of insanity for years but he did not believe she required confinement. Patterson tended to dismiss Farnsworth because he was a well-known spiritualist. He was unable to dismiss Mary's other guests, the Bradwells.[96]

James Bradwell, a former Chicago judge, was a member of the Illinois House of Representatives and had been Mary's personal attorney when she returned from Europe. Myra Bradwell, who had already made an unsuccessful visit to Bellevue to see Mary, was the founder and editor of the highly successful *Chicago Legal News*, publisher of the biennial session laws of the Illinois General Assembly and a zealous advocate for women's causes. Myra Bradwell's application to practice law in Illinois had been rejected by the state Supreme Court because she was a woman. She sought a writ of error from the U. S. Supreme Court claiming her Fourteenth Amendment rights had been violated. Of the nine justices, including David Davis, eight concurred with the lower court ruling. In a dicta on the concurrence, Justice Joseph P. Bradley wrote, "The paramount destiny and mission of women are to fulfill noble and benign offices of wife and mother. This is the law of the Creator." The lone dissenter was Salmon P. Chase, another of Lincoln's appointees to the court.[97]

Being previously refused admittance to see her long-time friend failed to stop Myra Bradwell. She wrote an article that was published in the *Chicago Morning Courier* on September 4, 1875. The headlines read, "Mrs. Lincoln, Is the Widow of President Lincoln Being Held a Prisoner? No One Allowed to See Her Except By Order of Her Son."[98]

The "mischievous lawyer" Swett warned Arnold about at Mary's trial had appeared. Myra Bradwell, with her connections and backed by her husband, was Swett, Davis, Arnold and Robert's worst nightmare. All four men knew their questionable legal maneuverings could cause them grave harm if uncovered by the newspapers.

To counteract Myra Bradwell's newspaper article, Robert bragged about the beauty of the Fox River Valley, where Bellevue was located, that his mother did not have to mingle with the other patients that the sanitarium was more like a hotel than an insane asylum and convinced Sally Orne that his mother was not at all aware of her situation. After Robert's next visit, Mary asked to be driven into Batavia to mail a letter to her sister, Elizabeth. Up to her old tricks, she also mailed a note to Judge Bradwell saying, "May I request you to come out here just *so* soon as you receive this note. Please bring your dear wife, Mr. Wm. Sturgess [probably the Chicago banker] and any other friend. Can you not be *here*, tomorrow on the noon train. Also bring Mr. W. F. Storey [editor of the *Chicago Times*] with you. I am sure you will not disappoint me. Drive up to the house. Also telegraph Genl Farnsworth to meet you here." She added that she would pay the expenses of their trip from Chicago.[99]

Left: Judge James Bradwell, Mary's attorney, was not notified of the legal action taken against Mary by Robert Lincoln. *Right:* Myra Bradwell, Chicago women's rights activist and editor/publisher of the *Chicago Legal News* beginning in 1868, was Mary Lincoln's champion and, acting on her behalf, made all the right moves to obtain the president's widow's release from the Batavia, Illinois, insane asylum in September 1876. Myra Bradwell was the "dangerous" person Supreme Court associate justice David Davis warned Robert Lincoln about acting on his mother's behalf (*Album of Genealogy and Biography, Cook County Illinois* [Chicago: Calumet Book and Engraving Company, 1897]).

Patterson had no choice but to admit the Bradwells for a visit with Mary and they did not leave until 7:30 that evening. They told Patterson that Mary should be set free and allowed to live with her sister, Elizabeth, in Springfield. If she remained at Bellevue, James and Myra Bradwell thought she would be driven insane.[100]

Rushing to tell Robert about his mother's visitors, Patterson thought Myra Bradwell was behind Mary's request to go to Springfield to live with the Edwardses. But, Myra had only just begun her campaign to free Mary from Bellevue. She made several visits to Batavia in late July, and in early August she spent the night there with Mary. Patterson was correct in his assumptions that Myra had written Elizabeth Edwards saying that Mary wanted her to come to visit her and that she wanted to return to Springfield with her sister. "She feels her incarceration most terribly and desires to get out from behind the *gates and bars,*" Myra wrote on July 30. "I cannot feel that it is necessary to keep her thus restrained. Perhaps I do not look at the matter rightly, but let this be my excuse—I love her most tenderly and feel sorry to see one heartache added to her already burdened soul." James Bradwell wrote John T. Stuart on the same day and told him that Mary wished to see him. "I believe a visit from you would do her good and I hope you may be able to make it."[101]

Myra took the next step and visited Robert in his Chicago law office. "On the surface, Robert was calm and deliberate," Charles Lachman wrote, "but surely he was seething inside, and about to make the critical mistake of underestimating Myra Bradwell's lawyerly skills. Myra presented Robert with an interesting proposition: would he, as Mary's conservator, permit his mother to live with Lizzie Edwards in Springfield? Robert thought about it and said he would raise no objections, assuming his Aunt Lizzie was agreeable, which he quickly maintained he was certain she would not be. In fact, he said, with a trace of condescension in his voice, he would personally go to Batavia and escort his mother to Springfield if Aunt Lizzie ever agreed to allow his mother to live with her. Then he laid out a condition that he probably assumed could never be met. He said that Dr. Richard Patterson would have to sign a 'certificate of recover' before Mary Lincoln could be released."[102]

Myra Bradwell had already outmaneuvered Robert setting the wheels in motion for Mary to visit Elizabeth.

Elizabeth Edwards answered Myra's letter on August 3, saying she was unable to visit Mary, as she had been bedridden from surgery. "My heart rebelled at the thought of placing her in an asylum; believing that her sad case merely required the care of a protector whose companionship would be pleasant to her. Had I been consulted, I would have remonstrated earnestly against the step being taken." Elizabeth added that she would write Mary at once. "It is my opinion, that she should be indulged in a desire to visit her friends as the surest means of restoring her to health and cheerfulness. Accept my thanks, for your interest in my sister and the suggestions you have made to me."[103]

Patterson was about to suffer the same fate as Robert. Myra spent Friday night, August 6, with Mary at Bellevue. The next day Patterson caught the train to Chicago, where he held office hours once a week, on Saturdays. Myra went into Batavia telling the staff she could return that afternoon. When Myra returned, she was accompanied by Franc B. Wilkie who, she told the staff, was a friend of Mrs. Lincoln. Actually, Mary did know him from the Washington press corps during the war. He was then a reporter for the *Chicago Times*. Wilkie, Myra and Mary spent two hours undisturbed in her room without the customary attendant. When Patterson returned, he was outraged and not at just being duped by Myra. Nonetheless, he sent her an angry letter saying future visits, if there were any, she wished to make to see Mary had to be on some day other than Saturday, when he was away.[104]

Robert decided on August 6, 1875, to write Elizabeth Edwards a letter that would absolutely dissuade her from asking Mary to visit or even live with her. At this stage there was nothing left to do but wash all his dirty linen before his aunt. Myra Bradwell, Robert told his aunt, belonged to a gang of spiritualists who were only interested in Mary's money. If that was not enough, he told her that when Mary came to live with he and Mary Harlan, after Tad's death, she almost destroyed his marriage—Mary Harlan did not return to Chicago for nearly two years—because she and his mother became angry at each other over some trifle. A year earlier, Robert continued, Mary threatened to kidnap little Mamie and run away. "Such a freak would be no more astonishing than a good many I could tell you that you have never heard of. I would be ashamed to put on paper an account of many of her insane acts—and I allowed only so much as was necessary to be establish the case."[105]

He explained why he had not sought assistance from Mary's sisters. It was because, he said, of Mary's estrangement from them. Should Mary come to Elizabeth's, he doubted "she would receive a call from any one of her sisters. Keep this letter & see if I am not correct when the time comes."[106] Robert railed that if his mother was released, she might go off to Europe or someplace. Robert's primary concern seemed to be that his mother's actions might possibly damage his reputation.

Elizabeth Edwards, after receiving Robert's letter warning her of the complications of even having Mary for a visit, backed off the idea. On August 11, Elizabeth apologized for causing him any annoyance by agreeing to Myra Bradwell's plan and declined to accompany him to go see Mary. The next day, Elizabeth again wrote Robert that she was unwilling to assume responsibility for her sister. At the same time, Myra wrote Elizabeth that Mary had not one symptom of insanity. "I am so sorry for the dear woman," she said, "shut up in that place. When they tell me she is not restrained, I want to ask how they should like it themselves."[107]

Assuming he had stopped the Bradwells' efforts to allow Mary to even visit Elizabeth, Robert made sure he and Patterson were pursuing the same goal—keeping the judge and Myra away from Mary. On August 14, Robert wrote Myra that on his recent visit his mother exhibited "a degree of the same appearance which marred her in May and which I had not noticed in my last few visits." Intimating Myra and her husband were the cause of this supposed decline, he continued, "I am compelled to request that you visit her less often and not at all with persons with whom I am not acquainted and especially that you do not aid her in corresponding with persons other than her relatives." The next day, Patterson wrote Judge Bradwell, "I am quite willing to believe that the objects of your visits and the numerous letters of Mrs. Bradwell are well meant, and not designed to promote unrest and discontent. But I have become fully convinced that such is their tendency and result. My opinion is that, for the present at least, those visits be discontinued. Mrs. Lincoln may be written to assigning reasons for not repeating visits. I understand that R. T. Lincoln, conservator of Mrs. Lincoln, will be absent from home about two weeks. I will suggest that, at least until his return, Mrs. Lincoln simply be left alone."[108]

Everything taken care of, or so he thought, Robert took his family for a two week vacation at Rye Beach, New Hampshire.[109]

Myra Bradwell was undeterred by either Robert or Patterson. She took the train to Springfield on August 17 and carefully explained the entire situation to Elizabeth Edwards— Robert's use of spiritualists, kidnapping plots, Mary's supposed regression and the fact that she did not receive a fair trial. Mary's sister changed her mind and wrote Robert that she would be glad to have his mother for a visit and asked that he hire a companion to accompany her. Judge Bradwell replied to Patterson's letter and left no doubt about his actions. "I am satisfied that Mrs. Lincoln does not require to be confined in a house for the insane, and that it would be greatly for her good to be allowed to visit her relatives and friends. She pines for liberty. Some of the best medical men in America say that it is shameful to lock Mrs. Lincoln up behind gates as she has been and I concur with them. I believe that such confinement is injurious to her in the extreme and calculated to drive her insane." The judge asked if Patterson intended to allow Mary to visit her sister. If she was not allowed to make the visit the judge left no doubt about his actions, saying, "I, as her legal advisor and friend, will see if a habeas corpus cannot open the door of Mrs. Lincoln's prison house."[110]

Patterson and Robert's efforts to keep Mary at Bellevue and away from her friends and family were pulverized by articles, arranged by the Bradwells, in the *Chicago Times* and *Chicago Post & Mail*. Franc Wilkie's article appeared in the *Chicago Times* on August 24, under a headline that read, "MRS. LINCOLN. Her Physicians Pronounce Her Entirely Sane." Wilkie wrote that he engaged Mary in conversation covering a wide range of topics, pleasant and painful and found no abnormal manifestations of mind. Mary remembered meeting Wilkie in Washington in 1862, when she spoke of Tad and the assassination with no difficulty.

The reporter said Mary explained that, the previous May, she had been suffering from a fever and a shattered nervous system when she returned from Florida. Wilkie concluded that whatever had happened to her, "she was unquestionably compos mentis and ought not to be deprived of her freedom."[111]

Judge Bradwell's release of his letter to Patterson brought a *Chicago Post & Mail* reporter to his office on August 23, asking for clarifications. "Mrs. Lincoln ought not to be where she is now and never ought to have been placed there," he told the reporter. "It was a gross outrage to imprison her behind grates and bars in a place understood to be for mad people. Why to be shut up and guarded and locked at night, with the feeling that it may last for life, is enough to make any aged and delicate woman crazy. She is no more insane today than you and I are." Bradwell mentioned he and his wife had received several letters from her and he had seen Mary within the past week. When the reporter asked what the late president's wife had to say, the judge replied, "She sighed and plead[ed] for liberty like a woman shut up without a cause. Said she to me, 'Mr. Bradwell, what have I done that I should be kept here in this prison behind these grates, my footsteps followed, and every action watched by day and my bedroom door locked upon the outside at night and the key taken away by my jailor. I am not mad, but soon shall be. I want liberty to be among my friends.'"[112]

When the reporter asked if Mary would be allowed to visit her sister, Bradwell replied that he hoped that would happen. Then, he put the onus on Patterson and Robert. "Dr. Patterson has signed a certificate of her fitness to go; but she had not got it, and I have not, but he told me he had signed it. Mrs. Edwards wrote her that she could come and live with her and it is expected that when Robert Lincoln returns from the East, about the middle of the week, he will go to Batavia and accompany his mother to Springfield." Bradwell elaborated on restrictions imposed on Mary's mail. "You can't tell what motives may bend to keep her there. Human nature is human nature. But if she is not out soon, there will be some startling developments not to be mentioned now. Let her out of danger first."[113]

The Bradwells felt so strongly about their efforts to free Mary that the gauntlet had been publicly thrown down and it was now up to Robert and Patterson to respond. Robert's brilliant legal team of Davis, Swett, Arnold and Ayer, so prominently involved three months earlier, were conspicuous by their absence. Patterson, anticipating unfavorable publicity that could hurt his business at Bellevue, folded first. He told Robert, "Inasmuch as Mrs. Lincoln has had the promise that on certain condition she can go and live with her sister, and as those conditions, so far as I know, have been complied with, I suppose the experiment ought to be made." That Robert made one last effort, when his mother's case had become such a national cause celeb, was puzzling. If, as he had often stated, he wanted to avoid unpleasant publicity and protect his family, the wise action would have been to agree for Mary to leave Bellevue quietly. But, he chose to make one last effort by calling for the opinion of two of the most eminent psychiatric authorities in the nation—Andrew W. McFarland, who operated Oak Lawn Retreat, a private sanitarium in Jacksonville, Illinois, and was president of the Association of Medical Superintendents of American Institutions for the Insane, and A. G. McDill, superintendent of the Wisconsin State Hospital for the Insane. McDill was busy and only McFarland went to see Mary.[114]

After his interview with Mary, McFarland wrote Robert what he wanted to hear.

> It is fully my opinion that all steps taken, growing out of her unhappy mental condition, have been absolutely necessary for her interests, her safety and her hope of restoration. All the measures now in use in her case are no more than her helpless and irresponsible state of mind render

unavoidable, and will bear the fullest inspection on the part of her innumerable sympathizers, the country over. I am pained to add that there are features of her case that give me grave apprehension as to the results unless the utmost quietude is observed. For the few ensuing months, beyond which all reasonable hope of restoration must be abandoned unless success within that period is achieved.[115]

Either sound reason prevailed in Robert Lincoln's head or all the fight had gone out of him at being bested, for the most part, by two women—one of them his mother. He did not use McFarland's letter of September 8.[116]

Mary walked out of Bellevue Place, along with her nurse Anna Kyle, on September 11, 1875, and took the 9:00 train to Chicago, where Robert met them. He had engaged the railroad president's private car, which he saw that Mary paid for, to take them to Springfield and bring him back to Chicago. Not only did Elizabeth and Ninian Edwards welcome Mary to their home but Frances Wallace and Ann Smith were also there to greet and dine with her.[117]

Robert, who appeared to suffer severe attacks of apoplexy whenever mention was made of Mary' clothing purchases, seemed to regard it as utterly useless that she should buy clothes. He decided she could take three trunks with her to Springfield and arranged to store eleven others at Bellevue without knowing whether they contained clothing she needed. Apparently, it never occurred to Robert that the contents of those trunks were the only real possessions Mary had in the world. They held precious memories for her since, for all practical purposes, she had been deprived of a home by Davis and her oldest son.

Mary settled in quite well in Springfield, receiving visitors, returning their calls, seeing some of Lincoln's old friends such as Jesse K. Dubois, having dinner at the Smiths' home, taking tea with Frances Wallace—normal things she had done since 1839.

There was something else she normally handled, the Lincolns' finances, and she was aggrieved her money and bonds were still under Robert's control. On November 5, Elizabeth wrote Robert that his mother was doing exceedingly well. "I have no hesitation in pronouncing her sane and far more reasonable, and gentle, than in her former years—She bears up with quiet patience under the oppressive weight of restraint, which to her proud spirit is very galling—awaiting the time, when the right of person and property, will be restored to her. Surely the evidence of derangement exhibited last Spring must have arisen from physical disorder—she informs me that her health was poor before going to Florida, and during her stay there, and on her return, was often conscious, of the fever—more-over had used Chloral very freely for the purpose of inducing sleep. Those causes, had doubtless much to do with producing the sad result." Elizabeth told Robert she was not monitoring Mary's expenditures. "I will state that she is too much *herself* to allow many suggestions. I quite agree with her that her dust-soiled veil and bonnet & shawl were too shabby for *her* to wear visiting or church going. She stated that she had no fresh substitute in her trunks."[118]

Mary's battle against Robert was only partially won with her release from Bellevue. He still controlled her money and her bonds. Being her conservator, Robert could keep his mother from traveling, such as trips to Florida and perhaps even back to Europe, and expenditures for clothing, for which he saw no necessity. Mary wanted complete control of what rightfully belonged to her and she intended to get it one way or another. Her painful Bellevue incarceration, although she outwitted him, fortified her sense of determination and reinforced his need of domination.

She had not won the release from Bellevue by making any stupid moves. Mary allowed

Elizabeth and Ninian Edwards to push her cause with Robert. In a November 12, 1875, letter to Robert, Elizabeth addressed his problems point by point. She told him that Jacob Bunn, a longtime Lincoln friend and banker, agreed handle her finances at no charge. Mary, more or less, declined to discuss spiritualism. The silver plate mentioned earlier by Robert, Elizabeth said Mary had given to a charitable home. "I perfectly understand you, with regard to her reckless expenditure of money, for the purpose of adding to the contents of her trunks— It has always been a prominent trait in her character to accumulate a large amount of clothing and now that she has the means, it seems to be the only available pleasure. Is it not best that she should be indulged in it, as a matter of expediency?"[119]

As to Robert's concerns about Mary's traveling, Elizabeth had some good advice for him. "Should she again show a roving propensity, I would advise, that she should not be interfered with. If you determine, to become indifferent—to what you cannot prevent— you will insure yourself, a greater degree of response of mind, than you have known for years."[120]

Ninian Edwards, after talking with his brother-in-law, Clark M. Smith, and John Todd Stuart, wrote Robert and suggested that he consider Mary going before former Gov. John M. Palmer, whom Lincoln appointed military governor of Kentucky; current Gov. John L. Beveridge; Shelby M. Cullom, a state representative and Kentucky native; Ozias Hatch and Jesse K. Dubois, long time Lincoln friends and political supporters; or appearing before the Cook County Court to show that she was a fit person to have the care and control of her property.[121]

Things were not working out in Springfield as Robert had hoped—the Edwardses were under the illusion that Mary was cured. So, he called in his principal advisors, Davis and Swett. Robert sent the Edwards' three November letters to Davis. This letter was another example of Robert's fixation about Mary's clothing. "I long ago told her it was not necessary to scrutinize my Mother's expenditures so long as they were not palpably outrageous, so that there was no need of her mentioning the bonnet and shawl purchases. I merely mention it to you to say that one of the last deliveries when before she went to Batavia was four new bonnets all of which were in her trunks at Mrs Edwards & none of which she had even worn. It is an indication to my mind that no radical change has taken place since last spring but only opportunity is wanting to develop the same trouble."[122]

Either Robert or the Pinkerton detectives he hired had pawed through her possessions and searched Mary's trunks before she left the Grand Pacific Hotel to go to Bellevue. Otherwise, how would he have known about her bonnets. More importantly, what difference did it make—she could certainly afford them. Robert was in Chicago and Mary was in Springfield and there was no way he knew exactly what articles of clothing his mother wore unless she was still under surveillance. Complaining to Davis about such a minor issue as Mary's bonnets raised a point of whose sanity was in question.

Still on the subject of Elizabeth, Robert told Davis she was trying to relieve herself of responsibilities. "I cannot help feeling that she is taking a pretty short turn on me to relieve herself at all hazards of the trouble. How great the trouble is I well know, but last summer without speaking to me my aunt sent my mother a letter by the hand of Mrs. Bradwell inviting her to visit her. Of course, I could only acquiesce." He also told Davis that Swett had been to see Judge Wallace and, although the conservator statute required one year to pass before he could entertain an application for relief, "He will order whatever Mr. Swett and I think best." Robert then outlined four options which were rather revealing.[123]

The first option was to remove all restraints on travel and residence. The second was to make payments to her in monthly installments. An annuity payment to her from the principal which would leave no estate at her death was the third option. Most interesting was the fourth option, "To deliver when as being necessary for her comfort all of her personal effects which consist of clothing and jewelry."[124]

The fourth option, which Robert outlined to Davis, clearly indicated that however many trunks Mary had at the Edwardses, not all of her personal possessions were contained therein. That option further reinforced the notion that all of her personal effects had been searched at the Grand Pacific Hotel before or after she went to Bellevue.

Davis replied to Robert, "No one sympathizes with you more or is more willing to share responsibility with you in whatever concerns your mother. The present posture of affairs is not encouraging, but I was not prepared for it. I expected from the first the intermeddling of officious people who do things in ignorance of the real situation. Mrs. Edwards brought the difficulty about when she sent a letter to your mother inviting her to visit her without consulting you in advance of the proposition." Davis went on to say that Elizabeth had no concept of Mary's real condition and "evidently does not believe that Spiritualism has anything to do with it while you and I know differently."[125]

Davis thought Mary's visit to Springfield was an embarrassment and probably damaged the case they wanted to continue to make that she was insane. "Your mother has evidently convinced Mrs Edwards & her other relatives that she is unjustly restrained of her liberty— Persons in her condition can generally restrain their impulses when they have an object in view. And I have no doubt yr mother from the first has acted in a way to convince all who have been brought in contact with her that she ought not to be confined. You cannot now send her back to Batavia and Mrs Edwards must be relieved of the trouble."[126]

Elizabeth Edwards had not asked to be relieved of her responsibility.

Gov. Palmer, as Mary's attorney, wrote Robert asking that the Cook County proceedings be set aside and her conservator discharged. Elizabeth and Ninian Edwards were urging Robert to lift the restriction on Mary. After the first of the year, Mary began pressing for action. She wrote Robert with a specific list of items she wanted returned to her. On January 14, 1876, Ninian Edwards wrote Robert that Mary was very embittered against him and had threatened to hire men to take his life. "Gov. Palmer advises me to inform you of her threats and of her carrying the pistol. He is of the opinion that by consent her bonds may be restored to her. If you think it best to come down you had better not come direct to our house but advise me where to meet you. Except on the subject of her bonds and her purchases she is as rational as I have ever known her." Edwards added that she spent a half of every day with dressmakers and in stores.[127]

Mary had a plan. She wanted travel restrictions lifted so she could attend the Centennial Exposition at Fairmount Park in Philadelphia beginning May 10. She was replenishing her wardrobe for the trip. After that, she planned to go to Europe. Mary had always traveled when she wanted to and where she wanted and chaffed at such severe restrictions. She wrote Robert and asked for the return of six paintings, a clock, two candelabras and more than 115 books, including multi volumes of Shakespeare and Dickens. Elizabeth, experiencing a storage problem, said they had a library of 5,000 volumes, and she asked Robert not to send them. He sent them regardless. In another letter, Mary asked for the return of the many gifts she had sent Mary Harlan since they were married.[128]

Everybody's tempers were wearing thin. Robert was angry at just about his entire clan in Springfield. The Edwardses were caught in the cross fire. Ninian Edwards went to see Davis in Bloomington in late May telling him that they believe she was sane, that she should be discharged and given her bonds and possessions. "Can we oppose it? Ought we to oppose it?" Davis asked Robert in a May 23 letter.

> Can we afford to have a [general trial] which is sure to come? I think she has enlisted Marshal O. Roberts in her behalf who has employed a lawyer in New York to assist Gov. Palmer if the discharge is resisted. Mr E. says she still purchases things, chiefly dresses that she does not need, but he says she always did this. Mr E. does not believe that your mother will squander the principal. He says she intends to spend her income hereafter but to trench on the principal. I have after mature reflection, come to the conclusion that it is better for your happiness to give free consent to the removal of all restraints on person and property and trust to the changes of time.

Davis outlined the steps Robert needed to take.[129]

Even Davis was quaking at the idea of another public confrontation with Mary and an even more formidable legal team working with the Bradwells.

June 15, 1876, arrived and Ninian Edwards presented Mary's petition to Judge Wallace. Swett offered no opposition and the matter went to the jury. While Wallace picked the jury, this one bore no resemblance to the carefully selected panel in May 1875, except that it included a physician.

Robert was surprised that the jury's verdict not only gave May possession of her bonds and money but also legally restored her sanity. He expected the proceedings to require the return of just her bonds and money. Swett knew Illinois law required a finding of sanity in such cases before property could be restored to its rightful owner.[130] Whether he apprised Robert of that part of the statute is not known.

Robert, however, had ready his receipts and disbursements for the thirteen months he controlled Mary's funds as conservator and Judge Wallace approved it that day. Robert had returned the lace curtains from Hollister and Phelps, $363.83, and from Allen and Mackey, $213. Mary paid $729.39 to Patterson for her incarceration at Bellevue, and $234.52, including telegrams, to physicians, most of whom she had never seen, for testifying that she was insane. She also paid $151 for Pinkerton detectives to follow her for three weeks, $77.10 for moving and storing her trunks and $64 to the Grand Pacific Hotel for room and board for a special attendant for three weeks. Robert made sure Mary paid for the issuance of the arrest warrant, $1.00; the carriages they used to transport Mary to and from court and to the railroad station on May 19–20, $8.00; then there was $8.60 for the railroad sleeping car, and 80 cents for a telegram arranging her journey to Batavia. While Mary may have fumed over the above charges, she had no problem with the $4,599.28 Robert sent Ninian W. Edwards from September 12, 1875, to June 7, 1876. Ninian cashed the checks and gave Mary the money.[131]

Not only did Mary regain control of her bonds and money but she had been legally declared sane. Such a legal determination, however, certainly did not obliterate the humiliations she had suffered extending from the Swett and Arnold strip search to forever being viewed, by some, as insane. Her personality was such that she was unable to keep the high ground, to walk away leaving Robert with mud on his face. She wanted her pound of flesh.

Mary wrote Myra Bradwell on June 18 acknowledging her letter of congratulations.

> God is just, *retribution* must follow those who act wickedly in *this* life, sooner or later compensation surely awaits those who suffer unjustly, if not here, in a brighter & happier world. The

most villainous plot, has come to a close, but on Friday morning, when the young man, who perpetrated it came down to S. when I looked into his face, at a slight distance you may be sure, I saw the reluctance, with which he yielded up what he so ignominiously fought for—my poor pittance, as the world goes—so far as wealth is concerned—"a widow's mite," my bonds. Prayers will scarcely avail in his case I think. My heart fails me, when I think of the contrast between himself and my noble glorious husband and my precious sons who have only "gone before" and are anxiously I am sure awaiting the reunion, where no more separation comes—and so I told him he could not approach us in the other world—on account of his heartless conduct to the wife of a man who worshipped me—as well as my blessed sons did. *This* son as my beloved husband always said was so very different from the rest of us. Prided himself on his philosophical nature—not *satisfied* with the fortune I bequeathed him *in one morning* desiring the rest, brought false charges against me. The only trouble about me, in all my sorrows and bereavements has been that my mind has always been too *clear* and remembrances have always been too keen, in the midst of my griefs. As to *Swett*, he has proved himself to be the most unmitigated scoundrel & *hell* will be his portion & *doubtless,* he will have company. Never could such a creature approach my husband, who loved me so devotedly—in the other life—I have, my dear friend a very great favor to ask of yourself, your good husband and the gentleman who called with you at B. the City Editor of the *Times*.[132]

Mary was unable to savor her victory, the wounds were too deep and drove her to seek additional retribution against Robert and his attorneys. She wanted Myra to arrange another interview with Franc Wilkie.[133] Apparently, that did not happen.

The wrath Mary felt toward Robert was not permitted to cool. Four days after the Chicago court hearing in which she finally bested him, she wrote him a scathing letter further diminishing any possibility of reconciliation. She was so devastated at what had happened to her, she was unable to turn loose of the suffering. "Robert T. Lincoln," her June 19 letter began, "do not fail to send me without the *least* delay, *all* my paintings, Moses in the bulrushes included—also the fruit picture which hung in your dining room—my silver set with large silver waiter presented me by New York friends, my silver tetê-à-tetê set, also other articles your wife appropriated & which are *well known* to you, must be sent without a day's delay. Two lawyers and myself, have just been together and their list coincides with my own & will be published in a few days. Trust not to the belief that Mrs. Edwards' tongue, had not been rancorous against you all winter & she has maintained to the very last that you dared not venture into her house & our presence."[134]

Mary's next lines reinforced that, at some point, her jewelry had been seized. Her jewels included the diamond covered heart pendant the president gave her, as well the pearl ensemble he purchased for her from Tiffany's for the first inaugural.[135]

"Send me my laces, my diamonds, my jewelry—My unmade silks, white lace dress—double lace shawl & flounce, lace scarf—2 black lace shawls—one blk lace deep flounce, white lace sets ½ yd in width and eleven yards in length. I am now in constant receipt of letters from my friends denouncing you in the bitterest terms, six letters from prominent, *respectable*, Chicago people such as you do not associate with. No John Forsythe's & such scamps, including Scamman. As to Mr. Harlan—you are not worthy to wipe the dust off his feet. Two prominent clergy men have written me since I saw you—and mention in their letters they think it advisable to offer up prayers for you in church, on account of your wickedness against me and High Heaven. In reference to Chicago you have enemies & I chance to have friends there. Send me all that I have written for, you have tried your game of robbery long enough. On yesterday, I received two telegrams from prominent Eastern lawyers. You have injured yourself, not me, by your wicked conduct. Mrs. A. Lincoln."[136]

Mary's correspondence brought about a threatening letter from Swett to Ninian Edwards. Swett's lawyerly missive, while containing some facts, was filled with half-truths and untruths. "Prior to her recent mental troubles Mrs. Lincoln was exceedingly kind to her children. She had an income larger than she needed herself and since the death of her husband she has been [generously undertaking] presents to them." One of the bigger discrepancies in Swett's letter was contained in this sentence. "While Mrs. Lincoln was in Chicago in 1866 she bought and furnished a house but soon tiring of this mode of life she broke up her house and stored most of her household ornaments, some furniture and a large number of trunks containing a great variety of personal articles."[137] Mary, as has been previously stated, desperately attempted to keep that house as a home for Tad and herself.

Swett claimed Robert collected $5,000 for his mother in 1873, and Mary allowed him to use it to purchase a law library and other items. The attorney, in his recollections of Mary's gifts to her son, failed to mention in April 1874, Mary deeded Robert the Lincoln home in Springfield for $500. The home's assessed value in 1865 was $3,500.[138]

"Now assuming," Swett continued, "that we have done the right thing in our doubtful experiment of giving to her her [whole] in bonds have we not gone far enough in that line? If any misfortune happens to her Robert [will have] to support her and is it not proper that [having] given her seventy thousand dollars to experiment on when we all [agree] that she is not in her right mind, we should keep something for her in case of misfortune. Besides Robert cannot now pay back the money she has given and turn over to Mrs. Lincoln a law library which he needs and which she can have no need for."[139]

Swett's letter certainly indicated that something had been held back. Aside from her bonds, all that Mary had left of any value was her jewelry. Robert already owned their home in Springfield and was paying her on the purchase of her house on Washington Street in Chicago.

Finally, Swett outlined two options in which he carefully omits the word *jewelry* as being options for Mary. "If Mrs. Lincoln wishes specific articles of property such as pictures or ornaments or things of like character which she has once given Robert or his wife and will ask their return recognizing the gifts and not demanding them as a right, we will return them if it can reasonably be done. But we cannot return them upon the theory that they were improperly procured, improperly detained or under denunciation and threats."[140]

Then, Swett outlined his other option, which was rather successful in scaring Ninian Edwards into compliance. For extra emphasis, Swett said he showed David Davis his letter and he concurred.

> We both know that the removal of civil liability from Mrs. Lincoln is an experiment. It has been done to err upon the side of leniency towards her if we should err at all. It has been done with the hope that she would be quiet. If she will it is all right. If she will not but turns on her only son ... to destroy him, knowing that she is insane, I shall as a citizen irrespective of Robert or anyone in discharge of what I know to be my duty to her and her dead husband at the proper time have her confined as an insane person whatever may be the clamor or the consequence. Please state to her kindly and firmly my intentions.[141]

Swett's duty to Abraham Lincoln was reached only by an exceedingly long stretch of his own imagination.

Edwards replied immediately that all Mary wanted returned were some paintings and her case of silverware. Again, no mention of her jewelry. Edwards added that he had reason to now believe the story of Mary having a pistol was untrue. He said that Mary promised, "in the presence of her sister and niece Mrs, Clover, that she will neither bring any suit against Robert nor make any attack on him."[142]

Robert went through his mother's letters dating back to her first European trip, when she sent gifts to his wife and children, and compiled a file of complete letters and portions he had cut out of other correspondence from her. He tied the documents with a pink ribbon, called them the MTL Insanity File and put them away for someone else to find decades later.

CHAPTER 20

All That Remains

Robert clung to his carefully documented Insanity Files—a record of gifts Mary had given he and his wife—stashing them for someone to find years after his death. He seldom mentioned his mother's name. Mary lugged around scores of trunks, containing all her personal possessions, filled with memories of the past. She was unable to reconcile herself to Robert's betrayal. A cavernous abyss existed between them. Both were stubborn, convinced that each was right, and they went their separate ways. In Robert's case, he kept the break with his mother inside himself. Mary had no reservations about freely sharing with friends and family her deep feelings about her only surviving son. Mary was most aggrieved that she could never wash away the stigma of being labeled a lunatic.

She also knew that she could not remain in Springfield. "I cannot endure to meet my former friends, Lizzie," Mary told her sister, "they will never cease to regard me as a lunatic, I feel it in their soothing manner. If I should say the moon is made of green cheese they would heartily and smilingly agree with me. I love you, but I cannot stay." It must have broken Elizabeth's heart to hear her sister's next words, "I would be much less unhappy in the midst of strangers."[1]

Lurking in the back of her mind was always the idea that Robert might again try to drag her back to Bellevue and the dreadful Dr. Patterson and attempt to reclaim her bonds and money. She had good cause.

Undoubtedly, Mary went over Robert's accounting of her funds from the documents he posted with the Cook County Court in June. She must have fumed when she discovered Robert spent $974, of her own money, on medical consultants to send her to the asylum and to keep her there as long as he could. That act raised the question, if he was so determined to place his mother behind grates and locked doors why did he not use his own money? Instead, he spent $271,000 in 2012 dollars in an attempt to make sure his mother never regained her freedom.[2]

Mary made plans for another trip to Europe, did her shopping in Springfield and hired dressmakers. It took some time to assemble all her trunks, which had been in Robert's possession while she was in Belleview. He gathered trunks she had sent to Wisconsin for use during her planned summer vacation of 1875, those from the Grand Pacific Hotel and those from Batavia and, from his report to the court, placed them with the Fidelity Safety Depository, in Chicago, all at her expense.[3]

Mary missed the opening of the Centennial Exhibition in Philadelphia on May 10, 1876, but she included the nation's 100th birthday celebration in her travel plans later that year.

While living with the Edwardses, Mary became quite fond of young Edward Lewis Baker, Jr., who was living with his grandparents since his parents, Edward L. and Julia Edwards Baker, were in South America. The senior Baker had been appointed U.S. counsel to Argentina and they were residing in Buenos Aires. About the age of Tad when he died, and with much the same intellect and sunny disposition, the young man developed an attachment for his great-aunt.[4]

Mary needed an escort and Lewis Edwards wanted to see more of America. Leaving Springfield in September 1876, they traveled by train to Kentucky, where their first stop was Mammoth Cave. Most likely, they took the Louisville and Nashville Railroad, which had a station at the Glasgow Junction. From there a stage line ran to Mammoth Cave, which along with Niagara Falls and Green-Wood Cemetery, was one of the nation's most popular travel destinations.[5]

They likely stayed at the Mammoth Cave Hotel; a rambling structure with long porches in a pastoral setting. Though there is no record of their registration at the hotel, Elizabeth Edwards, in an October 29, 1876, letter to Robert, mentioned Mammoth Cave was their first stop in Kentucky.

"There were dining facilities at the hotel and meals were also taken into the cave for the visitors as the tours could be very long," Terry Langford, curator of the Mammoth Cave Museum said describing the tours of the 1870s. "The guides were available any time to take visitors into the cave. Because it was a cave with only minimal improvements in the trails, it was possible to rent caving costumes to wear, thus saving their clothing from wear, tear and soil."[6]

Mary may have taken her meal in the ballroom area of the cave, where orchestras played when the supper dances were held. It is doubtful that she accompanied Lewis to the "Fairy Grotto," reached by crawling on hands and knees.[7]

From Mammoth Cave, they went to Lexington. Most of the Todds had died or moved away but Lyman Beecher Todd was there. Probably some Parker relatives still lived in town. Elizabeth told Robert they had remained in Lexington only one or two days and that she took Lewis to the scenes of her childhood and went to the cemetery where their parents were buried. Her stepmother, Betsy Humphreys Todd, had died two years earlier and had left funds for her daughters to erect an individual marker for her in the family plot. On one side of the twenty-one foot monument was her name, Elizabeth Humphreys Todd, and on the other side was a tablet reading, "In memory of my beloved sons—All Confederate soldiers—Samuel B. Todd, David H. Todd and Alexander H. Todd."[8]

Mary and Lewis took in Philadelphia and the magnificent Centennial Exposition. Ten years in the planning, the exposition had 50,000 exhibits in buildings spread over 450 acres and was visited by more than 10 million people. Among the popular exhibits were Alexander Graham Bell's new 1876 invention of the telephone and the Corliss engine. The monstrous steam engine furnished the power for running the exposition machinery. When President Grant and Brazilian Emperor Dom Pedro II started the engine on opening day, they were accompanied by a 1,000-voice choir singing Handel's "Hallelujah" chorus, a 150-piece band playing Wagner's "Centennial March" followed by a 100 gun salute.[9]

From Philadelphia, Mary and Lewis went to New York, where she remained for about a week, as Elizabeth described it, "spending much of the time in dining—and I presume as is her unfortunate custom, too much time and money shopping."[10]

Mary did shop in New York but she contacted none of her friends there, unquestionably due to the stigma of having been publicly branded a lunatic at Robert's instigation. She was also publicly restored to sanity but the second announcement failed to either get the press coverage of the first or eliminate the mortification she felt.

Half a century later, Mary Harlan, when presented with Myra Bradwell's granddaughter's manuscript about Mary's confinement to Bellevue, questioned whether Mary ever made the second trip to Europe. That question could have also been a ploy to reduce the price she would ultimately pay for the manuscript so she could destroy it. Mary Harlan had her Washington lawyer, Frederic N. Towers, checked with the State Department to see if her mother-in-law had been issued a passport for the trip. Tower, in a January 1928, letter to Katherine Helm, said he had been informed by the State Department that no passport was issued to Mary between 1876 and 1879. "It is possible, however, that Mrs. Lincoln went to Europe on an extended passport, that is to say a passport which had previously been issued to her and was simply continued to meet the necessity of her later trip. I personally can have no doubt of the fact that she was there, but we are going to make a little further investigation to find out."[11]

Mary Harlan's suspicions about Mary's passport probably accounts for Helm devoting just one paragraph in her book—published in 1928—to her aunt's last sojourn in Europe.[12] The hundreds of letters Mary wrote to family and friends are more than ample documentation that she was indeed in Europe from 1876 to 1880.

Mary Harlan was not the only one in her family that ignored Mary's second trip to Europe. Robert in a 1914 interview with a New York journalist failed to refer to her four-year sojourn. "My father's death had deranged my mother so much that she had become dangerous to herself," Jean Baker quoted him as saying. "She was placed in a private asylum and after a prolonged stay there she went to my aunt's. Her health seemed to improve so much there that my aunt undertook to care for her in her house. This she did until my mother's death in 1881."[13]

It was apparently easier for Robert to aver that his mother was a lunatic in need of confinement at her sister's home. Otherwise, how could one explain that she freely operated on her own and traveled the states with her nephew, as well as journeying to Europe, with no apparent drama? He could not reconcile both views of Mary, so he expeditiously chose to delete any proof against his version of her.

After leaving New York on October 1, 1876, Mary again experienced another stormy Atlantic crossing on the SS *Labrador*. She remained in Le Havre for a while recovering, as she wrote Lewis Baker a cheerful letter on October 17. "Our elegant & kind hearted friend Louis de Berbieu had written several letters to the agents here & they immediately took me in charge, without opening an article of baggage. They were equally as gentlemanly and distingué in appearance as Mr. de Berbieu, the latter I am told, is of royal descent, is a widower, certainly, a very cheerful looking one, with a beautiful young daughter, an only child."[14]

She told Lewis that she planned to take the steamer *Columbia* to Bordeaux the next day. From there she would take a train to Pau, located near the French-Spanish border. Sally Orne had taken a sick daughter to Pau six years earlier and recommended Mary try the resort because of the clear mountain air, constant levels of climate, the mineral baths and medical facilities. Pau not only had an English newspaper but there were 164 British families living there permanently and thirty-nine Americans. Mary rented a furnished room or apartment and began adding her own touches, such as a black and gilt mantle clock.[15] She wrote:

Each day since I have been here about eleven each morning, a carriage with coachman & foot-man in livery, has called for me to drive, accompanied always by the owner. It is pleasant to be *thus* received, although of course, I am aware, it is entirely my own fault, as in *N.Y & Phil*, in keeping myself aloof from dear friends, who love me well. I propose to act in a more *civilized* manner in the future, which conclusion will greatly please your *very dear* Grandma. I fear the small sum of $27 scarcely, returned you, My dear Louis [Lewis] to S. *Words*, are impossible to express *how* dear you are to my heart. Such attention, Such kindness, as you have shown me in the past year I can say no more, I am indeed a broken, bereaved woman, but God in his "Own Time," will restore me to my beloved ones. Please write at once & direct to Pau, France. Present my best love to all your precious home circle—write me everything. I have just received from Galignani's at Paris, Guizot's History of France in 5 large volumes, handsomely bound, the latest history of this beautiful land.[16]

Mary was fifty-eight years old, had experienced and survived traumas that really would have driven a person of lesser fortitude and determination crazy, she was headed for a strange city, and she planned to read a five-volume history of France. As long as she could see, she was a voracious reader.

By December, Mary had settled quite well into the social life of Pau. Her letter of December 1, 1876, to Myra Bradwell was filled with interesting bits about her life in France. "I believe I told you that I already had some friends residing in Pau," she wrote.

They have received me with great affection and I have made some new acquaintances whom I like very much but if I could *only* see you, dear precious friend, this day, not to speak of your dear husband, I will not allow myself to dwell on so pleasant a picture. This place is very beauti-ful to me surrounded by the Pyranees [Pyrenees] whose distant peaks are already covered with snow. I sleep under *four* soft blankets, the air growing a little *cool*, yet, during my six weeks stay I have never heard the least wind. One of the peculiarities I am told of the climate. The *drives* are simply enchanting, two days since I drove out six miles to Gau and returned and the lovely Chateaus built upon the hills all facing the mountains I cannot attempt to describe clearly. I am situated at one of the finest hotels, most accommodatingly landlord, very near the chateau of Henry 4th where I frequently wander through the grand rooms, so filled with historical interest, and beyond a park of miles—with seats under the beautiful old trees.[17]

Close your doors some day, my bright and appreciative friend, take your husband's arm, bring your talented daughter and son with you and rest. I have received some delightful letters from friends, and some distinguished ones who dwell in this land and most of them are natives, who give me so cordial a welcome to their shores. On my table lies a card received today from a gen-tleman and his wife who reside in Pau, an Austrian, Baron de Benneke, who was in Washington when we were. They often visit me and are very accomplished—plain and *so elegant* and conse-quently so unassuming. I fear that I am wearying you with so long a letter.[18]

Mary was at the end of the letter before she made any mention of Robert. "Would that I could see you again but I am allowed tranquility here and am not harassed by a *demon*," she concluded.[19]

Over the next four years, Mary conducted an extensive correspondence—ninety-two letters have been preserved—with Jacob Bunn, in Springfield, who took care of her business affairs. She followed the price of gold, market trends and interest rates in the French and American newspaper she read daily. "I observe, by my Daily Galignani of Paris, which receives constant news, from America, that gold on the 8th of Dec. was 107¼—quite a decline, mak-ing it however, so much better, if it continues, for the number of my francs." She told Bunn that she was saddened to hear of the death of Jesse K. Dubois and asked him to extend her remembrances to his family.[20]

Death was not only taking some of the Lincolns' friends but Elizabeth Edwards lost two of her granddaughters to scarlet fever in early 1877, and that appeared to plunge Mary back into her grief-stricken mode. Annie Edwards, age four, daughter of Albert Edwards, died January 17, 1877, and Florence, age four, daughter of Charles Edwards, died February 21. 1877. Mary wrote Elizabeth a second letter on March 19 expressing her sorrow about Florence's passing, which she read about in the *Illinois State Journal*. "The information saddened me greatly & rendered me quite ill," she wrote. "I have drank so deeply of the cup of sorrow, in my desolate bereavements, that I am always prepared to sympathise, with all those who suffer, but when it comes *so close* to us, & when I remember that precious, happy child, with its loving parents—what can I say? In grief, words are a poor consolation—silence & agonizing tears, are all, that is left to suffer." Mary closed the letter by saying, "My *Gethsemane* is ever with me & God can *alone* lighten the burden, until I am united to my dearly beloved husband, and children. Write as soon as possible."[21]

Writing Myra Bradwell in April 1877, Mary gently chides her for not having written and tells her about the deaths of Elizabeth's granddaughters. Ever the politician, Mary suggests that Myra nudge her husband toward the Supreme Court vacancy which occurred a month earlier when David Davis resigned and was elected to the Senate. "You with your great talents and diplomacy, could so well arrange affairs. Judge B. is far too modest for the age in which he lives, and so much care and work would be spared him by the *change*," she wrote. Between the lines is the vigor with which Mary would have pushed such an appointment. "A wife can do so much for her husband, which you have undoubtedly done," she continued. "It would gratify me so much to have that *vacant* seat assigned him. I believe a few quiet words would secure it. You know how greatly I prize you both and what interest I take in you and yours."[22]

April 1877 was a busy month for Mary, aside from her numerous letters to Jacob Bunn. Delia Dubois, daughter of the late Jesse Dubois, asked her to find her some lace suitable, from all indications, for a graduation dress. "I have searched in vain for lace suitable for your dress, there are only two lace stores here in the winter and, at the close of the season, they return to Paris," Mary wrote her on April 28. "After careful inquiry, I have ascertained that one store closed on the 12th of this month & the other on the 20th—You can scarcely imagine my disappointment, it would have been such a pleasure [for] me to have been able to procure the lace, *especially* for the occasion of which you wrote. You have been such an indefatigable student & I feel well assured, will have a triumphant success at your examination. Your mother has been owing me a letter for a long time, and I hope ere long, will write me. Please present her my best, and also remember me most kindly to Mr Hatch."[23]

Having been exceedingly well educated herself, Mary, whenever the opportunity presented itself, encouraged her young friends to complete their schooling. Earlier in that month, Mary wrote Lewis Baker after she received his letter saying he was not going to attend college. "You will pardon me for expressing also a regret, that you, with your talents, are not attending college. Perhaps, before the close of the *present* year such will be the case. Journalism, will naturally lead to a love for politics, & I think, *that* is anything, *but* desirable in a young man. You always find me expressing myself, very sincerely to you on all subjects."[24]

While writing to Lewis, Mary's thoughts turned to another young man, her son Robert. "How frequently, I wish I could see & converse with you all, once more, the kindness showered upon me in the days, when I was so cruelly persecuted, by a bad son, on whom I had bestowed, the greater part of my all, rankles, *still,* deeply in my heart. It is impossible to forget, the love shown us in our days of sorrow! That wretched young man, but *old* in sin, has a fearful account *yet to render* to his Maker! And, God does not allow sin to go unpunished."[25]

Mary's recollections about Robert, revealed in her letter to Lewis, gave a picture of family life in the Lincoln household during the Springfield years. "In our household, he was always trying to obtain the mastery, on all occasions—never daring, of course, to be insolent to my amiable devoted children or myself, when my beloved husband, was near, it was a great relief to us all, when he was sent East to school, *then* we had a most loving peace—So different from our other sons—he was always persecuting them and my husband so tender and loving—always said he never knew, from whence, such a mean nature came. Talents are not everything. My darling sons, were perfect in that respect & so worshipping to us both. *Distance* or time does not weaken *remembrance*."[26]

Mary's remarks about Robert in her letter above seemingly conflict with statements she made about him to Hannah Shearer in an 1859 letter and to Adeline Judd in an 1860 letter. Mary wrote Hannah Shearer about Robert going away to college, "I am feeling quite lonely, as *Bob* left for College in *Boston*, a few day since, and it almost appears as if the light & mirth, had departed with him, I will not see him for ten months, without I may next spring go to see him." Mary, in her letter the next year to Adeline Judd, wrote, "Our eldest boy, has been absent almost *a year*, a *long year*, & at times I feel *wild* to see him, if I went anywhere in the next few weeks, I should wish to visit him."[27]

In comparing these letters, it is important to note that Lewis Baker was family; Hannah Shearer and Adeline Judd were not. In fact, Adeline Judd, married to Norman Judd, was not a close friend and Mary would have never discussed her intimate feelings with her. Hannah Shearer had lived near the Lincolns in Springfield for a while. Why would Mary open a wound the woman probably already knew about? Also, there is a sixteen or seventeen year gap between the letters and Mary had endured an enormous amount of trauma during those years. Robert had not yet railroaded his mother into the lunatic asylum and had that occurred when those letters were written, the tone would have been most different.

Mary, during the winter of 1877–1878, spent some time in Sorrento, Italy. She wrote to Myra Bradwell on April 22:

> A few weeks since, I came around by sea, from Marseille to Naples, and as it was my second visit to the latter place within the last few years. I remained there only a week, but will return there in a few days. It is my season of sadness [month of Lincoln's assassination] and Naples with its noise was unendurable. With guide book in my hands, some years since I visited all places that were considered to be of interest, and it is well for me that I did not do so, for I could not interest myself *now* as I did *then*, in visiting each place. My heart was then filled with great sorrow, but since that time the crushing hand of bereavement has been laid so heavily upon me, that it is only by strong effort of will that I revisit places. I went to the Herculaneum, before I left Naples also to the Castle of St. Elmo.[28]
>
> Stopped at the Hotel de Rupie which commands the finest view of Vesuvius and the Bay of Naples but nothing equals, I think, the charming scenery of Sorrento. Even Mrs. Stowe's imaginative pen has scarcely done it justice. In front of my hotel in full view lies a grand chain of mountains, Vesuvius, rising above them all. The bay in full view, and orange and lemon grove within these grounds, trees bowed down with their fruit, of so much larger size and better flavor than we have with us. The villa of Aristides was the sole object of interest to me at Herculaneum.[29]

Mary encouraged Myra and her family to visit Europe. "My beloved husband and myself for hours would sit down and anticipate the pleasant time we would have in *quietly* visiting places and in *halting* at such spots as this, when his difficult labors were ended. God works in such a mysterious way and we are left to bow to His will. But to some of us, *resignation* will never come. But perhaps for the tears *shed* here, compensation will succeed the grief for the *present time*."[30]

For about the third time, Mary asked Myra about Ellen Johnson. "She was a faithful friend to me and I hope she is doing well. I wrote her a year since and have received no reply. I miss her good washing. I assure you when you see her remember me to her. Tell her I have a whole trunk of clothes for her, she will understand."[31] Ellen Johnson was Mary's laundress in Chicago.

When Mary returned to Pau from the spas at Vichy the last of June, she had a letter from Myra saying she was sailing to England on the June 12, 1878. On July 4, she wrote Myra that the Vichy waters had done her no good and she had been in bed for two days with boils under her left arm.[32]

Mary, from all indications, did quite a bit of traveling in 1879, being acutely aware of her mounting health problems. She described one trip in a letter to Lewis Baker.

> I passed a week on the seashore at St Jean de Luz, on the border of Spain, the *Spanish* mountains, overhanging the old town—it is four miles from Biarritz, & a much more quiet place, notwithstanding all along the seashore, crowds have now congregated. I stopped at Biarritz for three days, where the Ex Empress Eugenie has a fine Chateau—which she will never see again, it is supposed. To the deeply bereaved, grand mansion & broad lands, enter but little into the thoughts—and yet whilst we have life, there is a positive necessity for the means of subsistence. I think I will visit Biarritz early in October & then I will go through the Chateau. It is only open on Mondays. Some time or other, I will send your grandmother, views of the Chateau, here at Pau, the different sides. Tomorrow I am going to the mountains for the month of August, from one point to another—yet in some places, we have to return to Pau to take the railroad.

Mary added in a post script, "The Hotel where I stopped at St. Jean de Luz was so near the sea, my window opening out upon it that oftentimes I felt myself quite sea sick. A *further distance* would have been more agreeable.[33]

She commended Lewis for taking a summer vacation from his job at the *Illinois State Journal* and exploring the upper Mississippi.

> It is always pleasant to anticipate in *advance*. Therefore, permit me to suggest that *next* summer, you visit the White Mountains, returning home by way of Lake George, so unrivaled in scenery, I wish you to pass *your fourth* of July at the *Tip Top House* on the White Mountain—(Do I give it the right name?). I am sure you will not think it amiss, if I offer for your acceptance, at the time stated, sufficient means for four weeks of enjoyment, the month of July. Starting the 26th of June, you will easily reach the White Mountains by our patriotic fourth. If you write me on receipt of this letter, accepting my proposition for this *especial* journey, it will all be made right. Mr. Phillips (the newspaper editor) will be well pleased to acquiesce. The rent of June 1st, will be handed you on starting & Mr Bunn will forward my July rent to Boston to you, which is paid the first of *each* month. This is writing in a business like manner, but in this world of reality the *practical* is always the best. Of course it is for the present, entirely, entre nous, your Grandfather and Grandmother included.[34]

Mary lingered too long in the mountains in the summer of 1879 and returned to Pau with a severe cold. "I am enveloped in flannels from head to foot," she wrote Lewis Baker in October. "My throat is almost closed at times, continued pain & soreness in the chest—& am coughing most of the time. I am well paid for my love of mountain scenery, & detestation of town in summer. Rather a poor prospect for me, for the coming winter." Mary said she had lost weight and weighed the same, about 100 pounds, as when the Lincolns went to Washington in 1861. She was delighted that Lewis had accepted her offer to pay for his 1880 summer vacation.[35]

> Without a doubt, I must have been considered *quite* ill—as numerous cards are daily handed me and notes of enquiry, flowers, &&. I lead a life of such great quiet here that the *pleasant* thought occurs to me *sometimes* that I am not supposed to be in *this* latitude. How much I long to see you all—to have a taste of your dear Grandma's good food—*waffles, batter cakes,* egg corn break—are all unknown here—as to biscuits, light rolls && they have never dreamed of—*not* to speak of *buckwheat* cakes. It needs no assurance of mine, to convince you, that a long period of absence from America, is not agreeable—but to an oppressed, broken heart woman it is simply an *exile.* You are spared a very long letter, my dear Lewis, for I cannot sit up a moment longer. Since the commencement of this letter, the enclosed card has been sent up to me. These *dignitaries* around here are so courteous.[36]

Mary's eyesight was failing her, as she told Lewis that she no longer saw American newspapers and asked him to send her slips of news. However, she had heard that Roscoe Conkling, a senator from New York who opposed Rutherford B. Hayes for the presidency two years earlier, might make another run for the office. "I hope our country—will never nominate for the presidency, SO BAD a man as Roscoe Conkling." Conkling was allegedly involved in an affair with Kate Chase Sprague.[37]

Pau had other distinguished American guests in December 1879, but they neglected to call on Mary. Former President U. S. Grant and his wife, Julia, were making their two-year world tour and came to Pau for a parade, reception and dinner at the Hôtel de France. Mary Lincoln was not invited. "It was almost inconceivable that the Grants were not made aware of her presence in the tiny village, as she was certainly the most famous American to be living in permanent residence there," Lachman wrote. "Julia Grant tried to explain this unforgivable breach of etiquette in her memoirs. 'I learned the night before we left that Mrs. Abraham Lincoln was there and I was very, very, very sorry we had not learned of this sooner, as it was now too late to make her a visit. We had out tickets and our train, a party was going with us and we could not at this late hour change our plans.'"[38]

In January 1880, after injuring her back in a fall from a stepladder in her apartment in Pau, Mary realized it was time to think about going home. She wrote Jacob Bunn that she expected to be in Naples during February. After that, according to her letters, Mary divided her time in southern France between Pau, Avignon and Marseille.

Mary wrote Lewis Baker on January 16 that she had spent three weeks in bed in Avignon, France, with plasters on her back and left side. "When I am sufficiently recovered (which I trust will be soon as it is *still* cold here), I will proceed to Marseille & take the steamer to Naples. Two years since I was here for a few days, when I was not *so* bowed down with bodily pain, drove around, saw all the churches, viewed the quaint old town so filled with historical associations, the house of the noble *John Stuart* Mills [Mill] where he now rests from life's cares & ingratitude. I only wish that you, dear Lewis, were here in my place, with your young, bright, intelligence, & I a broken hearted sorrowing woman in *your* place, with your dear Grandma, my own good, sweet sister. Tell her to take a good rest, retire early & sleep well— How much we have to talk over, when we are once more together."[39]

While Mary claimed she was not reading the newspapers so much anymore, she did notice that Julia Tyler was campaigning for a government pension. "A woman, who was so bitter against our cause during the war, with much Northern property & money—as well as the South—but so *fearful* a Secessionist. Our Republican leaders will, I am sure, remember ALL THIS—& the country will not have fallen upon such 'evil times,' as to grant her impudent request."[40]

According to another letter to Lewis, on January 19, Mary was back in Pau. She wrote of her appreciation that he would be meeting her in New York and that his grandfather had arranged for her trunks to be exempt from custom duties. "The extremely cold weather & unusual amount of pain forces me in a week or two to leave for Naples." On January 29, she was still in Pau. Mary again began her trip to Naples and got as far as Marseille, France. She wrote Jacob Bunn on March 5, "I am too ill, to travel & have not the least wish to do so. Kindly pardon these details—as it is necessary to explain to you, that I have abandoned *all* idea of proceeding to Naples."[41]

Mary slowly made her way back to Avignon and finally to Pau. "Please direct to Pau, France, all letters this summer, as I am remaining *here* for the next four months," she wrote Jacob Bunn on June 5. By the time she returned to Pau, her physician ordered bed rest for two months. Mary had stored some trunks at the closed Hotel de la Paix which she wanted to examine and have repaired if necessary. She sent for a woman who had been her companion previously and, as they were descending the stairs, Mary fell again. The concierge, from her Hotel Henry Quatra, carried her to a carriage. "The bonne went for the physician, who ordered a warm bath, the bonne placed me in bed, & gave me a cup of warm soup, the physician returned toward evening, with fresh plasters & I am now sitting propped up on my lounge," Mary wrote Lewis proposing that, instead of the trip to the White Mountains, that he travel to France for a few months the next summer. "I shall never be satisfied until you see the beautiful Pyrénées & have a four or five months, journey, on *this* side of the water—and, dear Lewis, it will not be my fault, be assured, if it is not accomplished. But I must first return to American, straigen [straighten] out my bonds and settle down, THEN, I shall be only too pleased if you will undertake the journey by yourself."[42]

Due to her illness, Mary was unable to sail in early October as she hoped. She made arrangements with Ninian Edwards and Jacob Bunn to advance Lewis $125 to meet her in New York, and shipped her trunks. She sailed on the SS *Amerique* from Le Havre on October 16. Mary suggested that Lewis stay at the Fifth Avenue Hotel and when she arrived they would find another lodging place. "So many associations of happier days with my beloved children at some of these places," she wrote.[43]

Mary never seemed to have calm seas crossing the Atlantic and the *Amerique* voyage was no different. Mary expected the crossing to take nine days. The *Amerique* encountered a snowstorm during the crossing and reached New York three days late. The French actress Sarah Bernhardt was among the passengers and wrote in her memoirs that she saved Mary from falling down steps on board the ship.[44]

Mary's Springfield homecoming was not what she expected. Like herself, Elizabeth and Ninian Edwards had aged: she was sixty-seven and he was seventy-one. Despite the fact that neither was capable of looking after Mary, they rented her four rooms in their house plus storage for her sixty-seven trunks. Mary required personal care that Elizabeth was unable to give her. Much of that care was lovingly administered by Josephine Edwards, the wife of Elizabeth's son Albert, and their sixteen-year-old daughter, Mary.[45]

Christmas 1880 found Mary enclosed with warm family connections in the Edwards household in Springfield. The holiday must have been an improvement over the previous years in Europe. While Mary and Elizabeth were infirm with age, it was Ninian who became seriously ill that winter as he was attempting to finish the biography of his father and early Illinois history. His book, *The Edwards Papers*, was finished in 1884 and was edited by Elihu B. Washburne.[46]

Justin G. Turner and Linda Levitt Turner, in their book *Mary Todd Lincoln: Her Life and Letters*, write that Robert, with his twelve-year-old daughter, Mamie, visited Mary in Springfield in May of 1881.[47]

"She is undoubtedly far from well," Robert wrote Sally Orne, "& has not been out of her room for more than six months and she thinks she is very ill. My own judgment is that some part of her trouble is imaginary." Elizabeth was also of the opinion that Mary was exaggerating her condition, which she said took every minute of her time.[48]

There was nothing imaginary about the fact that Mary was nearly blind from cataracts and could hardly walk as a result of injuries to her back. Lachman quoted the *Chicago Tribune* as saying, "Immediate friends here consider her ailments to some extent imaginary." Mary was being so well cared for by the Edwardses, according to the newspaper, that Americans could rest assured that she was well provided for financially and medically. The *New York Times* opined that she was not really sick but suffering from a hysterical condition and could live for many years.[49]

In July, Mary consulted Philadelphia ophthalmologist Hermann Knapp, who diagnosed cataracts in both eyes. She traveled on to St. Catherines, near Niagara Falls, for spa treatments, which were unsuccessful. How she managed to return to New York was a mystery. When her train arrived in the city, Mary wrote Josephine Edwards on October 23, "I was so thoroughly exhausted that the Hackman lifted me in his arms into the carriage—also lifted me into the Clarendon Hotel—Dr. Miller insists that his man shall lift me upstairs from the baths—indeed it could not be otherwise."[50]

Regardless of her ailments, Mary received friends. "Some former Washington friends are stopping here, Mr & Mrs [Silas] Robbins & Judge & Mrs [Joseph G.] Bowman," she wrote. "I have received several calls from them. Mrs Dr Sayre comes often to see me—I decline many callers, with painful sores & and an aching back—it is necessary to do so." When Mary wrote Joe, as she called her, she was in Dr. Miller's Hotel, where she was being treated for her spinal injuries with electric baths.[51]

Perhaps because of her ailments, Mary began to nitpick Elizabeth and Ninian about the pittance she was paying them to store her trunks. "I am frightened with the great expenses I am passing through—Baths a nurse physician's bill hotel &&—The 5 dollars a month for the two rooms where my baggage is stored. Of course I have nothing whatever to do with the room, which I occupied as a chamber at Mr Edwards. I pay for no place I left open that as, you know was the agreement—I left 4 nails for the windows—to secure any party, who might occupy the room & to avoid the entrance from the roof. The agreement was to pay $3-a month for rooms where the baggage was stored. Wherever I AM I have *more asked* than I should pay for—I pay for NO room, I do not occupy & leave open." Elizabeth and Ninian Edwards' names were omitted from her closing words. "Dear Joe—I can write no more—The weather is as sunny & beautiful as September—I am too ill to ride out—Write—Love to Allie [and the] children—Frances Wallace & Mary Baker."[52]

Mary was soon engaged in another cause, her last, and rent for trunk storage lost its importance. President James A. Garfield, in whose cabinet Robert was secretary of war, was shot July 2, 1881, at a Washington railroad station by Charles J. Guiteau, a disgruntled office-seeker. Garfield lingered on and died on September 21, 1881. Vice-President Chester A.

Arthur was immediately sworn in to office. Robert and other members of the cabinet tendered their resignations but Arthur refused them, although he gradually began weeding them out with his own selections. Lucretia Garfield was left with seven children—two daughters and five sons—ranging in age from fourteen to twenty-two. National efforts to raise money for Garfield's family reached $360,000, in addition to a proposed $5,000 pension for Lucretia.[53]

Mary was blind and crippled but she still had her political acumen and her brain—if Lucretia Garfield was entitled to $5,000, then she deserved the same. Mary began making plans, just as she did at Bellevue. She needed three people: a spokesman about her medical condition, someone to write letters for her and a person to lobby Congress for an increase in her pension. The Edwardses, once again, gave her their support. Mary did not need the additional money. She had managed her money very well during those years in Europe and had not touched the principal. When Robert turned over her bonds in June 1876, the amount was $68,750. Her 1882 estate was worth $84,035.[54]

With Mary, it was not the money; it was the principle of the matter.

Her New York physician, Dr. Lewis A. Sayre, was the founding father of orthopedic surgery in America. He helped found the American Medical Association and was its president in 1880, and had known Mary since he attended Transylvania College, in Lexington, in 1837–1838. Sayre's book, *Spinal Disease and Spinal Curvature*, educated a generation of orthopedists and was printed in the United States, England and Germany.[55]

The daughter of Rhonda White, Mary's long-time friend in New York, Rhonda Mack was there to write her letters on her daily visit to Miller's Hotel. The Rev. Noyes W. Miner, Hannah Shearer's bother and Baptist minister, came to New York to attend a ministerial conference, visited Mary there and was shocked. "He was appalled at her wasted appearance, her weakened condition and her apparent lack of friends, and, after leaving her, delivered a moving speech in her defense before the assembled clergymen. He put himself at her disposal asking if there was anything he could do to help her."[56]

Dr. Lewis Sayre, one of the founders of orthopedic surgery in America, was Mary's New York physician and told reporters she was not insane (Library of Congress Prints and Photographs Division).

When a reporter asked Sayre about Mary's mental health, the physician replied rather tartly, "She is no more insane than you or I are and if you come with me to talk with her you would understand that."[57]

Robert and Mary Harlan were with President Arthur, the cabinet, the diplomat corps, generals and other dignitaries at Yorktown to celebrate the centennial of the British surrender at the end of the Revolutionary War, when renewed attention was drawn to Mary's illnesses.

"Much to her discomfort," Lachman wrote, "Mary [Harlan] found herself engaged in a discussion about her mother-in-law with President Arthur and the American businessman Cyrus W. Field. Interestingly, after the festivities, Mary Harlan Lincoln went directly to New York and for the first time in years, visited her mother-in-law."[58]

Sayre, at the request of Rep. William M. Springer, from Springfield, who proposed an increase in Mary's pension, assembled a team of physicians to examine her. The team of physicians included Sayre, Dr. Meredith Clymer, neurologist and professor at both New York Medical and Albany Medical colleges; Philadelphia ophthalmologist Hermann Knapp, a pioneer in his field who taught at New York University Medical College, and Dr. William Pancoast, a surgeon and professor of anatomy at Jefferson Medical College in Philadelphia.[59]

Summarizing their findings, Sayre wrote, "There is no probability that there will be any improvement in Mrs. Lincoln's condition, considering her age and the nature of her disease. She is now quite helpless, unable to walk with safety without the aid of an attendant, or indeed to help herself to any extent. She requires the continued services of a competent nurse and also constant medical attention."[60]

Mary, after Sayre's report, wrote Miner advising him, "NOT to say a word about bonds—ONLY urge the $10,000 a year & the 5 year & four months back pension *with interest*." She gave Miner a list of representatives and senators to talk with, told him not to talk with Robert and said she heard Davis was starting a rumor that she received the remainder of Lincoln's 1865 salary. "I never received a dollar of the 3 years pay of my husband," she wrote.[61] Apparently cooler heads prevailed and Mary agreed to accept, if offered, an annual increase in her pension to $5,000.

Two weeks later, Mary moved from Miller's Hotel to the Grand Central Hotel, since she was stopping the electric baths, and remained there until March 22, 1882. She claimed the food at Miller's was terrible and he was overcharging her. Mary knew about New York hotels and her selection of the Grand Central was baffling, as the hostel had a terrible reputation. When the Grand Central Hotel opened in August 1870, after being destroyed by fire three years earlier, it was the city's largest with 650 rooms spread over eight floors.[62]

Before Mary moved to the Grand Central Hotel, her pension increase to $5,000 was approved, along with $15,000 in restitution money, by Congress on January 24, 1882. A month later she wrote Miner anxious about the money. "I wrote you several days since—requesting you to write to Mr Springer regarding my new Pension paper & the $15,000—which both houses of Congress unanimously voted me—*Where* is the money—Please let me hear from you without any further delay. With best love to your family, believe me very truly—Mary Lincoln."[63]

On March 21, 1882, Mary wrote Lewis Baker with instructions to meet her train in Springfield. "May I request you to have a supervision over a box containing an invalid's chair & a smaller box—also a very small package of medicine. I leave here tomorrow Wednesday evening at 5 ½ o'clock for Springfield. I find that I must rest from the Electric Baths, for a few weeks. I go west by way of the Hudson River railroad—to Buffalo, Cleveland Detroit & Toledo arriving in Decatur before daylight Friday morning and Springfield at 7 o'clock in the morning. I dread the journey greatly, with my limbs still in so paralyzed state."[64]

Hopefully, Mary traveled with a nurse. The constant jolting of the train must have caused her terrible pain. Mary Edwards Brown recalled that Mary continued to have terrible headaches at the Edwardses. "Her fingers swelled up so she had to take off her wedding ring," she said. Mary's Springfield physician was Dr. T. W. Dresser, whose father married Mary and Lincoln and built the house where they lived. Bedridden and her body covered with boils, Mary suffered a stroke. On July 15, 1882, at 8:15 p.m., with Dr. Dresser holding her hand, Mary passed away to her long-awaited reunion with her husband and sons.[65] She died on the eleventh anniversary of Tad's death.

"After Aunt Mary died," Mary Edwards Brown recalled, "mother hunted it up [her wedding ring] and got it back on her finger. Mother laid Aunt Mary out, too. The newspapers wrote about the ring when she was lying in her coffin in Grandmother's parlor with the wedding lamps lighted how the ring was Etruscan gold and was shining on her finger and there was a smile on her face." Josephine Edwards smoothed back Mary's hair and cut off a lock.[66]

Robert came to Springfield for his mother's funeral; Mary Harlan remained in Chicago due to ill health. Mary's casket sat on a white velvet bier in the First Presbyterian Church as the Rev. James A. Reed's eulogy likened Mary and Abraham Lincoln to two pine trees reaching for the sky, whose roots and branches were intertwined. When one tree was struck down by lightning, he said, the other lingered for a few years, dying from the slow death that killed the first. Robert led the procession from the church to the Lincoln Tomb at Oak Ridge Cemetery, where Mary's casket was placed with that of her husband and sons.[67]

Whether David Davis, Leonard Swett or Isaac Arnold attended her funeral is not known. Arnold was, from all indications, somewhat disturbed about the pain and suffering the three of them, along with Robert, had inflicted upon Mary. Arnold addressed the situation in an oblique manner in his book *The Life of Abraham Lincoln*, as he shifted the blame the four of them bore to the newspapers. "There is nothing in American history so unmanly, so devoid of every chivalric impulse as the treatment of this poor, broken-hearted woman, whose reason was so shattered by the great tragedy of her life," he wrote. "One would have supposed it to be sufficient to secure the forbearance, the charitable construction, or the silence of the press, to remember that she was the widow of Abraham Lincoln."[68]

Davis, Swett, and Arnold and even her own son could no longer inflict either their assumed authority or bruising wounds upon Mary. She was once again with Abraham Lincoln, who said, "Wherever that woman lives is my home."[69]

Chapter Notes

Chapter 1

1. Thomas F. Schwartz, "Mary Todd's 1835 Visit to Springfield, Illinois," *Journal of the Abraham Lincoln Association*, Vol. 26, No. 1, Winter 2005.

2. "Ninian W. Edwards," bioguide.congress.gov.

3. Schwartz.

4. Katherine Helm, *Mary, Wife of Lincoln* (New York: Harper and Brothers, 1928), 97.

5. Telephone interview with Edwards House curator Erika Holst, 28 January 2013.

6. Richard E. Hart, "Springfield's African Americans as a Part of the Lincoln Community," *Journal of Abraham Lincoln Association*, Vol. 20, No. 1, Winter 1999.

7. *Transactions of the Illinois State Historical Society for the Year* (Springfield, Illinois, 1904), 488–490.

8. *The New York Times*, 1 December 1900.

9. Ibid.

10. Ibid.

11. "A Toast Volunteered at a Public Dinner at Springfield, Illinois." *Collected Works of Abraham Lincoln*. Vol. 1, 87.

12. Helm, 67–70.

13. Ibid.

14. Ibid.

15. Ibid.

16. Ibid.

17. "Ward Hill Lamon," usmarshals.gov/history. "John T. Stuart," "O. H. Browning," bioguide.congress.gov. "Stephen T. Logan," lrc.ky.gov/record. "Ninian Wirt Edwards," Day. O. Kellogg, *The Encyclopedia Britannica* (New York: Werner Company, 1902), 497.

18. "Stephen A. Douglas," "James Shields," bioguide.congress.gov. Justin G. Turner and Linda Levitt Turner, *Mary Todd Lincoln: Her Life and Letters* (New York: Alfred A. Knopf, 1972), Mary Lincoln to Mercy Ann Levering, 19 December 1840, 19–20. Hereafter cited as Turners.

19. John C. Power and Sarah H. Power, *History of the Early Settlers of Sangamon County, Illinois* (nc, 1876), 79. *The State Journal-Register*, 18 July 2010.

20. Douglas L. Wilson, "William H. Herndon and Mary Todd Lincoln," *Journal of the Abraham Lincoln Association*, Vol. 22, No. 2, 3.

21. Draft of the Helm manuscript, William H. Townsend Papers, Special Collections, University of Kentucky.

22. Merwin Roe, editor, *Speeches and Letters of Abraham Lincoln 1832–1865* (New York: E. P. Dutton, 1912), 8.

23. Roy P. Basler, ed., *The Collected Works of Abraham Lincoln* (New Brunswick, New Jersey: Rutgers University Press, 1853–1955), Vol. 1, Abraham Lincoln to Mary S. Owens, 13 December 1836, Vol. 1, 55–56. 17 May 1837, Vol. 1, 79–80. 16 August 1937. Abraham Lincoln to Mrs. O. H. Browning, Vol. 1, 1 April 1838. 23 January 1841, Vol. 1, 118–120.

24. Paul M. Angle, "Lincoln's Power With Words," *Journal of the Abraham Lincoln Association*, Vol. 3, No. 1, 1981.

25. Abraham Lincoln to James C. Conkling, 3 September 1863. *Collected Works of Abraham Lincoln*, Vol. 6, 430.

26. David Herbert Donald, *Lincoln* (New York: Simon and Schuster, 1995), 84.

27. Perrin, 314.

28. Emilie Todd Helm, "Historic Sketches of Edwards and Todd Families," typescript. Mary Todd Lincoln House, Lexington, Kentucky.

29. *McClure's Magazine*, March 1896, Vol. 45, No. 4.

30. Helm, 74–75.

31. Helm, 75.

32. Helm, 77.

33. Ibid.

34. Helm, 78.

35. Earl S. Miers, editor, *Lincoln Day by Day: A Chronology 1809–1865, Vol. 1* (Washington, D.C., Lincoln Sesquicentennial Commission, 1960), 142.

36. Miers, 143.

37. Walter Williams, *A History of Northeast Missouri*, Vol. 1 (Chicago: Lewis, 1913), 243. Wayne C. Temple, *Mary Lincoln's Travels* (nc, 1959), 181. Betty Boles Ellison, *A Man Seen but Once: Cassius Marcellus Clay* (Bloomington, Indiana: AuthorHouse, 2005), 35.

38. Williams, 243.

39. Helm, 79. Miers, on page 143 of his book, has Lincoln and Fields reaching Waterloo on Sunday, August 23, 1840. He listed his source as the *Register*, 4 September 1840. Lincoln spoke in Waterloo on Tuesday, August 25.

40. Mary Lincoln to Mercy Ann Levering, 23 July 1840, Turners, 14–19.

41. Mary Todd to Mercy Ann Levering, 15 December 1840. Turners, 19–22.

42. Helm, 81.

43. Ibid.

44. Ibid.

45. Ibid.

46. Ibid.

47. Helm, 81–82.

48. Helm, 82.

49. Ibid.

50. Ibid.

51. Helm, 88.

52. Lincoln to John T. Stuart, 23 January 1841. *Collected Works of Abraham Lincoln*, Vol. 1, 230–231.

53. Ibid. "John Todd Stuart," bioguide.congress.gov.

54. Lincoln to Joshua Speed, 19 June 1841, *Collected Works of Abraham Lincoln*, Vol. 1, 254–255.

55. Turners, 25–27.

56. Turners, 26–29.

57. Lincoln to Joshua Speed, 19 June 1841, *Collected Works of Abraham Lincoln*, Vol. 1, 260–261.

58. Helm, 85.

59. Lincoln to Mary Speed, 27 September 1841. *Collected Works of Abraham Lincoln*, Vol. 1, 260–261.

60. Helm, 90. Turners, 29.

61. Lincoln to Joshua Speed, 3 January 1842. *Collected Works of Abraham Lincoln*, Vol. 1, 265–266.

62. Ibid.

63. Lincoln to Joshua Speed, 3 February 1842. *Collected Works of Abraham Lincoln*, Vol. 1, 267–268.

64. Ibid.

65. Ibid.

66. Lincoln to Joshua Speed, 25 February 1842. *Collected Works of Abraham Lincoln*, Vol. 1, 280–281.

67. Lincoln to Joshua Speed, 27 March 1842. *Collected Works of Abraham Lincoln*, Vol. 1, 282.

68. Lincoln to Joshua Speed, 4 July 1842. *Collected Works of Abraham Lincoln*, Vol. 1, 289–290.

69. Ibid.

70. Turners, 29.

71. Ibid. Helm, 92.

72. Letter From the Lost Townships, 27 August 1842, *Collected Works of Abraham Lincoln*, Vol. 1, 291–297.

73. Shields to Lincoln, 17 September 1842. *Collected Works of Abraham Lincoln*, Vol. 1, 300–301.

74. Ibid.

75. Ibid.

76. Ibid.

77. Memorandum of Duel Instructions to Elias H. Merryman, 19 September 1842. *Collected Works of Abraham Lincoln,* Vol. 1, 301–303.

78. Donald, 91.

79. Attributed to the *Sangamon Journal*, 16 September 1842, in Douglas L. Wilson's *Honor's Voice: The Transformation of Abraham Lincoln* (New York: Alfred A. Knopf, 1998), 269–270.

80. Donald, 92. Memorandum of Duel Instructions to Elias H. Merryman, 19 September 1842. *Collected Works of Abraham Lincoln*. Vol. 1, 301–302.

81. Ibid.

82. J. Winston Coleman, *Famous Kentucky Duels* (Lexington, Kentucky: Henry Clay Press, 1969), 74–87.

83. Ibid.

84. Turners, 295–296.

85. John T. Bennett, "Transitional Philosopher of the Old South," *Methodist History* (nc, nd). Stewart Sifakis, *Who Was Who in the Civil War* (New York: Facts on File, 1988), 59.

86. Ron Schrepfer, "Abraham Lincoln's Forgotten Duel: Early Lessons of a Future President," Duke University, Fuqua School of Business.

87. Donald, 92.

88. Sophia Bledsoe Herrick, "The Illinois of Lincoln's Time," *The Century Illustrated Monthly Magazine*, March 1892, Vol. 43, 796–797. Herrick was an associate editor for *The Southern Review*, which her father founded in 1877. After his death that year, she joined the editorial staff of *Scribner's*, which later became *The Century*.

89. Ruth Painter Randall, *Mary Lincoln: Biography of a Marriage* (Boston: Little, Brown, 1953), 59.

90. Email to author from Lt. Col. Michael Wills, 5 March 2013. "Weapons: Dragoon Weapons," National Park Service, Fort Scott National Historic Site.

91. Lincoln to John J. Hardin, 1 May 1843. *Collected Works of Abraham Lincoln*, Vol. 1, 322–323.

92. Lincoln to Joshua Speed, 5 October 1842. *Collected Works of Abraham Lincoln*, Vol. 1, 302–303.

93. Ibid.

94. Helm, 94.

95. Thomas Schwartz, *Mary Todd Lincoln: First Lady of Controversy* (Springfield, Illinois: Abraham Lincoln Presidential Library Foundation, 2007), 16.

96. Turners, 30.

97. Gamaliel Bradford, "The Wife of Abraham Lincoln," *Harper's Magazine,* September 1925, 489–498. A draft of Helm's manuscript, in the William H. Townsend Papers, Special Collections, M. I. King Library, University of Kentucky, was quite critical of Bradford. "In short, he has evidently made up his mind to believe nothing to Mary's credit and sneers at any and all who find anything to commend; he just as unfailingly given credence to her detractors."

98. Lincoln to Samuel D. Marshall, 11 November 1842. *Collected Works of Abraham Lincoln*, Vol. 1, 304–305.

Chapter 2

1. Helm Family Papers, Special Collections, M.I. King Library, University of Kentucky. A drawing of the Todd family coat of arms contained the written notation, "Todd family Coat of Arms used by Robert S. Todd branch of the family." Katherine Helm, *Mary, Wife of Lincoln* (New York: Harper and Brothers, 1928), 1–8.

2. "The Covenanter Revolution," scottish-heratland. com.

3. Ibid.

4. "Battle of Drumclog, 1 June 1679," UK Battlefield Resource Center, The Battlefield Trust.

5. Ibid.

6. Ibid.

7. David M. Ferguson, *Shipwrecks of Orkney, Shetland and the Pentland Firth* (North Pomfret, Vermont: Newton, Abbott, Devon, 1988), 33. The King James II statement Ferguson referred to must have been made at a later date, as Charles II was king from 1660 to 1685, and James II succeeded him in 1685, in a short reign of three years.

8. *The Orcadian*, October 1988.

9. Ibid.

10. Ibid. See also David Dobson, *The Original Scots Colonists of Early America, 1612–1783* (Baltimore: Baltimore Regional Publishing, 1989), 33.

11. Helm, 10–11. Helm, 7–9, emphasized the prominence of English Todds. Thomas M. Green, *Historic Families of Kentucky* (Baltimore: Baltimore Regional Publishing, 1964), 208–215.

12. Green, 208–209.

13. Green, 209–210.

14. Ibid.

15. *Calendar of the George Rogers Clark Papers,* Draper Collection of Manuscript, Wisconsin Historical Society, Vol. 4, 151, 188, 192.

16. Ibid., 202, 206, 210.

17. Kentucky Papers of the Draper Collection of Manuscripts, State Historical Society of Wisconsin (Madison, 1925), 35.

18. Ibid.

19. Pennsylvania State Historic Preservation Office, "Governor David Rittenouse Porter." It was said that the Porter family was so successful that the governor's opponents complained he had an unfair advantage.

20. *The Kentucky Encyclopedia,* 887–888.

21. Ibid.

22. Calendar, Papers of George Rogers Clark, Draper Manuscript Collection, Vol. 4, Wisconsin Historical Society.

23. *Atlas of Historic County Boundaries* (nc, nd), 244.

24. *The Kentucky Encyclopedia,* John Kleber, editor (Lexington: University Press of Kentucky, 1992), 535.

25. John Todd Papers, University of Kentucky, Special Collections, M.I. King Library.

26. Richard C. Cox, ed., "Two Letters of Levi Todd, 1784, 1788," *Register of the Kentucky Historical Society* (Frankfort: Kentucky Historical Society), Vol. 76, No. 3, 216–222, July 1978.

27. *The Kentucky Encyclopedia,* 330. Charles Kerr, *History of Kentucky* (Chicago: American Historical Society, 1922), Vol. 1, 296. Staples, 12–17. J. Winston Coleman, *Lexington's First City Directory 1808* (Lexington, Kentucky: Winburn Press, 1953), 1–9.

28. Clay Lancaster, *Ante Bellum Homes of the Blue Grass* (Lexington: University of Kentucky Press, 1961), 30, and *Vestiges of the Venerable City of Lexington* (Lexington: Lexington-Fayette County Historic Commission,1978), 2. Some sources list William Wallace's birthplace as being Paisley, Renfrew, Scotland, and others place the event at Ellerslie, Renfrew, and Scotland. See newworldencyclopedia.org/William_Wallace or *Encyclopedia Britannica.*

29. Lancaster, 30.

30. William H. Townsend, *Lincoln and the Bluegrass* (Lexington: University of Kentucky Press, 1955), 26–28. *Journals of the House of Representatives of the Commonwealth of Kentucky,* 1813 to 1845 (Frankfort, Kentucky: S.L.M. Major, 1869).

31. Samuel M. Wilson, "Sesqui-centennial Sketches," *Lexington Herald,* 1941.

32. Ibid.

33. Cox, "Two Letters of Levi Todd, 1784, 1788."

34. Wilson, "Sesqui-centennial Sketches."

35. Lexington Fayette Urban County Government Office of History Preservation on the various courthouses. The current Fayette County clerk's office was unable to provide a list of the clerks who succeeded Levi Todd or provide a reason why the original clerk's office was separate from the courthouse other than to say it might have been for convenience. Charles R. Staples, *The History of Pioneer Lexington 1779–1806* (Lexington: University Press of Kentucky, 1996), 287–290.

36. Staples, 287–280.

37. Index to "Burnt Records," Fayette County clerk's office.

38. Levi Todd to Thomas Allin, Calendar of the Kentucky Papers in the Draper Collection of Manuscripts. *The Kentucky Encyclopedia,* 837, 927, 955–956. Merrill D. Peterson, *Thomas Jefferson and the New Nation* (New York: Oxford University Press, 1875), 346. Benjamin Sebastian Papers, Indiana Historical Society, Collection #SC 1728, OM0094.

39. *The Kentucky Encyclopedia,* 839.

40. Wilson, "Sesqui-centennial Sketches."

41. Jason Emerson, *The Madness of Mary Lincoln* (Carbondale: Southern Illinois University Press, 2007), 101, 221. *The Kentucky Encyclopedia,* 279, 625–626, 839.

42. *Acts Passed at the First Session of the Second Kentucky General Assembly for the Commonwealth of Kentucky* (Frankfort, Kentucky: John Bradford, 1793), Chapter 11, 16.

43. Levi Todd Estate Inventory, Will Book A, 436–438, 441. Fayette County clerk's office. Silver plate was the term given to items of coin silver in Lexington's early days and is not the same as silver plate of today. Some of Todd's silver probably came from Lexington's famous early silversmith, Asa Blanchard.

44. Ibid. measuringworth.com.

45. Townsend, 27–28. Widow Parker could have sent her daughters to Mrs. Lucky Gray's academy, which opened in 1797. Gladys V. Parrish, *The History of Female Education in Lexington and Fayette County,* master's thesis, 1932, University of Kentucky, 5, 8–9.

46. William A. Leavy, "A Memoir of Lexington and Its Vicinity," *Register of the Kentucky Historical Society,* 40: 132, July 1942, 257. Mary Menessier Beck was born in France and educated in England where she met her husband, artist-educator George Beck. The Becks had a school in Philadelphia before coming to Lexington. One of their teachers in Lexington was Mme. Charlotte Mentelle, who later opened her own school. Various dates are listed for the opening of the Becks' school from 1804 to 1806. Edna T. Whitley, "Mary Beck and the Female Mind," *Register of the Kentucky Historical Society,* 77: 1, Winter 1979, 15–20. Eugene C. Barker, "Stephen Fuller Austin," *The Handbook of Texas Online.*

47. James F. and Mary W. Hargreaves, editors, *The Papers of Henry Clay* (Lexington: University Press of Kentucky, 1959), Vol. 1, 598–599.

48. Townsend, 27–28. riverraisinbeattlefield.org. *The Kentucky Encyclopedia,* 784, 877.

49. Townsend, 28–29.

50. Townsend, 29.

51. Hargreaves, *The Papers of Henry Clay* (Lexington, 1959), Vol. 2, 865.

52. Townsend, 46.

53. Deed Book P, 357–358. *The Kentucky Encyclopedia,* 45–47.

54. Hargreaves, Vol. 2, 717.

55. Deed Book M, 118–119.The Kentucky Insurance Company was approved by the 1802 legislature to issue paper money but it was primarily an insurer of products shipped on boats on the Western waters and on the seas. The company was initially so successful that forty-three shares of its stock were sold in 1804 for $105 each. It was succeeded by the Band of the Commonwealth of Kentucky in 1822. An 1837 lawsuit, *Briscoe v. Bank of the Commonwealth,* in the Supreme Court validated the constitutionality of state bank notes and opened the door to greater state control of banking and currency in the antebellum period. Kermit L. Hall, editor, *The Oxford Companion to the Supreme Court of the United States* (New York: Oxford University Press, 1992), 91–92.

56. *Journals of the House of Representatives Commonwealth of Kentucky* (Frankfort, Kentucky, 1813 to 1834.)

57. Townsend, 47.

58. Townsend, 48. Collections of Funeral Notices, Lexington Public Library.

Chapter 3

1. Ishbel Ross, *The President's Wife: Mary Todd Lincoln* (New York: Putnam, 1973), 17.

2. Ibid. Other sources, such as William H. Townsend, stated that it was Robert Todd's unmarried sister, Ann Marie, who supervised the household.

3. Turners, 588.

4. Greene, 272–273. Reference Desk, Kentucky Room, Lexington Public Library.

5. Mrs. Charlotte Mentelle, *A Short History of Mrs. Mary O. T. Wickliffe* (Lexington, Kentucky, privately published,1850), 4.

6. Townsend, 53. Lancaster, 131. "John C. Breckinridge," *The Kentucky Encyclopedia*, 116.

7. Lancaster, 31, 38, 66.

8. Lancaster, 53. Townsend, 52.

9. Dan Meinwald, *Mememonto Mori: Death and Photography in Nineteenth Century America*. vv.arts.ucla.edu;terminal/meinwald.

10. William A. LaBach, *Ancestry of Alexander Humphreys (1757–1802)* (Lexington, n.p., 2000), 2. Jennie C. Morton, "Second Street, South Frankfort." *Register of the Kentucky Historical Society*, 11: 33, September 1913, 31–40.

11. Helm, 17.

12. Robert Peter, *Transylvania University: Origin, Rise, Decline and Fall* (Louisville, Kentucky: J. P. Morton, 1896), 77. Thomas D. Clark, *Footloose in Jacksonian America: Robert W. Scott and His Agrarian World* (Frankfort: Kentucky Historical Society, 1989), 218.

13. "John Brown," *The Kentucky Encyclopedia*, 128–129. bioguide.congress. When Brown died at his home, Liberty Hall, in Frankfort in 1837, he was the last surviving member of the Continental Congress.

14. "James Brown," bioguide.congress.gov. James Brown was also a brother-in-law of Henry Clay. The Brown brothers were the cousins of John and James Breckinridge.

15. *Journals of the House of Representatives of the Commonwealth of Kentucky*, 1813–1835.

16. Townsend, 49. "Matthew Jouett," *The Kentucky Encyclopedia*, 480–481.

17. Townsend, 49.

18. Townsend, 50.

19. Ibid.

20. Marie Innes Todd's connections to President James Madison and his wife, Dolley, came from both sides of her family. Her father, Harry Innes, the first federal district judge in Kentucky, was a childhood friend of James Madison. Marie Todd's former mother-in-law, Lucy Payne Washington, was a sister of Dolley Madison, and her first husband, George Steptoe Washington, was a nephew of George Washington. vclh.virginia.edu/Madison/exhibits/widowhood/letters. Justice Todd, appointed to the court by Jefferson, did not enjoy distinguished service. In his nineteen years on the court, he wrote one dissent, all of five lines, in 1810. Otherwise, he always agreed with Chief Justice John H. Marshall. See James MacGregor Burns, *Packing*

the Court (New York: Penguin Press, 2009), 35. Damon R. Eubank, *In the Shadow of the Patriarch: The John J. Crittenden Family in War and Peace* (Macon, Georgia: Mercer University Press, 2009), 2–3.

21. "John J. Crittenden," *The Kentucky Encyclopedia*, 240–241.

22. Helm, 17.

23. Helm, 2.

24. Ibid.

25. Ibid.

26. Helm, 3.

27. Ibid.

28. Ibid.

29. Helm, 4.

30. Ibid.

31. Parrish, 46. John D. Wright, *Lexington: Heart of the Bluegrass* (Lexington, Kentucky: Lexington-Fayette Historic Commission, 1982), 33–34.

32. Townsend, 51.

33. 8 April 1827, *Kentucky Gazette*.

34. Townsend, 145.

35. Helm, 17, 55.

36. Helm, 28.

37. Helm Papers, William H. Townsend Collection, Special Collections, M.I. King Library, University of Kentucky.

38. Helm, 25.

39. Helm, 21.

40. Helm, 30.

41. Robert V. Remini, *Henry Clay: Statesman for the Union* (New York: W. W. Norton, 1993), 653. McCalla was appointed U.S. marshal for Kentucky by President Andrew Jackson. 6 March 1829, *Observer and Reporter*.

Chapter 4

1. Helm, 41.

2. Helm, 21. "Richard M. Johnson," *The Kentucky Encyclopedia*, 475.

3. Helm, 21.

4. Helm, 22–23.

5. Helm, 39–40.

6. Helm, 40.

7. Deed Book 17, 194–195.

8. General Index to Deeds, Mortgages, Etc., Fayette County, Kentucky, 1794–1903, Book T. (Hereafter referred to as General Index to Deeds).

9. Ibid.

10. Will Book S, 576.

11. Helm, 36–38.

12. "Richard M. Johnson," *The Kentucky Encyclopedia*, 475. Mark O. Hatfield, *Vice-Presidents of the United States* (Washington, D.C.: Government Printing Office, 1997), 3–10. bioguide.congress.gov. Townsend, 75–78.

13. Townsend, 76.

14. Townsend, 76–78.

15. Townsend, 74–75, 95–96. Deed Book 1, 150. *1838–39 Lexington City Directory*, 134.

16. nola.com/lalaurie/archives. *Washington Post*, 24 October 2004.

17. Helm, 38–39.

18. Ivan E. McDougle, *Slavery in Kentucky 1792–1865* (Lancaster, Pennsylvania: Press of the New Era, 1918), 8. The act was repealed in 1849 and reinstated in 1864.

19. Ellison, *A Man Seen But Once: Cassius Marcellus Clay*, 40, 58.

20. Ibid. Townsend, 92.

21. Ellison, 40, 47.

22. McDoulel, 19.

23. *Acts Passed at the Second Session of the General Assembly for the Commonwealth of Kentucky* (Frankfort, Kentucky: J. H. Holeman, 1823.) Chapter 69, 49–50.

24. Mentelle, 5–6. Mme. Mentelle wrote that Russell, as far as she knew, was possibly known only to the prominent Lexington man who introduced him to the heiress.

25. Ibid. *New York Times*, 29 October 2002. woburn. co.uk/abbey/history.

26. Mentelle, 6–7. General Index.

27. Mentelle, 6.

28. Mentelle, 6–7.

29. Townsend, 180, 373.

30. Mentelle, 12. Townsend, 180.

31. Bill of sale for slaves Millie and Alfred from B. R. McIwaine to Mary O. Russell, 8 April 1825. Wickliffe-Preston Family Papers, Special Collections, M. I. King Library, University of Kentucky.

32. General Index to Deeds.

33. Copy of note, Wickliffe-Preston Family Papers. On November 22, 1825, Mary O. Russell sold Henry Clay fifty acres on Todd's Road.

34. Hargreaves, Vol. 1, 135.

35. Breckinridge, 70–71.

36. Ibid.

37. "Battle of Blue Licks," *The Kentucky Encyclopedia*, 951. Townsend, 177.

38. Richard H. Chinn to Robert Wickliffe, 9 September 1827, Fayette County Deed Book 5.

39. Deed Book 5, 118–119.

40. Deed Book, 11, 241. Wickliffe-Preston Family Papers, Box 4.

41. Mentelle, 17.

42. Statement of Mary O. Wickliffe, 9 March 1841. Wickliffe-Preston Family Papers.

43. Turnbull-Bowman Family papers, Subseries 2, Louisiana State University libraries.

44. *The African Repository and Colonial Journal*, Vol. 27 (Washington City: Way & Gideon, 1851), 149. There were 99 Kentucky slaves listed on the brig *Ajax*'s manifest.

45. Wickliffe Preston Family Papers. Munsell's 1835 map of Kentucky. Special Collections, M. I. King Library, University of Kentucky.

46. Ibid.

47. Alfred Francis Russell, African American Registry. liberiapastandpresent.org/19thcColonists.

48. Helm, 30.

49. C. Quisenberry, *The Life and Times of Hon. Humphrey Marshall* (Winchester, Kentucky: Sun Publishing, 1892), 100–102.

50. J. Winston Coleman, *Famous Kentucky Duels* (Lexington, Kentucky: Winburn Press, 1969) 49–50.

51. Townsend, 53.

52. Coleman, 73–74.

53. Coleman, 74.

54. Coleman, 75.

55. Coleman, 75.

56. Coleman 76. Townsend, 54.

57. Coleman, 77. Townsend, 55.

58. John L. Wilson, *The Code of Honor or Rules for the Government of Principals and Seconds in Dueling* (Charleston, South Carolina: J. Pinney, 1858).

59. Coleman, 78–79. Townsend, 56–57.

60. Coleman, 81–83. Townsend, 57.

61. Coleman, 85.

62. Coleman, 87.

Chapter 5

1. Fayette County Deed Book 19, 270.

2. *Kentucky Gazette*, 31 August 1827.

3. Fayette County clerk's office, Deed Book 8, 130–131, 133–134. Fact Sheet, Mary Todd Lincoln House media folder, June 9, 1977. There was an additional 2,162 square feet of space in the basement.

4. Dunn, 611.

5. Clay Lancaster, "Analysis for the Restoration of The Palmateer-Todd House" (privately prepared, November 1975), 1, 4. Fact Sheet, Mary Todd Lincoln House, June 9, 1977.

6. The octagonal bricks were found by the author during the renovation of the house in 1976–1977.

7. Lancaster, Analysis. The family could have added a kitchen cooking stove, as they were being manufactured in the East in the late 1820s and early 1830s. Marcus Benjamin, *Appleton's New Practical Encyclopedia* (New York: D. Appleton, 1887), 99. The author's observations, before the house was renovated in 1976–1977, indicated the kitchen fireplace hearth had collapsed into the basement.

8. 1849 Robert S. Todd Estate Sale Inventory, Fayette County clerk's office.

9. Ibid.

10. Marcus Benjamin, *Appleton's New Practical Encyclopedia* (New York: D. Appleton, 1887), 99. See also "Classifications of Cooking Ranges, Stoves and Ovens," U.S. Department of Homeland Security (Washington, D.C., 2009), 8.

11. Lancaster, 47. "John Wesley Hunt," *The Kentucky Encyclopedia*, 447. One of Hunt's sons, Francis Key Hunt (named for his mother's cousin, Francis Scott Key) used $30,000 of his inheritance in 1852 to build Louduon, the first castellated Gothic Revival villa in Kentucky and one of only five in the south. "Louduon House," U.S. Register of Historic Places.

12. Lancaster, 49. *Journal of the House of Representatives of the Commonwealth of Kentucky* (Frankfort, Kentucky: John Bradford, 1828), 4.

13. Lancaster, 61–62. "William Morton House," U.S. Register of Historic Places. Todd family friend and emancipationist Cassius M. Clay purchased Morton House in 1838, two years after the builder died, for $18,000.

14. Lancaster, 32–34, 53–55, 64–65. Dunn, "Coolavin."

15. Turners, 447.

16. Townsend, 58. Charlotte C. Mentelle, *Voyages, Adventures, and Situations of the French Emigrants from the Year (17)89 to (17)99* (Lexington, Kentucky: self-published, 1800).

17. Gladys V. Parrish, "The History of Female Education in Lexington and Fayette County," master's thesis, 1940, University of Kentucky, Special Collections, 20.

18. Helm, 45–46.

19. Ibid.

20. *Lexington Herald*, 15 August 1915. Lindsey Apple,

"The French in Central Kentucky: The Myth and Reality of Assimilation," *Journal of the Kentucky-Tennessee American Studies Association* (Murfreesboro: Middle Tennessee State University, 1983), No. 4, 9. John D. Wright, *Lexington: Heart of the Bluegrass* (Lexington, Kentucky: Lexington-Fayette Historic Commission, 1983) 39. Wright wrote that Giron was a former grenadier in Napoleon's army.

21. Helm, 47.

22. Helm, 52–53.

23. Apple, 12.

24. Ibid.

25. Ibid.

26. Charlotte Mentelle to C. C. Moore, 12 December 1836. Special Collections, M.I. King Library, University of Kentucky. Moore, an ordained minister, was an interesting character who was later sentenced to two years in an Ohio prison in 1899 for sending obscene material through the mail. President William McKinley commuted his sentence to six months. A reporter for several Lexington newspapers, Moore began the *Bluegrass Blade* in 1884, in which he espoused women's suffrage, prohibition, sex education and agnosticism. "Charles C. Moore," *The Kentucky Encyclopedia*, 647.

27. Baker, 44.

28. Mary Lincoln to Mary Harlan Lincoln, 29 January 1871. Turners, 58–583.

29. Lumsford P. Yandall, "An Account of Spasmodic Cholera," *Transylvania Journal of Medicine* (Lexington, Kentucky: J. Clarke), Vol. 6, 1833, 198.

30. Helm, 54. Wright, 45.

31. Helm, 49–50.

32. Helm, 50.

33. Ibid.

34. Helm, 51.

35. Ibid.

36. Ibid.

37. James Lane Allen, "King Solomon of Kentucky," *The Outlook* (New York: Outlook Printing, December 1909), 884–886.

38. Helm, 52–53.

39. Townsend, 58.

40. uky.edu/kentuckyatlas/ky-crab-orchard.

41. J. Winston Coleman, *The Springs of Kentucky* (Lexington, Kentucky: Winburn Press, 1955), 39, 67, 80–81. Michael Wallis, *The Real Wild West* (nc, 2000), 18. Young E. Allison, *The City of Louisville and a Glimpse of Kentucky* (Louisville, Kentucky: Committee on Industrial and Commercial Development of the Louisville Board of Trade, 1887), 145.

42. Allison, 145. "Crab Orchard Springs," *The Kentucky Encyclopedia*, 238.

43. Art Wrobel, *Journal of the Kentucky-Tennessee American Studies Association*, No. 11, 1999.

44. Helm, 54.

45. Helm, 54.

46. csx.history. catskillarchive.com.

47. Thomas F. Swartz, "Mary Todd's 1835 Visit to Springfield, Illinois," *Journal of the Abraham Lincoln Association*, Vol. 26, No. 1, Winter 2005, 42–45.

48. *Journal of the House of Representatives of the Commonwealth of Kentucky, 1835–1836* (Frankfort, Kentucky: Albert G. Hodge, 1835), 5.

49. Townsend, 59–60.

50. Ibid.

51. *Inventory of the Records of the Bank of Kentucky 1806–1835*, Lexington Public Library. From 1820 to 1830, the Bank of the Commonwealth of Kentucky was active. The bank ceased to function in 1830, but the legislature kept extending its charter until 1855 when accounts were finally settled. The importance of the bank was a 1837 U.S. Supreme Court lawsuit, *Briscoe v. Bank of the Commonwealth of Kentucky*, which upheld the issuance of circulating notes by a state chartered bank even when the bank's stock, funds and profits belonged to the state and whose officers and directors were appointed by the state legislature. By validating the constitutionality of state bank notes, the court opened the door to greater state control of banking and currency. *Inventory of the Records of the Bank of the Commonwealth of Kentucky*, Lexington Public Library. Kermit L. Hall, *The Oxford Companion to the Supreme Court of the United States* (New York, 1992), 91–92.

52. Ibid.

Chapter 6

1. Lincoln to Joshua Speed, 18 May 1843, *Collected Works of Abraham Lincoln*, Roy Basler, editor (New Brunswick, New Jersey: Rutgers University Press, 1953), Vol. 1, 324–325. Hereinafter referred to as *Collected Works of Abraham Lincoln*.

2. James T. Hickey, "The Lincolns' Globe Tavern," *Journal of the Illinois State Historical Society*, 56: 4, Winter 1963, 638–658.

3. Ibid.

4. Ibid.

5. Ibid.

6. Helm, 97.

7. Lincoln to Joshua Speed, 18 May 1843. *Collected Works of Abraham Lincoln*, Vol. 1, 324–325.

8. Lincoln to Joshua Speed, 24 March 1843. *Collected Works of Abraham Lincoln*, Vol. 1, 319.

9. Ibid.

10. Turners, 30.

11. Richard L. Miller, *Lincoln and His World: The Rise to National Prominence 1843–1853* (Jefferson, North Carolina: McFarland, 2011), 38.

12. Ibid.

13. Daniel Mark Epstein, *The Lincolns: Portrait of a Marriage* (New York: Ballantine Books, 2009), 81. Randall, 72–73.

14. Pass for Mrs. Harriet C. Bledsoe, *Collected Works of Abraham Lincoln*, Vol. 8, 218.

15. Lincoln Chronology, Lincoln Home National Historical Site, National Park Service.

16. Ruth Painter Randall, *Mary Lincoln: Biography of a Marriage* (Boston: Little, Brown, 1953), 98.

17. Deed of Conveyance to Mary Lincoln, 18 March 1844. *Collected Works of Abraham Lincoln*, Vol. 1, 334.

18. William H. Townsend, *Lincoln and the Bluegrass: Slavery and the Civil War* (Lexington: University of Kentucky Press, 1955), 82. Probate File, Estate of Robert S. Todd, Fayette County Clerk's Office.

19. Pratt, 66.

20. Miller, 39.

21. Townsend, *Lincoln and the Bluegrass: Slavery and the Civil War*, 97–98.

22. "The Contenders: Henry Clay 1777–1852." c-span. org. "Henry Clay," bioguide.congress.gov.

23. Thomas F. Schwartz, "An Egregious Political Blun-

der," *Journal of the Abraham Lincoln Association*, Vol. 8, No. 1, 1986.

24. lawpracticeofabrahamlincoln.org/reference/refer ence$20html1 percent20files.

25. Pratt, 65–66.

26. Sale contract by Charles Dresser and Abraham Lincoln, 16 January 1844. *Collected Works of Abraham Lincoln*, Vol. 1, 321.

27. Ibid.

28. Warrantee Deed, with Relinquishment of Dower. *Collected Works of Abraham Lincoln*, Vol. 1, 336.

29. "Abraham Lincoln Home," nps.gov. Richard S. Hagen, "What a Pleasant Home Abe Lincoln Has," *Journal of the Illinois State Historical Society*, Spring 1955, 5. "Lincoln Home Historic Site," Illinois Channel Network, 6 June 2005.

30. Helm, 108.

31. Randall, 77.

32. Ibid.

33. L. Bowen, "A. Lincoln: His House," a speech delivered before the Lincoln Centennial Association, Springfield, Illinois, 12 February 1925. http://quod.lib.umich.edu/a/alajournals/0526334.1925.001?rgn=main;view=fulltext.

34. Helm, 98.

35. A few of her Meissen pieces are in the Mary Todd Lincoln House in Lexington.

36. "The Lincolns Go Shopping," edited by Henry E. Pratt, *The Journal of the Illinois State Historical Society*, Spring 1955, 59–70.

37. Pratt, "The Lincolns Go Shopping," 66.

38. Ibid.

39. Pratt, "The Lincolns Go Shopping," 72–75.

40. Bowen.

41. "Sewing Machines," Museum of American Heritage, Palo Alto, California.

42. Randall, 84.

43. Eliza Leslie, 1787–1858, The Library Company of Philadelphia.

44. The Project Gutenberg EBook, *Directions for Cooking in its Various Branches*, by Eliza Leslie. Michigan State University Libraries, January 2004.

45. Mary Lincoln to Edward Lewis Baker, Jr., 4 October 1879. Turners, 686.

46. Hickey.

47. Pratt, *Personal Finances of Abraham Lincoln*, 94–95.

48. Eliza Leslie, *The Home Book: A Manual of Domestic Economy for Town and Country* (Philadelphia, Pennsylvania: Carey and Hart, 1844), 9–14.

49. Ibid., 27–34.

50. Leslie, 229–244.

51. Ibid.

52. Lincoln to Joshua Speed, 22 October 1846. *Collected Works of Abraham Lincoln*, Vol. 1, 390–391.

53. Ibid.

54. The address of Oregon Senator Mark Hatfield to the Abraham Lincoln Association's Annual Banquet, February 12, 1984 (Abraham Lincoln Association, Springfield, Illinois, 1985).

55. Lincoln to John J. Hardin, 7 February 1846, 19 January 1846. *Collected Works of Abraham Lincoln*, Vol. 1, 331–332.

56. Lincoln to Benjamin F. James, 24 November 1845, 16 January 1846. *Collected Works of Abraham Lincoln*, Vol. 1, 350–351, 357–357.

57. Richard J. Carwardine, "Lincoln, Evangelical Religion, and American Political Cultural in the Era of the Civil War," *Journal of the Abraham Lincoln Association*, Vol. 18, No. 1, Winter 1997.

58. William H. Townsend, *Lincoln and the Bluegrass: Slavery and the Civil War in Kentucky* (Lexington: University of Kentucky Press, 1955), 121.

59. Ibid.

60. Pratt, *Personal Finances of Abraham Lincoln*, 100.

61. Ibid.

62. Randall, 92. *Report of Civil and Criminal Cases Decided by the Court of Appeals of Kentucky, 1785–1951*, Vol. 11, No. 118 (Frankfort, Kentucky: J. Bradford, 1906), 322.

63. Randall, 92–93. Townsend, 123–124. Helm, 101–102.

64. Helm, 100.

65. Townsend, 129–130.

66. J. Winston Coleman, "Lexington's Slave Dealers and Their Southern Trade," *Filson Club History Quarterly* (Louisville, Kentucky, 1938), Vol. 12, No. 1, January 1938, 15.

67. Helm, 101. Townsend, 123–136.

68. Townsend, 129–140.

69. Clinton, 78. Randall, 94–96.

70. Lincoln to Mary Lincoln, 2 July 1848. *Collected Works of Abraham Lincoln*, Vol. 1, 495–496.

71. "Dolley Madison," firstladies.org/biographies.

72. Robert W. Merry, *A Country of Vast Designs: James K. Polk, the Mexican War and the Conquest of the American Continent* (New York: Simon and Schuster, 2009), 411.

Chapter 7

1. Lincoln to Mary Lincoln, 16 April 1848. *Collected Works of Abraham Lincoln*, Vol. 1, 465–466.

2. Ibid. Townsend, 146.

3. Lincoln to Mary Lincoln, 16 April 1848. *Collected Works of Abraham Lincoln*. Vol. 1, 465–466.

4. Ibid.

5. Robert S. Todd, *Mr. Todd's Reply to Mr. Wickliffe* (*Observer and Reporter*, Lexington, Kentucky, 1845), 5.

6. Ibid., 6, 7.

7. Lincoln to Mary Lincoln, 16 April 1848. *Collected Works of Abraham Lincoln*, Vol. 1, 465–466.

8. Ibid.

9. Ibid.

10. Ibid.

11. Ibid.

12. Ibid. Lancaster, 96. Bell Family Papers, 1843–1920, Special Collections, University of Kentucky Libraries.

13. Turners, 38.

14. Lincoln to Mary Lincoln, 12 June 1848. *Collected Works of Abraham Lincoln*, Vol. 1, 477–478.

15. Ibid.

16. Ibid.

17. Lincoln to Mary Lincoln, 2 July 1848, *Collected Works of Abraham Lincoln*, Vol. 1, 495–496.

18. Ibid.

19. Ibid.

20. Ibid.

21. thelincolnlog.org/calendar. Clinton, 84.

22. Townsend, 155. David W. Howe, "Why Abraham Lincoln Was a Whig," *Journal of the Abraham Lincoln Asso-*

ciation (Urbana: University of Illinois Press, 1995), Vol. 16, No. 1, Winter 1995. Anonymous, *Narrative of the Life of General Leslie Combs of Kentucky* (Washington, D.C.: J.T. and Lem. Towers, 1855), 22. Edward L. Bowen, *Legends of the Turf: A Century of Great Thoroughbred Breeders* (Lexington, Kentucky: Eclipse Press, 2004), Vol. 2, 129. "Lewis Cass," ohiohistorycentral.org.

23. Yanek Mieczkowski, *The Routledge Historic Atlas of Presidential Elections* (Oxford, England: Routledge, 2001), 45–46.

24. Townsend, 155.

25. Randall, 113.

26. Hickey, Chronology.

27. Turners, 39.

28. Thomas F. Schwartz, "An Egregious Political Blunder: Justin Butterfield, Lincoln and Illinois Whiggery," *Journal of the Abraham Lincoln Association*, Vol. 8, No. 1, Winter 1986. Lincoln to Josiah M. Lucas, 25 April 1949. Collected Works of Abraham Lincoln, Vol. 2, 57.

29. Lincoln to Thomas Ewing, 22 June 1849. *Collected Works of Abraham Lincoln*, Vol. 1, 481.

30. Hickey, Lincoln Chronology. Turners, 39–40. *Pacific Monthly* (Portland, Oregon: Pacific Monthly Publishing, 1902), Vols. 7–9, 282. Kentucky Historical Marker #1194, Boone County. Gaines, a former congressman and Mexican War veteran, became Oregon's first governor.

31. Helm, 108.

32. Townsend, 172. "Crab Orchard Springs," *Kentucky Encyclopedia*, 238.

33. *Lexington Observer and Reporter,* 18 July 1849.

34. Ibid.

35. *Illinois State Journal*, 17 June 1848.

36. *Albany Argus*, 19 June 1848.

37. Townsend, 176–177.

38. Townsend, 177.

39. Townsend, 178.

40. Townsend 178–179.

41. Randall, 123.

42. Townsend 185.

43. Ibid.

44. Fayette County Will Book S, 576. Townsend, 189–190.

45. James T. Hickey, "Lincolniana," *Journal of the Illinois State Historical Society*, Vol. 77, No. 1, Spring 1984. Harry E. Pratt, "Little Eddie Lincoln—'We Miss Him Very Much," *Journal of the Illinois Historical Society*, Vol. 47, No. 3, Autumn 1954. Samuel P. Wheeler, "Solving a Lincoln Literary Mystery: 'Little Eddie,'" *Journal of the Abraham Lincoln Association*, Vol. 33, No. 2, Summer 2012. *The Daily True Delta* (New Orleans), 9 July 1852.

46. Randall, 124. *American Journal of Physiology* (American Journal of Physiology Society, n.c., 1905), 332.

47. Turner, 41. Randall, 124–125. Wheeler, "Solving a Lincoln Literary Mystery: Little Eddie."

48. Turners, 41.

49. Harry E. Pratt, "Little Eddie Lincoln—'We Miss Him Very Much," *Journal of the Illinois State Historic Society*, 1954, Autumn, Vol. 47, No. 3. Samuel P. Wheeler. "Solving a Lincoln Literary Mystery: 'Little Eddie,'" *Journal of the Abraham Lincoln Association*, Summer 2012, Vol. 33, No. 2.

50. Pratt, "Little Eddie Lincoln."

51. Randall, 128.

52. Robert J. Havlik, "Abraham Lincoln and the Reverend Dr. James Smith: Lincoln's Presbyterian Experience

in Springfield," *Journal of the Illinois State Historic Society*, Vol. 92, No. 3, Autumn 1999. Townsend, 194.

53. *Parker v. Richardson et al.* (L05935), Fayette County, Kentucky, Circuit Court, Partition, April 1850.

54. Townsend, 196.

55. Fayette Circuit and Kentucky Appeals Court documents in the Townsend Collection, Box 1, Special Collections, University of Kentucky. *Lexington Observer and Reporter*, 9 April 1845.

56. Pratt, 86.

Chapter 8

1. Randall, 130.

2. Lincoln to John D. Johnson, 12 January 1851. *Collected Works of Abraham Lincoln*, Vol. 2, 96–97.

3. Mary Lincoln to Rhonda White, 2 May 1868, Turners, 475.

4. Randall, 132.

5. Ibid.

6. "Marseille White Corded Quilting," International Quilt Study Center and Museum, College of Education and Human Services, University of Nebraska–Lincoln.

7. Randall, 82–82.

8. Henry B. Rankin, *Personal Recollections of Abraham Lincoln* (New York: G.P. Putnam's Sons, 1916), 181–182.

9. Kansas-Nebraska Act, loc.gov. R. D. Monroe, "The Kansas-Nebraska Act and the Rise of the Republican Party, 1854–1856," Lincoln.lib.mie.edu/biography6text.html.

10. Monroe.

11. Rankin, 182.

12. Ibid.

13. Ibid.

14. Ibid.

15. Dominic Cascaini, "The History of Suffragettes," BBC, 2 October 2012.

16. *The 1971 World Almanac* (New York: Newspaper Enterprise Association, 1971), 214.

17. Lewis L. Gould, editor, *American First Ladies: Their Lives and Their Legacy* (Oxford, England: Taylor and Francis, 2001), 116.

18. William E. Gienapp, *The Origins of the Republican Party 1852–1856* (Oxford, England: Oxford University Press, 1987), 174–175. Matthew Pinsker, "Senator Abraham Lincoln," *Journal of the Abraham Lincoln Association*, Vol. 13, No. 2, Summer 1993. Helm, 107–108. Lincoln to Elihu B. Washburne, 9 February 1855, *Collected Works of Abraham Lincoln*, Vol. 2, 304–306.

19. Lincoln to Elihu B. Washburne, 9 February 1855, *Collected Works of Abraham Lincoln*, Vol. 2, 304–306.

20. Ibid.

21. John M. Lamb, "The Great Canal Scrip Fraud," *The Magazine of Illinois*, Vol. 16, No. 9, November 1977, 57–60.

22. Ibid.

23. Ibid. Lamb added that a grand jury of courthouse "hangers-on" was impaneled in Springfield in April 1859, but Matteson was not called to testify nor were any of the people from whom he allegedly purchased the scrip. The first grand jury vote was 16–7 to indict. Then, the grand jury voted to reconsider but again returned a true bill. On the third vote, the outcome was 12–10 not to indict.

24. *Illinois Times*, 11 March 2009.

25. Ibid. Matteson's mansion later burned to the ground.

26. Turners, 46–47.

27. Turners, 61.
28. Pinsker, "Senator Abraham Lincoln." Helm, 108.
29. Turners, 258, 264.
30. Guy C. Frakes, "The Real Lincoln Highway: The Forgotten Lincoln Circuit Markers," *Journal of the Abraham Lincoln Association*, Vol. 25, No. 1, Winter 2004.
31. Richard S. Hagen, "What a Pleasant Home Abe Lincoln Has," *The Journal of the Illinois State Historical Society*, Vol. 48, No. 1, Spring 1955. *Illinois State Journal*, 6 January 1857.
32. Hagen, "What a Pleasant Home Abe Lincoln Has."
33. Pratt, *Personal Finances of Abraham Lincoln*, 147–148, 92.
34. Ibid.
35. *New York Herald*, 13 August 1860, as included in Kenneth Scott's "Lincoln's Home in 1860," *Journal of the Illinois State Historical Society*, Vol. 41, No. 1, Spring 1953.
36. Pratt, *Personal Finances of Abraham Lincoln*, 95.
37. Ann Liberman, *Governor's Mansions of the Midwest* (Columbia: University of Missouri Press, 2003), 4–6.
38. Pratt, *Personal Finances of Abraham Lincoln*, 95–96.
39. Ibid.
40. Pratt, *Personal Finances of Abraham Lincoln*, 96–97.
41. Mary Lincoln to Emilie Todd Helm, 16 February 1857, Turners, 48.
42. Ibid., 49.
43. Charles V. Darrin, "Your Truly Attached Friend, Mary Lincoln," *Journal of the Illinois State Historic Society*, Vol. 44, No. 1, Spring 1951.
44. Ibid.
45. Ibid.
46. Katherine B. Menz, *The Lincoln Home* (Harper Ferry Center, National Park Service, U.S. Department of the Interior, Washington, D.C, 1983), 21–22.
47. Mary Lincoln to Mary Brayman, September 1857, Turners, 51.
48. Menz, 18–19.
49. nps.gov/liho/historyculture/debates. F. Lauriston Bullard, Edward Everette Hale, "Lincoln's Conquest of New England," *Abraham Lincoln Quarterly*, Vol. 3, No. 2, 49.
50. Henry B. Rankin, *Personal Recollections of Abraham Lincoln* (New York: Putnam's Sons, 1916), 184.
51. Rankin, 159–160.
52. Rankin, 185.
53. Allen Gueizo, *Lincoln and Douglas: The Debates that Defined America* (New York: Simon and Schuster, 2008), 257.
54. Gustave Koerner's Recollections of the 15 October 1858 Alton Debate, housedivided.dickinson.edu/node/27535.
55. Lincoln to Gustave Loerner, 15 July 1858. *Collected Works of Abraham Lincoln*, Vol. 2, 503–504.
56. White, 283.
57. Lincoln v. Douglas, Election Results of the 1858 Campaign for the United States Senate, Lincoln.lib.niu.edu/elect58_resw_040701_400.
58. Rankin, 185–186.
59. Lincoln to Dr. Anson G. Henry, 19 November 1858. *Collected Works of Abraham Lincoln*, Vol. 3, 339–340.
60. Ibid.
61. Irving Stone, "Mary Todd Lincoln: A Final Judgment?" *Lincoln Monographs* (Springfield, Illinois: Abraham Lincoln Association, 1973).

Chapter 9

1. Rankin, 181.
2. Ronald C. White, Jr., *A Lincoln: A Biography* (New York: Random House, 2009), 340.
3. Ibid.
4. Stephen A. Douglas to Lincoln, 30 July 1858; Lincoln to S. A. Douglas, 31 July 1858, *Collected Works of Abraham Lincoln*, Vol. 2.
5. Seventh Debate: Alton, Illinois. nps.gov/liho/historyculture/debate7.htm.
6. Darrin, 13.
7. White, 308. cooper.edu/about/history. nyc-architecture.com/LES/LES025.htm.
8. "Address at Cooper Institute, New York City," *Collected Works of Abraham Lincoln*, Vol. 3, 522–550.
9. Lincoln to Mary Todd Lincoln, 4 March 1860. Abraham Lincoln Papers at the Library of Congress.
10. Ibid.
11. White, 305.
12. Geoffrey Johnson, "Forgotten Fate of the Place Where Lincoln Won His Party's Nomination," *Chicago Magazine*, 25 May 2010. "Wigwam, 1860," *The Electronic Encyclopedia of Chicago* (Chicago, 2005). "Republican Wigwam Erected at Chicago," Chicago History Museum.
13. "Sarah Childress Polk," tennesseeencyclopedia. net, version 2.0. whitehouse.org/about/firstladies/sarah polk. Aside from being tutored at home, Sarah Childress attended the Murfreesboro Common School and the Bradley Academy in Murfreesboro, Abercrombie's Boarding School in Nashville, and the Moravian Female Academy, in Salem, North Carolina, for eleven years of formal education.
14. White, 328.
15. Pratt, *The Personal Finances of Abraham Lincoln*, 109–110.
16. White, 325–326.
17. White, 329.
18. Rankin, 191–192.
19. John Grinspan, "Young Men for War: The Wide Awakes and Lincoln's 1860 Presidential Campaign," *Journal of American History*, Vol. 96, September 2009, 357–378.
20. *The Independent*, 4 April 1895.
21. Rankin, 194.
22. Pratt, 110.
23. lawpracticeofabrahamlincoln.org/reference/reference percent20html percent20files. From 1862 to 1865, the law practice of Lincoln and Herndon dropped from less than a hundred cases a year to practically nothing.
24. Pratt, 110. The committee also paid the ninety-seven-dollar Chenery House bill of the delegation, which came to Springfield to formally notify Lincoln of his nomination, picked up the tabs of prominent politicians who visited and the basic charges of the big Republican rally in Springfield in August.
25. William H. Smith, "Old-time Campaigning and the Story of a Lincoln Campaign Song," *Journal of the Illinois State Historical Society*, Vol. 13, No. 1, April 1920, 23–31.
26. Ibid.
27. Ibid.
28. Ibid.
29. White, 343.
30. White, 340.
31. Goodwin, 265–266.
32. Mary Lincoln to Hannah Shearer, 30 October 1860, Turners, 65–66.

33. The Canal-Scrip Fraud, 16 October 1860. *Collected Works of Abraham Lincoln*, Vol. 4, 129.

34. White, 341.

35. Goodwin, 271.

36. White, 341.

37. White, 346.

38. *Presidential Elections, 1789–2008* (Washington, D.C.: Congressional Quarterly Press, 2010), 134, 224.

39. *The Kansas Chief*, 8 November 1860.

40. Harold Holzer, "Presidential Gifts, Circa 1860," *New York Times*, 12 February 2001. Lincoln to Cornelius F. McNeill, 6 April 1860. *Collected Works of Abraham Lincoln*, Vol. 4, 38.

41. Lincoln to Speed, 19 November 1860, *Collected Works of Abraham Lincoln*, Vol. 4, 141, 136.

42. Ibid.

43. White, 353.

44. *Executive Documents, House of Representatives, Second Session, Forty-Second Congress* (Washington, D.C.: Government Printing Office,), 400–402. The building was so well constructed, although destroyed in the Chicago Fire of 1871, that the wall refused to fall.

45. Epstein, 274.

46. Rankin, 185.

47. Epstein, 274.

48. Ibid.

49. William A. Evans, *Mrs. Abraham Lincoln: A Study of Her Personality and Her Influence on Lincoln* (New York: Alfred A. Knopf, 1932), 169.

50. Mary E. Latrobe to Dolley Madison, 12 April 1809. The Papers of James Madison Digital Edition, J.C. A. Stagg, editor, University of Virginia. Bernadine Morris, "How First Ladies Dressed for the Ball," *New York Times*, 16 February 1990.

51. measuringworth.com. This Internet site, recommended by reference librarian Denise Shanks at the Lexington Public Library, was funded by the University of Illinois–Chicago, headed by two UI–C economics professors and had a board of advisors that included respected economists from institutions across the nation.

52. White, 164.

53. Lincoln Home, Historical Furnishings Report, Section D: Evidence of Original Furnishings, National Park Service, Department of the Interior, 14.

54. Helm, 155–156.

55. "Lincolniana, Furniture from the Lincoln Home," *Journal of the Illinois Historical Society*, Vol. 44, No. 1, 61–63, Spring 1951.

56. National Park Service, Lincoln Home, Historic Furnishings Report, 14.

57. Baker, 164. Brian Wolly, "Lincoln's Whistle-stop Trip to Washington," *Smithsonian Magazine*, 9 February 2011.

58. Helen Nicolay, *Personal Traits of Abraham Lincoln* (New York: Century Company, 1912), 154.

59. Epstein, 278.

60. On February 3, 1862, Lincoln wrote Herndon, "Yours of January 30th. is just received. Do just as you say about the money matters. As you well know, I have not time to write a letter of respectable length. God bless you, says your friend, A. Lincoln." *Collected Works of Abraham Lincoln*, Vol. 5, 118. On February 19, 1863, Lincoln telegraphed Herndon, "Would you accept a job of about a month's duration at St. Louis, five dollars a day & mileage. Answer. A. Lincoln." *Collected Works of Abraham Lincoln*, Vol. 6, 111.

61. Farewell Address at Springfield, Illinois, 11 February 1861, *Collected Works of Abraham Lincoln*, Vol. 4, 190.

62. Helm, 162–163; Wolly, "Lincoln's Whistle-Stop Trip to Washington."

63. William T. Coggeshall, *Lincoln Memorial* (Columbus: Ohio State Journal, 1865), 25.

64. Helm, 164.

65. Coggeshall, 55.

66. Wolly, "Lincoln's Whistle-stop Trip to Washington." Paul Grondahl, "150 Years Later, Abe Remembered in Albany," *Albany Times-Union*, 18 February 2011.

67. Donna D. McCreary, *Fashionable First Lady: The Victorian Wardrobe of Mary Lincoln* (Charlestown, Indiana: Lincoln Presentations, 2007), 27.

68. Wolly, "Lincoln's Whistle-stop Trip to Washington."

69. Christopher Gray, "Where Lincoln Tossed and Turned," *New York Times*, 27 September 2009. McCreary, 27–28.

70. Ibid. Mary Lincoln to Hannah Shearer, 28 March 1861, Turners, 81.

71. Ibid. Thomas Allen, *Intelligence in the Civil War* (Washington, D.C.: Central Intelligence Agency, 2007), cia.gov/library/publications/additional-publications/civil-war/SML.

72. Christopher Gray, "Where Lincoln Tossed and Turned." Fred Nicklarson, "The Secession Winter and the Committee of Five," *Pennsylvania History* (University Park: Pennsylvania Historical Association), Vol. 38, No. 4, October 1971. Edward C. Papenfuse, Maryland State Archives, Special Collections, "Ferrandini, Cipriano (1823–1910)." 3520–14473.

73. Allen, *Intelligence in the Civil War*. Wolly, "Lincoln Whistle-Stop Trip to Washington."

74. *New York World*, 25 February 1861.

75. *National Intelligencer*, 26 February 1861.

76. Papenfuse, "Ferrandini, Cipriano (1823–1910)."

77. *National Intelligencer*, 26 February 1861.

78. White, 382–383.

79. William O. Stoddard, *Inside the White House in War Times* (New York: Charles L. Webster, 1890), 52.

80. "Willard Hotel," *National Register of Historic Places*, National Park Service. A.K. Sandoval-Strausz, *Hotel: An American History* (New Haven, Conn.: Yale University Press, 2007), 253. Elizabeth Smith Brownstein, "The Willard Hotel," *White House History*, No. 31, 5–19.

81. Ronald. D. Rietveld, "The Lincoln White House Community," *Journal of the Abraham Lincoln Association*, Vol. 20, No. 2, Summer 1999. Brownstein, "The Willard Hotel."

82. Rietveld, "The Lincoln White House Community."

Chapter 10

1. Helm, 168. White, 387–388.

2. White, 388.

3. White, 350.

4. Mary Lincoln to David Davis, 17 January 1861, Turners, 71–72.

5. Ibid.

6. White, 396.

7. William Seward to Abraham Lincoln, *Collected Works of Abraham Lincoln*, Vol. 4, 273. Allen Gueizo, *Abraham Lincoln: Redeemer President* (Grand Rapids, Michigan: Wm. B. Eerdmans, 1999), 256. Daniel W. Crofts, *Reluctant Confederates: Upper South Unionists in the Seces-*

sion Crisis (Chapel Hill: University of North Carolina Press, 1993), 221–224.

8. Lincoln to William H. Seward, 4 March 1861. *Collected Works of Abraham Lincoln*, Vol. 4, 273.

9. Holtz, "Presidential Gifts, Circa 1860," *New York Times*, 12 February 2001. White, 388. Wheatland, a seventeen-room, Federal-styled brick house was Buchanan's home near Lancaster, Pennsylvania. "Wheatland," nps.gov.

10. *Washington Evening Star*, 2 March 1861.

11. Ibid.

12. "Clerks of the House," house.gov/people/office/clerks. "Benjamin B. French," loc.gov/service.

13. Helm, 171. White, 388–389. Grimsley, "Six Months in the White House," 46. Allan Nevins, "He Did Hold Lincoln's Hat," *American Heritage*, Vol. 10, No. 2, February 1959.

14. "An Observation of Lincoln's Inaugural Ceremony," loc.gov/exhibits/treasures/inaugural-exhibit.

15. *New York Times*, 5 March 1861.

16. Albert G. Riddle, *Recollections of War Times: Reminiscences of Men and Events in Washington* (New York: G. P. Putnam's Sons, 1895), 15, 17.

17. William Seale, *The President's House* (Washington, D.C.: White House Historical Association, 1986), Vol. 1, 363. Grimsley, 46.

18. "Reply to a New York Delegation." 4 March 1861. *Collected Works of Abraham Lincoln*, Vol. 4, 272–273.

19. Ibid.

20. Grimsely, 48.

21. *Washington Evening Star*, 5 March 1861.

22. "Mrs. President Lincoln," Collection Number P 0406. Indiana Historical Society. McCready, 28–30.

23. *New York Times*, 5 March 1861.

24. Lincoln to Winfield Scott, 9 March 1861. *Collected Works of Abraham Lincoln*, Vol. 4, 279.

25. *Washington Evening Star*, 5 March 1861.

26. Grimsley, 47.

27. Betty G. Monkman, *The White House: Its Historic Furnishings and First Families* (New York: Abbeville Press, 2000), 20. Seale, Vol. 1, 39–47.

28. Monkman, 26–27.

29. Monkman, 28–30.

30. Monkman, 110–121. Seale, Vol. 1, 341, 346.

31. Annual Reports, Commissioner of Public Buildings, Requisition Book 22, National Archives and Records Administration, RG 42.

32. Measuringworth.com.

33. Monkman, 123. Rietveld, "The Lincoln White House Community."

34. Glyndon G. Van Duesen, "The Life and Career of William Henry Seward 1801–1872," *University of Rochester Library Bulletin*, Vol. 31, No. 1, Autumn 1978. Grimsley, 49.

35. *Washington Evening Star*, 9 March 1861.

36. Ibid. Stoddard, 53.

37. *Washington Evening Star*, 9 March 1861.

38. Ibid.

39. Ibid.

40. Helen Nicolay, *Lincoln's Secretary: A Biography of John G. Nicolay* (New York: Longmans, Green and Company, 1949), 79.

41. *Washington Evening Star*, 10 March 1861.

42. "President Lincoln's Cottage at the Soldiers' Home," nps.gov.

43. Mary Lincoln to Hannah Shearer, 28 March 1861, Turners, 81–82.

44. Chester G. Hearn, *Lincoln, the Cabinet and the Generals* (Baton Rouge: Louisiana State University Press, 2010), 47, 55–59. David H. Donald, *Lincoln* (New York: Simon and Schuster, 1996), 259.

45. William Howard Russell, *My Diary, North and South* (Boston: T.O.H.P. Burnham, 1863), 43–44.

46. Seale, Vol. 2, 367.

47. Ibid.

48. Grimsley, 49–50.

49. Grimsley, 51

50. Russell, 41–42.

51. Ellison, *A Man Seen But Once: Cassius Marcellus Clay* , 111.

52. Grimsley, 52.

53. John Speer, *The Life of Gen. James Lane, Liberator of Kansas* (Garden City, Kansas: John Speer, 1896), 236–238. "Long Bridge, Lincoln's Time, Washington, D.C. Union Troops Guarding a Bridge Over the Potomac River to Virginia to Prevent Infiltration by Confederate Spies," National Archives and Records Administration, Commission of Fine Arts, Identifier 518223. Grimsley, 51.

54. Lincoln to Thomas H. Hicks and George W. Brown, 20 April 1861, *Collected Works of Abraham Lincoln*, Vol. 4, 340–341. Grimsley, 53.

55. James Blake to Simon Cameron, 26 April 1861. National Archives and Records Administration, Record Group 42.

56. Grimsley, 55.

57. Ibid.

58. Ibid.

59. "John J. Crittenden," *Kentucky Encyclopedia*, 240–241. Helm, 175.

60. Grimsley, 56.

61. Grimsley, 56–57.

62. Robert J. Schneller, *A Quest for Glory: A Biography of Rear Admiral John A. Dahlgren* (Washington, D.C.: Navy Institute Press, 1995), 185. "Rear Admiral John A. Dahlgren," Naval History Heritage Command, history. navy.mil/bios/dahlgren. Robert V. Bruce, *Lincoln and the Tools of War* (Champagne-Urbana: University of Illinois Press, 1989), 210. Schneller, Dahlgren's biographer wrote that Lincoln often dropped by the Navy Yard because gadgets, weapons and munitions were most interesting to him.

63. *Washington Evening Star*, 10 May 1861.

64. Grimsley, 58. green-wood.com/about/history.

65. Grimsley, 58.

Chapter 11

1. Allen C. Guelzo, *Abraham Lincoln: Redeemer President* (Grand Rapids, Michigan: Wm. B. Eerdman, 2002), 112.

2. Monkman, 19–23.

3. Monkman, 25.

4. Ibid.

5. Monkman, 26–28.

6. "Abigail Adams," firstladies.org/biographies/first ladies.

7. William Seale, *The President's House* (Washington, D.C.: White House Historical Association, 1986), Vol. 1, 115.

8. Monkman, 32–41.

9. Benjamin H. Latrobe to Dolley Payne Todd Madison, 21, 22 March 1809, Mary Elizabeth Latrobe to Dolley Payne

Todd Madison, 12 April 1809. *The Dolley Madison Digital Edition*, Holly C. Shulman, editor (Charlottesville, Virginia: University of Virginia Press, rotunda, 2004).

10. Seale, Vol. 1, 115. Mary Jane M. Dowd, *Records of the Office of Public Buildings and Public Parks of the Nation's Capital* (Washington, D.C.: National Archives and Records Administration, 1992), 28–29.

11. Seale, Vol. 1, 152–154. Monkman, 71.

12. Harry Ammon, *James Monroe: The Quest for National Identity* (Charlottesville: University of Virginia Press, 1990), 533–535. Seale, Vol. 1, 152–156. Monkman, 74.

13. Monkman, 51–74; Annon, 533–535.

14. Monkman, 74.

15. Monkman, 85.

16. Seale, Vol. 1, 315–316, 318.

17. Seale, Vol. 1, 318.

18. Seale, Vol. 1, 320–322.

19. Reports of the Secretary of the Interior, Serial Sets 741, 746, Misc. Doc. 11.

20. Seale, Vol. 1, 329–330.

21. Mary Lincoln to Ward Hill Lamon, 11 April 1861, Turners, 83.

22. Lincoln to Salmon P. Chase, 10 April 1861. *Collected Works of Abraham Lincoln*, Vol. 4, 407.

23. Grimsley, 58. "Memorandum: Appointment of Harrison G. Fitzhugh or Captain Johnson," *Collected Works of Abraham Lincoln*, Vol. 4, 71.

24. Mary Jane Dowd, *Records of the Office of Public Buildings and Public Parks of the Nation's Capital* (Washington: GPO, 1992), 28–29.

25. Monkman, 124.

26. Monkman, 125.

27. Monkman, 125, 129, 130.

28. Monkman, 132–133.

29. *Statement of Appropriations and Expenditures from the National Treasury for Public and Private Purposes in the District of Columbia from July 16, 1790, to June 30, 1876*, 45th Congress, Second Session, Ex. Doc. No. 84 (Washington, D.C., Government Printing Office, 1878), 39. Treasury of the United States, Ledgers and Cancelled Checks, 1851–1866, National Archives and Records Administration, RG 42.

30. Lincoln to Salmon Chase, 15 June 1861. *Collected Works of Abraham Lincoln*, Vol. 4, 407.

31. Epstein, 342–343.

32. Public Laws of the United States of America Passed at the First Session of the Thirty-seventh Congress, 1861 (Boston: Little, Brown, 1862), 350–352.

33. Ibid. Treasury of U.S., Ledgers and Cancelled Checks. NARA, RG42.

34. Grimsley, 61.

35. After the octagonal mausoleum was built in downtown Chicago in 1881, Douglas's remains were moved in the tomb that featured a nine-foot-tall statue of Douglas atop a forty-five foot tall column. "Douglas Tomb," Illinois Historic Preservation Agency.

36. *New York Times*, 4 June 1861.

37. *Washington Evening Star*, July 1861.

38. *New York Herald*, 11 July 1861. *Washington Evening Star*, 17 July 1861.

39. William Watts Hart Davis, *History of the 104th Pennsylvania Regiment* (Philadelphia, Pennsylvania: J.H. Rogers, 1866), 32–33.

40. *Washington Evening Star*, 18 December 1861. The *Trent* incident occurred the previous month when Capt.

Charles Wilkes, commander of the USS *San Jacinto* intercepted the British mail steamer with Confederate Commissioners James M. Mason and John Slidell on board. They were on their way to Europe to solicit funds for the Confederate States of America. The two men and their secretaries were brought to shore and placed in prison in Boston. Britain demanded release of the prisoners and ordered troops into Canada to prepare for a conflict because the seizure took place in international waters. Seward apologized for the incident and all was well. "The Trent Affair," loc.gov.ammem/today/nov08.

41. *Baltimore Sun*, 19 December 1861. *New York Herald*, 16 December 1861.

42. *New York Times*, 16 December 1861.

43. *Daily Alta California*, 12 May 1862.

44. Ibid.

45. Monkman, 83–84.

46. *Daily Alta California*, 12 May 1862.

47. Monkman, 125–129.

48. *Daily Alta California*, 12 May 1862.

49. Monkman, 132.

50. Stoddard, 63.

Chapter 12

1. Seale, Vol. 1, 142–156. Harry Ammon, *James Monroe: The Quest for National Identity* (Charlottesville: University of Virginia Press, 1990), 533–535.

2. Stephen Dragget, *Congressional Research Service Report for Congress* (RS22926) (Washington, D.C.: Congressional Research Service, Library of Congress, Washington), 1.

3. Monkman, 74.

4. Ibid.

5. Ammon, 533–535.

6. *Statement of Appropriations and Expenditures from the National Treasury for Public and Private Purposes in the District of Columbia from July 16, 1790 to June 30, 1876*, 38–39, 40–41. (Washington, D.C.: Government Printing Office, 1862). measuringworth.com.

7. *Statement of Appropriations and Expenditures from the National Treasury for Public and Private Purposes in the District of Columbia from July 16, 1790 to June 30, 1876* (Washington, D.C.: Government Printing Office, 1878), 13.

8. *Reports of Committees of the House of Representatives Made During the Second Session of the Thirty-Seventh Congress* (Washington, D.C.: Government Printing Office, 1862) Committee Report 16, Loyalty of Clerks and Other Persons Employed by the Government, 1. (Hereafter, *Reports of the Committee*.)

9. Ibid., 2.

10. Ibid., 84–85.

11. House of Representatives Bills 388, 302, 617. Thirty-seventh Congress, First Session.

12. *Public Laws of the United States of America Passed at First Session of the Thirty-Seventh Congress; 1861* (Boston, Massachusetts: Little, Brown, 1861), 350–352.

13. Ibid., 350–352, 366–367.

14. Ibid. measuringworth.com.

15. Epstein, 342.

16. Mary Lincoln to Caleb B. Smith, 8 September 1861, Turners, 101–102.

17. Mary Lincoln to Simon Cameron, 12 September 1861, Turners, 102.

18. *Reports of the Committee*, 29.

19. *The Alleghanian*, 30 May 1861. *Reports of the Committee*, 29.

20. *Reports of the Committee*, 29.

21. Mary Lincoln to John F. Potter, 13 September 1861, Turners, 103–104.

22. *Reports of Committee*, 84–85. Charles F. Anderson testified against both Thomas Burns, a doorkeeper and _____ Edwards. A messenger, as uttering disloyal comments.

23. Pratt, 82.

24. Lincoln to Lorenzo Thomas, 16 November 1861, *Collected Works of Abraham Lincoln*, Vol. 5, 25.

25. *New York Herald*, 10 August 1862.

26. John D. Lawson, *American State Trials* (St. Louis, Missouri, F. H. Tomas Law Book Company, 1918), Vol. 12, 494.

27. Asher L. Hinds, *Hinds' Precedents of the House of Representatives, Including Reference to Provisions of the Constitution, The Laws and Decisions of the United States Senate* (Washington, D.C.: Government Printing Office, 1907), Vol. 3, 25–26.

28. Robert Spellman, "Defying the Law in the 19th Century: Journalistic Culture and Source Protection Privilege," paper presented to the International Communications Association, 26 May 2004, New Orleans Sheraton, New Orleans, Louisiana, 21–23.

29. Spellman, 27. W. A. Swanberg, *Sickles, The Incredible* (New York: Charles Scribner's Sons, 1956), 137–138.

30. "Sitting Presidents and Vice-Presidents Who Have Testified Before Congressional Committees" (prepared by the Senate Historical Office and the Senate Library, 2004), 1.

31. Lincoln to Caleb B. Smith, 8 January 1863, *Collected Works of Abraham Lincoln*, Vol. 6, 49–50.

32. Mary Jane M. Dowd, *Records of the Office of Public Buildings and Public Parks of the Nation's Capital* (Washington, D.C.: Government Printing Office, 1992), 28–28. The Office of the Commissioner of Public Buildings was abolished in 1871 and the duties and functions were transferred to the office of the Chief Engineer of the Army.

33. French Family Papers, Benjamin B. French's Diary, Library of Congress, 385.

34. Ibid.

35. French Diary, 374.

36. Ibid., 377.

37. Report of the Secretary of the Interior, Commissioner of Public Buildings, November 8, 1861. Serial Set, 1117, 603, 849.

38. French Diary, 381.

39. Michael Spangler, "Benjamin Brown French in the Lincoln Period," *White House History*, No. 8, Fall 2000, 13.

40. Ibid., 385, 389.

41. Ibid., 385.

42. Ibid., 383.

43. French Diary, Sunday, December 22, 1861, 383.

44. *Message of the President of the United States and Accompanying Documents to the Two Houses of Congress, at the Commencement of the First Session of the Thirty-eighth Congress* (Washington, D.C.: Government Printing Office), 1863, 661–662.

45. Lincoln to Benjamin B. French, 25 March 1864, *Collected Works of Abraham Lincoln*, Vol. 7, 266–267.

46. Ibid.

47. Spangler, 9.

48. *Statements of Appropriations and Expenditures from the National Treasury for Public and Private Purposes in the District of Columbia from July 16, 1790 to June 30, 1876* (Washington, D.C.: Government Printing Office, 1878), 43.

49. Spangler, 10.

50. French Diary, Sunday, December 16, 1862, 382.

51. *National Intelligencer*, 14, 18 December 1861.

52. French Diary, 382–383.

53. Ibid.

54. Ibid.

55. *Statement of Appropriations and Expenditures from the National Treasury for Public and Private Purposes in the District of Columbia from July 16, 1790 to June 30, 1876* (Washington, D.C.: Government Printing Office, 1878), 39, 41.

Chapter 13

1. Stoddard, 173.

2. Stoddard, 174.

3. Stoddard, 52.

4. Mary Lincoln to John Fry, 20 June 1861, Turners, 91.

5. Records of the Chief of Ordnance, 1861. National Archives and Records Administration, RG 156.

6. Stoddard, 62.

7. Ibid.

8. Mary Clemmer Ames, *Ten Years in Washington, Life and Scenes in the National Capital as a Woman Saw Them* (Hartford, Connecticut: A.D. Worthington, 1874), 234–235.

9. Ames, 238.

10. Ibid.

11. Ibid. "Julia Gardiner Tyler," britannica.com. "Julia Gardiner Tyler," firstladies.org/biographies.

12. Stoddard, 60.

13. Noah Brooks, *Washington in Lincoln's Time* (New York: Century Company, 1895), 4–7.

14. Stoddard, 88.

15. "Abraham and Mary Lincoln: A House Divided," Public Broadcasting System documentary produced by David Grubin, 2001.

16. thelincolnlog.org, March 1861 to April 1865.

17. Jennifer Fleischner, *Mrs. Lincoln and Mrs. Keckly* (New York: Broadway Books, 2003), 204. Harry E. Pratt and Ernest E. East, *Mrs. Lincoln Refurbished the White House* (Harrogate, Tennessee: Lincoln Memorial University, 1945), 2.

18. *Washington Evening Star*, 2, 8, 10, 15, 22, 23, 23 and 29 January.

19. *New York Times* 16 December 1861. Mary Lincoln to Ruth Harris, 21 November 1861, Turners, 115.

20. *New York Times*, 9 February 1862.

21. Ibid.

22. *The Washington Evening Star*, 6 February 1862.

23. William O. Stoddard, *Dispatches From Lincoln's White House* (Lincoln, Nebraska: University of Nebraska Press, 2002), 58.

24. Adam Goodheart, "A Peevish Prince, A Hairy-handed President, A Disastrous Dinner Party," *New York Times*, 2 August 2011.

25. Ibid.

26. Ibid.

27. Ibid.

28. Frederick W. Seward, *Seward: At Washington, Senator and Secretary of State* (New York: Derby and Miller, 1890), 607.

29. Grimsley, 70.

30. Grimsley, 69.

31. Goodheart.

32. Grimsley, 70.

33. Goodheart.

34. Ibid.

35. *Washington Evening Star*, 17 August 1861.

Chapter 14

1. *Baltimore Sun*, 24, 27 May 1861. Elmer E. Ellsworth biography, Elmer E. Ellsworth Archival Connection, Kenosha Civil War Museum Archives, Kenosha, Wisconsin. Ellsworth had recruited and trained a precision drill team that toured twenty cities in 1860. By giving drill exhibitions in New York and Boston, Ellsworth had enough money to take his team of Zouaves to the Wigwam in Chicago when Lincoln was nominated. He entered Lincoln's law office, not to really study law, but to organize an Illinois militia for what he saw as the coming war. Charles A. Ingraham, "Colonel Elmer E. Ellsworth, First Hero of the Civil War," *Wisconsin Magazine of History*, Vol. 1, No. 4, June 1918, 18–20.

2. *Baltimore Sun*, 27 May 1861. Drawing of Ellsworth's funeral in the East Room, Library of Congress, Waud, No. 527.

3. Lincoln to Ephraim D. and Phoebe Ellsworth, 25 May 1861, *Collected Works of Abraham Lincoln*, Vol. 1, 386.

4. Ibid.

5. Harry C. Tarshis and Rebecca Blair, *Lincoln's Constant Ally: Colonel Edward D. Baker* (Portland: Oregon Historical Society, 1960), 157–158, White, 456–457. Elijah R. Kennedy, *The Contest for California: How Colonel E. D. Baker Saved the Pacific States for the Union* (Whitefish, Montana: Kessinger, 2005), 166.

6. Tarshis and Blair, 157–158. senate.gov/artand history/history/minute/Senator_Killed_In_Battle. When the sculpture of was completed in 1868, the manuscript he was holding contained these words from the last speech he gave in the Senate in August 1861. "There will be some graves reeking with blood, watered by tears of affection. There will be some privation. There will be some loss of luxury. There will be somewhat more need of labor to procure the necessaries of life. When that is said, all is said. If we have the country, the whole country, the Union, the Constitution, Free Government, with all these will return all the blessings of a well ordered civilization. The path of the country will be a career of greatness and glory, such as our Fathers in the olden time foresaw in the dim vision of years yet to come; and such as would have been ours today had it not been for the treason for which Senator [John Breckinridge] too often seeks to apologize." *Washington Evening Star*, 13 April 1868.

7. *Washington Evening Star*, 28, 29 October 1861.

8. Epstein, 345.

9. White, 457. Helm, 191. The other four verses of Willie's poem are as follows. "His voice is silent in the hall, Which oft his presence graced, No more he'll hear the loud acclaim Which rang from place to place. No squeamish notions filled his breast, The Union was his theme, No surrender no compromise, His day thought and night dream.

His country has her part to play, To'rds those he left behind, His widow and children all, We must always keep in mind." Helm, 191–192.

10. *New York Herald*, 29 November 1861. thelincolnlog.org, December 1861.

11. Turners, 155.

12. *Washington Evening Star*, 2, 8, 10, 15, 22, 23, 24 29, 1862. *New York Herald*, 29 January 1862. *Journal of Benjamin B. French*, French Family Papers, Library of Congress, 385.

13. White, 475. M. D. Burkhart, "Lincoln's First Levee," *Journal of the Illinois State Historical Society*, Vol. 11, April 1918, 386–390.

14. Stoddard, 121.

15. knox.news.com/2012/feb/04/union-scores-major-victories-at-two-tennessee-forts.

16. *Washington Evening News*, 4 February 1862. Baker, 206.

17. restaurant-ingthroughhistory.com2008/11/6/famous-in-its-day-maillard. Baker, 206.

18. *Washington Evening Star*, 6 February 1862. Burkhart, 388.

19. Erika Holst, "One of the Best Women I Ever Knew: Abraham Lincoln and Rebecca Pomeroy," *Journal of the Abraham Lincoln Association*, Summer 2000, Vol. 31, No. 2.

20. *Washington Evening Star*, 7, 10 February 1962. Holst, "One of the Best Women I Ever Knew."

21. Holst, *Washington Evening Star*, 21 February 1862.

22. *The Diary of Edward Bates*, edited by Howard K. Beale (Washington, D.C.: Government Printing Office, 1923), 235.

23. Helm, 197–198.

24. *Gettysburg Times*, 25 February 1964. French Diary, Sunday, March 2, 1861, 389.

25. Ibid.

26. Holst, "One of the Best Women I Ever Knew." Lincoln to Ninian Edwards, 19 June 1861, *Collected Works of Abraham Lincoln*, Vol. 4, 412. Lincoln appointed Edwards captain and commissary of subsistence. Pratt 165.

27. Baker, 212–213.

28. *Washington Evening Star*, 20 March 1862.

29. Holst, "One of the Best Women I Ever Knew."

30. Mary Lincoln to Ruth Harris, 17 May 1862; Mary Lincoln to Ruth Harris, May 1862, Turners, 125–126.

31. Mary Lincoln to Julia Ann Sprigg, 29 May 1862, Turners, 127–128.

32. Ibid.

33. *Washington Evening Star*, 28 April 1862. *New York Herald*, 4 May 1862. David. R. Barbee, "The Musical Mr. Lincoln," *Abraham Lincoln Quarterly*, Vol. V, No. 8, December 1949, 442.

34. Mary Lincoln to Mrs. Charles Eames, 26 July 1862. Turners, 130–131.

35. Mary Lincoln to Benjamin B. French, 26 July 1862. Turners, 129–130. *New York Herald*, 17 July 1862.

36. Mary Lincoln to Benjamin B. French, 26 July 1862. Turners, 129–130.

37. *New York Herald*, 17 July 1862. *New York Tribune*, 10, 12 July 1862.

38. *Washington Evening Star*, 29 August 1862. *Philadelphia News*, 30 October 1862. A. Lincoln to Hiram P. Barney, 16 August 1862, *Collected Works of Abraham Lincoln*, Vol. 5, 378. Lincoln first met Barney, an associate of Thurlow Weed, when he gave the Cooper Union speech. Barney raised $35,000 for his 1860 campaign, and he was appointed collector for the Port of New York. James E.

Adams, "Lincoln and Hiram Barney," *Journal of the Illinois State Historical Society*, Winter 1957, Vol. 50, No. 4, 343–376. *New York Times*, 28 December 1863.

39. Mary Lincoln to Abraham Lincoln, 13 November 1862, Turners, 140–141.

40. Mary Lincoln to Hannah Shearer, 20 November 1864, Charles V. Darbin, "Your Truly Attached Friend, Mary Lincoln," *Journal of the Illinois State Historical Society*, Vol. 44, No. 1, Spring 1951, 25.

41. David R. Barbee, "The Musical Mr. Lincoln," *The Abraham Lincoln Quarterly* (Abraham Lincoln Association, Springfield Illinois, 1949), Vol. 5, No. 8, December 1949, 437–439.

42. Helm, 199.

43. Barbee, "The Musical Mr. Lincoln."

44. Thomas Moore, *Irish Melodies* (London: Longman, Brown, Green and Longmans, 1852), 58.

45. Barbee, "The Musical Mr. Lincoln."

46. Ibid.

47. Elizabeth Smith Brownstein, *Lincoln's Other White House: The Untold Story of the Man and His Presidency* (Hoboken, New Jersey: John Wiley, 2005), 77–78.

48. Noah Brooks, *Glimpses of Lincoln in War Time* (New York: Century, 1895), 47.

49. whitehouse.gov/history/firstladies. Seale, Vol. 1, 307. Joan E. Cashman, *First Lady of the Confederacy* (Cambridge, Massachusetts: Belknap Press of Harvard University Press, 2006), 64. Monkman, 115.

50. Monkman, 115.

51. Brooks, 47–48.

52. Ibid.

53. Mary Lincoln to Abraham Lincoln, 2 November 1862, The Abraham Lincoln Papers at the Library of Congress.

54. Ibid.

55. Ibid.

56. Lincoln to Margaret Wickliffe Preston, 21 August 1862, *Collected Works of Abraham Lincoln*, Vol. 5, 386. Guthrie was president of the Louisville and Nashville Railroad and had been Pierce's secretary of the treasury. Boyle, for much of the war, was commander of Union troops in Kentucky. Mary Lincoln to Jeremiah T. Boyle, 21 August 1862, Turners, 131.

57. Charles Moore, editor, *Joint Select Committee to Investigate the Charities and Reformatory Institutions in the District of Columbia* (Washington, D.C.: Government Printing Office, 1898), 32–36.

58. Mary Lincoln to Elizabeth Grimsley, 29 September 1861, Turners, 105–106.

59. Ibid.

60. Mary Lincoln to Gen. Daniel Sickles, 31 (?) September 1862. Turners, 133–132.

61. "President Lincoln's Cottage at the Soldiers' Home," npr.gov.

62. Lincoln to Mrs. A. Lincoln, 9 November 1862, *Collected Works of Abraham Lincoln*, Vol. 5, 492.

63. "President Lincoln's Cottage at the Soldiers' Home," nps.gov.

64. loc.gov/ammem/cwphtml/tl1862.

65. *Boston Journal*, 12 November 1862. *Philadelphia Press*, 27 November 1862. Helm, 204.

66. Glenna R. Schroeder-Lein, *Lincoln and Medicine* (Carbondale: Southern Illinois University Press, 2012), 66. Moore, 32–36.

67. Mary Lincoln to Edwin D. Morgan, 13 November 1862. Turners, 141–142.

Chapter 15

1. Edward Rosewater Diaries, 1860–1865, Thursday, January 1, 1863, War Department, Library of Congress, Manuscript Collection. White, 535.

2. White, 534–535. Benjamin B. French Diary, Sunday, January 3, 1863.

3. White, 535. Benjamin B. French Dairy, Sunday, January 3, 1863. McCreary, 81. The Emancipation Proclamation, Library of Congress. The Emancipation Proclamation, National Archives and Records Administration.

4. Mary Lincoln to Edwin M. Stanton, 11 February 1863; Mary Lincoln to Montgomery Meigs, no date; Mary Lincoln to Charles Harrington, March 30 and April 22, 1863. Turners, 146–150. *New York Herald*, 20 March 1863.

5. *New York Herald*, 11 February 1863.

6. Ibid. McCreary, 82.

7. Neil Harris, *Humbug: The Art of P. T. Barnum* (Chicago: University of Chicago Press, 1981), 163. *Frank Leslie's Illustrated Newspaper*, 28 February 1963. McCreary, 82.

8. Epstein, 387–391.

9. Ibid.

10. *New York Herald*, 3 March 1863. Benjamin B. French Diary, Tuesday, March 3, 1963.

11. *Washington Evening Star*, 6 April 1863.

12. Benjamin B. French Diary, Monday, February 18, 1863.

13. Noah Brooks, *Washington in Lincoln's Time* (New York: Century Company, 1895), 45–46, 55.

14. Brooks, 46–47.

15. Brooks, 47.

16. Ibid.

17. Brooks, 48.

18. Brooks, 54–55.

19. Brooks, 56.

20. Abraham Lincoln to Charles Sumner, 22 April 1863, *Collected Works of Abraham Lincoln*, Vol. 6, 185. Epstein, 394–395.

21. Epstein, 395. *Washington Evening Star*, 9 June 1863. Abraham Lincoln to Mary Lincoln, 9 June 1863, *Collected Works of Abraham Lincoln*, Vol. 6, 256.

22. Abraham Lincoln to Mary Lincoln, 11, 15 June, *Collected Works of Abraham Lincoln*, Vol. 6, 260, 277.

23. Abraham Lincoln to Mary Lincoln, 16 June 1863, *Collected Works of Abraham Lincoln*, Vol. 6, 283. *Washington Evening Star*, 22 June 1873.

24. Brownstein, 93.

25. *New York Times*, 3 July 1863. Epstein, 397. Clinton, 202–203.

26. Epstein, 398, Clinton 202–203.

27. Abraham Lincoln to Robert Lincoln, 3 July, 1863, *Collected Works of Abraham Lincoln*, Vol. 6, 314.

28. Stoddard, 206–207.

29. Stoddard, 207.

30. *New York Times*, 4 July 1863.

31. Epstein, 398. Holst, "One of the Best Women I Ever Knew."

32. Epstein, 400.

33. "White Mountains," plymouth.edu/museum-of-the-white-mountains. U.S. Forest Service Research Paper, NE-299 (U.S. Forest Service, Upper Darby, Pennsylvania, 1974), 4.

34. Abraham Lincoln to Mary Lincoln, 8 August 1863, *Collected Works of Abraham Lincoln*, Vol. 6, 371–372.

35. Ibid.

36. Ibid.

37. Allen C. Clark, "Abraham Lincoln in the National Capitol," *Journal of the Columbia Historic Association* (Washington, D.C.: The Society, 1925), 35. Whitman spent hundreds of hours visiting wounded in hospitals, writing letters for them and raising money to buy them food, clothes and other needed articles the government was unable to furnish. loc.gov/exhibits/treasures/whitman-wounddresser.

38. Abraham Lincoln to Mary Lincoln, 29 August 1863, *Collected Works of Abraham Lincoln*, Vol. 6, 421.

39. Abraham Lincoln to Mary Lincoln, 3 September, 6 September, 21 September 1863, *Collected Works of Abraham Lincoln*, Vol. 6, 431, 434, 474.

40. Abraham Lincoln to Mary Lincoln, 22 September 1863, *Collected Works of Abraham Lincoln*, Vol. 6, 474.

41. Abraham Lincoln to Mary Lincoln, 24 September 1863, *Collected Works of Abraham Lincoln*, Vol. 6, 479.

42. Abraham Lincoln to Mary Lincoln, 24 September 1863, *Collected Works of Abraham Lincoln*, Vol. 6, 479.

43. Helm, 216–217.

44. Turners, 155.

45. *Washington Chronicle*, 30 September 1863.

46. *Washington Evening Star*, 7 October 1863.

47. Leonard Grover, *Lincoln's Interest in the Theatre* (number ten of twenty-five numbered copies, Lincoln Financial Foundation Collection, 1909).

48. Abraham Lincoln to Lyman B. Todd, 15 October 1863, *Collected Works of Abraham Lincoln*, Vol. 6, 517.

49. Ibid.

50. Ibid.

51. Helm, 219.

52. Abraham Lincoln to Lyman B. Todd, 31 October 1863, *Collected Works of Abraham Lincoln*, Vol. 6, 553.

53. *Washington Evening Star*, 17 October 1863.

54. Abraham Lincoln to Judge Stephen T. Logan, 9 November 1863, *Collected Works of Abraham Lincoln*, Vol. 7, 7. *Washington Chronicle*, 19, 28 November 1863.

55. *Washington Chronicle*, 18, 21 November 1863.

56. Harvard's Unitarian Presidents, "Edward Everett (1846–1849)," harvardsquarelibrary.org.

57. Abraham Lincoln to Edward Everett, 20 November 1863, *Collected Works of Abraham Lincoln*, Vol. 7, 25.

58. Armond Goldman and E.J. Schmalstieg, "Abraham Lincoln's Gettysburg Illness," *Journal of Medical Biography* (Thousand Oaks, California: SAGE Publications, 2007), 15: 104–110.

59. Allen Nevins, editor, *Diary of the Civil War 1860–1865: George Templeton Strong* (New York: Macmillan, 1962), 239. Helm, 234. *Washington Evening Star, Washington Chronicle*, 28 November 1863. *New York Herald*, 29 November 1863. *New York Times*, 30 November 1863. *Chicago Tribune*, 1 December 1863. *Washington Evening Star*, 1, 3 December 1863. Telegrams between the Lincoln, *Collected Works of Abraham Lincoln*, Vol. 7, 34–35.

60. *Washington Chronicle*, 11 December 1863. *Washington Evening Star*, 15 December 1863.

61. Amnesty to Emily T. Helm, 14 December 1863. *Collected Works of Abraham Lincoln*, Vol. 7, 63–64. Lincoln signed the Proclamation of Amnesty and Reconstruction, with exceptions, on December 8, 1863. *Collected Works of Abraham Lincoln*, Vol. 7, 55–56.

62. Ibid.

63. Martha Todd White to Abraham Lincoln, 19 December 1863, Papers of Abraham Lincoln, Library of Congress.

64. Ibid.

65. Ibid.

66. Benjamin F. Butler to John G. Nicolay, 21 April 1863, Papers of Abraham Lincoln, Library of Congress.

67. "Benjamin Franklin Butler, 1818–1893." encyclopediavirginia.org/Butler-Benjamin_F_1818–1893.

68. O. Stewart to Abraham Lincoln, 27 April 1864. Papers of Abraham Lincoln, Library of Congress.

69. Grimsley, 57.

70. Helm, 181–182.

71. Helm, 182. Mrs. S. B. French to Abraham Lincoln, 20 April 1864, Papers of Abraham Lincoln, Library of Congress.

72. Helm, 182–183.

73. Randall, 307.

74. Martha Todd White to Abraham Lincoln, 14 March 1865, Papers of Abraham Lincoln, Library of Congress.

75. Randall, 307–308.

76. Levi Owen Todd to Abraham Lincoln, 12 September 1864, Abraham Lincoln Papers, Library of Congress.

77. Emilie Todd Helm to Abraham Lincoln, 30 September 1864, Abraham Lincoln Papers, Library of Congress.

78. Ibid.

79. Katherine Todd to Abraham Lincoln, 5, 18 September 1864, Papers of Abraham Lincoln, Library of Congress.

80. *The War of the Rebellion: A Compilation of the Official Records of the Union and Confederate Armies* (Washington, D.C.: Government Printing Office, 1880), Vol. 7, 1295, Vol. 8, 13–15.

81. Lincoln to Maj. Gen. Stephen G. Burbridge, 8 August 1864. *Collected Works of Abraham Lincoln*, Vol. 7, 484–485.

82. Mark E. Neely, Jr., "The Secret Treason of Abraham Lincoln's Brother-in-Law," *Journal of the Abraham Lincoln Association*, Vol. 17, No. 1, Winter 1996.

83. Nathaniel Henry Rhodes Dawson Collection, #00210, The Southern Historical Collection, University of North Carolina, Chapel Hill.

Chapter 16

1. Rivetveld, "The Lincoln White House Community."

2. *New York Times*, 2 January 1864.

3. Col. William H. Crook, edited by Margarita S. Gerry, *Through Five Administrations* (New York: Harper and Brothers, 1923), 17.

4. Crook, 5.

5. Crook, 6.

6. *Washington Evening Star, Washington Chronicle*, from 1 January through April 30, 1864.

7. *Washington National Republican*, 30 January 1864.

8. smithsonianmag.com/threaded/2013/04.

9. Epstein, 457.

10. Rivetveld, "The White House Community."

11. Mary Lincoln to Emmanuel Uhlfelder, Edwin A. Brooks, 1 April 1864, Turners, 173. Stoddard, *Inside the White House in War Times,* 175.

12. Mary Lincoln to George A. Hearn, 1 August 1864. Turners, 179.

13. Mary Lincoln to (possibly) A. T. Stewart, 16 April 1864, Turners, 174–175.

14. Mary Lincoln to Mary Jane Wells, 27 May 1864, Turners, 176.
15. Remarks at Opening of Patent Office Fair. *Collected Works of Abraham Lincoln*, Vol. 7, 198.
16. Epstein, 424.
17. Epstein, 426. Fred D. Grant, "Reminiscences of Gen. U. S. Grant," speech to the Illinois Commandry Loyal Legion of the United States, January 29, 1910, *Journal of the Illinois State Historical Society*, Vol. 7, April 1914. *The Century Magazine* (New York: The Century Company, 1897), 819.
18. Abraham Lincoln to William B. Astor and Robert B. Roosevelt, 8 November 1863, *Collected Works of Abraham Lincoln*, Vol. 7, 4. *New York Times*, 25 November 1863. green-wood.com/2011/august-birthdays.
19. John Niven, *Salmon P. Chase: A Biography* (London: Oxford University Press, 1955), 322. Thomas G. Belden and Marva R. Belden, *So Fell the Angels* (Boston: Little, Brown, 1956), 36. "Jay Cooke Story," stonelab.osu.edu/jay.cooke.
20. Belden and Belden, 18–28.
21. Ibid.
22. Belden and Belden, 101, 105. Peg A. Lamphier, *Kate Chase and William Sprague: Politics and Gender in a Civil War Marriage* (Lincoln: University of Nebraska Press, 2005), 121. Lamphier wrote that Sprague's treasonable activities were brushed under the rug after he voted guilty in Andrew Johnson's impeachment trial.
23. John Niven, "Lincoln and Chase: A Reappraisal," *Journal of the Abraham Lincoln Association*, Vol. 12, No. 1, 1991.
24. Belden and Belden, 104.
25. Belden and Belden, 110.
26. Belden and Belden, 170.
27. Belden and Belden, 80.
28. Belden and Belden, 108.
29. Thomas G. Belden, "Kate was Too Ambitious," *American Heritage*, Vol. 7, No. 5, August 1956.
30. Kerry L. Bryan, "Philadelphia Sanitary Fair of 1864," philadelphiaencycopedia.org/archives/civil-war-sanitary-fairs.
31. *Washington Evening Star*, 8 June 1864. White, 633.
32. Abraham Lincoln to Mary Lincoln, 19, 24 June 1864. *Collected Works of Abraham Lincoln*, Vol. 7, 401, 405.
33. Abraham Lincoln to Mary Lincoln, 29 June 1864. *Collected Works of Abraham Lincoln*, Vol. 7, 417. Brownstein, 75.
34. nps.gov/mono/history/culture/battle. White, 637.
35. *Washington Chronicle, Washington Evening Star*, 13 July 1864. White, 637.
36. *Washington Evening Star*, 15 July 1864. Brownstein, 69–72.
37. Brownstein, 76.
38. Abraham Lincoln to Mary Lincoln, 31 August, 8 September 1864, *Collected Works of Abraham Lincoln*, Vol. 7, 526, 544.
39. Abraham Lincoln to Mary Lincoln, 11 September 1864. *Collected Works of Abraham Lincoln*, Vol. 7, 547.
40. Epstein, 449–450.
41. Epstein, 450.
42. *Washington Evening Star*, 10 November 1864. usaelections.org/RESULTS/national.
43. *Washington Chronicle*, 5 December. *New York Herald*, 29 December 1864.
44. Abraham Lincoln to Gen. William T. Sherman, 26 December 1864. *Collected Works of Abraham Lincoln*, Vol. 8, 182.
45. *Washington Evening Star*, 2 January 1865. Ammi B. Young to Dr. William Whelan, 2 January 1865. oldnavyhospital.org/mrsoe/18650102–1.
46. McCready, 111. *Washington National Republican*, 13 January 1865.
47. Crook, 8.
48. Crook, 9.
49. Ibid.
50. *Washington Chronicle*, 9 February 1865.
51. *New York Herald*, 4 March 1865. Edwin M. Stanton to Ulysses S. Grant, 3 March 1865, *Collected Works of Abraham Lincoln*, Vol. 8, 330–331. U.S. Capitol Visitor's Center Timeline.
52. *Washington Evening Star*, 5 March 1865. Second Inaugural Address, *Collected Works of Abraham Lincoln*, Vol. 8, 332–333.
53. White, 667.
54. Ibid.
55. Ibid.
56. Ibid.
57. French Diary, Sunday, March 5, 1865.
58. White, 666–667.
59. Crook, 27.
60. Ibid.
61. *New York Times*, 7 March 1865. inaugural.senate.gov/day-event. si.edu/2008/06the-last-waltz.
62. *New York Times*, 8 March 1865.
63. Megan Bambino, "Document Deep Dive: The Menu from President Lincoln's Second Inaugural Ball," *Smithsonian*, January 15, 2013.
64. Ibid.
65. *Washington Evening Star*, 11 March 1865.
66. Abraham Lincoln to U.S. Grant, 23 March 1865. *Collected Works of Abraham Lincoln*, Vol. 8, 372–373. George P. A. Healy painting, "The Peacemakers," White House Historical Association.
67. Edwin Stanton to Abraham Lincoln, 25 March 1865, *Collected Works of Abraham Lincoln*, Vol. 8, 374.
68. Badeau was known for being belligerent, arguing with superiors and later suing Grant for a percentage of his memoirs, for which Badeau claimed he did the majority of the writing. *The New York Times*, 21 March 1895. William S. McFeely, *Grant: A Biography* (New York: W. W. Norton, 2002), 505.
69. Crook, 41–44.
70. Captain John S. Barnes, "With Lincoln," *Appleton's Magazine*, Vol. IX, No. 5, May 1907, 521–524, 743–751.
71. Abraham Lincoln to Mary Lincoln, 2 April 1865. *Collected Works of Abraham Lincoln*, Vol. 8, 381–382.
72. Abraham Lincoln to Mary Lincoln, 2 April 1865, *Collected Works of Abraham Lincoln*, Vol. 8, 384.
73. Crook, 58.
74. Crook, 65.
75. Crook, 66–67.
76. Ibid.

Chapter 17

1. nps.gov/foth/the-petersen-house.
2. Crook, 69.
3. Epstein, 504–509

4. memory.loc.gov/ammem/al/html/airtime.
5. Crook, 69.
6. Crook, 69–70.
7. Epstein, 458. Edward Seers, Jr., *Blood on the Moon: The Assassination of Abraham Lincoln* (Lexington: University Press of Kentucky, 2005), 270. *New York Times*, 14 March 1909.
8. Seer, 271.
9. Seer, 272–273.
10. Turners, 224.
11. Nancy Hill, "The Transformation of the Lincoln Tomb," *Journal of the Abraham Lincoln Association*, Vol. 27, No. 1, Winter 2005. Turner, 240.
12. Ibid. "Washington's Tomb," mountvernon.org.
13. Seer, 272–273. *Washington Evening Star*, 22 April 1865. French's Diary, 19 April 1865.
14. Thomas Schwartz, "First National Lincoln Monument Association: Part 1," Abraham Lincoln Presidential Library and Museum, 30 May 2011.
15. Hill, "The Transformation of the Lincoln Tomb."
16. Stephen B. Oats, *Abraham Lincoln: The Man Behind the Myths* (New York: Harper Collins, 2009), 180.
17. Crook, 70.
18. Mary Lincoln to Andrew Johnson, 29 April, 3 May 1865. Turners, 226–228.
19. Noah Brooks, *Lincoln Observed: Civil War Dispatches of Noah Brooks* (Baltimore, Maryland: JHU Press, 2002), 197.
20. Crook, 70–71.
21. *Statement of Appropriations and Expenditures from the National Treasury for Public and Private Purposes in the District of Columbia from July 16, 1790 to June 30, 1876*, 195.
22. Mary Lincoln to Gov. Richard J. Oglesby, 5 June 1865. Turners, 241–242.
23. Mary Lincoln to Gov. Richard J Oglesby, 10 June 1865. Turners, 243–244.
24. Mary Lincoln to Alexander Williamson, 15 June, 26 June, 17 August (2), 30 August, 9 September, 20 October, 9 November, 11 November, 26 November, 28 November, 1 December, 7 December, 13 December, 15 December, 16 December, 26 December, 29 December, 31 December 1865, Turners, 250–520.
25. Crook, 71.
26. Turner, 237–238.
27. James Cornelius, "Two New Stories about the Lincolns, 4 April 2011, Abraham Lincoln Presidential Library and Museum.
28. Pratt, 139–140.
29. Baker, 279.
30. Pratt, 134.
31. Mary Lincoln to David Davis, 27 June 1865. Turners, 254–255. William L. King, *Lincoln's Manager: David Davis* (Cambridge, Massachusetts: Harvard University Press, 1960), 233–234.
32. King, 233–234.
33. Mary Lincoln to David Davis, 12 September 1865. Turners, 273–274.
34. Ibid.
35. Ibid.
36. Ibid.
37. King, 233–234.
38. *New York Tribune*, 25 May 1865. King, 233–234.
39. Mary Lincoln to Dr. Anson Henry, 17 July 1865, Turners, 259–262.
40. Ibid. Mary Lincoln to Noah Brooks, 11 May 1866, Turners, 362.
41. Mary Lincoln to Sarah Bush Lincoln, 19 December 1867, Turners, 464–465.
42. Mary Lincoln to Sarah Bush Lincoln, 20 December 1867, Turners, 465.
43. Pratt, 138.
44. Mary Lincoln to Sally Orne, 31 August 1865, Turners, 269–270.
45. Mary Lincoln to Leeds and Miner, 11 November 1865, Turners, 281.
46. digitalhistory.uh.edu/exhibits/reconstruction/section1. David H. Fischer, *Liberty and Freedom: A Visual History of America's Founding Ideas* (London: Oxford University Press, 2005), 468–470. De Laboulays was instrumental in beginning the Statue of Liberty project.
47. Pratt, 135–136.
48. King, 237. Mary Lincoln to Alexander Williamson, 3 January 1866, Turners, 321.
49. Monkman, 134–135.
50. Mary Lincoln to Alexander Williamson, 26 January 1866, Turners, 330.
51. Turners, 312.
52. Mary Lincoln to David Davis, 11 January 1886, Turners, 324–325.
53. Mary Lincoln to Noah Brooks, 18 December 1865, Turners, 310–311. James Cornelius, "Newly Discovered Letters about Mary Lincoln's Desperation and Debt," 4 November 2012, Abraham Lincoln Presidential Library and Museum. King, 237.
54. King, 237.
55. Mary Lincoln to David Davis, 24 February 1867, Turners, 410.
56. Ibid.
57. Pratt, 140–141.
58. Charles Lachman, *The Last of the Lincolns: The Rise and Fall of a Great American Family* (New York: Union Square Press, 2008), 94. David Davis Mansion, daviddavismansion.org/history.
59. Lachman, 100–101.
60. Lachman, 103–104.
61. Lachman, 106–107.
62. King, 239. Turners, 412.
63. Mary Lincoln to David Davis, 4 March 1867. Turners, 414.
64. Mary Lincoln to David Davis, 6 March 1867, Turners, 315–416.
65. Lachman, 110.
66. Lachman, 110–111.
67. Turners, 431–475. Lachman, 110–119.
68. Mary Lincoln to W. H. Brady, September 1867, Turners, 434.
69. Mary Lincoln to W. H. Brady, 14 September 1967, Turners, 435. *New York World*, 7 October 1867. "Adam Wakeman," bioguide.congress.gov.
70. *New York World*, 7 October 1867.
71. Mary Lincoln to W. H. Brady, 18 September 1867, Turners, 435–436.
72. Mary Lincoln to W.H. Brady, 22 September 1867, Turners, 436.
73. Mary Lincoln to W. H. Brady, 25 September 1867, Turners, 437.
74. Baker, 280.
75. Mary Lincoln to David Davis, 17 November 1867, Turners, 457–458.

76. Lachman, 120.

77. James T. Hickey, "His Father's Son: Letters from the Robert Todd Lincoln Collection of the Illinois State Historical Library," *Journal of the Illinois State Historical Society*, Vol. 73, No. 3, Autumn 1980.

Chapter 18

1. Rankin, 185.

2. Mary Lincoln to Rhoda White, 2 May 1868. Turners, 475–477.

3. Lachman, 131. Baker, 280.

4. Linus P. Brockett and Mary C. Vaughn, *Woman's Work in the Civil War: A Record of Heroism, Patriotism and Patience* (Philadelphia: Ziger, McCurdy, 1867), 676–678. Lachman, 134–135, 154.

5. Lachman, 136.

6. gregormacgregor.com/tod&Macgregor/city_of_baltimore. Lachman, 138.

7. Isaac Markens, *America and the Jews* (New York: Isaac Markens, 1900), 31.

8. Markens, 31. Seligman Archives, University of Oklahoma Libraries. Included in the Seligman Archives are a photograph of Mary Lincoln and Seligman's correspondence with Grant.

9. Turners, 489–490. Lachman, 140–141.

10. Mary Lincoln to Eliza Slataper, 13 December 1868, Turners, 493–493.

11. Turners, 474.

12. Mary Lincoln to Eliza Slataper, 13 December 1868, Turners, 493–494.

13. Ibid.

14. *Brainard's Music World* (Baltimore, Maryland: S. Brainard & Sons, 1885), 255.

15. Lachman, 141.

16. Mary Lincoln to Eliza Slataper, 13 December 1868, Turners, 493–494.

17. Ibid.

18. Lachen, 144. Turners, 491.

19. Mary Lincoln to David Davis, 15 December 1868. Turners, 496–498. Baker, 121. Pratt, 139–141.

20. Mary Lincoln to David Davis, 15 December 1868, Turners, 496–498.

21. Mary Lincoln to Eliza Slataper, 17 February 1869, Turners, 500–502.

22. Ibid. burg-hohenzollern.com/castle-history.

23. Turners, 499–400.

24. *New York Times*, 20 May 1894.

25. Ibid.

26. Mary Lincoln to Charles Sumner, 27 March 1869, Turners, 506–507.

27. "The Forgotten Connections Between Abraham Lincoln and Robert Burns," April 2006. scotland.org/features/theforgotten-connections-between-abraham-lincoln-and-robert-burns. Turners, 508.

28. robertburns.org/encyclopedia/burnscottagealloway. robertburns.org/encyclopedia/Campbell/highlandmary.

29. Historicscotland.gov.uk.

30. southernhebrides.com/staffa. gatekeeperkey.org/scotlandduncanI.

31. covenanters.org/greyfriars.

32. bbc.co.uk/britishempire_seapower/battle_waterloo_01.

33. Lachman, 148.

34. Lachman, 148–149.

35. Lachman, 149.

36. Ibid.

37. Ibid.

38. Turners, 512–517.

39. Mary Lincoln to Sally Orne, 11 February 1870. Turners, 546–549.

40. Lachman, 153.

41. Ibid.

42. Turners, 556.

43. Thomas F. Schwartz and Anne V. Shaughnessy, "Unpublished Mary Lincoln Letters," *Journal of the Abraham Lincoln Association*, Vol. 11, No. 1, 1990.

44. Lachman, 152–153.

45. Turners, 572. Lachman, 154.

46. Ibid.

47. Ibid.

48. Mary Lincoln to James H. Orne, 16 July 1870. Turners, 576–577.

49. Mary Lincoln to Sally Orne, 17 August 1870. Turners, 575.

50. Lachman, 156. Mary Lincoln to Mrs. Paul R. Shipman, 27 October 1870, Mary Lincoln to Eliza Slataper, 7 November 1870, Turners, 578–580.

51. Mary Lincoln to Mrs. Paul R. Shipman, 13 January 1871. Turners, 582. Gen. George B. McClellan, "Princes of the House of Orleans," *The Internal Rev-enue Report and Customs Journal* (New York: W. C. and F. P. Church), 4 February 1884, Vol. 30, No. 5, 32.

52. Mary Lincoln to Mary Harlan Lincoln, 26 January 1871, Turners, 582.

53. Mary Lincoln to Mary Harlan Lincoln, November 1870, 26 January 1871, 12 February 1871; Mary Lincoln to Mrs. Paul R. Shipman,13 January 1871. Turners, 58–584. musuemsflorence.com/musei/pitti_palace. lincolntomb.org.

54. Lachman, 157–158, Turners, 584.

55. Lachman, 158, Turners, 584–585.

56. Lachman, 157–158, Turners, 585.

57. Lachman, 160.

58. Ibid.

59. Turners, 587–588. Lachman 161. Robert T. Lincoln to Mary Harlan Lincoln, 14 July 1871. Townsend Collection, Special Collections, University of Kentucky. Helm, 291–292.

60. Turners, 585–586. Lachman, 162–163.

61. Lachman, 164. Pratt, 184.

62. *New York Tribune*, 17 July 1871. Lachman, 166–167.

63. *New York Tribune*, 17 July 1871.

64. Robert T. Lincoln to Mary Harlan Lincoln, 18 July 1871. Townsend Collection.

65. Ibid.

66. Ibid.

67. Pratt, 184.

Chapter 19

1. Mary Lincoln to Eliza Slataper, 27 July, 13 August 1871, Turners, 591–592.

2. Mary Lincoln to Eliza Slataper, 4 October 1871; Turners, 596

3. Lachman, 170. "The Chicago Fire," chicagohs.org/history/fire.

4. Lachman, 171.

5. Lachman, 171–172. "The Chicago Fire," chicago.org/history/fire

6. Jeanne Schultz-Angel, "Aftermath of the Civil War: Mrs. May," *History of St. Charles: The First 100 Years* (St. Charles, Illinois: St. Charles Heritage Center, 2006). Lachman, 174–175.

7. Mary Lincoln to David Davis, Mary Lincoln to C. L. Farrington, 9 November 1871, Turners, 596–597.

8. Mary Lincoln to Mrs. George Eastman, 26 May 1872, Turners, 598.

9. *New York Times*, 3 December 1904.

10. Mary Lincoln to James F. Knowlton, 3 August 1872, Turners, 598–599.

11. William E. Barton, *The Paternity of Abraham Lincoln* (New York: George H. Doran, 1920), 303–322.

12. Turners, 602. Mary T. Kelly, *Washington County, Kentucky Bicentennial History, 1792–1992* (Springfield, Kentucky: Washington County Bicentennial Commission 1992), 10–12.

13. Mary Lincoln to Norman Williams, 8 August 1872. Turners, 599–600. Lillian Krulger, "Mary Lincoln Summers in Wisconsin," *Journal of the Illinois State Historical Society*, Vol. 34, No. 2, June 1841. "Mrs. Lincoln Grieves in Wisconsin," wisconsinhistory.org/odd/archives/002649.

14. Joyce Hackett Smith-Moore, "Seances: Another First for Auburn," *The Citizen*, 12 October 2008.

15. Raymond Buckland, *The Spirit Book: The Encyclopedia of Clairvoyance, Channeling and Spirit Communication* (Canton, Michigan: Visible Ink Press, 2008), 7. J. Gordon Melton, "Mary Andrews," *Gale Encyclopedia of Occultism and Parapsychology* (Detroit, Michigan, 2000), Vol. 1, 51.

16. Joyce Smith-Moore. "In Memoriam, John Hotaling, M.D.," *Albany Medical Annals* (Albany, New York: Press of Brandow Printing Co., 1907), Vol. 28, 577. Dr. Hotaling was described as "a man of spotless character, a citizen ready to assist in the moral and spiritual uplift of the community and a physician of marked ability and great success."

17. Louis Kaplan, *The Strange Case of William Mumler, Spirit Photographer* (Minneapolis: University of Minnesota Press, 2008), xii, 10, 132–233.

18. Lachman, 181. peterspioneers.com/eddiefoy.

19. Lachman, 177. Clinton, 296. Mark E. Neely, Jr., and R. Gerald McMurtry, *The Insanity File: The Case of Mary Todd Lincoln* (Carbondale: Southern Illinois University, 1986), 6.

20. Lachman, 178.

21. Ibid.

22. Ralph Gary, *Following in Lincoln's Footsteps* (New York: Basic Books, 2000), 164. arlingtonnationalcemetery.org. Samuel A. Schreiner, Jr., *The Trial of Mrs. Lincoln* (New York: Donald I. Fine, 1987), 309.

23. Lachman, 178. Baker, 311. An August 7, 1985, speaking engagement with the Kentucky Mansions Preservation Foundation brought Dr. James T. Hickey, curator of the Illinois State Historical Society Library, to Lexington, Kentucky. In a conversation with the author, the foundation's secretary, and Mrs. Lou Holden, the foundation's treasurer and director of the Mary Todd Lincoln House, Dr. Hickey related a visit with the Lincolns' great-grandson, Robert Todd Lincoln Beckwith, at the family home, Hildene, in Manchester, Vermont. They were in the basement, Dr. Hickey said, when he opened a door to a crawl space, which held nothing but vast numbers empty whiskey bottles. He asked Beckwith if somebody in the family was rum-running

during Prohibition. Beckwith said that was not the case; the whiskey bottles belonged to his grandmother, Mary Harlan Lincoln.

24. Mary Lincoln to John Todd Stuart, 15 December 1873. Turners, 603–604.

25. B. F. Irwin, *Lincoln's Religious Belief* (Springfield, Illinois: B. E. Baker, 1918), 1–11.

26. Mary Lincoln to John Todd Stuart, January 21, 1874. Turners, 606–607.

27. Lachman, 179. Schreiner, 76.

28. "Chloral Hydrate," *Encyclopedia Britannica: A Dictionary of Arts, Sciences and General Literature* (New York: Henry G. Allen, 1890), 677.

29. Lachman, 179.

30. Lachman, 180.

31. Mary Lincoln to Isaac N. Arnold, 20 October 1874, Turners, 607–608.

32. Ibid.

33. Baker, 314. greencovesrings.com/index.

34. Jason Emerson, *The Madness of Mary Lincoln* (Carbondale: Southern Illinois University Press, 2007), 161–162.

35. Turners, 609. Lachman, 182. Baker, 314.

36. Molly W. Berger, *Hotel Dreams: Luxury, Technology and Urban Ambition, 1829–1929.* (Baltimore, Maryland: Johns Hopkins University Press, 2011), 175. Lachman, 185. Baker, 316.

37. Neely and McMurtry, 8, Lachman, 186.

38. James A. Rhodes and Dean Jauchius, *The Trial of Mary Lincoln* (Indianapolis, Indiana: Bobbs-Merrill, 1959), 32–49.

39. Neely and McMurtry, 8. Lachman, 186.

40. Neely and McMurtry, 8–12. Lachman, 186–187.

41. Neely and McMurtry, 8.

42. Neely and McMurtry, 12. Lachman, 187.

43. Neely and McMurtry, 13. Baker, 317–318.

44. Schreiner, 38–39.

45. Ibid.

46. Schreiner, 40.

47. Schreiner, 52.

48. Lachman, 194.

49. Schreiner, 50. Neely and McMurtry, 115. Lachman, 189–190.

50. Rhodes and Jauchius, 11–19. Baker, 317–318. Lachman, 191–192.

51. Jason Emerson, *Mary Lincoln's Insanity Trial* (Champaign: University of Illinois Press, 2012), 44–49; Leonard Swett to David Davis, 24 May 1875.

52. Ibid.

53. Ibid.

54. Ibid.

55. Ibid.

56. Ibid.

57. Ibid.

58. Ibid.

59. Ibid.

60. Ibid.

61. Ibid.

62. Ibid.

63. Ibid.

64. Ibid.

65. Ibid.

66. Ibid.

67. Ibid.

68. Ibid.

69. Ibid.
70. Ibid.
71. Ibid.
72. Ibid.
73. Ibid.
74. Ibid.
75. Baker, 319. Lachman, 195.
76. Leonard Swett to David Davis, 24 May 1875.
77. Lachman, 200.
78. Edith Mayo, editor, *The Smithsonian Book of First Ladies* (New York: Macmillan, 1996), 87.
79. Lachman, 200.
80. Lachman, 202.
81. Leonard Swett to David Davis, 24 May 1875.
82. Ibid.
83. Ibid.
84. Ibid.
85. Ibid.
86. Ibid.
87. Schreiner, 132.
88. Schreiner, 133–134.
89. Leonard Swett to David Davis, 24 May 1875.
90. Cook County in re Mrs. Mary Lincoln, Inventory. Insanity File Collection, Lincoln Financial Foundation Collection, Allen County Public Library, Fort Wayne, Indiana. Hereafter referred to as the Insanity File Collection.
91. Ibid.
92. Robert T. Lincoln to Hon. J. M. Palmer, 23 December 1875. Schreiner, 232–233.
93. Lachman, 208–209. "Mary Todd Lincoln at Bellevue," bataviahistoricalsociety.org. Baker, 336.
94. Schreiner, 148–159. Lachman, 212.
95. *Chicago Post and Mail*, 13 July 1875.
96. Neely and McMurtry, 148–151. Baker, 358–359.
97. Kermit L. Hall, editor, "Bradwell v. Illinois," *The Oxford Companion to the Supreme Court of the United States* (New York: Oxford University Press, 1992), 82–83. It was almost a century later before the Court began to use the Fourteenth Amendment to overturn state laws discriminating against women. See Reed v. Reed, 1971. Neely and McMurtry, 59.
98. *Chicago Morning Courier*, 4 September 1875.
99. Emerson, 162–193, 236.
100. Lachman, 221, Schreiner, 158.
101. Emerson, 163.
102. Lachman, 222.
103. Emerson, 164.
104. Lachman, 222–223. Schreiner, 158–159. Neely and McMurtry, 60–61.
105. Schreiner, 160. Neely and McMurtry, 61.
106. Ibid.
107. Emerson, 87. Neely and McMurtry, 162–163. Schreiner, 162.
108. Schreiner, 163–165. Emerson, 86.
109. Emerson, 91.
110. Lachman, 226–227. Schreiner, 166–167.
111. *Chicago Times*, 24 August 1875. Neely and McMurtry, 63–64.
112. Schreiner, 167–169. Neely and McMurtry, 167169.
113. Ibid.
114. Neely and McMurtry, 170–171. Schreiner, 178. Lachman, 230.
115. Schreiner, 179–180, Neely and McMurtry, 172.
116. Neely and McMurtry, 172. Lachman, 230.
117. Schreiner, 182. Neely and McMurtry, 73.

118. Schreiner, 212–213. Neely and McMurtry, 75–76.
119. Schreiner, 213–215. Neely and McMurtry, 76–77.
120. Schreiner, 214–215. Neely and McMurtry, 77.
121. Neely and McMurtry, 77.
122. Schreiner, 215–217. Neely and McMurtry, 79.
123. Schreiner, 217. Neely and McMurtry, 81–82.
124. Ibid.
125. Ibid.
126. Schreiner, 219. Neely and McMurtry, 82.
127. Neely and McMurtry, 91–92. Schreiner, 233–234.
128. Schreiner, 239–240. Neely and McMurtry, 97–98.
129. Schreiner, 241–242. Neely and McMurtry, 99–101.
130. Neely and McMurtry, 103. Schreiner, 146.
131. Robert T. Lincoln Conservator Report, Insanity File Collection.
132. Emerson, 168–169.
133. Ibid.
134. Mary Lincoln to Robert Todd Lincoln, 19 June 1876. Turner, 615–616.
135. Thomas F. Schwartz, *Mary Lincoln: First Lady of Controversy* (Springfield, Illinois: Abraham Lincoln Presidential Library Foundation, 2007), 37.
136. Mary Lincoln to Robert Todd Lincoln, 19 June 1876. Turners, 615–616.
137. Schreiner, 259–265. Neely and McMurtry, 105–107.
138. Schreiner, 259–265. Mary Ann Pohl, Lincoln cataloger, Abraham Lincoln Presidential Library and Museum, to author 22 July 2013. Pratt, 137.
139. Schreiner, 259–265.
140. Ibid.
141. Ibid.
142. Schreiner, 265.

Chapter 20

1. Helm, 298.
2. Robert T. Lincoln's Conservator Accounting to Cook County Court, 20 June 1876. Insanity File Collection, Lincoln Financial Foundation Collection, Allen County Public Library, Fort Wayne, Indiana, hereafter referred to as Insanity File Collection. measuring worth.com/us/compare.
3. Robert T. Lincoln Conservator Accounting. Insanity File Collection.
4. Elizabeth Edwards to Robert T. Lincoln, 29 October 1876. Insanity File Collection.
5. Edward King Baker, *The Southern States of North America: A Record of Journeys in Louisiana, Texas, the Indian Territory, Missouri, Arkansas, Mississippi, Alabama, Georgia, Florida, South Carolina, North Carolina, Kentucky, Tennessee, Virginia, West Virginia and Maryland* (London: Blackie and Son, 1875), 45, 700.
6. Terry Langford email to author, 27 March 2013.
7. King, 701.
8. Baker, 354.
9. "Exhibition Facts," library.phila.gov/CenCol/exh. "The Corliss Engine," pbs.org/americanexperience.
10. Elizabeth Edwards to Robert T. Lincoln, 29 October 1876, Lincoln Collection, Allen County Public Library, Fort Wayne, Indiana.
11. Frederick N. Towers to Katherine Helm, 27 January 1928. Townsend Collection, Special Collections, University of Kentucky.

12. Helm, 298–299
13. Baker, 365.
14. Mary Lincoln to Edward Lewis Baker, Jr., 17 October 1876. Turners, 617–618.
15. Barker, 356–357. christies.comlotfinders/books manuscripts/Lincoln-mary-todd-mantle-clock-of5382318-details.
16. Mary Lincoln to Edward Lewis Baker, Jr., 17 October 1876. Turners, 617–618..
17. Mary Lincoln to Myra Bradwell, 1 December 1876. Emerson, 172–173.
18. Mary Lincoln to Myra Bradwell, 1 December 1876. Emerson, 172–173.
19. Ibid.
20. Mary Lincoln to Jacob Bunn, 12 December 1876. Turners, 622–623.
21. Mary Lincoln to Elizabeth Edwards, 19 March 1877. Turners, 626–627. Mary Lincoln to Edward Lewis Baker, Jr., 11 April 1877. Turners, 632–633.
22. Mary Lincoln to Myra Bradwell, 12 April 1877. Emerson, 173–174.
23. Mary Lincoln to Delia Dubois, 28 April 1877. Turners, 636.
24. Mary Lincoln to Edward Lewis Baker, 11 April 1877. Turners, 632–634.
25. Ibid.
26. Ibid.
27. Mary Lincoln to Hannah Shearer, 28 August 1859; Mary Lincoln to Adeline Judd, 13 June 1860. Turners, 57–58, 64–65.
28. Mary Lincoln to Myra Bradwell, 22 April 1878. Emerson, 174–175.
29. Ibid.
30. Ibid.
31. Ibid.
32. Mary Lincoln to Myra Bradwell, 4, 6 July 1878. Emerson, 175–176.
33. Mary Lincoln to Edward Lewis Baker, Jr., 3 August 1879. Turners, 686–688.
34. Mary Lincoln to Edward Lewis Baker, Jr., 3 August 1879. Turners, 686–688.
35. Mary Lincoln to Edward Lewis Baker, Jr., 4 October 1879. Turners, 690–691.
36. Ibid.
37. Ibid.
38. Lachman, 260.
39. Mary Lincoln to Edward Lewis Baker, Jr., 16 January 1880. Turners, 694.
40. Ibid.
41. Mary Lincoln to Edward Lewis Baker, Jr., 19 January 1889. Turners, 695. Mary Lincoln to Jacob Bunn, 26 January, 5 March 1880. Turners, 695–696.
42. Mary Lincoln to Jacob Bunn, 5 June 1880. Mary Lincoln to Edward Lewis Baker, Jr., 12 June 1880. Turners, 698–700.
43. Mary Lincoln to Edward Lewis Baker, Jr., 29 August 1880, 7 October 1880. Mary Lincoln to Jacob Bunn, 6 September, 7 October 1880. Turners, 701–703.
44. Lachman, 262–262. Sarah Bernhardt, Memories of My Life (New York: D. Appleton, 1907), 369. Olivia Laing, "Sarah: The Life of Sarah Bernhardt by Robert Gottlieb," review, The Observer, 25 October 2010.
45. Dorthy M. Kunhardt, "An Old Lady's Lincoln Memories," Life, 9 February 1959.
46. Baker, 265. Ninian Wirt Edwards, The Edwards Papers (Chicago: Fergus Printing, 1884).
47. Turners, 706. Lachman, 274.
48. Turners, 705–706.
49. Lachman, 272.
50. Hirschborn and Feldman. Lachman, 274. Mary Lincoln to Josephine Remann Edwards, 23 October 1881. Turners, 708.
51. Mary Lincoln to Josephine Remann Edwards, 23 October 1881. Turners, 708
52. Ibid.
53. New York Tribune, 3 July 1881. The Evening Critic (Washington), 21 September 1881. "Lucretia Garfield," first-ladies.org/biographies.
54. Pratt, 184–185.
55. "Lucretia Garfield," firstladies.org/biographies. Lewis A. Sayre, Spinal Disease and Spinal Curvature (Philadelphia: Lippincott, 1877). "Lewis A. Sayre," ncbi.nlm.nih.gov/pubmed. B.J. Gooch, director, Special Collections, Transylvania University, to author, 24 July 2013.
56. Turners, 707.
57. Baker, 366.
58. Lachman, 276.
59. Norbert Hirschorn and Robert G. Feldman, "Mary Lincoln's Final Illness: A Medical and Historic Reappraisal," Journal of the History of Medicine, Vol. 54, October 1999, 511–542.
60. Ibid.
61. Mary Lincoln to Noyes W. Miner, 3 January, 3 February 1882. Turners, 710–712.
62. Mary Lincoln to Noyes W. Miner, 21 February 1882. Turners, 714–715. New York Times, 1 June 1871; 7 January, 22 December 1872; 24 February 1874; 16 April 1877.
63. Mary Lincoln to Noyes W. Miner, 24 February 1882. Turners, 715.
64. Mary Lincoln to Edward Lewis Baker, Jr., 21 March 1882. Turners, 716.
65. Turners, 716.
66. Mary Edwards Brown interview.
67. Turners, 717. Lachman, 278–279.
68. Schreiner, 316–317.
69. Mary Edwards Brown interview.

Bibliography

Allison, Young E. *The City of Louisville and a Glimpse of Kentucky*. Louisville, Kentucky: Committee on Industrial and Commercial Development, 1887.

Ames, Mary Clemmer. *Ten Years in Washington: Life and Scenes in the Nation's Capital as a Woman Saw Them*. Hartford, Connecticut: A. D. Worthing, 1874.

Ammon, Henry. *James Monroe: The Quest for National Identity*. Charlottesville: University of Virginia Press, 1990.

Baker, Edward K. *The Southern States of North America*. London: Blackie and Son, 1875.

Baker, Jean H. *Mary Lincoln: A Biography*. New York: W. W. Norton, 1987.

Barton, William E. *The Paternity of Abraham Lincoln*. New York: George H. Doran, 1920.

Basler, Roy P., editor. *The Collected Works of Abraham Lincoln*. New Brunswick, New Jersey: Rutgers University Press, 1955.

Beale, Howard K., editor. *The Diary of Edward Bates*. Washington: Government Printing Office, 1923.

Belden, Thomas G., and Marva R. Belden. *So Fell the Angels*. Boston: Little, Brown, 1956.

Benjamin, Marcus. *Appleton's New Practical Encyclopedia*. New York: D. Appleton, 1887.

Berry, Stephen W. *House of Abraham: Lincoln and the Todds, A Family Divided by War*. Boston: Houghton Mifflin, 2007.

Bowen, Edward L. *Legends of the Turf: A Century of Great Thoroughbred Breeders*. Lexington, Kentucky: Eclipse Press, 2004.

Brockett, Linus P., and Mary C. Vaughn. *Women's Work in the Civil War: A Record of Heroism, Patriotism and Patience*. Philadelphia: Ziger, McCurdy, 1867.

Brooks, Noah. *Abraham Lincoln: The Nation's Leader in the Great Struggle Through Which Was Maintained the Existence of the United States*. New York: G. P. Putnam's Sons, 1888.

_____. *Glimpses of Lincoln in War Time*. New York: The Century Company, 1895.

_____. *Washington in Lincoln's Time*. New York: The Century Company, 1895.

Brownstein, Elizabeth S. *Lincoln's Other White House*. Hoboken, New Jersey: John Wiley and Sons, 2005.

Bruce, Edward L. *Lincoln and the Tools of War*. Champaign-Urbana: University of Illinois Press, 1989.

Burlingame, Michael. *Abraham Lincoln: A Life*. Baltimore: Johns Hopkins University Press, 2008.

_____. *Honest Abe, Dishonest Mary*. Racine, Wisconsin: Lincoln Fellowship of Wisconsin, 1994.

_____. *The Inner World of Abraham Lincoln*. Champaign-Urbana: University of Illinois Press, 1994.

Burns, James MacGregor. *Packing the Court*. New York: Penguin Press, 2009.

Cashman, Joan E. *First Lady of the Confederacy*. Cambridge, Massachusetts: Harvard University Press, 2006.

Clark Thomas D. *Footloose in Jacksonian America: Robert W. Scott and His Agrarian World*. Frankfort: Kentucky Historical Society, 1989.

Clinton, Catherine. *Mrs. Lincoln: A Life*. New York: Harper, 2009.

Coleman, J. Winston. *Famous Kentucky Duels*. Lexington, Kentucky: Henry Clay Press, 1969.

_____. *Lexington's First City Directory, 1808*. Lexington, Kentucky: Winburn Press, 1953

_____. *The Springs of Kentucky*. Lexington, Kentucky: Winburn Press, 1955.

Crofts, Daniel W. *Reluctant Confederates: Upper South Unionists in the Secession Crisis*. Chapel Hill: University of North Carolina Press, 1993.

Crook, William H., and Margarita S. Gerry, editor. *Through Five Administrations*. New York: Harper and Brothers, 1923.

Dobson, David. *The Original Scots Colonists of Early America, 1612–1783*. Baltimore: Baltimore Regional Publishing, 1989.

Donald, David H. *Lincoln*. New York: Simon and Schuster, 1995.

_____. *Lincoln at Home: Two Glimpses of Abraham Lincoln's Family Life*. New York: Simon and Schuster, 2000.

Dowd, Mary Jane M. *Records of the Office of Public*

Buildings and Public Parks of the Nation's Capital. Washington: Government Printing Office, 1992.

Edwards, Ninian W. *The Edwards Papers.* Chicago: Fergus Printing, 1884.

Ellison, Betty B. *A Man Seen But Once: Cassius Marcellus Clay.* Bloomington, Indiana: AuthorHouse, 2005.

Emerson, Jason. *The Madness of Mary Lincoln.* Carbondale: Southern Illinois University Press, 2007.

Epstein, Daniel M. *The Lincolns: A Portrait of a Marriage.* New York: Ballentine, 2008.

Eubank, Damon R. *In the Shadow of the Patriarch: The John J. Crittenden Family in War and Peace.* Macon, Georgia: Mercer University Press, 2009.

Evans, William A. *Mrs. Abraham Lincoln: A Study of Her Personality and Her Influence on Lincoln.* New York: Alfred A. Knopf, 1932.

Ferguson, David M. *Shipwrecks of Orkney, Shetland and the Pentland Firth.* North Pomfret, Vermont: Newton, Abbot, Devon, 1988.

Fleischner, Jennifer. *Mrs. Lincoln and Mrs. Keckly.* New York: Broadway Books, 2003.

Gary, Ralph. *Following in Lincoln's Footsteps.* New York: Basic Books, 2000.

Gienapp, William E. *Origins of the Republican Party 1852–1856.* Oxford, England: Oxford University Press, 1987.

Goodwin, Doris Kearns. *Team of Rivals: The Political Genius of Abraham Lincoln.* New York: Simon and Schuster, 2005.

Green, Thomas. *Historic Families of Kentucky.* Baltimore, Maryland: Regional Publishing, 1964.

Gueizo, Allen. *Abraham Lincoln: Redeemer.* Grand Rapids, Michigan: William B. Eerdmans, 1999.

_____. *Lincoln and Douglas: The Debates That Defined America.* New York: Simon and Schuster, 2008.

Hall, Kermit L., editor. *The Oxford Companion of the Supreme Court of the United States.* New York: Oxford University Press, 1992.

Hargreves, John F., and Margaret W., editors. *The Papers of Henry Clay.* Lexington, Kentucky: University Press of Kentucky, 1959.

Hay, John, and William R. Thayer. *With Lincoln at the White House: From the Unpublished Diaries of John Hay.* New York: Harper and Brothers, 1915.

Hearn, Chester G. *Lincoln, the Cabinet and the Generals.* Baton Rouge: Louisiana State University Press, 2010.

Helm, Katherine. *Mary, Wife of Lincoln.* New York: Harper and Brothers, 1928.

Herndon, William H., and Jesse W. Weilk. *Herndon's Life of Lincoln: The True Story of a Great Life.* Chicago: Clarke, 1889.

_____, _____, Douglas L. Wilson, and Rodney O. Davis. *Herndon's Lincoln.* Champaign-Urbana: University of Illinois Press, 2006.

Hinds, Asher L. *Hinds' Precedents of the House of Representatives, Including References to the Constitution, the Laws and Decisions of the United States Senate.* Washington: Government Printing Office, 1907.

Kaplan, Louis. *The Strange Case of William Mumler.* Minneapolis: University of Minnesota Press, 2008.

Kebler, John, editor. *The Kentucky Encyclopedia.* Lexington: University Press of Kentucky, 1992.

Kellogg, Day O., editor. *Encyclopedia Britannica.* New York: Werner, 1902.

Kelly, Mary T. *Washington County Kentucky Bicentennial History.* Springfield, Kentucky: Washington County Bicentennial Commission, 2008.

Kennedy, Elijah R. *The Contest for California: How Colonel E. D. Baker Saved the Pacific States for the Union.* Whitefish, Montana: Kessinger, 2005.

Kerr, Charles. *History of Kentucky.* Chicago: American Historical Society, 1922.

King, Willard L. *Lincoln's Manager, David Davis.* Cambridge, Massachusetts: Harvard University Press, 1960.

Lachman, Charles. *The Last of the Lincolns: The Rise and Fall of a Great American Family.* New York: Union Square Press, 2008.

Lamon, Ward Hill, and Chauncey F. Black. *The Life of Abraham Lincoln: From His Birth to His Inauguration as President.* Boston, Massachusetts: James R. Osgood, 1872.

Lamphier, Peg. *Kate Chase and William Sprague: Politics in a Civil War Marriage.* Lincoln: University of Nebraska Press, 2005.

Lancaster, Clay. *Ante Bellum Homes of the Blue Grass.* Lexington: University of Kentucky Press, 1978.

_____. *Vestiges of the Venerable City of Lexington, Kentucky.* Lexington, Kentucky: Lexington Fayette County Historic Commission, 1978.

Lawson, John D. *American State Trials.* St. Louis, Missouri: Thomas Law Book Company, 1918.

Leslie, Eliza. *The House Book: Or a Manual of Domestic Economy.* Philadelphia: Carey and Hart, 1840.

_____, and Louis Szathmary. *Direction for Cookery, in Its Various Branches.* New York: Arno Press, 1973.

Lien, Glenna R. Schroeder. *Lincoln and Medicine.* Carbondale: Southern Illinois University Press, 2012.

Mayo, Edith, editor. *The Smithsonian Book of First Ladies.* New York: Macmillan, 1996.

McCreary, Donna D. *Fashionable First Lady: The Victorian Wardrobe of Mary Lincoln.* Charlestown, Indiana: Lincoln Presentations, 2007.

McDougal, Ivan E. *Slavery in Kentucky 1792–1865.* Lancaster, Pennsylvania: Press of the New Era Printing Company, 1918.

McFeely, William S. *Grant: A Biography.* New York: W. W. Norton, 2002.

Mentelle, Charlotte C. *Adventures and Situations of the French Emigrants from the Year 1789–1790.* Lexington, Kentucky: privately published, 1800.

Mieczowski, Yanek. *The Rourtledge Historic Atlas of Presidential Election.* Oxford, England: Routledge, 2001.

Miers, Earl S. *Lincoln Day by Day.* Washington: Lincoln Sesquicentennial Commission, 1996.

Monkman, Betty G. *The White House, Its Furnishings and First Families.* New York: Abbeville Press, 2000.

Moore, Thomas. *Irish Melodies.* London, England: Longman, Brown, Green, Longmans, 1852.

Neely, Mark E., Jr., and R. Gerald McMurtry. *The Insanity File: The Case of Mary Todd Lincoln.* Carbondale: Southern Illinois University Press, 1986.

Nevins, Allen, editor. *Diary of the Civil War 1860–1865: George Templeton Strong.* New York: Macmillan, 1963.

Nicolay, Helen. *Lincoln's Secretary: A Biography of John G. Nicolay.* New York: Longmans, Green, 1949.

Niven, John. *Salmon P. Chase: A Biography.* London: Oxford University Press, 1955.

Oats, Stephen B. *Abraham Lincoln: The Man Behind the Myth.* New York: Harper Collins, 2009.

Parrish, Gladys. *The History of Female Education in Lexington and Fayette County.* Master's thesis, University of Kentucky, 1932.

Peter, Robert. *Transylvania University: Origin, Rise, Decline and Fall.* Louisville, Kentucky: J. P. Morton, 1896.

Peterson, Merrill D. *Thomas Jefferson and the New Nation.* New York: Oxford University Press, 1970.

Power, John C., and Sarah H. Power, *History of the Early Settlers of Sangamon County, Illinois.* Springfield, Illinois: Edwin A. Wilson, 1876.

Pratt, Henry E. *Lincoln, 1840–1846, Being the Day-to-Day Activity of Abraham Lincoln.* Springfield, Illinois: Abraham Lincoln Association, 1939.

_____. *The Personal Finances of Abraham Lincoln.* Springfield, Illinois: Abraham Lincoln Association, 1943.

_____, and Ernest E. East. *Mrs. Lincoln Furnishes the White House.* Harrogate, Tennessee: Lincoln Memorial University, 1945.

Public Laws of the United States of America at the Thirty-seventh Congress. Boston: Massachusetts: Little, Brown, 1861.

Randall, Ruth P. *Mary Lincoln: A Biography of a Marriage.* Boston, Massachusetts: Little, Brown, 1953.

Rankin, Henry B. *Personal Recollection of Abraham Lincoln.* New York: Putnam's Sons, 1916.

Remini, Robert V. *Henry Clay, Statesman for the Union.* New York: W. W. Norton, 1993.

Reports of the Committees of the House of Representatives During the Second Session of the Thirty-seventh Congress. Washington: Government Printing Office, 1862.

Rhodes, James A. and Dean Jauchius. *The Trial of Mary Lincoln.* Indianapolis, Indiana: Bobbs-Merrill, 1959.

Riddle, Albert G. *A Recollection of War Times: Reminiscences of Men and Events.* New York: G. P. Putnam's Sons, 1895.

Roe, Merwin, editor. *Speeches and Letters of Abraham Lincoln.* New York: E. P. Dutton, 1912.

Ross, Ishbel. *The President's Wife: Mary Todd Lincoln.* New York: Putnam, 1973.

Russell, William A. *My Diary, North and South.* Boston, Massachusetts: T.O.H.P. Burham, 1863.

Sandbery, Carl, and Paul M. Angle. *Mary Lincoln: Wife and Widow.* New York: Harcourt, Brace, 1932.

Sayre, Lewis A. *Spinal Disease and Spinal Curvature.* Philadelphia, Pennsylvania: Lippincott, 1977.

Schneller, Robert J. *A Quest for Glory: A Biography of Rear Admiral John A. Dahlgren.* Washington: Naval Institute Press, 1995.

Schriener, Samuel A. *The Trial of Mrs. Lincoln.* New York: Donald I. Fine, 1987.

Seale, William. *The President's House.* Washington: White House Historical Association, 1986.

Seers, Edward, Jr. *Blood on the Moon: The Assassination of Abraham Lincoln.* Lexington: University Press of Kentucky, 2005.

Seward, Frederick W. *Seward at Washington: Senator and Secretary of State.* New York: Derby and Miller, 1890.

Sifakis, Stewart. *Who Was Who in the Civil War.* New York: Facts on File, 1988.

Speer, John. *The Life of Gen. James Lane.* Garden City, Kansas: John Speer, 1896.

Staples, Charles R. *A History of Pioneer Lexington.* Lexington: University Press of Kentucky, 1996.

Statements of Appropriations and Expenditures for the National Treasury for Public and Private Purposed in the District of Columbia from June 16, 1790 to June 30, 1876. Washington: Government Printing Office, 1878.

Swanberg, W. A. *Sickles the Incredible.* New York: Charles Scribner's Sons, 1956.

Tarshis, Harry C., and Rebecca Blair. *Lincoln's Constant Ally, Edward D. Baker.* Portland: Oregon Historical Society, 1960.

Townsend, William H. *Lincoln and His Wife's Hometown.* Indianapolis, Indiana: Bobbs-Merrill, 1929.

_____. *Lincoln and Liquor.* New York: Press of the Pioneers, 1934.

_____. *Lincoln and the Bluegrass.* Indianapolis, Indiana: Bobbs-Merrill, 1929.

_____. *Lincoln and the Bluegrass: Slavery and Civil War In Kentucky.* Lexington: University of Kentucky Press, 1955.

_____. *Lincoln the Litigant.* New York: Houghton Mifflin, 1925.

Turner, Justin G., and Linda Levitt Turner. *Mary Todd Lincoln: Her Life and Letters.* New York: Alfred A. Knopf, 1972.

War of the Rebellion: A Compilation of the Official Records of the Union and Confederate Armies. Washington: Government Printing Office, 1880.

White, Ronald C., Jr. *Lincoln: A Biography.* New York: Random House, 2009.

Williams, Walter A. *A Story of Northwest Missouri.* Chicago, Lewis Publishing, 1913.

Wilson, Douglas L., Rodney O. Davis, Terry Wilson, William H. Herndon, and Jesse W. Weilk. *Herndon's Informants: Letters Interviews and Statements about Abraham Lincoln.* Champaign-Urbana: University of Illinois Press, 1998.

Winkle, Kenneth J. *Abraham and Mary Lincoln.* Carbondale: Southern Illinois University Press, 2011.

Journals, Periodicals, Magazines

Albany Argus.
Albany Times-Union.
American Heritage.
Baltimore Sun.
Boston Globe.
Boston Journal.
Century Illustrated Magazine.
Chicago Inter Ocean.
Chicago Magazine.
Chicago Post and Mail.
Chicago Times.
Chicago Tribune.
Daily Alta California.
Frank Leslie's Illustrated Newspaper.
Gettysburg Times.
Harper's New Monthly Magazine.
Illinois State Journal.
Illinois State Register.
Internal Revenue Report and Customs Journal.
Journal of American History.
Journal of the Abraham Lincoln Association.
Journal of the History of Medicine.
Journal of the Illinois State Historical Society.
Journals of the House of Representatives of the Commonwealth of Kentucky.
Kentucky Gazette.
Lexington Herald.
Lexington Observer and Reporter.
Life.
Magazine of Illinois.
McClure's Magazine.
New York Herald.
New York Times.
New York Tribune.
New York World.
The Orcadian.
Pacific Monthly.
Philadelphia News.
Register of the Kentucky Historical Society.
Smithsonian Magazine.
Transylvania Journal of Medicine.
Washington Chronicle.
Washington Evening Star.
Washington Intelligencer.
Washington Post.

Archived Collections

Abraham Lincoln Presidential Library and Museum, Springfield, Illinois.
    Mary Lincoln's Jewelry.
Allen County Public Library, Fort Wayne, Indiana.
    The Insanity File Collection, Lincoln Financial Foundation Collection.
Fayette County Clerk's Office, Lexington, Kentucky.
    Will Books, Deed Books and Records of Manumissions.
Lexington Public Library, Kentucky Room, Lexington, Kentucky.
    Collection of Funeral Notices.
Library of Congress, Washington, D.C.
    Abraham Lincoln Papers.
    French Family Papers.
Louisiana State University, Special Collections, Baton Rouge, Louisiana.
    Turnbull-Bowman Family Papers.
National Archives and Record Administration, Washington, D.C.
    Record Groups, 42, 146.
    Commissioner of Public Buildings, Requisition Books, 19, 20, 21, 22.
    Commissioner of Public Buildings, Cancelled Checks, Treasurer of the United States.
Pennsylvania State Office of Historic Preservation, Harrisburg, Pennsylvania.
    Papers of Gov. David Rittenhouse Porter.
Transylvania University, Lexington, Kentucky.
    Bullock Photography Collection.
    J. Winston Coleman Collection.
United States Senate, Forty-fifth Congress, Second Session, Executive Document No. 84: Statement of Appropriations and Expenditures from the National Treasury for Public and Private Purposes in the District of Columbia from July 16, 1790, to June 30, 1876.
University of Kentucky, Lexington, Kentucky.
    Congressional Serial Sets, Reports of the Commissioner of Public Buildings: Serial Set Volumes: 11, 302, 464, 432, 482, 499, 540, 598, 599, 641, 685, 741, 746,840, 893, 942, 974, 974, 1023, 1078, 1117, 1157, 1220.
University of Kentucky, Special Collections, Lexington, Kentucky.
    Bell Family Papers.
    Breckinridge Family Papers.
    Cassius Marcellus Clay Papers.
    Henry Clay Papers.
    William H. Townsend Papers, Helm Collection.

Index

279